Mao's Invisible Hand

Harvard Contemporary China Series 17

Mao's Invisible Hand

The Political Foundations of Adaptive Governance in China

edited by

Sebastian Heilmann and Elizabeth J. Perry

Published by the Harvard University Asia Center
Distributed by Harvard University Press
Cambridge (Massachusetts) and London 2011

Printed in the United States of America

The Harvard Contemporary China Series is designed to present new research that deals with present-day issues against the background of Chinese history and society. The focus is on interdisciplinary research intended to convey the significance of the rapidly changing Chinese scene.

Library of Congress Cataloging-in-Publication Data

Mao's invisible hand : the political foundations of adaptive governance in China / edited by Sebastian Heilmann and Elizabeth J. Perry.
    p. cm.
Includes bibliographical references.
ISBN 978-0-674-06063-0 (alk. paper)
1. Public administration—China. 2. Communism—China. 3. China—Politics and government—1949- I. Heilmann, Sebastian. II. Perry, Elizabeth J.
JQ1510.M35 2011
320.53'230951—dc22
2010052574

Published by the
Harvard University Asia Center
1730 Cambridge Street
Cambridge, MA 02138

Distributed by
Harvard University Press
79 Garden Street
Cambridge, MA 02138

♾ Printed on acid-free paper

Last figure below indicates year of this printing
19 18 17 16 15 14 13 12 11

For Nancy Hearst

Contents

Acknowledgments

Edited books are by definition collaborative ventures, and we acknowledge with genuine appreciation the many institutions and individuals that have contributed to the publication of this volume. For generous financial support, we thank Trier University and Harvard University's Weatherhead, Asia and Fairbank Centers. For expert logistical and administrative assistance and oversight, we thank especially Adelaide Shalhope, Kristen Wanner and William Hammell at Harvard; and Ruth Wabschke, Dirk Schmidt and Lea Shih at Trier. We are also deeply grateful to the many scholars who participated as paper writers and discussants in the conferences at Trier and Harvard from which this volume emerged. Above all, we express our profound appreciation to Fairbank Center Librarian Nancy Hearst for her extraordinary curatorial, editorial and scholarly contributions to our work. For this — and so much more — we dedicate this book to her.

Sebastian Heilmann, Trier University
Elizabeth J. Perry, Harvard University

Contributors

Jae Ho Chung, Department of International Relations, Seoul National University

Nara Dillon, Department of Government, Harvard University

Joseph Fewsmith, Department of International Relations, Boston University

Sebastian Heilmann, Department of Political Science, Trier University

Benjamin L. Liebman, Columbia Law School

Elizabeth J. Perry, Department of Government, Harvard University

Patricia M. Thornton, Department of Politics and International Relations, Oxford University

Wang Shaoguang, Department of Government and Public Administration, Chinese University of Hong Kong

Yuezhi Zhao, School of Communication, Simon Fraser University

Tables and Figures

Abbreviations

CCP	Chinese Communist Party
CCTV	China Central Television
CESRRI	Chinese Economic System Reform Research Institute
CHE	*Zhongguo weisheng jingji* (China Health Economics)
CMS	cooperative medical system
CNNIC	China Internet Network Information Center
CR	Cultural Revolution
CRHM	*Zhongguo nongcun weisheng shiye guanli* (China Rural Health Service Management)
GAPP	General Administration for Press and Publications
GLF	Great Leap Forward
GMD	Guomindang
JCRR	Joint Commission on Rural Reconstruction
LD	*Jiefang ribao* (Liberation Daily)
MEM	Mass Education movement
NCMS	New Cooperative Medical Scheme
NEP	New Economic Policy
NGO	non-governmental organization
NPC	National People's Congress
PLA	People's Liberation Army
PRC	People's Republic of China
RMRB	*Renmin ribao* (People's Daily)
RRM	Rural Reconstruction movement
SARFT	State Administration of Radio, Film, and Television
SGAP	State Administration of Press
SMA	Shanghai Municipal Archives
SPC	Supreme People's Court
WTO	World Trade Organization

Mao's Invisible Hand

CHAPTER I

Embracing Uncertainty: Guerrilla Policy Style and Adaptive Governance in China

Sebastian Heilmann and Elizabeth J. Perry

Observers have been predicting the imminent demise of the Chinese political system since the death of Mao Zedong more than thirty years ago. Such forecasts gained currency and urgency with the Tiananmen Uprising twenty years ago, when it did appear that the regime was tottering on the verge of collapse.[1] Although the People's Republic of China (PRC) managed to outlast both Eastern European and Soviet variants of communism, predictions of its impending demise did not disappear. In the last several years we have seen a steady parade of books with titles such as *The Coming Collapse of China, China's Trapped Transition, China: Fragile Superpower,* or, more optimistically, *China's Democratic Future: How It Will Happen and Where It Will Lead.*[2]

The rapid economic growth of the post-Mao era generated expectations of a commensurate political transformation. To sustain such economic progress in the face of mounting social unrest, it was widely believed, would require jettisoning an outmoded Communist Party in favor of liberal democratic institutions. With each passing decade, however, the characterization of the Chinese Communist system as exhausted and about to expire rings a little more hollow. Far from decrepit, the regime — having weathered Mao's death in 1976, the Tiananmen Uprising in 1989, Deng's death in 1997, and large-scale ethnic riots in 2008–9 — seems over time to have become increasingly adept at managing tricky challenges ranging from leadership succession and popular unrest to administrative reorganization, legal institutionalization, and even global economic integration. Contrary to expectations, the PRC regime has proven surprisingly capable of surviving serious unanticipated crises, from the Asian financial crisis of 1997–99 through the SARS epidemic of 2003, to the global economic downturn of 2008–9. These challenges would have sounded the death knell to many a less hardy regime.

To be sure, the phenomenon of rapid economic growth without political liberalization comes at a high price. The absence of civil liberties for ordinary Chinese citizens is perhaps the most obvious and egregious of these costs. But the lack of political restraints also contributes to numerous other serious problems in the contemporary PRC, from cadre corruption to the weakness of consumer protection and environmental degradation. It is certainly conceivable that some combination of these vulnerabilities sooner or later will lead to systemic change.

We hazard no predictions about how long Communist Party rule in China may persist. The vagaries of historical contingency render any such exercise of limited utility. Nor do we speculate about what an alternative future political system might look like. Such prescriptions are better left to Chinese policy makers and political reformers themselves. Instead, as social scientists we intend to take a fresh look at the reasons and, more precisely, the policy mechanisms[3] behind the staying power of Communist Party rule *up to this point*: How has the Communist Party in China achieved such rapid and profound organizational, economic, and social change over the last three decades? What political techniques and procedures has the authoritarian regime employed to manage the unsettling impact of the fastest sustained economic expansion in world history — a transformation that has brought with it not only greater wealth and global clout, but also political-ideological contestation, growing income and regional inequality, and rampant popular protest?

China as a "Black Swan"

Conventional political science models of regime types and regime transitions, constructed around dichotomous systemic categories stemming from the Cold War period ("from dictatorship to democracy," "from plan to market," and so forth), assign almost no adaptability to Communist party-states. Institutionally speaking, Communist political systems are judged to be inflexible and incapable of continuous improvements in administrative organization, economic coordination, technological innovation, and international competitiveness.[4] This explanatory framework has not proven particularly useful in understanding the complex dynamics of an innovative, competitive, and powerful China, however. In light of the country's unusual development record, it has become increasingly problematic to try to shoe-horn China into the shop-worn categories of Cold War regime types, even by adding numerous attributes to the original categories.[5]

China has not taken the road anticipated by Western social scientists and desired by Western publics. Marketization has not spelled democratization. Although the intense ideological pressures, struggle campaigns, and organized dependency[6] of the Mao era have given way to a more regular administrative and technocratic, and in some fields even consultative, mode of governance, China has made no transition in the direction of electoral, pluralist democracy. It remains an authoritarian party-state, characterized by Leninist institutions. Yet China's Soviet-inspired formal institutions are combined with distinctive governance methods shaped by the Chinese Communists' own revolutionary and post-revolutionary past and, during the post-Mao era, complemented by selective borrowing from "advanced" foreign organizational and regulatory practices. It is these governance techniques, we argue, that account for the otherwise puzzling pattern of spectacular economic success under the aegis of an institutionally unreformed Communist system.

Though market coordination has gained considerable ground in China's economy, the state still controls the "commanding heights" in key industries (from infrastructure to telecommunications, to finance) through public property rights, pervasive administrative interference, and Communist Party supervision of senior managers. China's political economy thus diverges fundamentally from the Anglo-American marketization-cum-privatization paradigm. Moreover, China's Communist Party–guided capitalism also deviates from core features of the Japanese and South Korean "developmental state," in which state enterprises, public property, and political control over senior executives played only a very limited role and in which foreign trade liberalization was introduced at a much more mature state of development than that in China.[7]

As this volume will detail, many contemporary methods of governance crucial to sustaining Communist Party rule in a shifting and uncertain environment can be traced back to formative revolutionary experiences. China's governance techniques are marked by a signature Maoist stamp that conceives of policy-making as a process of ceaseless change, tension management, continual experimentation, and ad-hoc adjustment. Such techniques reflect a mindset and method that contrast sharply with the more bureaucratic and legalistic approaches to policy-making that obtain in many other major polities.

Due to its idiosyncratic developmental pathway over the past thirty years, contemporary China presents an enigma not only to the field of Chinese politics, which did not predict the surprising resilience of the Communist system under reform and has yet to provide a convincing explanation for it. It also poses a major puzzle to the field of comparative politics, where prevailing theories of modernization, democratization, and regime transition to date offer little illumination for the case of post-Mao China.[8]

China stands as a "Black Swan" challenge to the social sciences.[9] The political resilience of the Communist party-state, in combination with a rapidly expanding, internationally competitive, and integrated economy, represents a significant deviant and unpredicted case with a huge potential impact not only on the global distribution of political and economic power but also on the global debate about models of development. Framed in terms of social science methodology, China's exceptional development trajectory represents an "extreme value on an independent or dependent variable of general interest."[10] As such, it challenges conventional wisdom as well as conventional models of political change.

In relying upon concepts and theories derived from more familiar historical trajectories (e.g., the triumph of Western liberal democracies over Communist regimes at the end of the last century) to examine a political economy that emerged from very different experiences, analysts have tended to dismiss potentially powerful innovations as irregularities, deviations, externalities, or simply dead-ends. But what if China is in fact pursuing a unique path, and — due to its size, history, and surprising success — introducing important unconventional, non-Western techniques to the repertoire of governance in the twenty-first century? Whether the PRC's institutional and policy solutions over the past three decades turn out to be transitional remains uncertain, but in any case they have served the Communist Party's management of economic and social change remarkably effectively *so far*, and for that reason alone they deserve our serious attention as social scientists. If these techniques persist much longer, they will surely command widespread public interest and concern as well.

With this volume, we wish to sound a cautionary note against the common tendency among Western observers to trivialize the contributions of political leadership and policy initiatives in China by reducing that country's politics to an unremitting interplay of repression and resistance. We seek neither to condemn nor to celebrate the reform record of the PRC, but to understand it. Such understanding requires in the first instance an investigation of its origins. Identifying the roots of contemporary methods of governance is important for analyzing both the genesis and the generalizability of the specific array of solutions, institutions, and processes at work in China today. These roots are firmly planted, we will argue, in the fertile soil of the Maoist past. The usual practice of restricting the study of contemporary Chinese political economy to the reform period has had the unfortunate effect of obscuring key sources of its dynamism. By contrast, this volume focuses on the formative legacy of revolutionary (1927–49) and early PRC (1949–76) techniques of policy creation and implementation that we label, in shorthand, "Maoist."[11]

There were important variations within that eventful half century of "Maoist" political history, to be sure. At certain moments both before and after the political victory of 1949, Mao Zedong's distinctive mass mobilization methods were challenged by a more orthodox Soviet style of bureaucratic control. That Mao's approach won out repeatedly in these conflicts did not necessarily redound to the benefit of the Chinese people. The disastrous elements of the Great Leap Forward exemplified the negative consequences of an unbridled Maoist mode of development. Leadership and ideology would prove decisive in determining whether the power of revolutionary governance would be put toward destructive or productive ends.

Prevailing Institutional Explanations

In highlighting the importance of revolutionary experience for contemporary practice, we depart from mainstream explanations of regime resilience. As scholars have begun to seek an answer to the puzzling vigor of the Chinese Communist system, they have generally concentrated on the role of institutional factors. According to Andrew Nathan, the Chinese regime's surprising resilience can be attributed to its institutionalization of the elite succession process and containment of factionalism as well as its success in fostering a "high level of acceptance" through various "input institutions" — local elections, letters-and-visits departments, people's congresses, administrative litigation, mass media, and the like.[12] David Shambaugh also sees the Chinese Communist Party as "a reasonably strong and resilient institution" and suggests that "a range of intraparty reforms, as well as reforms affecting other sectors of the state, society and economy" have contributed to the party's ruling capacity.[13] Barry Naughton and Dali Yang point out that "China has retained a core element of central control — the *nomenklatura* system of personnel management" — and argue that "this nomenklatura personnel system is the most important institution reinforcing national unity."[14] As Andrew Walder has observed, although the *composition* of the political elite has changed dramatically since Mao's day (reflecting, among other things, an exponential growth in its educational credentials), its organizational *structure* has been remarkably stable.[15]

Whereas the above scholars have looked to formal institutions as the basis of regime resilience, others have emphasized the role of informal institutions. Kellee Tsai, for example, credits the contribution of "informal adaptive institutions," such as the transitional practice of private entrepreneurs registering their enterprises as collectively owned, with convincing the central authorities to adopt new measures (e.g., admitting private entrepreneurs as members of the Chinese Communist Party) that have inadvertently served to strengthen state stability.[16] Lily Tsai notes the value of local "informal institutions of accountability" (e.g., temple associations and lineages) for the provision of public goods in rural China. According to her analysis, these solidary groups (which include local officials as well as ordinary villagers) generate increased support for the government in the Chinese countryside.[17]

A full answer to the resilience of the Chinese Communist system to date is of course complex, varying over time under different leaders and with respect to different challenges. We do not discount the role of either formal or informal institutions in this process. But why has China alone benefited from such institutions? After all, a defining feature of Communist systems is their common institutional structure: Leninist party, collectivized production, command economy, centralized propaganda apparatus, coercive public security apparatus, and so forth. What, then, accounts for the glaring difference between the contemporary Chinese experience and that of the other formerly Communist countries? Why has China proven more tolerant of informal institutions than many of its erstwhile counterparts elsewhere in the world? And why did China — in contrast to the Soviet Union and Eastern Europe — not only survive the 1989 crisis with its party-state system intact, but then in the space of a single generation manage to engineer an economic and social transformation of such stunning proportions?

We believe that much of the explanation for this singular achievement lies in the creative adaptation of key elements of China's revolutionary heritage. Unlike Russia and Eastern Europe, the imposition of a national Communist regime in China required nearly three decades of revolutionary mobilization and struggle. In the course of that protracted process, which took the Communists out of the major cities into the rural hinterland and on a Long March from the southern to the northern regions of the country, invaluable lessons in adapting to a wide range of different environmental conditions and challenges were learned. That these rich revolutionary experiences led directly to the dramatic successes — as well as the dismal failures — of Chairman Mao's radical programs during the initial years of the PRC is well recognized.[18] The origins of the mass campaigns of the 1950s and 1960s, which brought improved literacy and basic health care but also the worst famine of the twentieth century and severe environmental damage,[19] are readily traceable to the revolutionary policies of the wartime base areas.

Less widely acknowledged, however, is the continued importance of revolutionary precedents in the techniques of rule- and policy-making employed by Mao's successors. Instead, reform-era China is usually characterized as a *post*-revolutionary society in which, with the notable exception of the Leninist party-state, Maoist ideas and initiatives have been thoroughly discredited and dismantled.[20] In the aftermath of the Cold War, with ideological conflict seemingly having been superseded by economic competition, the revolutionary past is generally regarded as a historical curiosity at most.

Despite the institutional commonalities among Communist countries, China from its revolutionary days to the present has chosen a singular path. Unlike the Soviet Union and its Eastern European satellites, Mao's China exhibited a trademark policy style that favored continual experimentation and transformation (or "permanent revolution") over regime consolidation. The erratic and idiosyncratic course navigated by the Great Helmsman in his quixotic quest to continue the revolution after 1949 was terribly disruptive and destructive to be sure, but the underlying protean approach remained available for more productive uses. China's long revolution gave rise to a "guerrilla-style policy-making"[21] approach that proved capable of generating an array of creative — proactive as well as evasive — tactics for managing sudden change and uncertainty. With new political leadership and policy priorities, these familiar practices could lead to very different outcomes.

The wartime base areas' formula of encouraging decentralized initiative within the framework of centralized political authority proved highly effective when redirected to the economic modernization objectives of Mao's successors. Unlike other countries saddled with the rigid top-down legacies of Leninist parties and command economies, some of whose leaders also proposed bold reforms, the Chinese polity has been singularly adept in adjusting to the demands of domestic economic reform and global market competition. A major reason for this glaring difference is China's unusual receptivity to on-the-ground generation of new knowledge and practice — a feature, we believe, that derives in large measure from many of the same policy mechanisms that propelled the Chinese Communists' protracted revolutionary struggle.

From an institutional perspective, the Chinese polity fits the standard definition of an authoritarian Communist party-state. Yet China's vast and bureaucratically fragmented political system is animated by policy processes that allow for far greater bottom-up input than would be predicted from its formal structures. These processes are fundamental to the PRC's resilience and adaptability.

Political Resilience and Adaptive Governance

What do we mean by resilience and adaptability? *Resilience* can be defined as the capacity of a system to experience and absorb shocks and disturbances "while retaining essentially the same function, structure, feedbacks, and therefore identity."[22] In turn, *adaptability* can be defined as "the capacity of actors in a system to further resilience" through their actions and interactions, intentionally or unintentionally. The foundation of adaptability in this sense is *response diversity*: a variety of reactive, digestive, pre-emptive, and proactive operations and procedures that facilitate continual adjustment to and absorption of endogenous and exogenous challenges. In these agency-oriented definitions of resilience and adaptability, institutional mechanisms are only one, sometimes minor, element. Behavioral and cognitive processes are critical; adaptiveness depends upon people's readiness to venture forth into unfamiliar environments to act, experiment, and learn from changing circumstances.

Historical institutionalist Douglass North puts adaptive capacity at the center of his explanation of developmental success. He notes that in political and economic systems alike, adaptive capacity is facilitated by formal and informal institutions and norms that enable actors in the system to try out various options. A broad spectrum of plausible alternative solutions is needed to escape developmental blockages, tackle emerging challenges, and grasp new opportunities.[23] Nassim Taleb gives the discussion on adaptive governance a new twist by proposing that innovative strength varies not according to systemic features (market vs. plan, democracy vs. authoritarianism) but by the opportunities afforded for "maximum tinkering." The prerequisite to such tinkering in any political economy is an openness to random discoveries of novel solutions on the part of its institutions, processes, and actors. Intensive tinkering can take place in non-democracies so long as the rulers are willing to encourage the decentralized generation of new knowledge.[24] In this volume, we seek to show why China has provided a political setting conducive to the kind of broad-based tinkering that development theorists such as Dani Rodrik identify as essential for discovering policy alternatives that, if built into specific domestic conditions and adapted to a changing global environment, have the potential to propel economic and social development.[25]

The Potential of Retrospective Governance Studies

To explain the adaptive capacities of China's polity, the contributors to this volume look to the historical experiences and techniques of Communist Party rule under Mao Zedong, and their retention, reinvention, and renovation under Mao's successors. The chapters to follow will trace specific linkages between revolutionary precedents and contemporary practices in a range of policy areas: agricultural development, health care, social regulation, legal reform, media control, public opinion surveillance, sub-county governance, and central-local relations. Rather than rest content with vague analogies between past and present, the authors focus on concrete mechanisms of governance cast during the Maoist era and recast by the post-Mao leadership.

The approach adopted here bears some similarity to that of historical institutionalism inasmuch as we monitor continuities and changes in political trajectories over time. But the authors depart in important ways from that approach. Rather than trace the "path-dependent" evolution of an institution as it unfolded seamlessly from some previous "critical juncture,"[26] we start our analyses with prominent features of China's contemporary political scene and then work backward in search of their (often tortuous) historical origins. The chapters in this volume, although differing substantially in content and conclusions, comprise retrospective studies of governance in a variety of key policy arenas.

A major advantage of retrospective governance studies is their open research design. When new actors, interests, or ideologies enter the scene, the approach easily accommodates such additions — in contrast to the more deterministic, prestructured models of institutional political economy. Moreover, our approach promises to avoid the teleological tendency so pervasive in social science debates about China's transformation (ever on the outlook for signs of a "real" market economy or "real" democracy) by leaving open the future possibility of unorthodox mechanisms, overlooked actors, unexpected interactions, and random interventions. Rather than biasing expectations in light of familiar Western models, we adopt an inductive outlook that views modern and contemporary Chinese history as an uncertain process of discovery — not as a trajectory pre-ordained by past experiences (or present-day social science paradigms).

In adopting this open-ended approach, one discovers in contemporary China a complex amalgam of governance mechanisms that combine Maoist, post-Maoist, and borrowed foreign elements. Moving from the Mao era's "socialist construction" to the post-Mao era's "reform and opening," China has not simply jettisoned its revolutionary past as it "transits" toward a democratic future. Rather, a succession of post-Mao leaders have managed to fashion a surprisingly adaptive pattern of authoritarian rule capable so far of withstanding challenges, including grievous and growing social and spatial inequalities, which would surely have undone less robust or flexible regimes. We obviously do not claim that revolutionary origins will tell us everything we need or want to know about the Chinese regime's resilience. But we do believe that this particular focus provides an important complement — and in some cases corrective — to prevailing approaches.

Institutional Plasticity and Policy Style Continuity

Institutional and policy instability have been prominent features of Chinese politics throughout the last century. Except for a small number of crucial core institutions, such as the Communist Party's hierarchical cadre system that Naughton and Yang rightly identify as a pillar of the Chinese polity, few organizational arrangements have functioned continuously over the entire history of the PRC.[27] Party, government, and legal institutions were subject to frequent and sometimes wild shake-ups and reorganizations.[28] Policy volatility was extreme by any comparative standard until at least 1992 when China's leadership settled on the formula of a "socialist market economy."

If institutions and policies were so unstable under Communist rule, where then do we look for continuities and guiding principles? How have Chinese policy makers responded when facing challenges or initiating programs that could not be handled by bureaucratic "autopilot" procedures? The common ground that connects the contributions in this volume, beyond the historical legacy argument, is a focus on *policy style* — or a government's guiding methodology for tackling shifting policy tasks.[29] An important concern in public administration theory, the concept of "policy style," opens a revealing window on the issue of continuity and change in contemporary China. Although PRC institutions and policies have been subject to frequent shifts over time, major components of the Communist Party's policy style have remained surprisingly stable, even across the widely accepted watershed of the Mao and post-Mao eras.

In adopting a policy-style perspective, we are not simply imposing yet another abstract Western concept on China. The term *zuofeng* (作风) (usually translated as "work-style") permeates Chinese administrative practice. Pointing to durable policy-making routines and administrative habits that are neither formalized nor reflected upon, yet encompass a set of generally practiced problem-solving techniques, *zuofeng* is very similar in meaning to the concept of "policy style" in public administration studies.[30] Here we have a rare case where the technical terms of Western social science theory and the discourse of Chinese administrative practice actually intersect.

Once a mainstay of scholarship on Chinese politics, policy studies have been overshadowed in recent years by the field's fascination with "civil society," "social movements," "rights consciousness," and other phenomena often associated with the rise of a market economy. The relative research accessibility of such phenomena, when contrasted to the opaqueness of the Chinese political elite, has understandably contributed to the shift in scholarly priorities. The decline of policy studies is unfortunate, however, since in China's state-heavy political economy, administrative coordination and state intervention remain at least as decisive as market exchanges. The policy process holds special importance for explaining not only political interactions and rule-making, but also economic markets and social trends that in China are in no way independent of state interference. The policy process is a key mechanism for connecting (both empirically and analytically) formal hierarchies, informal networks, market transactions, and social interactions.

Guerrilla Policy Style

The exceptional institutional and policy instability of PRC history is usually attributed to the erratic and divisive behavior of the paramount leaders.[31] Such behavior, we propose, reflects a deeper *policy style* whose basic components stem in large measure from the formative experience of guerrilla warfare and revolutionary mobilization. In the course of surviving and surmounting seemingly impossible odds, Mao and his colleagues came to appreciate the advantages of agility over stability.

The *guerrilla policy style* of the PRC leadership includes a shared under-standing[32] about political agency and a distinctive methodology of policy generation that enabled success in the unpredictable military-combat settings of revolutionary times, and that bequeathed a dynamic means of navigating the treacherous rapids of transformative governance during both the Mao era ("socialist construction," "permanent revolution") and the post-Mao era ("four modernizations," "reform and opening," "socialist market economy," "joining the world" [*rushi*, also translatable as "joining the World Trade Organization"] [入世]). Core features of what we call guerrilla policy style continue to shape present-day policy-making and have contributed to the flexibility, and volatility, of Communist Party rule.

The proven ability of mobile guerrilla warfare to reap unexpected gains in a highly uncertain and threatening environment left an indelible imprint on Chinese policy makers who took part in the revolution (including the age cohorts of Mao, Deng, and Hu Yaobang, who dominated Chinese politics until at least the early 1990s). The Maoist guerrilla approach to problem-solving issued from almost thirty years of incessant political and military struggles that the Communists fought from a militarily inferior — and at times seemingly hopeless — position. It was marked by secrecy, versatility, speed, and surprise. Over the course of the revolution, continuous improvi-sation became a defining feature of Chinese Communist tactics. Moreover, Mao made abundantly clear that war and politics were to be played accord-ing to the same rules. As he stated in 1959: "Military affairs are politics under special conditions. They are a continuation of politics. Politics are also a type of war."[33]

The legacies of the guerrilla policy style in China have attracted scant attention by Western scholars.[34] Yet core features of contemporary Chinese policy-making are also defining characteristics of Chinese guerrilla warfare.[35] Beyond the well-known combination of centralized leadership and intensive popular mobilization ("mass line"), the guerrilla mode of political leadership and policy-making revolves around the following shared understandings:

- the political world and its power constellations are subject to eternal flux and ceaseless change that cannot be effectively halted or channelled by political-legal institution-building;
- policy-making should be kept fluid by trying to avoid binding con-straints (e.g., personal pre-commitments or legal-contractual obliga-tions) so as to retain political initiative and room for policy revision;
- policy-making is a process of continual improvisation and adjustment that "shapes itself in the making";[36]

- recurrent standard operating procedures that can be discerned by enemy forces should be avoided;
- advice derived from theory and abstract models is not to be trusted; instead, new methods of action are derived from pilot efforts and practical experience in concrete settings;
- strategic decisions are the preserve of the top leadership; yet operationalization and implementation require substantial latitude for local initiative and independence;
- tensions among political forces and within society should be actively manipulated to take full advantage of political opportunities;[37]
- unexpected opportunities should be ruthlessly exploited to weaken or eliminate political enemies; alliances should be forged or broken as conditions dictate;
- risk should be minimized by launching new campaigns and staging direct confrontations only in the most favorable environments.

The policy style that emerges from these stratagems is fundamentally dictatorial, opportunistic, and merciless. Unchecked by institutions of accountability, guerrilla leaders pursue their objectives with little concern for the interests of those who stand in their way.

But with regard to adaptive capacity, the approach produces maximum creativity since policy makers are required to:

- test and push constantly the limits of the status quo and seize every possible opportunity for changing the situation to their advantage;
- keep the core strategic objectives firmly in mind, yet be as agile and pragmatic as possible in choosing tactical and operational means;
- tinker with a full range of available operational tactics and organizational approaches, be they traditional, non-traditional, or even foreign;
- search for and exploit random opportunities and discoveries that promise to promote political power and strategic goals.

The policy style shaped by these basic features can be characterized as a change-oriented "push-and-seize" style that contrasts with the stability-oriented "anticipate-and-regulate" norm of modern constitutional government and rule-of-law polities (which typically aspire to a predictable environment where political leaders are held accountable for their actions). It shares, however, certain affinities with the "business as warfare" theme that permeates recent writing on market competition by today's captains of global capitalism.[38]

In the guerrilla policy style, political accountability is sacrificed to the goal of leadership flexibility, expressed in the Maoist formula of "politics in command" (*zhengzhi guashuai*, 政治挂帅). In theory, lower-level leaders are subject to supervision by their Communist Party superiors. Since oversight is sketchy and episodic, however, local policy makers are not credibly constrained. In post-Mao local government we find widespread evidence at the grassroots level of entrepreneurial, experimentalist, opportunistic, and ruthless policy makers who simultaneously advance both their careers and their material interests. In so doing, they embody classic features, including the downsides and risks, of the guerrilla policy style. The guerrilla fighter is a populist, not a democrat.

Mao's conversion of guerrilla warfare into a mode of political governance was driven by Machiavellian calculations. As Michel Oksenberg observes, "Mao's pattern of rule ... [was an] ... effort to control ... the process of policy-making by determining communication channels, personnel appointments and military deployment ... [to] avoid becoming the captive of the administrative apparatus. ... Mao had to use informal means (such as the use of personal ties) or counter-institutions (such as campaigns) in order to make the formal mechanisms which he only partially created responsive to his will."[39]

The guerrilla policy style stands in stark contrast to democratic norms of political accountability, legal consistency, and procedural stability. It also stands in clear tension with the formal bureaucratic norms that are an important part of the Soviet Communist tradition and that competed with Mao's free-wheeling style even in his own day.[40] Although bureaucracy has gained a more secure status in post-Mao China, comprehensive rounds of "rectification" and restructuring remain a conspicuous feature of Chinese politics.[41] Forceful top-down policy interventions and campaigns that disrupt bureaucratic routines and shake up bureaucratic organizations continue to occur.

In addition to its negative impact on political accountability and procedural predictability, guerrilla policy style generates difficulties for central-local interaction and inter-regional distribution. To maximize flexibility and reduce the burden (and accountability) of the central leadership, the division of labor among different command levels is un-clarified and under-institutionalized. In effect, localities are generally left to fend for themselves, receiving only erratic and episodic central support. Although this may work to boost local policy creativity and operational autonomy, the lack of centrally coordinated redistribution also generates stark inter-regional disparities and underequipped "local government on a shoestring."[42]

Guerrilla policy-making consists of malleable stratagems that are employed in multiple variations and applications in response to shifting constellations of political forces. These stratagems only work if they are used in such a way as to surprise one's competitors. Guerrilla-style policy-making calls for circumventing existing rules, overcoming constraints, and maximizing one's own maneuverability while minimizing or eliminating one's opponents' influence on the course of events.

Moving back beyond Communist Party history to probe more deeply into the Chinese past, one may observe that basic features of the guerrilla policy style are congruent with a long and influential line of traditional thought which stressed fluid, dialectical, and tactical approaches to managing ubiquitous tensions and contradictions.[43] The ancient *Book of Changes* presents an image of the world subject to continuous flux and driven by the ceaseless interaction of opposing elements. Sunzi's *Art of War* reflects a similar view in its military prescriptions: "All warfare is based on deception. Hence when able to attack we must seem unable; when using our forces, we must seem inactive; when we are near, we must make the enemy believe we are far away; when we are far away, we must make him believe we are near." What Iain Johnston has labeled the dominant *"parabellum* paradigm" of Chinese strategic culture assumes the ubiquity of conflict and the attendant advantages of "absolute flexibility" in the application of violence.[44] Thanks in part perhaps to these powerful cultural and intellectual legacies, Chinese leaders seem inclined toward a strategic outlook that differs markedly from that of many Western democratic politicians.

Preview of the Volume

The chapters to follow offer retrospective studies of a variety of important policy arenas in contemporary China. They do not pretend to be either comprehensive or consistent. Many critical governance issues (e.g., education, religion, and internal security to name but a few) are not covered. And the authors reach different conclusions on many points, from the particular origins of the various practices they examine to the degree of continuity and discontinuity in these practices over the Mao and post-Mao eras. Some of the disagreements can be attributed to the particular policies under consideration, whereas others reflect divergent interpretations on the part of the authors. Despite such inconsistencies, the chapters point to what we believe to be a coherent, fruitful, and under-utilized avenue for explaining the surprising resilience and adaptability of the Chinese Communist regime. Even in the "post-revolutionary" setting of the contemporary PRC, the often invisible hand of Chairman Mao merits serious analytical attention. Tamed, tweaked, and transformed, to be sure, his guerrilla policy style still plays an important role in China's governing practices.

Elizabeth Perry's opening chapter explores the legacy of a defining element of the Chinese revolutionary tradition: the mass campaign. Put to dramatic (and sometimes devastating) use by Mao and his comrades from the 1930s on, the mass campaign was declared defunct by Deng Xiaoping at the beginning of the reform era in 1978. Nonetheless, Perry argues, campaigns have continued to constitute an important and effective resource for policy experimentation throughout the reform era. Based on an examination of the contemporary rural development program to construct "a new socialist countryside," Perry suggests that mass campaigns have been modified into "managed campaigns" that are more eclectic in both sources of inspiration and methods of implementation than their Maoist forebears. Despite such adjustments, Chinese leaders' continued reliance on campaign methods perpetuates certain negative aspects of Maoism, including the often callous disregard for the actual (as opposed to imagined) preferences of rural inhabitants.

Sebastian Heilmann's chapter traces the distinctive "point-to-surface" method of Chinese policy-making back to the establishment of Mao Zedong's first rural base area in Jinggangshan in 1928. Operating in an impoverished remote mountainous setting where standard Leninist revolutionary prescriptions offered little guidance, the Chinese Communists developed an experimental brand of policy formulation that became a cornerstone of Maoist revolutionary strategy. In the guerrilla tradition, in response to the changing environment, the leaders made up policies as they went along. The method underwent important transformation during the early years of the PRC (with the imposition of centrally designated models for national emulation), but remained available for post-Mao leaders to redirect to the goal of economic modernization. Even today, thanks to this "experimentation under hierarchy" approach, trial implementation of controversial or risky reforms in limited domains regularly precedes the enactment of national laws: risky policies are tried out first, spread to larger areas secondly, and only written into national law as a last step.

Wang Shaoguang's chapter addresses one of the major rural development challenges for the contemporary Chinese state: ensuring affordable health care in the wake of the decollectivization of agriculture. Wang notes that a variety of cooperative medical schemes emerged as grassroots-initiated programs in the mid-1950s during the Maoist upsurge of rural collectivization, which (despite reversals in the 1960s) by the early 1970s provided nearly universal health-care coverage for Chinese villagers. Although this impressive system was largely dismantled under the market reforms of the 1980s, in very recent years the central government — drawing on the results of widespread experimental studies — has provided substantial subsidies to enable an unprecedented extension of the quasi-Maoist cooperative medical program.

Nara Dillon emphasizes the continuing importance of Maoist methods in the PRC's handling of voluntary associations, non-profits, and other elements of what is often termed "civil society." State control of this sector has been achieved not through the oftentimes inefficient and corrupt police apparatus or through universal bureaucratic enforcement, but through a low-cost, targeted approach that has served to isolate threatening social forces while sustaining the majority's compliance with Communist Party rule. In the 1950s, a series of mass struggle campaigns (an extension and elaboration of guerrilla tactics) proved to be an effective means of exerting authority over the voluntary sector. Because of their selectivity, uncertainty, and attacks on the legitimacy of their targets, such campaigns afforded the new Communist government considerable leverage. Despite important movement toward greater legalism in the post-Mao period, rectification reviews reminiscent of campaigns continue to serve as a critical instrument for taming this sector, thereby inhibiting the rise of an independent civil society. Dillon observes that these quasi-Maoist methods of control have been employed more frequently in the last few years.

If, as Dillon suggests, the NGO sector does not offer much ground for optimism about an imminent transition to democracy via an emergent civil society, what about the legal arena? Benjamin Liebman explores the legal reforms of the post-Mao era, finding in China's current emphasis on legal aid, public hearings, and education about the law — all of which are unusual practices for authoritarian regimes — evidence not of incipient democracy, but rather of the continued importance of the legacy of revolutionary legalism. He argues that the susceptibility of Chinese legal institutions to influence by public opinion, popular protest, and the media reflect an abiding appreciation for "legal populism" that has been a central feature of Chinese Communist legal theory and practice since the Jiangxi Soviet of the 1930s. According to Liebman, although the first twenty years of post-Mao reform were marked by attempts to break with the revolutionary past in favor of international norms, in very recent years the PRC has returned to an emphasis on its own unique legal model. The 2000s have seen a shift away from adjudication and legal procedure back toward the forms of mediation that were more typical of Mao's China. In the Maoist approach to legal institutions, law is designed to advance party policy, not to restrain it. Liebman concludes that contemporary Chinese courts diverge significantly from other comparative models — democratic and authoritarian alike — opening the possibility for an alternative trajectory of legal development.

If the seeds of Chinese democracy do not lie in the legal sphere, what about the media? Highlighting President Hu Jintao's recent turn to the Internet to "chat" with the populace, Yuezhi Zhao sees not the signs of political liberalization but instead "a digital age re-articulation of the CCP's revolutionary hegemony, especially its 'mass-line' mode of political communication." Zhao also detects the revival of Maoist populism in the voices of many ordinary Chinese Netizens, who have taken to the Internet to criticize the post-Mao reforms as a betrayal of the revolution. Somewhat counter-intuitively, perhaps, cutting-edge commercial technology has emerged as a powerful vehicle for conveying anti-market sentiments. Articulating a concern for social justice and socialist renewal, Internet discourse has rekindled a latent yearning for Maoist revolutionary values among some sectors of the population.

Like Yuezhi Zhao, Patricia Thornton notes the Chinese Communist Party's continuing interest to "construct public opinion." She emphasizes, however, the stark difference between Maoist social investigation efforts to stir class consciousness and post-Mao random survey methods that stifle mass criticism in favor of a "depoliticized choice-making on the part of respondents." According to Thornton, the mass line politics of Mao's age have been supplanted by an engineering approach in which public opinion polls serve to disaggregate, and thereby defuse, awareness of and anger toward the growing socioeconomic inequalities generated by reform. Although the Communist leadership retains its revolutionary-era concern for mass transformation, it seeks to achieve this familiar goal through new means. The party's epistemological and methodological shift toward "scientific development" may not hasten political liberalization, but in Thornton's words serve to "lubricate the global machinery of capitalism."

Courts of law, media, and public opinion polls are not the only means of channelling mass interests, of course. Grassroots government remains the primary mechanism for handling popular grievances. Yet, as Joseph Fewsmith details, sub-county governance in China is in serious trouble.

Because local administration is not well institutionalized — an outcome that Fewsmith attributes to the legacy of thin imperial rule followed by revolutionary efforts to control society — the system invites abuse on the part of unscrupulous cadres. In some places, local party secretaries even employ organized criminal networks to enforce their will on restive villagers. Although Fewsmith reviews a number of recent experiments to reform local government, he stresses that — absent a fundamental transformation of the political system — such efforts are unlikely to curb cadre misbehavior in any significant or systematic way. Instead, similar to guerrilla leaders of the revolutionary era, grassroots officials today are largely unaccountable to the people they ostensibly serve.

Like Fewsmith, Jae Ho Chung points to the lingering influence of both imperial and revolutionary governance practices to explain enduring patterns of central-local relations. Whereas Fewsmith highlights the negative consequences of these patterns for ordinary citizens, Chung underscores their positive contribution to political unity and stability. Despite a centrifugal tradition that has been an integral part of Chinese history, Chung observes, central directives consistently trumped local discretion throughout the Mao period. In the 1950s and 1960s in particular, centralized ideological control was so effective that it was "independent of the bureaucratic institutions and mostly self-policing in its mode of operation," even in the midst of severe disruptions in the administrative system. Although post-Mao reforms loosened Beijing's command over the localities and transformed central-local interactions, the center still wields a variety of effective controls (from communications channels to military might) for restraining regionalism and enforcing national policy. Chung offers no long-range prediction about the durability of the current political system. But he concludes with a haunting hypothesis: "in the long run, the features of a Chinese dynasty may eventually overshadow the characteristics of a Communist regime."

Conclusion

Whether they present the particular Maoist legacy under consideration in more negative or positive terms, the contributors agree on the value of investigating its continuing impact on contemporary practices. A range of governing techniques — political-administrative, legal, social, and economic — owe their origins to the Maoist past (see Table 1.1).

Despite the authors' emphases on the continued salience of Maoist influences, no one claims that guerrilla policy style explains everything or

Table 1.1

Distinctive Contemporary Governance Techniques That Originate from the
Revolutionary and Mao Eras (1927–1976)

Political-Administrative	Legal	Social	Economic
institutional plasticity; strong informal networks; weak bureaucratic rules	law and adjudication as malleable instruments to advance party policies	grassroots practices and on-site investigations as inputs into national policy-making	policy objectives set by party center; policy instruments developed by the localities
shifting balance in central-local policy initiatives; experiment-based policy generation	priority of party decrees over law in policy implementation	managed campaigns for policy implementation	policy implementation according to local circumstances
weakly institutionalized central-local interactions; prohibitions of collective action by local governments	emphasis on mediation, informality, and morality in dispute resolution	controlled social polarization; careful targeting and staging of political repression	generating economic policy change from experimental sites
extensive propaganda work; active construction of public opinion	judicial populism vs. judicial professionalism	discretionary approaches for dealing with social groups and organizations	achieving "hard targets" (e.g., the GDP growth rate) through cadre system incentives
political campaigns; circumvention of bureaucratic inertia through populist appeals	experimental regulation and legislation	guiding and educating society through model experiences	production and investment campaigns as short-term fixes to economic bottlenecks

Source: Selected findings from the contributions to this volume.

that it has remained unaltered. No one denies that this policy style has had a dreadful impact on political accountability and the legal system. And no one asserts that this policy style will save the Communist Party from political and social pressures that may result in future systemic transformation.

Two core components of guerrilla policy style — ideological control and mass mobilization — have been substantially diluted during the reform era. Under Mao, as Chung observes, centralized ideological control was at times so effective that "even in the middle of organizational breakdown and administrative disruption, the self-policing Maoist norms operated effectively to ensure mechanical conformity and to detect even slight deviations at the local level." That reservoir of popular enthusiasm, or ideological conformism, facilitated the regime's reliance on mass campaigns — in place of bureaucratic methods — during the Great Leap Forward and the Cultural Revolution. Ideological indoctrination and mass upheaval were seen by post-Mao leaders as among the most problematic elements of the Maoist legacy — responsible for preserving Communist Party rule at the expense of economic modernization. It was this conclusion that prompted Deng Xiaoping to declare an end to mass campaigns. Yet, although ideologically inspired mass mobilization no longer plays the same central role in routine policy-making and administration these days, the ambitious propaganda effort to shape and manipulate public opinion has never ceased, even if, as Thornton suggests, the goal has changed from mobilizing the masses for political action and personal sacrifice to promoting passive compliance and commercial consumerism.

The guerrilla policy style competes today (as it did intermittently even under Mao) with more conventional approaches: bureaucratic and law-based policy-making and implementation. "Regularizing" governance has become a core theme of the Chinese leadership since the 1980s. China's bureaucratic and legal systems have been extended and modernized to a degree well beyond anything during the Mao era. But, as the chapters of this volume argue, inherited and adapted elements of guerrilla policy still play a vital role in dealing with crucial policy tasks, from mobilization in times of perceived crisis to managing central-local interactions to facilitating economic policy innovation and reorganizing public health care. Designed to handle a changing, complex, and unpredictable environment in a proactive manner, the guerrilla policy approach — for better *and* for worse — remains politically potent.

What emerges from studying the legacies of revolutionary and Mao-era policy styles in contemporary Chinese governance is not a ready-made

"Chinese model" defined by replicable institutional variables. We find rather a fluid, context-, situation-, and agency-based *modus operandi*: a method of policy generation and implementation based on an acceptance of pervasive uncertainty, a readiness to experiment and learn (even from enemies and foreigners), an agility in grasping unforeseen opportunities, a single-mindedness in pursuing strategic goals, a willingness to ignore ugly side effects, and a ruthlessness in eradicating unfriendly opposition.

Because the guerrilla approach to policy generation and implementation is experimentalist and non-repetitive, it is not best conceptualized as an "informal institution."[45] Whether formal or informal, institutions are designed to *contain uncertainty* and stabilize actors' expectations about future interactions by specifying certain norms and rules. In contrast, the rationale behind guerrilla policy-making is precisely to *embrace uncertainty* in order to benefit from it. The guerrilla policy approach is driven by a determination to overcome or eliminate existing constraints, rather than to work within them.

Guerrilla policy style pursues a decidedly change- and agency-oriented agenda. It constitutes a type of *transformative* governance geared to overcoming the status quo. It is not directed to systemic and institutional consolidation, unlike polities that regard themselves as advanced or mature systems and therefore cling to an implicitly *protective* type of governance. Table 1.2 juxtaposes as ideal types the transformative and protective policy styles.

To reiterate, the Chinese guerrilla policy style is not a generic feature of Communist countries. In contrast to the PRC, the socialist states of the Soviet Union and Eastern Europe, after their Stalinist phase, strove to defend, and improve only incrementally on, the status quo. They made every effort to solidify their rule, not to reinvent it repeatedly. The latter is a uniquely Maoist imperative. Since the guerrilla policy style rests on fluid institutional arrangements, the adaptation of party-state institutions to new economic priorities proved much less problematic in China than in the former Soviet and Eastern European Communist party-states, despite a series of reform efforts from Khrushchev through Gorbachev.[46]

These important differences between the PRC and other Communist systems suggest that the preoccupation with institutional analysis and regime typologies characteristic of many Western studies of China's political economy may be misplaced. Communist Party rule has proven adaptive in China not because of its institutional foundations (which were as clumsy and fragmented as in the former Communist party-states of Eastern Europe) but because of a pervasive policy style that encourages diverse and flexible

Table 1.2
Transformative vs. Protective Policy Styles and Adaptive Capacity

	Transformative (Guerrilla) Policy Style	**Protective Policy Style**
overriding policy goal	overcoming status quo	defending/incrementally improving the status quo
institutional structure	fluid institutional arrangements	fixed institutional arrangements
	shifting division of labor between different administrative levels	constitutionally defined division of labor between different administrative levels
policy process	agency-oriented ("politics in command"; "push and seize")	structure-oriented (rigid institutional checks; "anticipate and regulate")
	policy makers with considerable discretionary powers	policy makers bound to formal rules
	experimentalist	legalistic
	active management of uncertainty through policy experimentation	attempt to contain uncertainty through extensive legal provisions
	maximum exposure to random discoveries of novel policy solutions	minimal exposure to random discoveries of novel policy solutions
adaptive capacity	policy-driven (ad-hoc, periodically volatile)	law-based (pre-stabilized), market-driven
	possibility of swift, "big leap" adaptation and innovation	incremental, "small step" adjustments
political accountability	cast aside to facilitate maximum policy flexibility	emphasized as foundation of rule of law

responses to fundamentally redefined development priorities and to large-scale changes in the domestic and global environments.

The difficulty in trying to force China's development experience into the procrustean bed of conventional institutional categories is not accidental: the dynamics and capacities of China's political system are driven by particular patterns that are ill-suited to such a taxonomic exercise. A

methodological alternative, whose advantages we hope to demonstrate in
this volume, is to intensify research on the deviant (unconventional or even
unique) and varying policy mechanisms that have propelled change in
important sectors of China's government, economy, society, and international relations. More generally, the power of policy creativity deserves
greater emphasis in discussions about how to facilitate change in developing,
emerging, and even advanced political economies.[47]

A serious analysis of China's transformative style of governance not only
helps to explain the peculiarities of the Chinese case (by going beyond static
and linear institutionalist, path-dependency perspectives). It also poses
a potential challenge to presently more-developed political economies
struggling to keep up with the accelerated pace of change in the twenty-
first century, while saddled with a strong institutional status-quo bias[48]
and weak policy corrective mechanisms. The adaptive capacity of China's
non-democratic political system offers a radical alternative to the bland
governance models favored by many Western social scientists who seem to
take the political stability and economic superiority of capitalist democracies
for granted. To increase policy agility and strengthen the resilience of democratic rule in the twenty-first century may require an intellectual effort
willing to question twentieth-century assumptions about systemic superiority by taking a sober look at the foundations of innovative capacity displayed
by non-democratic challengers such as China.

Again, the Chinese guerrilla policy style has fundamental flaws: lack of
political accountability, undue administrative discretion, and distributive
deficiencies that contribute to severe regional and social tensions. The most
serious long-term shortcoming, beyond its fundamentally undemocratic
nature, may lie in the single-minded pursuit of strategic policy goals (e.g.,
economic growth or demographic control) with little regard for the deleteri-
ous side-effects that often emerge only over time (e.g., environmental
destruction or gender imbalances). As the demand from Chinese society for
political accountability, legal entitlements, a social safety net, and environmental protection grows, public tolerance for guerrilla-style policy-making
may well decline. The hard test for China's adaptive capacity will be some
massive crisis in which not only economic and social learning, but also polit-
ical-institutional responsiveness and popular support for the government
are stretched to the limit. As Andrew Nathan warns in a recent essay on
"authoritarian impermanence":

> What keeps such crises of government from becoming crises of the regime are
> cultures of open dissent, the robust rule of law, and the institutional capacity to

change leaders in response to public discontent without changing the system.... Without them, the authoritarian regime must perform constantly like a team of acrobats on a high wire, staving off all crises while keeping its act flawlessly together. Today ... the regime is managing to do that. But it cannot afford to slip.[49]

In this volume, we make no predictions about the future of China's high-wire performance. Taking a page out of the Chinese policy makers' play-book, we too may be well advised to "embrace uncertainty." But, however long before the curtain closes on China's virtuoso acrobatic act, we do insist that it has been sufficiently sure-footed to date to merit a more complete explanation of its political foundations.

Endnotes

1. Roderick MacFarquhar, "The Anatomy of Collapse," *New York Review of Books*, 38, no. 15 (September 26, 1991): 5–9; Jack A. Goldstone, "The Coming Chinese Collapse," *Foreign Policy*, no. 99 (Summer 1995): 35–52.

2. Gordon G. Chang, *The Coming Collapse of China* (New York: Random House, 2001); Minxin Pei, *China's Trapped Transition: The Limits of Developmental Autocracy* (Cambridge, MA: Harvard University Press, 2006); Susan L. Shirk, *China: Fragile Superpower* (New York: Oxford University Press, 2007); Bruce Gilley, *China's Democratic Future: How It Will Happen and Where It Will Lead* (New York: Columbia University Press, 2004).

3. The concept of "mechanism" (policy, administrative, etc.) as used in this volume follows Jon Elster's definition as "frequently occurring and easily recognizable causal patterns that are triggered under generally unknown conditions or with indeterminate consequences." Cf. Jon Elster, *Explaining Social Behavior: More Nuts and Bolts for the Social Sciences* (New York: Cambridge University Press, 2007), p. 36.

4. Valerie Bunce, *Subversive Institutions: The Design and the Destruction of Socialism and the State* (New York: Cambridge University Press, 1999); Archie Brown, *The Rise and Fall of Communism* (London: Bodley Head, 2009).

5. The proliferation of "hybrid regime" types has also been of limited utility for understanding the Chinese case. See Larry Jay Diamond, "Thinking About Hybrid Regimes," *Journal of Democracy*, 13, no. 2 (April 2002): 21–35; Steven Levitsky and Lucan Way, *Competitive Authoritarianism: The Origins and Evolution of Hybrid Regime Change in the Post-Cold War Era* (forthcoming).

6. Cf. Andrew G. Walder, *Communist Neo-Traditionalism: Work and Authority in Chinese Industry* (Berkeley: University of California Press, 1986).

7. Cf. Mark Beeson, "Developmental States in East Asia: A Comparison of the Japanese and Chinese Experiences," *Asian Perspective*, 33, no. 2 (2009): 5–39.

8. On the limits of comparison see Elizabeth J. Perry, "Studying Chinese Politics: Farewell to Revolution?" *The China Journal*, no. 57 (January 2007): 2–5.

9. For the "Black Swan" concept and its significance for social science epistemology and methodology, see Nassim Nicholas Taleb, *The Black Swan: The Impact of the Highly Improbable* (New York: Random House, 2007).

10. Cf. John Gerring, *Case Study Research: Principles and Practices* (New York: Cambridge University Press, 2007), p. 101.

11. We are well aware that the term Maoism is not officially used in China. But because "Mao Zedong Thought" has been defined as representing the Communist leadership's "collective wisdom" derived from socialist revolution and construction, we take the liberty to label pre-1976 official political ideology and leadership doctrine with the popular Western term "Maoist."

12. Andrew J. Nathan, "Authoritarian Resilience," *Journal of Democracy* 14, no. 1 (2003): pp. 6, 13–15.

13. David Shambaugh, *China's Communist Party: Atrophy and Adaptation* (Washington, DC: Woodrow Wilson Center Press and Berkeley: University of California Press, 2008), pp. 2, 176.

14. Barry J. Naughton and Dali L. Yang, eds., *Holding China Together: Diversity and National Integration in the Post-Deng Era* (New York: Cambridge University Press, 2004), p. 9.

15. Andrew G. Walder, "The Party Elite and China's Trajectory of Change," *China: An International Journal*, 2, no. 2 (September 2004): 189–209.

16. Kellee S. Tsai, *Capitalism Without Democracy: The Private Sector in Contemporary China* (Ithaca, NY: Cornell University Press, 2007).

17. Lily L. Tsai, *Accountability Without Democracy: Solidary Groups and Public Goods Provision in Rural China* (New York: Cambridge University Press, 2007).

18. See, for example, Ping-ti Ho and Tang Tsou, eds., *China in Crisis*, 2 vols. (Chicago: University of Chicago Press, 1968, 1969); Michel Oksenberg, ed., *China's Developmental Experience* (New York: Praeger, 1973).

19. On the catastrophic famine of the 1959–62 period and its political ramifications, see Dali L. Yang, *Calamity and Reform in China: State, Rural Society, and Institutional Change since the Great Leap Famine* (Stanford, CA: Stanford University Press, 1996); and Jasper Becker, *Hungry Ghosts: Mao's Secret Famine* (New York: The Free Press, 1996). On severe environmental destruction produced by Maoist campaigns, see Judith Shapiro, *Mao's War against Nature: Politics and the Environment in Revolutionary China* (New York: Cambridge University Press, 2001). On progress made in basic educational skills and public-health standards from the 1950s to the 1970s, and the stark contrast with India, see Jean Drèze and Amartya Sen, *India: Economic Development and Social Opportunity* (New York: Oxford University Press, 1995).

20. Li Zehou (李澤厚) and Liu Zaifu (刘再复), *Gaobie geming: Ershi shiji duitan lu* (告別革命：二十世紀對談錄) (Farewell to Revolution: A Twentieth-Century Dialogue) (Taipei: Maitian chuban gufen youxian gongsi, 1999).

21. This term was employed by Roderick MacFarquhar in his comments on post-Mao policy experimentation during the July 2008 conference at Harvard.

22. The definitions in this paragraph are based on Brian Walker et al., "A Handful of Heuristics and Some Propositions for Understanding Resilience in Social-Ecological Systems," *Ecology and Society*, 11, no. 1 (2006): 2–3, 8–9.

23. Douglass C. North, *Institutions, Institutional Change and Economic Performance* (New York: Cambridge University Press, 1990), pp. 80–81; *Understanding the Process of Economic Change* (Princeton, NJ: Princeton University Press, 2005), p. 154.

24. Taleb, *The Black Swan*, p. xxi; Sebastian Heilmann, "Maximum Tinkering under Uncertainty: Unorthodox Lessons from China," *Modern China*, 35, no. 4 (July 2009): 450–462.

25. For a sophisticated conception of development as a large-scale process of self-discovery, see Dani Rodrik, *One Economics, Many Recipes: Globalization, Institutions, and Economic Growth* (Princeton, NJ: Princeton University Press, 2007).

26. For a critique of the notion of "path-dependence" in the social sciences, see Wolfgang Streeck and Kathleen Thelen, "Introduction," in Streeck and Thelen, eds., *Beyond Continuity: Institutional Change in Advanced Political Economies* (Oxford: Oxford University Press, 2005), pp. 4–9.

27. For detailed documentation of recurrent and comprehensive government restructurings throughout PRC history, see Guojia xingzheng xueyuan (国家行政学院), ed., *Zhonghua renmin gongheguo zhengfu jigou wushinian, 1949–1999* (中华人民共和国政府机构五十年, 1949–1999) (Fifty Years of Government Structures in the People's Republic of China, 1949–1999) (Beijing: Dangjian duwu chubanshe, 2000).

28. Harry Harding, *Organizing China: The Problem of Bureaucracy, 1949–1976* (Stanford, CA: Stanford University Press, 1981).

29. Cf. Jeremy Richardson, Gunnel Gustafsson, and Grant Jordan, "The Concept of Policy Style," in Jeremy Richardson, ed., *Policy Styles in Western Europe* (London: Allen and Unwin, 1982), p. 13; Michael Howlett and M. Ramesh, *Studying Public Policy* (New York: Oxford University Press, 1995), pp. 228–233.

30. In numerous interviews conducted in China's economic bureaucracies in recent years, the term *zuofeng* was raised to explain governmental practices that deviate from Western, or Soviet, conceptions and are rooted in historically grounded administrative routines. The impact of national and sectoral "administrative styles" on policy outcomes has become a subject of intense research and debate in European political science; cf. Christoph Knill, "European Policies: The Impact of National Administrative Traditions," *Journal of Public Policy*, 18, no. 1 (January 1998): 1–28.

31. See Roderick MacFarquhar, *The Origins of the Cultural Revolution*, 3 vols. (New York: Columbia University Press, 1974, 1983, 1997); Frederick C. Teiwes, *Leadership, Legitimacy, and Conflict in China: From a Charismatic Mao to the Politics of Succession* (Armonk, NY: M.E. Sharpe, 1984); Parris H. Chang, *Power and Policy in China* (University Park: Pennsylvania State University Press, 1975); Jürgen Domes, *The Internal Politics of China, 1949–1972* (New York: Praeger, 1973).

32. On a discussion of such shared understandings from an institutionalist perspective, see Kathleen Thelen, "How Institutions Evolve: Insights from Comparative Historical Analysis," in James Mahoney and Dietrich Rueschemeyer, eds., *Comparative Historical Analysis in the Social Sciences* (New York: Cambridge University Press, 2003), pp. 216–217; see also Paul Pierson, *Politics in Time: History, Institutions, and Social Analysis* (Princeton, NJ: Princeton University Press, 2004), pp. 38–39.

33. Quoted from Michel Oksenberg, "The Political Leader," in Dick Wilson, ed., *Mao Tse-tung in the Scales of History: A Preliminary Assessment* (Cambridge: Cambridge University Press, 1977), p. 78.

34. Among the most instructive studies on how guerrilla tactics shaped Maoist politics and policy-making are Samuel B. Griffith, trans., *Mao Tse-tung on Guerrilla War* (Champaign: University of Illinois Press, 2000; originally published in 1961); Oksenberg,

"The Political Leader," pp. 70–116; MacFarquhar, *The Origins of the Cultural Revolution,* 3: 326–330.

35. A particularly instructive and straightforward source on the Chinese Communists' guerrilla tactics, with special emphasis on operating under uncertainty and threat, the limits to central command, and the necessity of local operative autonomy is Mao Zedong (毛泽东), *Kang Ri youji zhanzheng de yiban wenti* (抗日游击战争的一般问题) (Yan'an: Jiefangshe, 1938). This publication (parts of which serve as the basis of Griffith's study on Chinese guerrilla tactics) gives a vivid impression of the extreme tactical flexibility, organizational plasticity, and opportunistic ruthlessness that were at the heart of the Communists' approach to war and politics. Strikingly, the straightforward wording and unprincipled tactics contained in this and other wartime pamphlets were significantly toned down and polished away in the collections of Mao's works that were published after the founding of the PRC. A useful sourcebook on the formative pre-1949 experiences of combining unconventional military and political approaches in revolutionary war is Gene Z. Hanrahan, comp., *Chinese Communist Guerrilla Tactics, A Source Book* (New York: Columbia University, 1952).

36. That is how Mao characterized his concept of "permanent revolution" in 1958; see the quote in Stuart Schram, "The Marxist," in Wilson, ed., *Mao Tse-tung in the Scales of History,* pp. 68–69.

37. Cf. Oksenberg, "The Political Leader," pp. 76–77.

38. See, for example, C. Kenneth Allard, *Business as War: Battling for Competitive Advantage* (Hoboken, NJ: John Wiley, 2004); Jack Welch, *Winning* (New York: HarperBusiness, 2005).

39. Oksenberg, "The Political Leader," pp. 86–87.

40. For classic studies of the bureaucracy's role in Chinese policy-making, see Kenneth Lieberthal and Michel Oksenberg, *Policy Making in China: Leaders, Structures, and Processes* (Princeton, NJ: Princeton University Press, 1988); Kenneth G. Lieberthal and David M. Lampton, eds., *Bureaucracy, Politics and Decision Making in Post-Mao China* (Berkeley: University of California Press, 1992); David M. Lampton, ed., *Policy Implementation in Post-Mao China* (Berkeley: University of California Press, 1987).

41. Cf. Guojia xingzheng xueyuan, ed., *Zhonghua renmin gongheguo zhengfu jigou wushinian* and Wang Yukai (汪玉凯) et al., *Zhongguo xingzheng tizhi gaige 30 nian huigu yu zhanwang* (1978–2008) (中国行政体制改革30年回顾与展望 [1978–2008]) (Prospects and Reflections on Thirty Years of Chinese Political Reform) (Beijing: Renmin chubanshe, 2008).

42. This term was coined by Lily Tsai in her comments at the July 2008 conference at Harvard.

43. For instructive studies that elaborate on these distinctive features in traditional and contemporary Chinese strategic thinking, see François Jullien, *A Treatise on Efficacy: Between Western and Chinese Thinking* (Honolulu: University of Hawai'i Press, 2004); Ralph D. Sawyer, trans. and ed., *The Essence of War: Leadership and Strategy from the Chinese Military Classics* (Boulder, CO: Westview Press, 2004).

44. Alastair Iain Johnston, *Cultural Realism: Strategic Culture and Grand Strategy in Chinese History* (Princeton, NJ: Princeton University Press, 1995).

45. We concur with Bo Rothstein's warning about the risks of conceptual overstretch in institutionalist explanations: "If 'institution' means everything, it means nothing."

Variable policy processes should be treated as distinct from durable and structured institutional arrangements. Cf. Rothstein, "Political Institutions: An Overview," in Robert E. Goodin and Hans-Dieter Klingemann, eds., *A New Handbook of Political Science* (New York: Oxford University Press, 1996), pp. 133–166, at p. 145. For a critique of the static and linear assumptions that characterize most explanations of institutional change, see Kurt Weyland, "Toward a New Theory of Institutional Change," *World Politics*, 60, no. 2 (January 2008): 281–314.

46. Cf. Peter Rutland, *The Politics of Economic Stagnation in the Soviet Union: The Role of Local Party Organs in Economic Management* (Cambridge: Cambridge University Press, 1993).

47. On the general challenge of linking and balancing structure and agency in social science analysis of large-scale change, see Ira Katznelson, "Periodization and Preferences: Reflections on Purposive Action in Comparative Historical Social Science," in Mahoney and Rueschemeyer, eds., *Comparative Historical Analysis in the Social Sciences*, pp. 270–301, especially p. 282.

48. For this argumentation, see Pierson, *Politics in Time,* pp. 30–31, 40–41.

49. Andrew J. Nathan, "Authoritarian Impermanence," *Journal of Democracy*, 20, no. 3 (July 2009): 40.

CHAPTER 2

From Mass Campaigns to Managed Campaigns: "Constructing a New Socialist Countryside"

Elizabeth J. Perry

Campaigns: A Relic of the Revolutionary Past?

It is often said that one of the most important differences between the Mao and post-Mao eras is the replacement of "revolutionary" campaigns by "rational" bureaucratic modes of governance. With the death of Mao Zedong and the gradual but steady substitution among the political leadership of younger engineers for elderly revolutionaries, China appeared to have settled into post-revolutionary technocratic rule. Hung Yung Lee wrote in 1991, "[D]uring the Mao era the regime's primary task — socialist revolution — reinforced its leadership method of mass mobilization and its commitment to revolutionary change .... [T]he replacement of revolutionary cadres by bureaucratic technocrats signifies an end to the revolutionary era in modern China."[1] A decade later, Cheng Li's study of the current generation of Chinese leaders reaches a similar conclusion, observing that "the technocratic orientation in the reform era certainly departs from the Mao era, when the Chinese Communist regime was preoccupied with constant political campaigns and 'mass line' politics."[2] This assertion that revolutionary campaigns have given way to rational-bureaucratic administration fits comfortably with comparative communism variants of modernization theory, in which the inexorable ascendance of "experts" over "reds" as a result of industrialization ensures that radical utopianism will give way to a less ambitious "post-revolutionary phase."[3]

Most China scholars (and surely most Chinese citizens) welcomed Deng Xiaoping's 1978 declaration that the campaign era had ended. A sound market economy, it seemed, would require a more orderly, less convulsive mode of policy implementation. Deng enjoined his comrades henceforth to "rely on the masses, but do not launch campaigns."[4] Over time, however, some scholars and citizens have detected certain problems with this presumed transformation in governance. In a recent book, Minxin Pei points to an "erosion of the CCP's mass mobilization capacity" in the reform period as symptomatic of a precipitous decline in the regime's ability to rule effectively. In sharp contrast to the Mao era, when "the CCP had an unusually strong capacity of mass political mobilization," Pei argues that the loss of its campaign capacity in the reform era has meant that the contemporary party-state "no longer can build broad-based social coalitions to pursue its policies and defend itself."[5]

Some Chinese villagers, mindful of the days when corrupt officials could be threatened with mass criticism, have even called for a revival of campaigns. In 1997, a Communist party journal reported a "cry [*husheng*, 呼声] for mass campaigns that at times is intense."[6] Kevin O'Brien and Li Lianjiang, writing two years later, observe that "many villagers remain nostalgic for a type of mobilization common in the Maoist era but little seen lately — vigorous mass campaigns.... More specifically, they say they yearn for agents of higher levels appearing in their villages to clean things up."[7] O'Brien and Li stress, however, that "[t]o this point, there is no indication that China's top leaders are considering anything approaching a large-scale mass movement (or even a focused, open-door rectification)."[8]

Whether one regarded post-Mao technocratic authoritarianism with relief or with reservation, it was generally agreed that campaigns had largely vanished from the contemporary Chinese political landscape. The one consistent exception appeared to be in the area of population control, where, as Tyrene White demonstrates, campaign methods continue to be employed.[9] The other notable exception was as a mode of "crisis" management, when the leadership drew upon campaign techniques to cope with sudden and unexpected challenges, such as during the Tiananmen protests of 1989, the Falun Gong protests of 1999, and the SARS epidemic of 2003.[10] Population control and crisis management involved the mobilization of grassroots party networks alongside an intensive propaganda blitz in an effort to enlist mass participation in overcoming what were deemed to be severe societal problems. In the arena of economic development, however, it was widely assumed that campaigns had been supplanted by technocratic approaches to policy implementation.

I would like to question this common assumption by proposing that the legacy of mass campaigns has remained an integral — and underappreciated

— instrument of rule in post-Mao China not only for population control and crisis management, but even in the realm of economic development. The tendency to dismiss campaigns as a discarded relic of the revolutionary past has, I believe, hindered our understanding of the ways in which the post-Mao engineers have both retained and reconfigured the revolutionary tradition. Maoist campaigns encompassed a wider variety of activities, objectives, and outcomes than is sometimes remembered, offering attractive resources for today's technocrats to rework this particular revolutionary mode of governance. The contemporary program to "construct a New Socialist Countryside" provides telling evidence of the manner in which post-Mao Chinese leaders, by means of what I call *managed campaigns*, adopt and adapt revolutionary campaign methods to current reformist agendas.

Maoist Campaigns

As many scholars have observed, the campaigns for which Mao's China is justly famous can be traced back to the years of revolutionary struggle. Although the origins were already visible in the Jiangxi Soviet,[11] it was during the Yan'an period that mass mobilization became a defining feature of Mao's revolutionary strategy.[12] In the wartime base areas, "the Chinese Communists launched a series of organized and planned campaigns with a view to mobilize the entire people in support of the Party leadership and its policies."[13] The Chinese Communist Party sponsored several different types of mass campaigns in the 1930s and 1940s: production campaigns intended to improve the economy; cultural or educational campaigns designed to combat illiteracy and heighten political consciousness; and so forth. Despite their diverse aims, all of these campaigns unfolded through a succession of more or less uniform stages.[14]

Typical of the campaigns of the wartime period was the to-the-countryside (*xiaxiang*, 下乡) movement in which cadres and cultural workers were sent down to base area villages to "squat on a point" (*dundian*, 蹲点) in order to promote economic development and raise literacy levels.[15] This kind of campaign, which combined economic and educational objectives, was continued and greatly expanded after the establishment of the PRC with the Up to the Mountains and Down to the Countryside program that sent some 1.2 million youths to the countryside between 1956 and 1966 and another 12 million between 1968 and 1975.[16] The program in many respects was costly, yet a Western economic analysis in 1975 observed that "agriculture is benefiting from the broadening of education and training in the rural areas, the increased experience of the work force with fertilizers and machinery, and the assignment to the countryside since 1968 of nearly 10 million middle-school graduates from urban areas."[17] In his comprehensive study of this campaign, political scientist Thomas Bernstein concurs that the program — despite evident inefficiencies — "undoubtedly" brought benefits to the rural sector.[18]

The Up to the Mountains and Down to the Countryside movement, although especially important for understanding today's effort to construct a New Socialist Countryside, was only one of numerous campaigns that punctuated the Maoist era. As John Gardner noted in his 1969 study of the Five-Antis Campaign in 1950s Shanghai, "the implementation of policy by means of mass mobilization is one of the most distinctive features of the Chinese Communist political process. Since 1949 the Chinese masses have participated in over one hundred mass movements, all of which, to some degree, have been designed to assist the revolutionization of society."[19] Gordon Bennett, in his monograph on the subject, offered the following definition of the seemingly ubiquitous Maoist mass campaign: "A Chinese *yundong* is a government-sponsored effort to storm and eventually overwhelm strong but vulnerable barriers to the progress of socialism through intensive mass mobilization of active commitment."[20]

As in the wartime era of guerrilla struggle, so too in the post-1949 Maoist period campaigns were carried out through a progressive series of identifiable stages: experimentation with competing policy proposals, designation of tasks summed up by catchy slogans, a draft of points distributed to all concerned agencies, and the establishment of keypoints (*zhongdian*, 重点) and representative models (*dianxing*, 典型). (For further discussion of this Maoist legacy of experimentation, see Sebastian Heilmann's chapter in this volume.) Cadres were dispatched to these keypoint and model sites for intensive training in the new movement, after which they were expected to implement the campaign in their own jurisdictions. Regular party organizations managed the majority of the campaigns, but in especially important campaigns detached cadres were temporarily transferred outside of their jurisdictions as "work teams" (*gongzuodui*, 工作队) that joined with local party leaders to form an ad-hoc leadership group. "Activists" (*jiji fenzi*, 积极分子) and "backbones" (*gugan*, 骨干) were selected from among the masses in the course of the campaign to facilitate "breakthroughs" (*tupuo kou*, 突破口) in grassroots implementation and to replenish the party ranks.[21] The aim was to prevent bureaucratic inertia by recruiting grassroots enthusiasts to augment (and in some cases override) local party and government cadres so as to advance the central leaders' agendas.

Although today we look back upon Mao's mass campaigns as a destructive style of governance that disrupted and nearly derailed China's development effort, an earlier generation of scholars was less negative in its assessment. In his 1977 book on Mao-era mobilization campaigns, Charles Cell identified three major types of campaigns: economic, ideological, and struggle. According to Cell, economic campaigns — in which "leaders talk of 'socialist construction'" — exhibited better results than the other two types. With the notable exception of the Great Leap Forward, Cell credits economic campaigns with a productive emphasis on construction, solidarity, and development.[22] In a similar vein, Gordon Bennett argued in 1976 that not only were Maoist campaigns an "effective vehicle for political participation," but they also "contribute more to economic development than they take away."[23]

Michel Oksenberg, in his 1969 dissertation on the mass irrigation campaign of 1957–58, provided a similar description of the goals of Maoist campaigns, although offering a less sanguine view of the actual results. In Oksenberg's account, campaigns shared one or more of three aims: to establish new or reorganize old organizations, to change the attitudes of leaders and masses, and to stimulate production. Oksenberg presents the Maoist campaign as posing a radical challenge to the claims of modernization theory: "In a fundamental sense, the Chinese experience under Mao is a litmus test of the relationship between modern bureaucratic practice and economic development. Need the former accompany the latter?" In the case of the water conservancy campaign, however, he concluded that "on balance, the campaign retarded the development of China's water resources." The revolutionary campaign style, Oksenberg argued, caused a deterioration of the reporting system and a denigration of the value of technical expertise, both of which "proved disastrous."[24] Although there were surely economically more efficient means of implementing water conservancy measures than the mass campaign, China's achievements in this realm — even during the devastating Great Leap Forward — were impressive nonetheless. In the three years from 1958 to 1960, more than 16.5 million additional *mou* of land were reportedly brought under irrigation through such means.[25]

A Chinese specialist in party history and rural issues has recently summarized the achievements of Maoist campaigns as follows:

> From the collectivization campaign through the Cultural Revolution, the construction of a New Socialist Countryside made certain advances. For example, the emergence of a whole group of models represented by Dazhai, together with

"new socialist peasants," represented by Chen Yonggui, Wu Renbao, Xing Yanzi, and others, and the promotion of ideas, such as "hydrology is the lifeblood of agriculture," "mechanization is the way forward for agriculture," the "eight character constitution" for agriculture, and the like ... gradually put in place a support system that included labor insurance, poverty subsidies, livelihood subsidies, social relief, and the village "five guarantees" as well as rudimentary social protective organizations, such as old-age homes and cooperative medical care.[26]

In this view, mass campaigns to construct a New Socialist Countryside during the Maoist era laid a solid infrastructural foundation for the subsequent gains of the reform period.[27]

Constructing a New Socialist Countryside in Historical Perspective

Considering that many campaigns of the Mao era were directed toward economic development and moreover that they evidently attained at least some modicum of success, it is perhaps not surprising that the engineers now responsible for managing China's economy have launched a "construction" initiative that bears a notable resemblance to earlier to-the-countryside campaigns. Although the current leaders, adhering to Deng Xiaoping's dictum to avoid "campaigns," do not use that particular term to characterize their comprehensive effort to transform the Chinese countryside, the parallels to Maoist campaigns are quite striking.

As a recent monograph on China's rural development policy observes, "the concept of a 'new countryside' dates back to the early days of the Communist revolution in the 1930s ... previous attempts to revitalize rural China ... have provided many of the lessons learned that are now finding their way into practice; and it is with those lessons in mind that China's leadership has developed both a long-term vision and plan and a menu of many urgent goals and immediate tasks."[28]

At the Fifth Plenum of the Sixteenth Party Congress in October 2005, the CCP announced its "great historic mission" of "constructing a New Socialist Countryside" (*jianshe shehuizhuyi xin nongcun*, 建设社会主义新农村). The announcement came five months after President Hu Jintao and Premier Wen Jiabao delivered separate speeches in which they invoked these phrases as part of an action plan for resolving the problem of the "three rurals" (*sannong*, 三农), i.e., agriculture, farmers, and villages. The following year, Central Document No. 1 of 2006 highlighted the construction of a New Socialist Countryside as the "struggle target" and "action plan" for socioeconomic development in the upcoming five years. A year later,

Central Document No. 1 of 2007 reiterated this commitment, noting that "developing modern agriculture is the chief task of New Socialist Country-side construction."[29] As party organs hastened to explain, although the "phrasing" (*tifa*, 提法) harked back to the 1950s, the current initiative was being launched under new historical conditions and under "a completely new conceptual direction."[30]

The government's worry that the new construction program might be mistaken for a Maoist throwback was understandable. The 1956–67 National Program for Agricultural Development, personally drafted by Mao Zedong in late 1955 and officially promulgated in October 1957, outlined ambitious goals for a New Socialist Countryside that included improvements in agricultural production, especially grain production; water conservancy and road building; new rural housing; public health and sanitation; and educa-tion.[31] In June 1956, the National People's Congress (NPC) embraced as its "struggle target" the goal of constructing a New Socialist Countryside. Mao's program became an integral part of the General Line for Socialist Construction with which the Great Leap Forward was launched in May 1958. Constructing socialism, it was emphasized, involved not only economic progress but also the cultivation of a "new socialist person" with "socialist consciousness." Two years later, at the height of the terrible famine, the National Program for Agricultural Development was formally adopted by the NPC. Vice Premier Tan Zhenlin, who played an important role in encouraging the excesses of the Great Leap Forward, praised Mao's National Program as imbued with "mass character for constructing a New Socialist Countryside."[32]

The late 1950s saw the start of a massive relocation and reeducation effort in which a large number of both students and cadres were sent down-to-the-countryside. In August 1957, for example, the city of Nanjing assigned hundreds of recent primary and middle-school graduates to serve as "new-style peasants" in remote villages as part of the effort to construct a New Socialist Countryside.[33] With the launching of the Great Leap Forward the next year, successive waves of party cadres were dispatched to rural areas to engage in labor and carry out intensive agit-prop among the peasants.[34] What these sent-down cadres actually accomplished during their rural sojourns is not entirely clear. Many of them were reportedly overly zealous in pushing the ill-conceived policies of the Great Leap in hopes that such displays of radicalism would expedite their return to the cities.[35]

Despite the horrendous consequences of the Great Leap famine, when several tens of millions of Chinese starved to death, the Communist leadership's commitment to New Socialist Countryside construction continued to reverberate in the years that followed. In December 1963, the party center announced a resolution to mobilize urban youth to participate in the construction of New Socialist Villages. Over the next decade, millions of young people, praised as the "newborn force" of the campaign, left the cities to head "up to the mountains and down to the countryside."[36] The initiative was accompanied by considerable cultural and propaganda effort. In 1964, for example, three new Peking operas were staged (in the cities of Changchun, Nanjing, and Nanchang) to celebrate the building of New Socialist Villages around the country.[37]

During the Cultural Revolution, the "Learn from Dazhai in Agriculture" campaign carried forward the Great Leap agenda by incorporating as one of its key objectives the building of a New Socialist Countryside. In 1966, for example, production brigades in impoverished areas of Shandong were congratulated for the spirit of "arduous struggle and self-reliance" that fueled the construction of "Dazhai-type New Socialist Villages."[38] The Dazhai model of agrarian radicalism remained salient throughout the Cultural Revolution decade.[39] The party secretary of Huaxi brigade in Jiangsu, Wu Renbao, was honored in 1975 for having constructed a New Socialist Village with "new-style peasants" imbued with "socialist con-sciousness" by applying the Dazhai model in his own village over the preceding ten years.[40] Other rural campaigns during the Mao period, from irrigation to tree planting, were framed in similar terms. In 1975, an editorial in the *Hebei Forestry Science and Technology* journal referred to Chairman Mao's 1958 call for constructing a New Socialist Countryside as the inspiration for the orchards that had been planted across the province in the intervening two decades.[41]

By the end of the Cultural Revolution, the language of rural socialist construction was pervasive across a spectrum of policy arenas. A student in the Physics Department at Shaanxi Normal University wrote in 1975 of his solemn pledge to form a "strike roots" (*zhagen*, 扎根) group to carry out the construction of a New Socialist Countryside and thereby "uphold Chairman Mao's revolutionary line in education."[42] Even after the Mao period, this discourse remained powerful. In 1977, a commune in North China was lauded as a New Socialist Village for having successfully implemented a public health and sanitation drive by a combination of "reviewing Chairman Mao's teachings" and "actual class struggle."[43] Although the introduction of the Household Responsibility System and the decollectivization of agricul-ture brought a temporary halt to this discussion, it was soon revived in the

Civilized Village Campaign: "Civilized villages are the basic form for constructing a New Socialist Countryside."[44] The Civilized Village Campaign of the mid-1980s, like the earlier Mao-era campaigns, specified both objective and subjective areas for "construction": the rural economy, ideology, culture, morals, public works, village beautification, and democracy.

In the 1990s, as the focus on economic growth favored the coastal cities at the expense of the hinterland, talk of constructing a New Socialist Countryside diminished. But it did not entirely disappear. In 1992, Fujian province was credited with advancing the cause of "building new socialist villages through common effort and unified struggle." Over the preceding year, more than 40 percent of the villages in Fujian were said to have carried out "socialist education activities" aimed at "cultivating a new style peasant."[45] Party theoreticians struggled to keep the concept alive by attributing to Deng Xiaoping the idea of "constructing a New Socialist Countryside with Chinese characteristics." While acknowledging that Deng, unlike Mao, had never actually engaged in a systematic discussion of rural socialist construction, the theorists nevertheless argued that Deng's pronouncements on rural industrialization and "socialist spiritual civilization" amounted to an elaboration of Mao's pioneering efforts in this vein.[46]

Constructing a New Socialist Countryside Today

Although contemporary proponents of the New Socialist Countryside initiative eschew the term "campaign," they do not deny the obvious Maoist inspiration.[47] A policy analyst at the Sichuan Academy of Social Sciences justifies the recent initiative by explicit reference to Mao Zedong's agricultural policies:

> After many years of exploration, Mao Zedong developed a program for rural construction: namely, villages should travel the collective economic path and use "people's communes" to systematize the collective economy. . . . After New China was founded . . . the party and state organized the peasantry to take the road of collectivization. This was the correct choice under those historical conditions and had a historically progressive meaning. It serves as a powerful example for our current construction of a New Socialist Countryside. In constructing new socialist villages, we must fully affirm and fully absorb Mao Zedong's thinking on agricultural cooperation.[48]

Today's socialist countryside program, like its forerunners, calls for improving rural infrastructure (with greater state investment in water conservancy, roads, and public utilities), free compulsory education, and new rural cooperative medical services. In terms reminiscent of the Great Leap's pledge to overcome the Three Great Differences and Walk on Two Legs, the current undertaking promises to redress the imbalance between city and countryside and between industry and agriculture. As the contemporary slogan puts it, "industry repays agriculture; cities bring along the country-side" (*gongye fanbu nongye*, 工业反哺农业; *chengshi daidong nongcun*, 城市带动农村).[49] The countryside is promised more favorable treatment with the slogan "give more, take less, enliven" (*duoyu*, 多予; *shaoqu*, 少取; *fanghuo*, 放活). As in earlier campaigns, however, the expressed goals — summed up by a twenty-character mantra — are not only economic but also social, cultural, and political: "develop production, enrich livelihood, civilize rural habits, tidy up the villages, democratize management" (*shengchan fazhan*, 生产发展; *shenghuo kuanyu*, 生活宽裕; *xiangfeng wenming*, 乡风文明; *cunrong zhengji*, 村容整洁; *guanli minzhu*, 管理民主).

Despite careful avoidance of the term "campaign" (*yundong*, 运动) and substitution of less politically charged terms such as "activity" (*huodong*, 活动) and "action" (*xingdong*, 行动), Maoist rhetoric and practices pervade the initiative. An ongoing "three down-to-the-countryside activity" to disseminate science, culture, and hygiene to backward villages is to be folded into a new "three strike-roots action" in which cadres are asked to "squat on a point" in order to institutionalize efforts in rural technology, education, and public health.[50] Implementation is said to require the identification of "breakthroughs" and the cultivation of "backbones." The need for mass activism and struggle is constantly invoked. Much of Premier Wen Jiabao's December 29, 2005 speech on constructing a New Socialist Countryside could have been mistaken for a Great Leap or Dazhai manifesto: "We must fully arouse the activism of the broad peasant masses, inspiring them to carry forth the spirit of arduous struggle and self-reliance."

To jumpstart the contemporary campaign, thousands of propaganda teams and lecture teams (*xuanjiangdui*, 宣讲队; *baogaodui*, 报告队) were organized in every province. In Guangdong, old revolutionaries were invited to accompany these groups down to the villages, to "carry out education in the revolutionary tradition." Places with "red resources" such as Hailufeng (site of China's first rural soviet) were selected as sites for conducting "advanced education activity" for village cadres. In Guangxi, more than 10,000 rural work cadres possessing "good political character and a certain theoretical level" as well as technical expertise were sent to the villages to educate grassroots party members.[51]

In Jiangsu's Xuzhou city, 3,078 "work teams," composed of 6,763 party members from every county, district, and township, were dispatched to all the villages in the municipality. In each village, "backbones" were selected from among the residents to carry out specific tasks. Additionally, some 10,000 cadres were sent down from the city agencies to "squat on a point" to carry out grassroots party education.[52] In Yan'an's Wuqi county, village speech competitions were held on the theme of "the party in my heart," while locally written and produced dramas were staged and three waves of "collective study sessions among the masses" were organized to publicize the many facets of the New Socialist Countryside project. This was followed by township-level mass meetings, "unprecedented in scale," to commend those villagers who had demonstrated the greatest enthusiasm and activism.[53]

From April 2006 to January 2007, for the first time since the end of the Maoist era, every county party secretary and county magistrate in the country (more than 5,300 cadres in total) was required to attend special week-long training sessions on the implementation of the new campaign.[54] Some of these sessions were held at the Central Party School in Beijing; others at the new branch of the Central Party School located at the site of the CCP's first revolutionary base area of Jinggangshan; and yet others at "model" villages famous for their continued adherence to collectivist practices such as Dazhai in Shanxi and Huaxi in Jiangsu.[55] In some instances, graduates of these training sessions reportedly restored elements of collective farming upon returning to their home jurisdictions.[56]

To provide the central leadership with comprehensive data for selecting "test-points" and "keypoints," the Ministry of Agriculture conducted its largest-ever national survey of villages, the summary report of which concluded that "we personally felt the peasant masses' ardor and creative energy."[57] In the "model agricultural city" of Guang'an, survey data permitted the identification of fifty relatively well-off keypoint villages along with sixty poverty-stricken test-point villages.[58]

This emphasis upon survey research, while hardly surprising for a campaign designed by engineers, has also been linked to Mao Zedong's own method of rural investigation. (For more on Maoist methods of gauging public opinion, see the chapter in this volume by Patricia Thornton.) From the mid-1920s on, Mao was of course a firm advocate of village surveys, having conducted several key investigations among peasants in Hunan and Jiangxi that had a significant impact on the course of the Chinese revolution.[59] A researcher in the Department of Law and Politics of Jimei University draws the connection:

In sum, Mao Zedong's investigative approach retains its extremely important guiding function in the effort to construct new socialist villages in the new era. It is precious spiritual wealth that Mao Zedong bequeathed to us. In the process of New Socialist Countryside construction, only by upholding Mao Zedong's investigative approach ... will the construction of a New Socialist Countryside develop in a comprehensive and healthy manner.[60]

Mao's "mass line" method — "from the masses to the masses" — is frequently invoked as the appropriate means of policy formulation and implementation in the building of new socialist villages.[61]

Scholars and officials are apparently not alone in sensing Chairman Mao's guiding hand in the contemporary program. The Chinese media have offered glowing descriptions of the peasants' response to the socialist countryside program, in which the spirit of Mao Zedong hovers over the current scene. A report from Jiangxi's famous "Red Well," which — according to revolutionary legend — was dug by Mao himself at the start of the Long March, is typical of these hortatory accounts:

> By the side of the Red Well in Shazhoubei Village in Ruijin city, an old villager named Yang Qingpo could scarcely believe his eyes when he strolled around the newly built cement roads of the village. How could a village where he had lived for over sixty years change overnight? The old toilets and dilapidated pigpens had been torn down and the garbage that had been piled high around all the houses was gone. Newly built houses were neat and clean. .... "The new socialist village construction has brought us old folks great benefit. Thanks be it to the Communist Party!" He touched the stone tablet next to the Red Well that read, "When drinking the water, don't forget the one who dug the well. Think often of Chairman Mao." He felt that it expressed his own deepest sentiments.[62]

Such rosy pictures notwithstanding, there is mounting evidence that the current New Socialist Countryside campaign — like its Maoist predecessors — is at times implemented coercively, with callous disregard for the desires of the local inhabitants. For example, to promote "village beautification," party leaders in Henan's Wen county ordered thousands of public officials, teachers, and medical personnel to return to their native villages to participate in an "uprooting movement" that entailed pulling out any crops planted in front of peasant homes, along roadways, or in vacant lots. Impoverished villagers who objected that they relied on the crops for their livelihood were threatened with having their welfare subsidies cut off if they did not comply with the directive.[63]

In many instances, lineage halls and village temples have been razed to make way for roads and housing developments. In some cases, villagers have been evicted from their own homes and forcibly relocated to concentrated mass housing complexes at considerable personal expense. Such resettlement projects afford an opportunity for land grabs by rapacious officials, triggering resentment and on occasion resistance.[64] The cadre corruption that has become pervasive in rural China these days (see the chapter by Joseph Fewsmith in this volume) is on full display in this campaign. The widespread illegal conversion of collective village lands into lucrative real estate developments (that line the pockets of unscrupulous cadres) has prompted its critics to characterize the New Socialist Countryside construction effort as a "fake urbanization leap forward" (*weichengshihua yuejin*, 伪城市化跃进).[65] The *Yan'an Daily* summed up the abuses bluntly, "In the course of New Socialist Countryside construction, some places have already shown signs of conducting a mass campaign. This calls for vigilance."[66]

Even well-meaning cadres are sometimes carried away by the campaign spirit. Overly exuberant local officials have been accused of harboring "Great Leap Forward expectations."[67] Their selection of test-points and models, for example, is said to overlook backward villages in favor of wealthier villages that can more easily be presented as success stories. As was the case during the Maoist campaigns, cadres in impoverished areas are said to be particularly prone to the practice of "blindly making false reports" (*mangmu di xubao*, 盲目地虚报).[68] Rich and poor villages alike have been saddled with onerous debts to pay for road building and other expensive construction projects, the costs of which may exceed their limited means.[69]

Criticisms of the insensitive manner in which the New Socialist Countryside initiative has sometimes been conducted echo the familiar litany of complaints from bygone campaigns. Cadres are accused of "formalism" (*xingshizhuyi*, 形式主义), "commandism" (*minglingzhuyi*, 命令主义), "bureaucratism" (*guanliaozhuyi*, 官僚主义), and "ossified conservatism" (*jianghua baoshou*, 僵化保守); and warned against "seeking rigid uniformity" (*qiangqiu yilu*, 强求一律), "cutting with a single knife" (*yidaoqie*, 一刀切), "running the whole show" (*baoban daiti*, 包办代替), or "trying to promote growth by tugging at the sprouts" (*bamiao zhuzhang*, 拔苗助长).[70] Local governments are criticized for reverting to old Mao-era habits in trying to force peasant compliance without due consideration for local conditions and preferences: "During the period of the planned economy, the government grew accustomed to treating the peasantry as peons who simply took orders; it controlled the peasants by issuing blanket directives and administrative rulings. Today many local government agencies cling to these outmoded methods, refusing to adapt to the rules of a market economy as though one can still get by with 'administration dominating everything.'"[71]

Managed Campaigns

Conceptually, today's managed campaigns perpetuate many features of revolutionary mass campaigns. Like their Maoist forerunners, managed campaigns posit a close connection between subjective consciousness-raising and objective economic gains. Intensive political propaganda, intended to arouse emotional enthusiasm and enlist widespread engagement, remains a central element.[72] So, too, does the call for struggle and sacrifice in service to a larger cause. In terms of implementation, there are also (sometimes unfortunate) continuities. Coercive enforcement by over-eager cadres is not uncommon.

But managed campaigns also depart from Maoist campaigns in significant ways. Although the main purpose is still to prevent bureaucratic ossification, the sources of inspiration and imitation are more eclectic than was once the case. Managed campaigns are unabashedly pragmatic, searching for workable models wherever they may be found. In addition to Maoist rhetoric and practice, a wide variety of other concepts and techniques are also employed. On top of the language of revolution is an overlay of new technocratic terminology. One sees frequent reference to "mechanisms" (*jizhi*, 机制), "propulsion mechanisms" (*yunxing jizhi*, 运行机制), "convey-ers" (*zaiti*, 载体), "dynamics" (*lidu*, 力度), "pressure points" (*zhuolidian*, 着力点), and other technical terms befitting a Communist Party led by engineers. The entire process is to be guided by a "scientific concept of development" (*kexue fazhan guan*, 科学发展观), the motto of Hu Jintao's administration.

In managed campaigns, the benefits of an engineering approach are sometimes explicitly contrasted to the pitfalls of improperly applied Maoist methods. One policy analyst, in discussing the latest effort to construct a New Socialist Countryside, complains of a pervasive "test-point discourse" (*shidianlun*, 试点论) that confuses the identification of experimental villages with the actual construction of new socialist villages. While acknowledging that "establishing test-points and models, accumulating experience, per-fecting policies, and moving from points to planes is a very important work method," the analyst notes that grassroots cadres are often under the mistaken impression that all they need to do is to develop a few successful test-points to show off to higher levels. Instead, cadres are urged to regard the construction of new socialist villages as "systems engineering" (*xitong gongcheng*, 系统工程), requiring "comprehensive planning" (*tongchou jiangu*, 统筹兼顾) and "scientific mastery" (*kexue bawo*, 科学把握).[73]

Although the current program has certainly drawn its share of criticism for insensitive and uniform enforcement, managed campaigns do appear to allow greater latitude for grassroots variation than was true of many of Mao's campaigns. In the promotion of "model new villages" in Jiangxi's Ruijin, for example, no fewer than eighteen different types of models have been identified: tourist villages, industrial villages, agricultural villages, cultural villages, and so forth. Policy priorities are supposed to vary in accordance with these diverse identities.[74]

The recent religious resurgence taking place across much of the Chinese landscape poses special problems for an engineering effort intended, among other things, to transform rural habits and culture. One way in which the discussion surrounding the current New Socialist Countryside initiative differs from previous incarnations is in the widely expressed concern for accommodating, rather than eradicating, popular religious beliefs and practices. In contrast to the Mao era, when "new villages" were expected to renounce all expressions of religion, today's more pragmatic approach shows a greater appreciation of the necessity — and even benefit — of religious toleration. Christianity in particular is sometimes credited with contributing to villagers' patriotism, morality, and enthusiasm for education.[75] But such tolerance coexists uneasily with calls for security organs to play a more active role in constructing a New Socialist Countryside by crushing "evil cults" perpetrated by geomancers, witch doctors, and other practitioners of "feudal superstition."[76]

In light of the challenge that religion presents for managed campaigns, one cannot help but wonder whether the current construction program, like the Great Leap Forward fifty years ago, will not generate a backlash in minority regions — particularly Tibet and Xinjiang — where religious beliefs and practices are especially pronounced and where government calls for rural modernization may readily be interpreted as an assault on traditional cultural values. As June Dreyer noted of the Great Leap, "There was . . . one crucial difference between the impact of the Leap in minority areas and that in Han areas: the Great Leap Forward in minority areas was perceived as having been imposed from outside in an attempt to erase native culture and ways of life."[77] A recent report from a Tibetan region of Gansu province charges that the Chinese government, "as part of the creation of the New Socialist Countryside," has called upon Tibetan nomads "to give up their ancestral lifestyle, calling it primitive and unproductive . . . ."[78]

The latest initiative is not simply a retread of previous mass campaigns, however. In contrast to the millenarian Great Leap Forward, today's New

Socialist Countryside program does not promise to deliver instant utopia. The central leadership emphasizes that the creation of socialist villages is a long-term mission that will require many years to complete. Moreover, despite the revolutionary origins of much of the program, violence and conflict are explicitly eschewed. Although there is much talk of "struggle" (*fendou*, 奋斗), there is no mention of "class struggle" (*jieji douzheng*, 阶级斗争); instead, the watchword is the omnipresent call for a "harmonious society" (*hexie shehui*, 和谐社会).[79]

Aside from the rejection of class struggle and quick fixes, perhaps the most significant difference between a managed campaign today and a Maoist mass campaign is the avowed eagerness with which contemporary policy makers attempt to identify, adopt, and adapt relevant historical and international experiences — regardless of their political bona fides. Whereas the Great Leap Forward and Learn from Dazhai campaigns were launched in a spirit of Communist correctness and autarkic defiance, the current initiative is openly receptive to a wide range of domestic and foreign exemplars — revolutionary and non-revolutionary alike.[80]

The appeal of traditional Chinese values in today's New Socialist Countryside construction is visible in the frequent references to Confucian ideals and institutions. Official directives speak of the classic Confucian goal of a "moderately comfortable society" (*xiaokang shehui*, 小康社会), of the need for "reverse nurturance" (*fanbu*, 反哺) in which the cities — like filial children — give back the support that they once received from the countryside, and of the deployment of "land literati" (*tianxiucai*, 田秀才) — an alternative term for local backbones with technical expertise.[81] In a village in Shanghai's Chuansha county, a ditty entitled "Song to Admonish the People" (*quanmin ge*, 劝民歌), composed and promoted by the village party committee, expresses a Confucian concern for filial piety and frugality:

> The loving kindness of parents is as deep as the ocean, Show deference to the elderly and boundless love to the young; Industriousness can make one rich, Gluttony and laziness lead to a lifetime of poverty. . . .

To popularize the ditty, famous opera singers were invited to make recordings, the CDs of which were then distributed to all the villagers. Each household in the village was also required to compose "family discipline phrases" (*jia xunci*, 家训词), encouraging its members to work hard and respect their elders.[82]

Imperial precedents are cited as the inspiration for a number of recent innovations. For example, the "new village construction councils" introduced in Jiangxi province are praised as an adaptation of the "gentry power" (*shenquan*, 绅权) of the Ming and Qing dynasties. Just as in that earlier period when Jiangxi villages were governed by a "Confucian" local elite composed of retired officials, literati, lineage elders, landlords, and other influential non-bureaucrats, so today's village councils are said to be led by a "Communist" local elite of non-officials: retired cadres and elderly school teachers, model workers, and non-cadre CCP members.[83]

Republican-era precedents are highlighted as well. Members of the so-called "Rural China School," composed of eminent agrarian economists such as Chen Hansheng, Xue Muqiao, and Feng Hefa, are lauded for their illuminating rural investigations.[84] The rural reconstruction programs of the 1920s and 1930s attract considerable attention as a fruitful source of contemporary lessons. The efforts by James Yen, Liang Shuming, Lu Zuofu, Huang Yanpei, Gao Jiansi, and Tao Xingzhi are credited with promoting mass education, economic cooperation, popular participation, an equitable land system, agricultural technology, household sideline production, and the construction of rural roads, bridges, and other public works. Yen and Liang elicit particular praise for the favorable international reputations (especially in the United States and Japan) that they enjoyed during their lifetimes. Even the central organs of the Guomindang have been commended for their officially sponsored experimental counties (*shiyanxian*, 实验县) in Jiangning, Lanxi, Qingdao, and elsewhere.[85] A researcher at the Shandong Institute of Technology summarizes the contributions of these Republican-era pioneers: "Their ideas about rural construction offer inspiration and meaningful exemplars for our efforts today to study and solve the 'three rurals' and to actively promote the construction of new socialist villages."[86]

It is not surprising that the experimental outlook of earlier rural reconstruction efforts, inspired in part by John Dewey's pragmatism, attracts admiration from aspiring social engineers today. But the primary lesson drawn from the Republican-period experience is the need for a new generation of altruistic intellectuals willing to devote their own lives to the cause of rural transformation: "What must be stressed particularly is that the New Socialist Countryside construction desperately demands a large group of truly talented and knowledgeable intellectuals endowed with a spirit of sacrifice who will really go deep into the villages, into the grassroots, and will — together with the rural cadres and masses — enthusiastically carry out investigations and experiments and develop plans and proposals to solve actual difficulties and problems."[87]

Unlike Mao's to-the-countryside campaigns, in which the resettlement of urban intellectuals was supposed to be permanent, government expectations today are less demanding.[88] University students are encouraged to take advantage of their summer vacations to conduct the "three down-to-the-countryside activity" by "marching off to battle" (*chuzheng*, 出征), "following in the footsteps of the Red Army and cherishing the memory of the martyrs." Brief (and sometimes bogus) as the experience may be, the revolutionary idealism underlying the contemporary program remains observable.[89] As Bernstein wrote of the Mao era, "a revolutionary is one who defines the transfer to the countryside not as a form of downward mobility but as a form of service to the nation and to its goals of building socialism and communism."[90]

Today's engineers are willing to look not only backward, but also outward, to identify promising models for emulation and adaptation. In terms of foreign exemplars, although reference is made to the experience of Western countries such as the United States, Canada, and France, far greater attention is paid to cases closer to home: Taiwan, Japan, and especially South Korea. A recent compendium of essays by Chinese social scientists on the political theory underlying the New Socialist Countryside program begins with the statement: "From the rural reconstruction movement of the twenties and thirties, to Japan's 'one village, one product' campaign of the 1960s and Korea's New Village Movement of the 1970s, to Taiwan's village construction effort, there is a common lineage and legacy; the influence on East Asian society as a whole has been profound and the implications are immense."[91]

The South Korean New Village Movement (or *Saemaul undong*) has attracted the greatest attention and admiration, both because of the leading role played by the Korean government under Park Chung-hee in formulating and implementing the program and because of its apparent success in improving the living standards of Korean villagers.[92] In May 2005, as the Chinese Communist Party prepared to launch the Eleventh Five-year Plan guided by "the historic mission of constructing a New Socialist Countryside," the State Council dispatched a high-level delegation to Seoul to evaluate the legacy of South Korea's New Village Movement. The delegation, which included representatives from the Central Research Group, the Central Agricultural Office, the Ministry of Finance, the Ministry of Construction, the People's Bank, and Guizhou province, returned to China with a highly favorable assessment, contributing to a flood of Chinese attention to the Korean experience.[93]

As a Chinese professor of public administration has observed, China's fascination with the Korean New Village Movement bears more than a passing connection to its own history of rural campaigns:

> Using a campaign mode to undertake economic construction, as in the "Great Leap Forward" of the 1950s or "Learn from Dazhai in Agriculture" of the 1960s and 1970s, is a method of social mobilization that is very familiar to the Chinese people, particularly the Chinese peasantry. Since 1978, although many types of campaigns have become extinct, the government still favors launching campaigns as a means of social control. But as a means of economic construction, campaigns have been repudiated by government officials and ordinary people alike. And yet the Korean New Village Movement, which is hailed as a successful model of rural construction, actually shares many similarities with China's "Learn from Dazhai" campaign in terms of both organization and mobilization.[94]

Korea's *Saemaul undong*, carried out between 1970 and 1980, is generally credited with many of the same achievements as the Republican-era rural reconstruction effort: improved rural roads and residences, the delivery of electricity and running water to remote villages, the introduction of advanced farming techniques, and the establishment of functioning village councils.[95] A critical ingredient in the success of the New Village Movement, again like China's own rural reconstruction experience, is said to lie in its mobilization of urbanites — from intellectuals and government officials to ordinary citizens — who ventured down-to-the-countryside in large numbers to make their own contributions to improving the quality of rural life.[96]

At least as intriguing to Chinese observers as the process and outcome of the Korean movement is the fact that it was conducted under the auspices of an authoritarian government operating in a historically Confucian society. A Chinese political scientist points out:

> The Chinese political system is similar to that of Korea in many respects. In the past we relied upon a central authority to launch a number of large-scale national campaigns, such as the "Great Leap Forward," "Learn from Dazhai in Agriculture," and so forth. Leaving aside the question of the pluses and minuses of a campaign mode of social control, under a centralized political system within a Chinese type of cultural tradition it is necessary to use central government authority to promote the provision of rural public goods. This is the valuable experience gleaned from the success of the East Asian countries, especially Korea.[97]

The combination of strong governmental initiative together with an emphasis on ethics and education is seen as a particularly attractive — and easily adapted — feature of the New Village Movement.[98] The *Saemaul undong* is credited with having awakened Korean villagers from a fatalistic and dependent mentality nurtured by a long history of Confucian traditional culture.[99] At the same time, a perceived failing of the Korean (and also Japanese) experience is spotlighted and cautioned against; namely, the massive rural-to-urban migration that occurred in those countries in the wake of rapid economic growth. Officials and policy analysts alike call for an end to the "hollowing out" (*kongxinhua*, 空心化) that is already threatening many Chinese villages, as the younger, stronger, and more capable members of the communities depart for the cities.[100]

Taiwan is in many respects a politically more problematic exemplar for the PRC than either South Korea or Japan, of course. Yet political sensitivities have not prevented serious interest in the Taiwanese record of rural development. Somewhat ironically, in light of the PRC's own socialist pretensions, it is Taiwan's achievements in the realm of grassroots collective organization that have attracted the greatest admiration from observers on the mainland. Taiwan's farmers' associations (*nonghui*, 农会), first established in 1900 under Japanese colonialism but systematized in the 1970s under Guomindang authoritarian rule, are held up as a model for how to bridge the concerns of government and peasantry. The associations are lauded for providing a channel for the articulation of peasant interests as well as for publicizing and promoting official policies, agricultural techniques, market conditions, and the like.[101] Taiwan's agricultural cooperatives (*nongye hezuoshe*, 农业合作社), albeit a more recent and less widespread institution than its farmers' associations, are also credited with important organizational and economic contributions.[102]

Conclusion

Although engineers have succeeded revolutionaries as the power elite in China, their ascendance has not brought an end to the campaign tradition. What we are witnessing in contemporary China, it seems, is not simply the replacement of an outmoded revolutionary style of politics with a modern technocratic mode, but rather a complex amalgam of the two (with a strong element of Confucianism and East Asian experience thrown in for good measure). Modernization theory, with its emphasis on the inexorable evolution of rational-legal bureaucratization, will therefore not take us very far in making sense of it. Managed campaigns should be studied seriously on their own terms, as a powerful method of governance — capable of impressive achievements yet entailing substantial human cost.

The continuing importance of the campaign tradition to China's current development drive cautions against drawing too definitive a distinction between the Mao and post-Mao periods. As the Chinese economy enters its fourth decade of stunning growth, while retaining and reshaping central components of its Maoist past, the question that Michel Oksenberg posed of campaigns forty years ago remains relevant today: Must economic development be accompanied by "modern bureaucratic practice"?

Why do campaigns, which appear so antithetical to "modern bureaucratic practice," persist in post-Mao China? Tyrene White observed in 1990 that the campaign method remained an important mode of policy implementation because of "the lingering memory that campaigns played during the Maoist era and the defining tendency of Leninist parties to rely on directed mobilization as the basic approach to political change and control."[103] Part of the explanation for the continuation of campaigns in contemporary China surely can be attributed to the powerful hold of the past. No less an authority than the former general secretary of the Chinese Communist Party, Zhao Ziyang, recalled the difficulty he faced in January 1987 in moving beyond familiar campaign methods: "I specifically stated that 'The Third Plenum resolved that there would be no more mass campaigns. However, people are accustomed to the old ways, so whenever we attack anything, these methods are still used.'"[104]

But managed campaigns are not a simple product of path dependence. As Tyrene White points out in her study of the one-child campaign, "mobilizational methods have been recast in ways that make them useful to the reformist elite."[105] Zhao Ziyang, in explaining how his approach to the anti-bourgeois liberalization campaign of 1987 would differ from past mass campaigns, promised that "From the beginning we will clearly define what can and cannot be done and declare specifically what the limits are."[106]

Managed campaigns are the result of an active and ongoing attempt to reconfigure elements of China's revolutionary tradition in order to address new challenges under changed conditions. Although the process by which China's leaders convert revolutionary legacies to contemporary purposes is sometimes opaque, recently available memoirs make clear that this has been a conscious and contested strategy within the political elite. According to the economic diaries of Zhao Ziyang's nemesis, former Premier Li Peng, at a September 1988 central work conference to deal with the then serious problems of inflation and panic purchasing, "someone suggested that we should undertake a campaign without announcing it as a campaign." As a result of this suggestion, Li observes, the emotional climate in the meeting hall "immediately turned tense." Nevertheless, Li Peng volunteered to take responsibility for this initiative. A few days later, he proposed a plan to control prices by inspections involving "keypoints" and "breakthroughs." As Li explains, "the method was to incite the masses to file reports, strengthen oversight, pursue clues, thoroughly investigate, analyze causes, adopt correct policies, prevent loopholes, and manage prices well."[107] Although campaign methods were but one weapon in the arsenal of central measures to control inflation,[108] they remained — albeit in altered form — a well-recognized approach to overcoming bureaucratic hurdles to solve economic challenges.

Today's rendition of constructing a New Socialist Countryside is one among a number of current programs that draw selectively upon past campaign practices in a manner both familiar and foreign. While this particular initiative may already be losing steam, it will surely be followed by other campaign-like efforts to harness the Chinese state's still significant mobilizing capacity to the pursuit of developmental goals.

Although today's managed campaigns differ in important respects from their Maoist forerunners, they still serve as a powerful tool for combating bureaucratic rigidity and resistance. The collapse of communism in Eastern Europe and the former Soviet Union is often attributed above all to bureaucratic entrenchment. The ossified Leninist party-state, we are told, stymied the best intentions of Gorbachev and other reform-minded leaders.[109] For this reason, the PRC's continued reliance on a campaign style of policy implementation may provide a telling clue about the relative resilience of the Chinese Communist political system.

As historian and sociologist Perry Anderson observes, the divergent paths of the Soviet Union and the People's Republic of China are among the most influential developments of our time:

> If the twentieth century was dominated, more than by any other single event, by the trajectory of the Russian Revolution, the twenty-first will be shaped by the outcome of the Chinese Revolution. The Soviet state . . . dissolved after seven decades with scarcely a shot, as swiftly as it had once arisen. . . . The outcome of the Chinese Revolution offers an arresting contrast. As it enters its seventh decade, the People's Republic is an engine of the world economy . . . for a quarter of a century posting the fastest growth rates in per capita income, for the largest population, ever recorded. . . . In the character and scale of that achievement, of course, there is more than one — bitter — irony. But of the difference between the fate of the revolutions in China and Russia, there can be little doubt.[110]

Critical as the Soviet model was for Chinese communism, Mao and his comrades — along with their successors — forged a distinctive (if ironic) revolutionary road.

Among the many ironies of managed campaigns in contemporary China is their reversal of Deng Xiaoping's dictum to "rely on the masses, but do not launch campaigns." Although campaigns continue to be launched as a key method for checking bureaucratic inertia and promoting economic development, they no longer elicit the same degree of mass involvement and enthusiasm. These days it is grassroots officials, rather than ordinary peasants, who appear to be the main objects and actors in state-managed campaigns. To be sure, the recruitment of backbones and activists from among the masses remains a high priority for the Communist Party, but contemporary Chinese villagers — allured by alternative channels of upward and outward mobility — have become a less receptive and less reliable target of state mobilization.

Endnotes

I owe a debt of appreciation to my former student and research assistant, Yan Xiaojun, for locating many of the materials on which this paper is based. I should also like to thank fellow participants at the Trier Workshop in the summer of 2007 — Nara Dillon, Zhang Jishun, Barry Naughton, Joseph Fewsmith, Patricia Thornton, and especially Sebastian Heilmann — for helpful comments on an earlier draft.

1. Hong Yung Lee, *From Revolutionary Cadres to Party Technocrats in Socialist China* (Berkeley: University of California Press, 1991), pp. 388, 407.

2. Cheng Li, *China's Leaders: The New Generation* (Lanham, MD: Rowman and Littlefield, 2001), p. 195.

3. Richard Lowenthal, "Development vs. Utopia in Communist Policy," in Chalmers Johnson, ed., *Change in Communist Systems* (Stanford, CA: Stanford University Press, 1970), pp. 33–116.

4. Deng Xiaoping, *Selected Works (1982–1992)* (Beijing: Foreign Languages Press, 1994), 3: 44.

5. Minxin Pei, *China's Trapped Transition: The Limits of Developmental Autocracy* (Cambridge, MA: Harvard University Press, 2006), p. 182.

6. Quoted in Kevin J. O'Brien and Lianjiang Li, "Campaign Nostalgia in the Chinese Countryside," *Asian Survey*, 39, no. 3 (May-June 1999): 376.

7. Ibid.

8. Ibid., p. 391.

9. Tyrene White, *China's Longest Campaign: Birth Planning in the People's Republic, 1949–2005* (Ithaca, NY: Cornell University Press, 2006).

10. Joan Kaufman, "SARS and China's Health-Care Response: Better to Be Both Red and Expert!" in Arthur Kleinman and James L. Watson, eds., *SARS in China: Prelude to Pandemic?* (Stanford, CA: Stanford University Press, 2006), pp. 66–67; Elizabeth J. Perry,

Challenging the Mandate of Heaven: Social Protest and State Power in China (Armonk, NY: M.E. Sharpe, 2001), introduction.

11. Ilpyong J. Kim, *The Politics of Chinese Communism: Kiangsi under the Soviets* (Berkeley: University of California Press, 1973).

12. Mark Selden, *The Yenan Way in Revolutionary China* (Cambridge, MA: Harvard University Press, 1971).

13. Govind S. Kelkar, "The Chinese Experience of Political Campaigns and Mass Mobilization," *Social Scientist*, 7, no. 5 (December 1978): 45.

14. Ibid., p. 50.

15. Ibid., p. 57.

16. Thomas P. Bernstein, *Up to the Mountains and Down to the Villages: The Transfer of Youth from Urban to Rural China* (New Haven, CT: Yale University Press, 1977), p. 2.

17. Arthur G. Ashbrook, Jr., "China: Economic Overview, 1975," in Joint Economic Committee, ed., *China: A Reassessment of the Economy* (Washington, DC: Government Printing Office, 1975), p. 30, quoted in Bernstein, *Up to the Mountains*, p. 238.

18. Bernstein, *Up to the Mountains*, p. 238.

19. John Gardner, "The *Wu-fan* Campaign in Shanghai: A Study in the Consolidation of Urban Control," in A. Doak Barnett, ed., *Chinese Communist Politics in Action* (Seattle: University of Washington Press, 1969), p. 477.

20. Gordon Bennett, *Yundong: Mass Campaigns in Chinese Communist Leadership* (Berkeley: Center for Chinese Studies, University of California, 1976), p. 18.

21. Ibid., pp. 39–41.

22. Charles P. Cell, *Revolution at Work: Mobilization Campaigns in China* (NY: Academic Press, 1977), pp. 8, 172.

23. Bennett, *Yundong*, p. 15.

24. Michel Charles Oksenberg, "Policy Formulation in Communist China: The Case of the Mass Irrigation Campaign, 1957–58," Ph.D. thesis, Columbia University, 1969.

25. E.L. Wheelwright and Bruce McFarlane, *The Chinese Road to Socialism: Economics of the Cultural Revolution* (New York: Monthly Review Press, 1970), p. 51.

26. Wang Shengkai (王盛开), *Nongcun gaige sanshinian: Zhengce quxiang yu liyi suqiu* (农村改革三十年: 政策取向与利益诉求) (Thirty Years of Rural Reform: Policy Trends and Interest Articulation) (Beijing: Zhongguo shehui kexue chubanshe, 2008), p. 203.

27. Ibid., pp. 203–204.

28. Minzi Su, *China's Rural Development Policy: Exploring the "New Socialist Countryside"* (Boulder, CO: First Forum Press, 2009), pp. 131–132.

29. Wang Shengkai, *Nongcun gaige*, pp. 208–214.

30. "Tongchou chengxiang fazhan zhongda jucuo, jianshe shehuizhuyi xin nongcun zongshu" (统筹城乡发展重大举措建设社会主义新农村综述) (A Major Review of Urban and Rural Development Initiatives and Building a New Socialist Countryside), Xinhua she (新华社) (New China News Agency), October 24, 2005, at http://www.gov .cn/jrzg/2005-10/24/content_82445.htm (accessed August 11, 2010).

31. Wang Shengkai, *Nongcun gaige*, pp. 202–203.

32. Wang Yanmin (王艳敏) and Xie Ziping (谢子平), "Jianshe shehui kexue xin nongcun de lishi huigu yu bijiao" (建设社会科学新农村的历史回顾与比较) (Historical Reflections and Comparisons of Constructing a New Socialist Scientific

Countryside), *Zhonggong zhongyang dangxiao xuebao* (中共中央党校学报) (Academic Journal of the Central Party School of the Chinese Communist Party), 10, no. 4 (August 2006): 55–59; Fu Chun (付春), "Shixi Mao Zedong dui shehuizhuyi xin nongcun jianshe de chubu tansuo" (试析毛泽东对社会主义新农村建设的初步探索) (Preliminary Analysis of Mao's Initial Explorations of Construction of a New Socialist Countryside), *Mao Zedong sixiang yanjiu* (毛泽东思想研究) (Studies of Mao Zedong Thought), 24, no. 5 (September 2007): 36.

33. Jin Miao (金描), "Nanjingshi zhongxiaoxue biyesheng dierpi xiaxiang canjia nongye shengchan" (南京市中小学毕业生第二批下乡参加农业生产) (The Second Group of Nanjing City's Middle and Elementary School Graduates to Go Down to the Countryside to Participate in Agricultural Production), *Jiangsu jiaoyu* (江苏教育) (Jiangsu Education), no. 17 (September 10, 1957): 30.

34. Chen Baoshan (陈宝善), "Jianshe shehuizhuyi xin nongcun de cujinpai" (建设社会主义新农村的促进派) (Advocates of New Socialist Countryside Construction), *Jiaoxue yu yanjiu* (教学与研究) (Teaching and Research), no. 8 (1958): 31–32.

35. Lynn T. White, III, *Careers in Shanghai: The Social Guidance of Personal Energies in a Developing Chinese City, 1949–1966* (Berkeley: University of California Press, 1978).

36. Fu Chun, "Shixi Mao Zedong," p. 38.

37. Xin Qiu (欣秋), "Kan sanchu fanying shehuizhuyi xin nongcun de jingju" (看三出反映社会主义新农村的京剧) (On Watching Three Peking Operas That Reflect the New Socialist Countryside), *Zhongguo xiju* (中国戏剧) (Chinese Theatre), no. 7 (1964): 46–48.

38. Shandongsheng jingji yanjiusuo nongye jingjizu (山东省经济研究所农业经济组) (Shandong Provincial Economics Institute, Agricultural Economics Group), "Ziligengsheng, jianshe shehuizhuyi xin nongcun" (自力更生, 建设社会主义新农村) (Self-Reliance, Construction of New Socialist Villages), *Wenshizhe* (文史哲) (Journal of Literature, History, Philosophy), no. 1 (1966): 50–57.

39. David Zweig, *Agrarian Radicalism in China, 1968–1981* (Cambridge, MA: Harvard University Press, 1989).

40. Zhonggong Jiangsusheng Jiangyinxian weiyuanhui (中共江苏省江阴县委员会) (Chinese Communist Party Committee of Jiangyin County of Jiangsu Province), "Chanchu jiushehui de henji jianshe shehuizhuyi xin nongcun" (铲除旧社会的痕迹建设社会主义新农村) (Eradicating Vestiges of the Old Society by Constructing New Socialist Villages), *Nongye keji tongxun* (农业科技通讯) (Bulletin of Agricultural Science and Technology), no. 9 (1975): 2–4.

41. "Zai shixing dadi yuanlinhua de daolushang jixu qianjin" (在实行大地园林化的道路上继续前进) (Advancing Down the Road of Large-Scale Afforestation), *Hebei linye keji* (河北林业科技) (Hebei Forestry Science and Technology), no. 3 (1975): 1–8.

42. Gao Yuanzong (高元宗), "Shizuo jianshe shehuizhuyi xin nongcun de 'zhagenpai'" (誓做建设社会主义新农村的"扎根派") ("Strike-roots Groups" Pledged to Construct a New Socialist Countryside), *Shaanxi shifan daxue xuebao* (陕西师范大学学报) (Journal of Shaanxi Normal University), no. 2 (1975): 54–56.

43. Fugouxian cuiqiao gongshe dangwei tongxunzu (扶沟县崔桥公社党委通讯组) (Communications Group of the Party Committee of Fugou County's Cuiqiao Commune), "Yige shehuizhuyi weishengcun" (一个社会主义卫生村) (A Socialist Sanitary Village), *Zhongyi kan* (中医刊) (Central Plains Medical Journal), no. 2 (1977): 30–32.

44. Shi Yunsheng (时运生), Li Wenqin (李文钦), and Dun Zhanmin (顿占民), "Qianyi wenmingcun jianshe neirong ji qi jiben tezheng" (浅议文明村建设内容及其基本特征) (Preliminary Discussion of the Content and Basic Characteristics of Civilized Village Construction), *Daode yu wenming* (道德与文明) (Morality and Civilization), no. 6 (1984): 8–10. For more on the 1980s campaign, see Ann Anagnost, "Defining the Socialist Imaginary: The 'Civilized Village' Campaign in Post-Mao China," paper presented at the American Anthropological Association meeting, 1988.

45. Lin Zhenping (林振平), Nie Shangying (聂尚颖), and Jiang Huakai (江化开), "Jianshe shehuizhuyi xin nongcun de shijian yu sikao" (建设社会主义新农村的实践与思考) (Experience and Reflections on Constructing New Socialist Villages), *Dongnan xueshu* (东南学术) (Southeast Academic Research), no. 1 (1992): 24–27.

46. Sun Yimei (孙以美) and Huang Yunyu (黄韵玉), "Deng Xiaoping zai jianshe shehuizhuyi xin nongcun lilunshang de tupo" (邓小平在建设社会主义新农村理论上的突破) (Deng Xiaoping's Theoretical Breakthrough in Constructing New Socialist Villages), *Weishi* (唯实) (Reality Only), no. 12 (1995): 5–7; "Wei jianshe you Zhongguo tese shehuizhuyi xin nongcun er nuli fendou" (为建设有中国特色社会主义新农村而努力奋斗) (Striving and Struggling to Construct New Socialist Villages with Chinese Characteristics), *Qiushi* (求是) (Seeking Truth), no. 20 (1998): 9–11; Fan Minhua (范敏华), "Shilun Deng Xiaoping guanyu jianshe shehuizhuyi nongcun de sixiang" (试论邓小平关于建设社会主义农村的思想) (A Preliminary Discussion of Deng Xiaoping's Thinking on the Construction of Socialist Villages), *Suzhou daxue xuebao* (苏州大学学报) (Suzhou University Journal), no. 4 (1999): 1–4. For a recent elaboration of this argument, see Zhou Dajiang (周达疆), "Shilun Deng Xiaoping dui Mao Zedong 'sannong' sixiang de xucheng he fazhan" (试论邓小平对毛泽东 '三农' 思想的继承和发展) (A Preliminary Discussion of Deng Xiaoping's Inheritance and Development of Mao Zedong's Thinking on the "Three Rurals"), *Zhongguo jiti jingji* (中国集体经济) (China Collective Economy), no. 1 (2007): 46–48.

47. In addition to Premier Wen Jiabao, the most outspoken advocate of New Socialist Countryside construction would appear to be Chen Xiwen, director of the Central Leadership Group for Rural Work and a close advisor to the premier on agricultural affairs. See, for example, Chen Xiwen (陈锡文), "Tuijin shehuizhuyi xin nongcun jianshe" (推进社会主义新农村建设) (Promote the Construction of New Socialist Villages), *Lilun* (理论) (Theory) (November 4, 2005): 9; and Zhang Yihua (张怡恬) and Yu Chunhui (于春晖), "Yixiangshi guan quanju de zhongda lishi renwu: Fang zhongyang caijing lingdao xiaozu bangongshi fuzhuren Chen Xiwen" (一项事关全局的重大历史任务: 访中央财经领导小组办公室副主任陈锡文) (A Matter Concerning the Overall Situation in the Great Historic Mission of Constructing a New Socialist Countryside: An Interview with the Deputy Director of the Office of the Central Leadership Financial Small Group, Chen Xiwen), *Renmin ribao* (人民日报) (People's Daily) (May 11, 2006): 8.

48. Fu Chun, "Shixi Mao Zedong," p. 37.

49. Sometimes the latter half of the slogan is rendered as "cities support the countryside" (*chengshi zhichi nongcun*, 城市支持农村).

50. Wang Fangjie (王方杰), "Hengshui: 'Sanxiaxiang' biancheng 'sanzhagen'" (衡水: "三下乡" 变成 "三扎根") (Hengshui: "Three Down to the Villages" Becomes "Three Strike Roots"), *Yaowen* (要闻) (Important News) (November 17, 2005): 4.

51. Li Yajie (李亚杰), "Weile dadi de fengshou: Disanpi xianjinxing jiaoyu huodong xuexi peixun jishi" (为了大地的丰收: 第三批先进性教育活动学习培训纪实) (For the Harvest of the Heartland: Annals of the Third Wave of Advanced Educational Study and Training Activity), *Yaowen* (December 27, 2005): 1.

52. Gong Yongquan (龚永泉) and Wang Yang (王杨), "Xuzhou jinwan ganbu zhucun zhidao xianjinxing jiaoyu huodong," (徐州近万干部驻村指导先进性教育活动) (Nearly 10,000 Xuzhou Cadres Are Stationed in Villages to Supervise Advanced Education Activities), *Yaowen* (December 31, 2005): 4.

53. Bai Shihu (白世虎) and Sun Shizhong (孙世忠), "Jianshe shehuizhuyi xin nongcun de youyi shijian" (建设社会主义新农村的有益实践) (Beneficial Practices of Constructing the New Socialist Countryside), *Yan'an ribao* (延安日报) (Yan'an Daily) (December 29, 2005): 1.

54. *Guangming ribao* (光明日报) (Enlightenment Daily) (April 28, 2006): 1.

55. Gong Yongquan (龚永泉), "Xianjinxing jiaoyu huodong dailai xin huoli" (先进性教育活动带来新活力) (Advanced Education Activities Bring New Dynamism), *Yaowen* (October 10, 2005): 4.

56. He Yong (何勇), "Laizi jiceng ganbu de xin sheng — Jianshe xin nongcun shuodao zanxin kanshang" (来自基层干部的心声—建设新农村说到咱心坎上) (Heartfelt Wishes from Grassroots Cadres — Building A New Socialist Countryside Speaks from the Bottom of Our Heart), *Renmin ribao* (November 29, 2005): 15.

57. Du Qinglin (杜青林), "Shenru diaocha yanjiu zongjie dianxing jingyan, buduan tansuo shehuzhuyi xin nongcun jianshe de xin luzi" (深入调查研总结典型经验不断探索社会主义新农村建设的新路子) (Sum Up the Typical Experiences of In-Depth Investigation and Continuously Explore the New Road of Construction for the New Socialist Countryside), *Nongyebu wangzhan* (农业部网站) (Ministry of Agriculture Online), June 16, 2006, at http://www.gov.cn/gzdt/2006-06/16/content_312096.htm (accessed August 11, 2010).

58. Luo Weiping (罗卫平), "Guang'anshi jianshe shehuizhuyi xin nongcun de xin tansuo" (广安市建设社会主义新农村的新探索) (New Exploration of New Socialist Countryside Construction in Guang'an City), *Nongcun jianshe* (农村建设) (Village Construction), no. 3 (2007): 18.

59. See, for example, Roger R. Thompson, trans., *Report from Xunwu* (Stanford, CA: Stanford University Press, 1990).

60. Lin Huadi (林华俤), "Lun Mao Zedong diaocha yanjiu sixiang yu xin nongcun jianshe" (论毛泽东调查研究思想与新农村建设) (On New Socialist Village Construction and Mao Zedong's Thinking on Investigative Research), *Sichuan nongye daxue xuebao* (四川农业大学学报) (Sichuan Agriculture University Journal), 25, no. 2 (June 2007): 134.

61. "Xin nongcun jianshe yao chuli hao sandui maodun" (新农村建设要处理好三对矛盾) (New Socialist Village Construction Must Solve Three Contradictions), *Jiangxi ribao* (江西日报) (Jiangxi Daily) (June 25, 2007): 3.

62. Zhang Xiufeng (张秀峰), Luo Lin (罗璘), and Gong Wenrui (龚文瑞), "Goujian hexie xin nongcun: Ganzhou yinxiang ji" (构建和谐新农村: 赣州印象记) (Constructing a Harmonious New Countryside: A Record of Impressions of Ganzhou [Jiangxi]), *Renmin ribao* (July 9, 2005): 8.

63. Wu Shan (吴珊), "Wei jianshe xin nongcun ganbu jiaoshi xiaxiang (bamiao)" (为建设新农村干部教师下乡 [拔苗]) (Cadre Teachers Sent Down to the Villages to "Tug at Roots" in Order to Construct a New Countryside), *Xiangzhen luntan* (乡镇论坛) (Township and Village Forum), no. 18 (September 2007): 13–15.

64. Han Jun (韩俊), "Zouchu xin nongcun jianshe de wuqu" (走出新农村建设的误区) (Avoiding Mistakes in New Countryside Construction), *Shanxi nongye* (山西农业) (Shanxi Agriculture), no. 10 (2006): 36–38.

65. Deng Weihua (邓卫华) and Deng Huaning (邓华宁), "Jianshe xin nongcun jinfang 'wei chengshihua yuejin'" (建设新农村谨防 "伪城市化跃进") (Constructing a New Socialist Countryside While Guarding Against a "Fake Urbanization Leap Forward"), *Xibu caikuai* (西部财会) (Western Finance and Accounting), no. 6 (2007): 73–74.

66. Chen Tao (陈涛), "Jingti nongcun jianshezhong xingshizhuyi" (警惕农村建设中形式主义) (Guard Against Formalism in the Construction of the New Socialist Countryside), *Yan'an ribao* (December 21, 2006): 2.

67. Long Bo (龙博), "Jingyi xin nongcun jianshe wuda wuqu" (警惕新农村建设五大误区) (Warning Against Five Big Mistakes in New Socialist Countryside Construction), *Nongcun shiyong jishu* (农村实用技术) (Practical Rural Technology), no. 9 (2007): 6–7.

68. Li Guiping (李桂萍), "Xin nongcun jianshezhong burong hushi de jige wenti" (新农村建设中不容忽视的几个问题) (Several Questions That Cannot Be Neglected in Constructing New Villages), *Qinghai jinrong* (青海金融) (Qinghai Finance), no. 6 (2007): 47.

69. Zhang Xiaolin (张小林), Liu Hejun (刘河军), and Zhang Chang'an (张长安), "Xin nongcun jianshe jiuda nanti jidai jiejue" (新农村建设九大难题亟待解决) (Nine Major Issues Awaiting Resolution in Constructing a New Countryside), *Renda jianshe* (人大建设) (People's Congress Construction), no. 8 (2007): 7–9.

70. Lei Xiaoying (雷晓鹰), "Xin nongcun jianshe xuyao de shi ruogan jia shigan" (新农村建设需要的是若干加实干) (The Building of the New Countryside Needs an Increase in Hard Work), *Yan'an ribao* (July 7, 2006): 2; Benbao pinglun yuan (本报评论员), "Zhunque bawo jianshe xin nongcun de kexue neihan" (准确把握建设新农村的科学内涵) (Accurately Grasp the Scientific Connotation of the Construction of the New Socialist Countryside), *Yan'an ribao* (March 23, 2006): 1; Benbao pinglun yuan (本报评论员), "Jianshe xin nongcun yao queli 'tejiuzhan' de guannian" (建设新农村要确立 "特久战" 的观念) (Construction of the New Countryside Needs to Establish the Concept of a "Special Battlefield"), *Yan'an ribao* (April 6, 2006): 1; Huang Jiansheng (黄建生), "Xin nongcun jianshe 'shiji shiyao'" (新农村建设 "十忌十要") (Ten Dos and Don'ts of New Countryside Construction), *Zhejiang tongji* (浙江统计) (Zhejiang Statistics), no. 7 (2007): 4–6.

71. Li Tongshan (李铜山), "Xin nongcun jianshe jinchengzhong de difang zhengfu xingwei guifan yanjiu" (新农村建设进程中的地方政府行为规范研究) (A Study of the Patterns of Local Government Activity in the Course of New Countryside Construction), *Zhongzhou xuebao* (中州学刊) (Academic Journal of Zhongzhou), no. 4 (July 2007): 44.

72. On the importance of "emotion work" in Mao's mass campaigns, see Elizabeth J. Perry, "Moving the Masses: Emotion Work in the Chinese Revolution," *Mobilization*, 7, no. 2 (Summer 2002): 111–128.

73. Qi Huiting (元慧亭), "Zouqu xin nongcun jianshe de renshi wuqu, tansuo xin nongcun jianshe de youxiao lujing" (走出新农村建设的认识误区, 探索新农村建设的有效路径) (Avoiding Misunderstandings in New Village Construction While Exploring an Effective Path for New Village Construction), *Shandong nongye daxue xuebao (Shehui kexue ban)* (山东农业大学学报 [社会科学版]) (Shandong Agricultural University Journal [Social Science Edition]), no. 3 (2007): 53–54.

74. Su Chunsheng (苏春生), "Ruijin xin nongcun jianshe jia 'supao'" (瑞金新农村建设加 "速跑") (Speeding up the Pace of New Village Construction in Ruijin), *Jiangxi ribao* (December 9, 2004). For other examples of different types of model villages, see Zhang Liyang (张利庠), "Kezi jiejian de bazhong xin nongcun fazhan moshi" (可资借鉴的八种新农村发展模式) (Eight Types of New Village Development Models Worth Emulating), *Lilun congheng* (理论纵横) (Theoretical Interconnections), no. 3 (2007): 62–63.

75. Zhang Jiancheng (张建成), "Dangqian shehuizhuyi xin nongcun jianshezhong zongjiao wenti de fansi" (当前社会主义新农村建设中宗教问题的反思) (Reflections on the Question of Religion in the Contemporary New Socialist Countryside Construction), *Qingdao nongye daxue xuebao (shehui kexue ban)* (青岛农业大学学报 [社会科学版]) (Journal of Qingdao Agricultural University [Social Science Edition]), 19, no. 2 (June 2007): 24.

76. Yang Huijie (杨辉解), "Lun gong'an jiguan zai shehuizhuyi xin nongcun jianshezhong de lishi shiming" (论公安机关在社会主义新农村建设中的历史使命) (On the Historical Mission of the Public Security Agencies in the Construction of the New Socialist Countryside), *Zhengfa xuekan* (政法学刊) (Journal of Politics and Law), 24, no. 3 (June 2007): 69.

77. June Teufel Dreyer, *China's Forty Millions: Minority Nationalities and National Integration in the People's Republic of China* (Cambridge, MA: Harvard University Press, 1976), p. 165.

78. "Human Rights Update and Archives," Tibetan Centre for Human Rights and Democracy, July 2007, at http://www.tchrd.org/publications/hr_updates/2007/hr200707.pdf (accessed July 7, 2010).

79. On the Confucian origins of contemporary state discourse, see John Delury, "'Harmonious' in China," *Policy Review*, no. 148 (April-May 2008): 35–44.

80. Xu Puying (徐璞英), "Guowai nongcun jianshe de youguan jingyan he zuofa" (国外农村建设的有关经验和做法) (Relevant Experience and Work Methods in Overseas Rural Construction), *Ziliao tongxun* (资料通讯) (Materials Bulletin), no. 4 (2006): 44ff; Zhou Jianfei (周建飞) and Xu Guangyi (徐广义), "Dangqian xin nongcun jianshe ge'an yu moshi yanjiu lilun shuping" (当前新农村建设个案与模式研究理论述评) (Theoretical Critique of Case Studies and Models of Contemporary New Village Construction), *Ningbo jingji (Sanjiang luntan)* (宁波经济 [三江论坛]) (Ningbo Economy [Three Rivers Forum]), no. 1 (2007): 32–38.

81. Sheng Ruowei (盛若蔚), "Beijing fa li peiyu 'tian xiucai' jianshe nongcun shiyong rencai duiwu" (Beijing Trains "Land Literati" to Build a Corps of Talent to Build the Countryside) (北京发力培育 "田秀才" 建设农村实用人才队伍), *Renmin ribao* (December 13, 2005): 15, at http://nc.people.com.cn/GB/5160687.html (accessed August 11, 2010).

82. Shao Yanjing (邵燕敬), "Jielongcun: Wenming xiangfeng pumianlai" (界龙村: 文明乡风扑面来) (Jielong Village: Winds of Rural Civilization), *Pudong fazhan* (浦东发展) (Pudong Development), no. 4 (2006): 39–40.

83. Li Yonghua (李勇华) and Huang Yunqiang (黄允强), "'Xin nongcun jianshe lishihui': Zhongguo chuantong cunzhi de chenggong jieyong yu gaizao" ("新农村建设理事会": 中国传统村治的成功借用与改造) ("New Village Construction Councils": Successful Adoption and Adaptation of Traditional Chinese Village Rule), *Xuexi yu tansuo* (学习与探索) (Study and Exploration), no. 3 (2007): 81.

84. Wang Jingxin (王景新), "Xiangcun jianshe de lishi leixing, xianshi moshi he weilai fazhan" (乡村建设的历史类型, 现实模式和未来发展) (Historical Typology of Rural Construction, Practical Models, and Future Developments), *Zhongguo nongcun guancha* (中国农村观察) (China Rural Survey), no. 3 (2006): 48.

85. Ibid., pp. 46–48; Xu Yuan (许圆) and Wang Zhengzhong (王正中), "'Xiangcun jianshe yundong' dui xin nongcun shequhua jianshe de qishi" ("乡村建设运动" 对新农村社区化建设的启示) (Lessons from the "Rural Reconstruction Movement" for New Village Community Construction), *Nongcun jingji yu kexue* (农村经济与科学) (Rural Economy and Science-Technology), no. 6 (2007): 79–80; Zhang Jingping (章敬平), "Cong Liang Shuming dao Lin Yifu: Sannong wenti bainian lishi" (从梁漱溟到林毅夫: 三农问题百年历史) (From Liang Shuming to Lin Yifu: One Hundred Years of History of the Three Rurals), *Xiandai rencai* (现代人才) (Modern Talent), no. 3 (2006): 48–49.

86. Zhang Bingfu (张秉福), "Minguo shiqi sanda xiangcun jianshe moshi: Bijiao yu jiejian" (民国时期三大乡村建设模式: 比较与借鉴) (Three Major Rural Construction Models during the Republican Period: Comparisons and Implications), *Xinjiang shehui kexue* (新疆社会科学) (Social Sciences in Xinjiang), no. 2 (2006): 97.

87. Ibid., p. 103.

88. Recently Premier Wen announced a new government policy, offering free tuition at six major normal universities to students who are willing to spend three years as teachers in rural villages. Xinhua News Agency, May 4, 2007.

89. Hailing Wu, "Student Teachers' Implementation and Perception of the Rural-Related Summer Social Practice Curriculum: A Case Study," paper presented at the annual meeting of the Association for Asian Studies, Chicago, 2009.

90. Bernstein, *Up to the Mountains*, pp. 7–8.

91. Fang Ming (方明) and Liu Jun (刘军), eds., *Xin nongcun jianshe zhengce lilun wenji* (新农村建设政策理论文集) (Collected Essays on the Policy Theory of New Village Construction) (Beijing: Zhongguo jianzhu gongye chubanshe, 2006), p. 16.

92. Articles advocating the South Korean New Village Movement model appeared as early as 1998. See Wang Siming (王思明), "Xin nongcun jianshe: Beijing, chengxiao, wenti he qishi — ZhongRiHan de bijiao yanjiu" (新农村建设: 背景, 成效, 问题和启示—中日韩的比较研究) (New Village Construction: Background, Results, Problems, and Implications — A Comparative Study of China, Japan, and South Korea), *Zhongguo nongshi* (中国农史) (Chinese Agricultural History), no. 2 (2007): 39–47; Guo Ru (郭汝), "Jiejian HanRi jingyan: Cujin woguo xin nongcun jianshe" (借鉴韩日经验: 促进我国新农村建设) (Drawing on the Korean and Japanese Experience: Promoting Our Country's New Village Construction), *Xiao chengzhen jianshe* (小城镇建设) (Development of Small Cities and Towns), no. 9 (2007): 75–77.

93. An Internet search by one Chinese scholar in March 2006 found more than 116,000 entries in Chinese concerning the Korean New Village Movement. See Bao Zongshun (包宗顺), "ZhongHan xin nongcun jianshe: Bijiao yu jiejian" (中韩新农村建设: 比较与借鉴) (New Village Construction in China and Korea: Comparisons and Lessons), *Dangdai Hanguo* (当代韩国) (Contemporary Korea), no. 3 (2006): 17.

94. Zheng Xinli (郑新立), "Hanguo 'xincun yundong' qishilu" (韩国 "新村运动" 启示录) (A Record of the Lessons from the Korean "New Village Movement"), *Renmin luntan* (人民论坛) (People's Tribune), no. 2 (2006): 9; "Hanguo 'xincun yundong' kaocha baogao" (韩国"新村运动"考察报告) (Investigation Report on Korea's New Village Movement), *Zhengce* (政策) (Policy), no. 2 (2006): 57–59.

95. Shi Lei (石磊), "Xunqiu 'linglei' fazhan de fanshi: Hanguo xincun yundong yu Zhongguo xiangcun jianshe" (寻求"另类" 发展的范式: 韩国新村运动与中国乡村建设) (In Search of an Alternative Development Model: Korea's New Village Movement and China's Rural Construction), *Shehuixue yanjiu* (社会学研究) (Sociological Research), no. 4 (2004): 39–49.

96. Zhou Jianfei and Xu Guangyi, "Dangqian xin nongcun," p. 33; Wu Keliang (吴可亮), "Xincun yundongzhong Hanguo zhengfu de xingzheng zuowei ji qi dui Zhongguo de qishi" (新村运动中韩国政府的行政作为及其对中国的启示) (The Actions of the Korean Government in the New Village Movement and the Implications for China), *Xingzheng yu fa* (行政与法) (Administration and Law), no. 2 (2008): 30–32; Li Shutong (李曙桐), "Hanguo xincun yundong: Yi nongmin wei hexin de shehui shijian" (韩国新村运动: 以农民为核心的社会实践) (Korea's New Village Movement: The Social Practice of Taking the Farmers as the Core), *Renmin luntan* (人民论坛) (People's Tribune), no. 4A (2006): 40–41.

97. Sun Haoran (孙浩然), "Hanguo xincun yundong ji qi dui woguo jianshe shehuizhuyi xin nongcun de qishi" (韩国新村运动及其对我国建设社会主义新农村的启示) (Korea's New Village Movement and Its Implications for Our Country's New Socialist Countryside Campaign), *Lilun xuekan* (理论学刊) (Theory Journal), no. 5 (2006): 76–77.

98. Zhang Qing (张青), "Nongcun gonggong chanpin gongji de guoji jingyan jiejian: Yi Hanguo xincun yundong weili" (农村公共产品供给的国际经验借鉴: 以韩国新村运动为例) (Lessons from the International Experience of Rural Public Goods Provision: Taking the Korean New Village Movement as an Example), *Shehuizhuyi yanjiu* (社会主义研究) (Socialism Studies), no. 5 (2005): 76; Liao Zhongchun (柳钟椿), "Hanguo de xincun yundong" (韩国的新村运动) (Korea's New Village Movement), *Dangdai Hanguo* (当代韩国) (Contemporary Korea), no. 1 (2006): 32–37; Li Shuishan (李水山), Huang Changchun (黄长春), and Li Que (李鹤), "Hanguo xincun yundong de hexin: Xincun jiaoyu" (韩国新村运动的核心: 新村教育) (The Core of the Korean New Village Movement: New Village Education), *Jiaoyu yu zhiye* (教育与职业) (Education and Occupation), no. 3 (2006): 23–25; Zhang Deqiang (张德强), "Lun Hanguo xincun yundong de jiaoyu benzhi" (论韩国新村运动的教育本质) (The Basic Nature of Education in Korea's New Village Movement), *Bijiao jiaoyu yanjiu* (比较教育研究) (Comparative Education Review), no. 9 (2007): 14–19.

99. Jin Yingji (金英姬), "Hanguo de xincun yundong" (韩国的新村运动) (Korea's New Village Movement), *Dangdai yatai* (当代亚太) (Contemporary Asia-Pacific Studies), no. 6 (2006): 19–20.

100. Chen Mingxing (陈明星), "Xin nongcun jianshe yao jinfang 'kongxinhua' qingxiang" (新农村建设要谨防 "空心化" 倾向) (New Village Construction Must Guard Against the Trend of "Hollowing Out"), *Nongjia guwen* (农家顾问) (Rural Household Advice), no. 9 (2007): 1–2.

101. Yu Jianrong (于建嵘), "Taiwan jingyan: Yikao nonghui jianshe nongcun" (台湾经验: 依靠农会建设农村) (Taiwan's Experience: Relying on Farmers' Associations for Rural Construction), *Nongcun, nongye, nongmin* (农村, 农业, 农民) (Country Agriculture, Farmers), no. 7 (2006): 31–32; Yu Jianrong (于建嵘), "Nonghui zuzhi yu jianshe xin nongcun" (农会组织与建设新农村) (Organizing Farmers' Associations and New Village Construction), *Zhongguo nongcun guancha* (中国农村观察) (China Rural Survey), no. 2 (2006): 71–78; Zeng Huangdong (曾煌东), "Dui jianshe xin nongcun de xianshi sikao: Cong Taiwan nonghui zuzhi zuoyong de shijiao kan" (对建设新农村的现实思考: 从台湾农会组织作用的视角看) (Practical Ideas about Constructing New Villages: A View from the Perspective of Taiwan's Farmers' Associations), *Tanqiu* (探求) (Academic Search for Truth and Reality), no. 1 (2007): 40–43.

102. Wu Limin (吴丽民) and Yuan Shanlin (袁山林), "Taiwan nongye hezuoshe de fazhan ji qi dui dalu de qishi" (台湾农业合作社的发展及其对大陆的启示) (The Development of Agricultural Cooperatives in Taiwan and the Implications for the Mainland), *Xiandai jingji tantao* (现代经济探讨) (Modern Economics), no. 5 (2006): 37–40; Dan Yuli (单玉丽), "Tuijin nongye hezuo zuzhi tizhi yu jizhi chuangxin: Taiwan fazhan nongye hezuo zuzhi zhi qidi" (推进农业合作组织体制与机制创新: 台湾发展农业合作组织之启迪) (Promoting a System of Agricultural Cooperative Organizations and Mechanical Innovation: Inspiration from Taiwan's Development of Agricultural Cooperatives), *Fazhan yanjiu* (发展研究) (Development Research), no. 10 (2006): 18–20.

103. Tyrene White, "Postrevolutionary Mobilization in China: The One-Child Policy Reconsidered," *World Politics*, 43, no. 1 (October 1990): 75.

104. Zhao Ziyang, *Prisoner of the State: The Secret Journal of Zhao Ziyang* (New York: Simon and Schuster, 2009), p. 185.

105. White, "Postrevolutionary Mobilization in China," p. 73.

106. Zhao Ziyang, *Prisoner of the State*, p. 185.

107. Li Peng (李鹏), *Shichang yu tiaokong: Li Peng jingji riji* (市场与调控: 李鹏经济日记) (Markets and Controls: Li Peng's Economic Diary) (Beijing: Xinhua chubanshe, 2007), 1: 576–578.

108. Yasheng Huang, *Inflation and Investment Controls in China: The Political Economy of Central-Local Relations During the Reform Era* (New York: Cambridge University Press, 1996).

109. Valerie Bunce, *Subversive Institutions: The Design and the Destruction of Socialism and the State* (New York: Cambridge University Press, 1999).

110. Perry Anderson, "Two Revolutions," *New Left Review*, no. 61 (January–February 2010): 59–96.

CHAPTER 3

Policy-Making through Experimentation: The Formation of a Distinctive Policy Process

SEBASTIAN HEILMANN

To explain the capability of China's party-state to generate institutional and policy innovations for economic reform and to adapt to a rapidly changing economic environment, many studies point to the crucial role of decentralized experimentation.[1] A policy process in which central policy makers encourage local officials to try out new ways of problem-solving and then feed the local experiences back into national policy formulation has been a pervasive feature of China's economic transformation. It has decisively shaped the making of policies in areas ranging from rural decollectivization, foreign economic opening, and promotion of private business to state-sector restructuring and stock-market regulation.[2] In some intensely disputed policy areas, such as state-sector bankruptcy, experimental programs with varying priorities came and went for more than twenty years until a finalized national law was eventually issued.[3] Over and over again, those national policy makers who attempted to change the way the economy was run instrumentalized the results of experimental programs for asserting the initiative and overcoming opposition from rival policy makers who tried to defend the old rules of the game.

The existence of a sophisticated indigenous methodology of "proceeding from point to surface" (*youdian daomian*, 由点到面) in making policy suggests an entrenched legitimacy of decentralized experimentation that goes far beyond the sporadic experiments that were carried out in other authoritarian polities or in the paradigmatic party-state of the Soviet Union. The Chinese point-to-surface approach entails a policy process that is initiated from individual "experimental points" (*shidian*, 试点) and driven by local initiative with the formal or informal backing of higher-level policy makers. If judged to be conducive to current priorities by party and government leaders, "model experiences" (*dianxing jingyan*, 典型经验) extracted from the initial experiments are spread through extensive media coverage, high-profile conferences, intervisitation programs, and appeals for emulation in more and more regions. This expansion process requires progressive policy refinement and effects a search for generalizable policy solutions. The tried-and-tested novel approaches emerging from this process are integrated into national policies after further revision, if they gain broad acceptance among top policy makers. Thus, the point-to-surface technique gives room for local officials to develop models on their own, while ultimate control over confirming, revising, terminating, and spreading the model experiments rests with top-level decision makers. Importantly, the mode of experimentation practiced in the PRC focuses on finding innovative policy *instruments*; it is not designed to define policy *objectives* which remain the prerogative of the party leadership.[4]

Although it is rarely disputed that experimentation has constituted a crucial mechanism for institutional and policy innovation,[5] the origins of the experimental policy process observed in China remain unexplained. In searching for the prerequisites of post-Mao experimentation, some scholars point to particular initial conditions, mainly the cellular economic structure, smaller state industry, and less comprehensive central planning at the outset of the economic reforms, to explain why China had the potential to introduce market competition with less disruption than that which occurred in the former socialist economies of Eastern Europe.[6] Others see China's economic rise in the post-Mao era characterized by extensive administrative decentralization that allowed local jurisdictions to launch economic policy innovations on their own.[7] A recent study argues that it was not decentralization but rather factional competition at the national level that gave rise to local experimentation based on patron-client networks reaching from the central policy makers down to the local administrators.[8]

However, research undertaken thus far does not explicate how the Chinese pattern of policy experimentation took shape and became an entrenched approach to generate new policy options. First, initial conditions do not determine how effectively policy makers made use of them and why Chinese policy makers chose a particular experimental approach to facilitate policy innovation. Second, so as to make decentralized experimentation work in an authoritarian party-state, there must be a special mechanism that legitimizes local initiative while leaving hierarchical control intact. As a

consequence, the patterns of central-local interaction differ from explanatory models that are derived from the context of advanced democratic
polities, such as "laboratories of federalism" or "decentralization." Third,
even if factional competition constitutes a driving force behind policy-
making, it does not help explain the distinctive historical and ideological
foundations and the concrete patterns of experiment-based policy-making
in China.

The methods and terminology used in experimental programs in China
are so idiosyncratic and unconventional in international comparison that an
exploration of their political origins may provide important clues as to why,
and under what conditions, local experimentation came to be accepted and
legitimized as a general method of leadership and policy-making in China,
even though the party center has not been willing to relinquish hierarchical
control over the polity and has never lost its power to impose drastic
sanctions on local policy makers and officials. Core elements of experimentation, such as "experimental points" or "proceeding from point to
surface," can serve as identifiers in our search for the origins of China's
experiment-based policy process.

In the first section of this chapter, I elaborate on the Chinese Communists' particular experience in experimentation to develop transformative
policies during their revolutionary struggles. Second, I turn to the non-
Communist intellectual context and administrative practices in which the
concepts of policy experimentation were pioneered in China. In the third
section, I explain core features of China's contemporary policy process
through the revolution-era repertoire that policy makers could draw upon
in their search for new policy instruments to facilitate rapid economic
modernization.

Revolutionary Antecedents of Experiment-Based Policy-Making

The Chinese Communist Party's mode of policy experimentation attests to
the persisting importance of formative historical experiences on China's
contemporary policy process. The methodology and terminology of policy
experimentation that continues to be used by present-day policy makers
(albeit often unaware of their historical roots)[9] date from the revolutionary
experience of the Chinese Communist Party and are not inventions of
reform-era leaders who after 1978 made energetic pleas for "vigorous"
(Deng Xiaoping) or more "cautious" (Chen Yun) experimentation.

EXPERIMENTING FOR SURVIVAL (1928–1943)

An elaborate mode of local policy experimentation under central guidance was developed in the context of experiments with land reform in the Communist base areas before the founding of the PRC in 1949. Due to the strict commandism and centralization of Stalin's Soviet Union, the Chinese Communists could not look to Soviet models of decentralized experimentation in rural revolution.[10] The Chinese Communists took over elements of the Soviet Stakhanovite movement in propagandizing "model units" and conducting emulation campaigns.[11] And they borrowed heavily from Soviet terminology, including the language of Soviet social engineering of the 1920s and 1930s that included terms such as "experimental station" (*opytnaia stantsiia*, a term that denotes pioneering state farms but was also widely applied to pilot projects in the educational and cultural systems)[12] and "experimental point" (*opytnyi punkt*), which came to assume a much broader significance in Chinese communism than it ever enjoyed in the Soviet Union. Since social experiments in Stalin's Soviet Union were "conducted behind a veil of secrecy," mostly confined to technological and educational innovation and never propagandized as a regular policy-making approach,[13] Chinese indigenous experiences had to provide the pattern for decentralized experimentation to reorganize rural society.

The experiments with alternative approaches to land reform that were undertaken by Mao Zedong in Jinggangshan and Deng Zihui in Minxi in 1928 constituted a pioneering experience for later Communist land policy.[14] Although Mao has been given most of the attention and credit for shaping the CCP's methods of land reform in official party historiography, recent research by Chinese historians and recollections by party cadres involved in early land reform work suggest that Deng Zihui, not Mao, may have been the first to initiate the point-to-surface type of controlled experimentation based on the establishment of "model villages," dissemination of "model experiences," and progressive refinement of policies in the course of expansion.[15] Due to constant military threats and shaky political support, Mao's attempts at land redistribution in Jinggangshan were confined to isolated places and short-lived efforts. The Minxi area provided more opportunity and time for systematic reforms. There Deng Zihui made a serious effort to develop novel policies from the bottom up by consulting the local populace and absorbing their suggestions on practicable measures, while reserving the decisions on policy acceptability and expansion for party bodies. By 1930, the Minxi experiences were already widely known in Communist publications and served as an important reference for land policies applied in the Jiangxi Soviet from 1931 to 1934. Moreover, the Minxi methods were later summarized in an official report that circulated in Yan'an from February 1943, at a time when the point-to-surface methodology was intensively discussed and eventually elevated to an official leadership technique in the Communist Party. Though Deng Zihui apparently did not coin the point-to-surface terminology, his consistent efforts at bottom-up experimentation, gradual model dissemination, and constant revision of policy instruments certainly influenced the intra-party debate on policy-making approaches and, more directly, the views of Mao, who maintained a close working relationship with Deng Zihui in rural matters until the mid-1950s.[16]

During the Communist Party's Jiangxi Soviet period, implementation of agrarian policies varied considerably from place to place. The party leadership, internally divided and insecure about concrete ways to make revolution in the countryside, came to accept the stark variations in policy implementation, encouraging party organs at each level to experiment with unconventional measures and to produce diverse models for emulation by other localities. On this basis, Mao Zedong drafted detailed reports on "model Soviet governments" that contained long sections on organizational techniques and their applicability to other locations.[17] The "Xingguo Model" (*mofan Xingguo*, 模范兴国), describing a county in the Jiangxi Soviet area that was praised by Mao in 1934 for its pioneering achievements in organizational, educational, and land reform work, became a reference for many other experimental sites in the late 1930s and 1940s.[18] Yet the proliferation of emulation campaigns undertaken in the Jiangxi Soviet did not result in systematic and uniform policy-making. There were myriads of model experiments, but the expansion of novel local approaches to larger areas remained patchy and piecemeal. In spite of these constraints, Mao refined an organizational technique during his Jiangxi years that later on was to become a principal revolutionary method: dispatching work teams consisting of "strong cadres" to selected sites so as to test and demonstrate methods of land reform in one small spot; simultaneously training party activists and potential new cadres in this spot; bringing the "masses" from other places to the model demonstration site; and sending cadres and activists from the model spot to adjacent areas, thereby spreading those practices that had been identified by top leaders as conducive to current party policies. One of Mao's collaborators during these early land reform endeavors retrospectively depicts this technique as "experimental point" work.[19] Yet the experimentalist terminology that would emerge in the 1940s was not yet used in the Jiangxi Soviet.

After the central leaders of the Communist Party established their headquarters in Yan'an, and with the intensification of the Japanese military campaigns, the many scattered guerrilla bases behind Japanese lines (mainly in North China) became centers of the Communist Party–led peasant movement and sites of a large variety of mass mobilization and land reform experiments. One major center of revolutionary experimentation, where numerous Chinese Communist leaders left a mark who later would become top reform-era policy makers, was the Taihang Base Area (on the border of Shanxi and Henan provinces). This base area operated under constant military threats and political uncertainty inflicted by Japanese attacks, an erratic provincial warlord (Yan Xishan), and KMT forces. In autumn 1939, taking the 1934 Xingguo Model as a reference, two "experimental counties" (*shiyan xian*, 实验县) reporting directly to the base area party committee were expected to provide a "model demonstration" (*dianxing shifan*, 典型示范) to guide the entire area to introduce new methods of mass mobilization and recruitment of party activists. The experimental sites were required to test a new "bottom-up work-style" based on consultation with the populace. "Contests in experimental work" were held among different party branches. Less successful branches were required to visit and to learn from the successful branches. Local party activists were expected to become "labor heroes in creating experiments." To achieve the objectives of strengthening the Communist Party's local mass base, the envisaged experimental period of six months was subdivided into two-month phases, each with clearly stated work objectives to be accomplished on schedule.[20] Because Deng Xiaoping was a prominent leader in this base area, it is very likely that the opportunistic but active experimentation in Taihang may have exerted considerable influence on his approach to policy-making in the later stages of his political career.[21]

ELEVATING EXPERIMENTATION TO A METHOD OF POLITICAL LEADERSHIP (1943–1953)

The Chinese Communists' experiments in the many administratively autonomous and, with regard to their land reform approaches and successes, widely differing base areas, decisively shaped revolutionary strategy and theory.[22] That policies had to be implemented "in accordance with local conditions" (*yindi zhiyi*, 因地制宜) became a core revolutionary tactic that created inevitable tension with the principle of hierarchical discipline.[23]

During the 1942–43 Rectification Movement, which resulted in major restatements of revolutionary leadership and strategy, decentralized policy experimentation was confirmed as a standard method of "creating model experiments" and "proceeding from point to surface." An authoritative, yet still vague, guideline on this method was published under Mao's name in June 1943.[24] In a general statement on "methods of leadership," Mao stressed that for any task party cadres must "make a breakthrough at some single point, gain experience, and use this experience for guiding other units."[25] In successive statements on this leadership method, Mao made it clear that it was not meant to justify unfettered trial and error and it had to be geared to the creation of "model experiments" that demonstrated effective and novel ways for realizing the policy objectives set by the party leadership.[26] In line with his practice-based epistemology, Mao held that policy implementation, not policy debate, provided the crucial device for learning and innovation.[27] In a 1948 directive to the party, Mao went so far as to proclaim that the "model experiences" produced by several Communist-controlled base areas were "much closer to reality and richer than the decisions and directives issued by our leadership organs" and should serve as an antidote against tendencies toward "commandism" within the party.[28]

That designing methods of effective implementation was largely left to local initiative was one of the practical lessons derived from the Communists' protracted land reform efforts. In the face of a highly fragmented and heterogeneous revolutionary process, the party leadership refrained from issuing standard implementation procedures that had already all-too-often proven to be impracticable. Broad discretionary powers were given to basic-level party organs to experiment with diverse measures of rural transformation, ranging from brutally repressive to more conciliatory approaches.[29] Even on the eve of the civil war victory, Mao stressed that land reform could not be achieved in just a few months and by one-size-fits-all measures. Instead, it needed to be based on a carefully designed point-to-surface approach, first by obtaining experience on the ground in a small number of selected sites and then by spreading the experience in a succession of increasingly broader and stronger wave-like movements.[30] During this time, as Vivienne Shue states, the point-to-surface method emerged as "one of the standard devices of the Party and the government for implementing important rural policies" in a "consciously experimental" but carefully controlled manner.[31]

The party center always reserved, and regularly exercised, the power to annul local experiments or to make them into a national model. The pursuit of an experiment-based policy approach resulted from necessity. The CCP simply did not have a sufficient number of well-trained rural cadres to dispatch to the hundreds of thousands of villages. And since the revolutionary process was driven from scattered base areas, the party lacked an integrated apparatus and capacity for standardized policy implementation.[32] Model villages and other basic-level model units were designated, supervised, and propagandized by higher-level party bodies that often did not have the means to give consistent material support from above. Thus model units were forced to support themselves and to come up with creative local problem-solving for many endeavors.[33] It was not the lack of political power or ideological determination on the part of the party center, but the lack of resources and personnel that forced the party center to give room to local initiative and even to tolerate ideological deviations as long as they strengthened overall Communist Party control in the respective localities.

CCP-controlled experimentation was elevated to a general method of leadership following the statements by Mao. But the concrete techniques and terms were specified by other party leaders based on their practical experiences. Over the 1940s, veteran rural revolutionary Deng Zihui refined the technique of spreading local experience to larger areas by reassigning work teams and local activists in a systematic way. Various "experimental zones for land reform" were in place beginning in 1947.[34] Between 1946 and 1948, both Chen Yun (in the Northeast) and Deng Xiaoping (in the Southwest) issued guidelines on implementing land reform that made full use of the point-to-surface methodology.[35] In 1950 CCP directives instructed top cadres to personally take the lead in implementing land reform experiments.[36] In East China, Rao Shushi supervised a total of 370 "model experiment townships" designed to find effective ways to prepare for full-scale land redistribution. The experimental process was supposed to last up to three months and Rao made it clear that, as in guerrilla war, "drastic" violent measures had to be taken at certain points to overcome resistance and to "achieve breakthroughs" at the rural experimental sites.[37] By 1951, the party guidelines for land reform had been consolidated into six steps, of which steps 2 to 6 are crucial to Chinese-style policy experimentation to the present day: (1) train work-team cadres and send them down to the localities; (2) carry out model experiments; (3) accomplish breakthroughs in a key point; (4) broaden the campaign from point to surface; (5) integrate point and surface with regard to applied measures; and (6) unfold the campaign in steady steps.[38]

By the early 1950s, the terms "model experiment" (*dianxing shiyan*, 典型试验), "experimental point," as well as "model demonstration," "proceeding from point to surface" (*youdian daomian* or *yidian daimian*, 以点带面), and "integrating point and surface" (*dianmian jiehe*, 点面结合) had emerged as key terms in the Chinese Communists' repertoire of policy experimentation.[39] All these terms are still widely used in official language today. However, "experimental point" has become by far the most prevalent term in reform-era policy experimentation. Beginning in the 1950s, the term "experimental point" was used as a synonym for the more formal term "model experiment," both of which have the meaning of obtaining experience through concrete work at one spot so as to guide general policy.[40]

In an earlier analysis, I characterize the term "experimental point" as an indigenous neologism introduced by the Chinese Communists.[41] After the article was published, Peter Kuhfus (a Sinologist specializing in the history of interactions between the Soviet and Chinese Communist parties) pointed out to me that the Russian term *opytnyi punkt* ("trial point" or "experimental point") had at least occasionally been used in local pilot projects of the 1930s and 1940s in the USSR. Despite an intensive search, the Chinese and Russian sources that Kuhfus and I have scrutinized do not give explicit clues on how the term "experimental point" made its way into China. As with other elements of Soviet terminology, it is likely that the Russian term was either transferred to China by Soviet advisors or by Chinese Communists who had learned about Soviet "experimental stations" and "experimental points" during their stays in the USSR. An electronic search of official Chinese Communist media reveals it is plausible that the Chinese term "experimental point" originated in the Soviet Union. The term *shidian* spread in China from first being widely used in the Northeast regions (the center of the Soviet advisors' activity in the early PRC and a place where many Soviet-inspired top Chinese cadres such as Gao Gang and Chen Yun worked at the time), and then, in the early 1950s, was adopted as a key term for local policy experimentation nationwide.[42]

Whereas "experimental point" has remained a widely used official term in China from the early 1950s to the present day, after the 1940s Soviet sources no longer prominently used it.[43] Most importantly, the Soviet Communists did not use the "point-to-surface" terminology that played a crucial role in Maoist experimentation. In Soviet policy-making, the "experimental point" method never had the significance that it had in the Chinese Communists' policy process. When economic reforms were considered in the Soviet Union in the 1960s, even very modest local experiments in the planning and allocation system met with stiff resistance from the bureaucracy and violent criticisms from prominent economists who castigated economic experimentation as a retreat from systematic theoretical analysis and comprehensive planning.[44] The centralized planning bureaucracy and rigid economic order that were founded on detailed laws and decrees in the Soviet Union clearly were a much less hospitable context for decentralized and informal experimentation than in the PRC where there was room for decentralized tinkering due to the constantly shifting institutional and legal environments.

Clearly, the indigenous, down-to-earth experiences with experiment-based policy generation in the Chinese Communists' base areas and in the plethora of non-Communist, Republican-era experimental units exerted a direct and powerful influence on the Chinese Communist pattern of experimentation. According to a 1953 cadre education journal, one of the core purposes of "experimental points" was to "bring welfare to society by making use of scientific patterns that have been discovered through practice . . . to be a reflection of objective processes." The strengths of the "experimental point" method were defined to prevent "blind" implementation of unfamiliar policies; give cadres an opportunity to learn and overcome old habits by trying out new solutions first on a small scale; "educate the masses" and win their support for new policies through active participation in local experiments; and help to save resources, manpower, and time in carrying out new policies. At the same time, it was emphasized that the success of "experimental point" work depended on appropriate preparation and timing (premature establishment would lead to failure), the selection of "typical" experimental sites that could teach credible lessons to "the masses" in other sites, a contingent of strong cadres and activists at the test spots, and sophisticated analysis to extract generalizable lessons.[45]

The point-to-surface technique became a cornerstone of Maoist policy-making theory that resurfaced over and over again in a series of post-1949 Mao statements.[46] As a method of revolutionary transformation, it was used not only in China but also exported in almost the exact form to Vietnam. In the context of extensive Chinese support to the Vietminh forces, the 1953–56 land reform in North Vietnam was designed by a team of experienced Chinese cadres and initiated by small-scale "experimental waves," including the initial establishment of "experimental points" (*thí điểm*, that is, *shidian*) and "typical models" (*điển hình*, that is *dianxing*) before scaling up the reforms in a phased manner, depending on the success of the experimental units and local circumstances.[47]

In sum, the "experimental point" and point-to-surface methodologies were firmly established through a series of statements by top Communist Party leaders, and refined and redefined by practical application during the 1943–53 period. Although these methodologies were the product of the distinctive historical context of revolutionary struggle, they came to be seen by the economic reformers of the 1980s as the "concretization" of the Chinese Communist Party's best tradition in "seeking truth from facts."[48] Deng Xiaoping, Chen Yun, and other powerful veterans, though holding differing views on the desirable extent, direction, and speed of economic reform, were in agreement that the success of the large-scale experimentation in the 1943–53 period provided valuable lessons about flexible and risk-minimizing methods of policy innovation that could be employed to modernize the country. This is why the terminology of experimentation and the slogan "crossing the river by groping for the stones"[49] were taken from their revolutionary contexts and made to serve the purpose of reforming the Chinese economy.

FROM DECENTRALIZED EXPERIMENTATION TO CENTRALLY IMPOSED MODEL EMULATION

The consolidation of the Communist Party's power and apparatus, combined with the gradual introduction of economic planning and an ideological hardening in Mao's stance over the course of the 1950s, provoked marked shifts in the pattern of policy-making.[50] Though central control over many sectors of the economy remained patchy, the proliferation of central decrees, investment plans, and production quotas weakened the corrective mechanisms inherent in the "experimental point" approach. "Experimental point work" undertaken in agriculture and industry during the 1953–57 period was designed to contribute to cooperativization, plan fulfilment, and overall technical and organizational innovation by producing "advanced units" for national popularization under central guidelines.[51] The political leeway for generating new policy approaches through decentralized experimentation became substantially circumscribed.

With the Great Leap Forward (GLF, 1958–60), bureaucratic centralization was pushed back and local initiative and experimentation were again encouraged. But the ideological and political contexts of experimentation were fundamentally different from those in the late 1940s and the early 1950s. The experiences of the GLF and the Cultural Revolution (CR) demonstrate the dialectic that is inherent in the point-to-surface technique:

it can be a very much bottom-up or very much a top-down affair, depending on the overall political and ideological constellation.

The severe political risks stemming from this ambiguity had already come to the fore during the campaign against "rightist" tendencies in summer 1957. There was much talk about local experimentation and the lessons to be learned from such experiments. But in reality there was no room politically for experiments that contradicted the ideological directives coming from Mao. In the second half of the 1950s, the core principles of the Chinese Communists' revolutionary experience, such as "implementing policies in accordance with local conditions" and "proceeding from point to surface," increasingly became empty slogans. Standardized implementation and swift total compliance became inevitable as a manifestation of political reliability and loyalty to Mao Zedong: "Once the centre (usually Mao) sent out a signal, a few model units were selected, increasingly higher targets disseminated, target over-fulfilment reported from below, and the task completed swiftly in a highly standardized manner."[52] Those who used methods of implementation that came to be judged as deviant were classified as people who had committed errors in "political line." Even the search for solutions and instruments in implementing party policy was regularly transformed into an issue of class and line struggle, although leading policy makers such as Chen Yun continued to plea for cautious experimentation in economic administration.[53]

An instructive case of how drastically the political climate for experimentation changed in 1957–58 is the fate of the "experimental points" for fixing agricultural output quotas for individual households in Wenzhou district (Zhejiang province). In an effort to counter a downslide in agricultural production that resulted from the collectivization policies, starting in spring 1956 the party committee of Yongjia county initiated experiments with new incentives for peasant households, after having obtained the informal consent of the district party committee. The experiments proved to be so popular and successful that they were rapidly extended from point to surface in the county. However, as soon as the political winds changed and ideological struggle stiffened with the advent of the anti-rightist campaign, starting in summer 1957 the experiments and the experimenters were severely attacked and crushed as "anti-socialist." Many local cadres were expelled from the party and some were sent to labor camps, along with those peasants who had been the most enthusiastic supporters of the experiments. Repression was carried out by the same district-level leaders who had benevolently tolerated the county-level experiments only a few months earlier, although carefully avoiding becoming closely associated with them.[54]

In such a feverish ideological context, there was only room for "working toward" the erratic party chairman[55] and no room for open experimentation. Significantly, the time horizon became ever narrower. Whereas the establishment of "model experiments" was expected to take several months during the land reform era, no time was allowed to prove the results of the policy experiments during the Great Leap. In addition, local officials ran a high risk in criticizing the drawbacks of their own local experiments. Such self-criticisms had contributed to the spread of the 1946–53 land reform movement that had also produced, beyond the usual official praise, insightful analysis about the failure of certain local and national policies.[56]

The GLF was identified by contemporaries as a deviation from the experiment-based policy process that had proven to be so useful to the CCP's rise to power. Critics complained that the People's Communes were established "too rapidly" without sufficient experience through prior experimentation. In 1960, the official press made a serious effort to dilute this criticism by pointing to a series of "experimental point-like communes" that had been set up at the start of the national movement.[57] The post-Mao leadership, however, sided with the early critics and held that the GLF had led to disaster because "serious investigations and experimental point work" had not been undertaken and policy implementation had been based on blind and subjectivist political enthusiasm.[58]

This is not the place to go into the details of the feverish emulation campaigns that were commonplace during the 1957–78 period. Yet some remarkable shifts in terminology indicate the differences between experimentation and emulation. During the GLF, the principle of taking action "in accordance with local circumstances" was superseded by the new slogan to treat "the whole country as one chessboard" (*quanguo yipanqi*, 全国一盘棋). All local efforts were to be unified in executing every new policy or ideological clue that came from the party center.[59] During the Cultural Revolution, the construction of national "templates" (*yangban*, 样板) according to orders from above was seen as an effective instrument in standardizing policy implementation: "Put templates to use, push forward across the board" (*yunyong yangban, tuidong quanpan*, 运用样板, 推动全盘).[60] Consequently, the rural and industrial model sites of Dazhai and Daqing were not called "experimental points" but rather were presented as "templates" and "models for achieving greater, faster, better, and more economical results."[61] Thus, not even the official terminology claimed that these two creations of top-level policy pushes could be treated as cases of experimentation. These were national projects imposed and supported by central will without conducting simultaneous test-runs in other sites and without regard to how these models might be replicated under different local circumstances. In responding to central signals, instant implementation and instant results were required. Neither time nor operative and ideological leeway for experimentation were allowed. This is why a number of notorious instant models, promoted by top-level initiative and Mao's personal attention, faded as suddenly as they sprang up, such as that of Xushui county whose goal in 1958 was to establish communism in one huge-and-quick leap, but had to announce the termination of this ambitious experiment only four months after starting it.[62]

Thus, in studying the historical development of policy experimentation under Communist Party leadership it is appropriate to distinguish between experimentation that is open-ended with regard to the instruments of policy implementation on the one hand, and pre-conceived, centrally imposed model propagation and emulation on the other. Most models of the GLF and CR eras, including Dazhai and Daqing, clearly belong to the latter category, since they were products of centralized sponsorship and amplification, and essentially served to demonstrate the vision and wisdom of the top leaders.[63]

Doing justice to the ambiguities of the GLF and CR periods, it should be mentioned that policy experimentation was not suffocated in all policy domains all of the time. The "experimental point" method was never formally abolished and it was always cherished as part of the mythical revolutionary tradition. It thus could serve to legitimate decentralized initiatives under the condition that high-level patrons and advocates were supportive and the policy domains in which the experiments were undertaken temporarily lay on the margins of the ideological battlefield. Certain programs of the 1960s and 1970s allowed meaningful experimentation to find new policy instruments when the policy context was more relaxed and top-level backing was present. In retrospect, certain instances of path-breaking experimentation during that period may be seen as trend-setting for the post-1978 reforms, such as the experiments with household-based agricultural production (1957 and 1961), family planning (1964), formation of industrial trusts (1964–65), rural cooperative health care (1966), and rural industry and trade (1969–70). Though these experimental programs, with the exception of rural cooperative health care, were subject to intense political-ideological strife and were terminated at an early stage, they provided precedents and experience that policy makers could draw on after 1978.

In sum, the GLF and CR experiences demonstrated that experimentation can be productive only if applied in a policy environment which allows step-by-step problem-solving over an extended period of time, tolerates deviant decentralized initiative, and is geared to well-defined and stable policy priorities. This is why Communist experimentation worked to strengthen party power as long as Mao maintained his pragmatism. But as soon as the politics of ideological outbidding and economic utopianism kicked in, experimentation turned into a fever of instant model creation and blind model emulation, both of which led to disaster.

Embedded Revolutionaries: Non-Communist Sources of Policy Experimentation

As Donald Munro succinctly states, the point-to-surface technique "differs fundamentally from Soviet socialist emulation theory" in terms of its decentralized and informal character.[64] Strikingly, experimentation is a blind spot in the Marxist-Leninist canon. Developing methods of revolution through experiments was neither debated nor proposed by Marx, Lenin, or Stalin.[65] In Lenin's entire collected works, the need for experimentation to find new policy solutions is mentioned only once and in a very specific context.[66] Stalin was vehemently hostile to "spontaneous" and "blind" local initiative.[67] A commandist top-down approach to policy generation and implementation represented the legitimate revolutionary strategy and administrative practice of the Soviet Union. Since revolution meant putting the laws of history into reality, revolutionaries knew what to do in advance of implementing policy and were not supposed to be distracted by experimentation.

Nevertheless, Chinese political intellectuals and activists came to perceive the Russian revolution as a huge experiment. Qu Qiubai, a prominent figure in the early Chinese Communist movement, characterized Soviet Russia as "a laboratory of communism," in which Bolshevik "chemists" remolded the Russian people in the "test tubes" of the Soviets and produced new "social-ist compounds."[68] Soviet Russia's New Economic Policy (NEP) attracted much interest among Chinese Communists. But the books that introduced the NEP to the Chinese public did not mention experimentation as a key element of Soviet governance.[69] In fact, the NEP was never conceived of as an experiment for developing policy tools in an open-ended manner. Rather, it was seen by Lenin as a package of emergency measures for economic survival and as a transitional arrangement that was to lead to "correct" socialist economic policies as soon as Communist power was consolidated.[70] The fact that an experimentalist approach to making revolution was not developed in the Marxist-Leninist classics makes it even more remarkable that the Chinese Communists turned to an experimental point-to-surface approach in their efforts to transform China.

In explaining the revolutionary experience and legacies of the Chinese Communists, Benjamin Schwartz, and many others in his wake, points to the distinctive circumstances, social forces, and political dynamics at work in the Chinese revolution that virtually forced unorthodox solutions onto the Communist leaders and provoked major deviations from standard Marxist-Leninist and Soviet recipes. From the perspective of official party historiography, it is clear who invented Chinese-style policy experimentation: Mao Zedong raised the basic concepts and other party leaders further developed Mao's concepts through practical application. However, this interpretation of the emergence of the point-to-surface methodology in China is untenable in the face of the ample evidence of social and administrative experimentation that preceded the Communists' activities. The findings presented in the following paragraphs are unequivocal: the transformation of social, political, and economic conditions by way of decentralized but controlled experimentation was not pioneered by the Communists. Instead, Communist experimentation is a part of a much bigger story about widespread efforts at experimentation in extremely uncertain times during China's Republican era.

THE DEWEYAN IMPRINT ON MAO'S EXPERIMENTAL APPROACH

The impact of John Dewey's pragmatist philosophy on political debate in China during the 1920s has been the subject of numerous scholarly works. The series of lectures that Dewey gave in major Chinese cities and universities in 1919 and 1920 influenced the thinking of a generation of political intellectuals and activists, including the founders of the Communist Party and Mao Zedong. One core theme in Dewey's lectures was the experimental method that he presented as the central innovative feature of modern science and the most important method for obtaining scientific knowledge. Chinese political activists eagerly picked up on his statements on experimentation which, according to Dewey, "is guided by intentional anticipation instead of being blind trial and error.... [i]t is experience marked by the intent to act upon the idea." Dewey contrasted classical philosophies that tended to be "isolated from the cold, hard facts of human experience" with modern approaches that stressed that ideas and theories had to be tested through practical application and experimentation: "There can be no true knowledge without doing. It is only doing that enables us to revise our outlook, to organize our facts in a systematic way, and to discover new facts."[71]

Dewey's Chinese followers presented experimentation as the core of the Deweyan approach to social reform and rendered Dewey's philosophy as *shiyanzhuyi* (实验主义), a term that in a literal translation means "experimentalism."[72] The most prominent interpreter and popularizer of Deweyan thinking, the American-trained philosopher Hu Shi, gave a decisive twist to the Chinese debate on pragmatism by extracting Dewey's methodological prescriptions from their Western normative context and stressing a one-sidedly instrumentalist understanding of pragmatist philosophy. Hu Shi presented Dewey's "experimentalism" as a methodology of social engineering that proved to be extremely attractive to a very broad spectrum of young Chinese intellectuals, ranging from American-inspired reformers to Soviet-leaning radicals. According to Yu Yingshi, Hu Shi's "reductionist" rendering of Deweyan philosophy has exerted a lasting influence on modern Chinese political thinking, including on Mao's steady emphasis on learning through practice and debates on "practice as the sole criterion for truth" that served to justify the initiation of the economic reform and opening.[73] Mao himself once admitted that he had been an ardent admirer of Hu Shi during the early May Fourth period.[74]

The influence of Deweyan ideas on Mao Zedong's epistemology, with its emphasis on learning through direct practical experience, has been noted in a number of academic works. With regard to Mao's article "On Practice," Herbert Marcuse holds that "there is more Dewey than Marx in all this."[75] Certain formulations and arguments appearing in "On Practice" are strikingly similar to what Dewey stated in his China lectures.[76] Recent works reveal that Mao attended at least one of Dewey's China lectures in 1920, and had read and recommended the Chinese edition of Dewey's *Five Major Lectures* and stocked this book when he opened a bookstore that year.[77] Dewey's 1920 dictum on modern science, "everything through experimentation" (translated by his disciples into Chinese as *yiqie dou cong shiyan xiashou* [一切都从实验下手])[78] was echoed in a 1958 directive by Mao that stated "everything through experimentation" (*yiqie jingguo shiyan*, 一切经过试验).[79]

Along with Mao, most other founding members of the CCP were deeply attracted to Dewey's epistemology that conveyed the message that learning and acting, that is, obtaining knowledge about the world and bringing change to the world, could be achieved through a well-conceived process of practical experimentation.[80] In the early version of Chinese communism, "experimentalism both as a philosophy and as a scientific method had . . . an upper hand over dialectic materialism." Even the idea of class struggle was initially rejected by most early Communist protagonists.[81] Dewey's "emphasis on methodology, logic, and practicality made it irresistibly attractive to the leaders of the intellectual revolution . . . and highly useful in promoting many social, ethical, and economic reforms."[82]

According to Munro, Dewey's idea of learning through practical experience, as popularized by Hu Shi in China, goes together well with the importance of teaching by example and learning through role models in the Chinese educational and administrative traditions. Cultivating, propagandizing, and emulating concrete models through a type of social and psychological conditioning process, instead of abiding by abstract moral or legal principles, doubtlessly has strong roots in premodern Chinese philosophy. From the late 1920s, these traditions were reinvigorated by Soviet-inspired movements that propagandized "labor heroes," "model factories," and "socialist competition" among all kinds of model units. Thus emerged the emulation of models built on both Chinese tradition and Soviet campaign methods.[83] However, the experimentation that became part and parcel of the Chinese Communists' point-to-surface technique sprang from efforts at social reform that were inspired more by Deweyan thinking than by traditional Chinese or Soviet governance practices.

NGO-REFORMISTS: EXPERIMENTAL SITES IN THE RURAL RECONSTRUCTION MOVEMENT

During the May Fourth era, as a result of Dewey's 1919–20 pleas for social experimentation and his disciples' vigorous efforts at application, numerous experimental sites were established all over China, with a focus on schools, agriculture, health care, and local administration. According to GMD government statistics, about 600 different para-governmental and non-governmental organizations (many supported by foreign funds) were involved in rural reform efforts and in more than 1,000 experimental sites that were scattered all over the country in the mid-1930s. In addition to many small experimental sites such as schools, agricultural stations, or health centers, about twenty full-scale, though mostly failing and short-lived, experimental counties were officially recognized by the central government prior to 1937.[84] Thus, before the Japanese invasion, social experimentation had become a popular activity in which Chinese political activists took a keen interest.

NGO-funded American agricultural reformers were pioneers in introducing the idea and practice of experimentation to Chinese administrators. The American system of establishing one agricultural experiment station in every state was transferred to the provincial-level units in China.[85] Although American advisors raised serious doubts about the success of China's experimental stations in trying out new agricultural methods and varieties,[86] the general approach of setting up one experimental unit per province was pursued in the experimental county program of the 1930s. Moreover, the Chinese terminology of experimentation was introduced in the 1910s and 1920s by agricultural experimenters who popularized "experimental extension" (*shixing tuiguang*, 试行推广) of technological and organizational innovations.[87]

The most prominent social experimenters of the Republican era emerged from the Mass Education movement (MEM) and the Rural Reconstruction movement (RRM) which established influential non-Communist antecedents for the point-to-surface approach in rural reform. By June 1925, the Yale-educated Chinese founder of the MEM, Yan Yangchu (James Yen), had laid out the basic principles of what later would become essential elements in the Communists' point-to-surface technique:

> The general plan of the [Mass Education] Movement is to select one or two typical rural districts in north, south, east, west, and central China, respectively, for intensive and extensive experimentations ... to make it a model district in education and in general social and economic improvement, so that it may be used as a demonstration and training center for other districts. While intensive experiments of this kind are being undertaken in the chosen areas, the Movement promotes its program extensively to as many villages as possible and as rapidly as possible.[88]

As early as the late 1920s, the terms "experimental county" and "experimental zone" were already employed by MEM/RRM leaders and other NGO initiators then active in rural China.[89] The experimental sites managed by the MEM and RRM exerted considerable influence on the Communists for a number of reasons that are not readily conceded by official party historiography. From the very beginning of MEM activities, there existed close personal relationships that crossed the boundaries between the Communist Party and the non-Communist MEM. One co-founder of the MEM who became the closest collaborator of James Yen from the 1920s to 1949 was an uncle of one of the eminent Communist Party leaders of the 1920s,

Qu Qiubai.[90] More importantly in terms of experimental practice, local MEM and RRM associations were systematically used as cover organizations by underground branches of the Communist Party in the 1930s. When rural reconstruction experiments reached their climax in the mid-1930s, the CCP was at a low historical point. At that time, the MEM and RRM had become big players in rural reform and were seen by CCP leaders as attractive partners. In May 1937, CCP strategist Liu Shaoqi encouraged party organs that operated in areas controlled by the Japanese or the GMD to take active parts in MEM and RRM rural work. Therefore, numerous CCP cadres became MEM activists who worked for the non-Communist rural reform movement during the day and held meetings with their CCP underground comrades during the night.[91]

At the leadership level, MEM and RRM leaders visited Yan'an for political exchanges with Mao Zedong on several occasions. When Mao received a delegation in 1938, he spoke of the MEM activists as the Communist Party's "friends" and, certainly for tactical reasons, expressed his appreciation of their endeavors.[92] In the same year, Mao met for several days of lively chats with Liang Shuming, the RRM leader, and obviously held Liang in high regard at the time.[93] Several Communist delegations visited Ding experimental county to study the social programs initiated there, and Mao certainly was well informed about the basic ideas and diverse experiments conducted by the RRM and MEM. In their search for policies that might generate mass support, Communist leaders used the MEM/RRM efforts to reorganize rural production, education, and health care as instructive references and in some cases appeared to copy directly social programs that had originally been developed in Ding experimental county.[94] In utilizing novel policies, recruiting political activists, and addressing the most pressing needs of the peasants, there was clearly a lot to learn from the non-Communist experimenters.[95]

ENEMY REFORMISTS: GMD-SPONSORED EXPERIMENTAL COUNTIES

During the 1930s, RRM and MEM leaders Liang Shuming and James Yen were courted by both the GMD and the Communists and were invited for talks not only with Mao Zedong but also with Chiang Kai-shek. Scores of GMD politicians and administrators visited and inspected the experimental sites managed by the RRM and MEM as part of a policy tourism in search of new organizational models for China's countryside.[96] Remarkably, not only the Communists were inspired by the MEM and RRM experimental sites; between 1932 and 1937 the GMD government also undertook some prominent efforts to test new ways of governing the countryside. Although the objectives and policies involved in the GMD-led effort at county administrative reconstruction met with a lot of distrust,[97] at least two experimental counties (of altogether twenty counties in eleven provinces) set up by the GMD, Jiangning in Jiangsu province and Lanxi in Zhejiang province, focusing on administration, education, welfare, and security, were promoted by determined county leaders with high-level backing.[98] These two government-sponsored rural reform efforts "from above" were regarded as producing much useful experience. But since these experiments relied on very generous subsidies and had to be terminated in the face of the Japanese invasion, they could not serve as models for other jurisdictions.[99]

After the Japanese defeat, individual GMD policy makers made efforts to re-launch a program of experimental counties. But the Communists were advancing rapidly and proudly announced that they had managed to nip the 1947 GMD experiments in the bud in northern Jiangsu.[100] However, non-Communist experimentation, due to James Yen's successful fund-raising and lobbying efforts in Washington in 1948, was taken up again under the auspices of the Sino-American Joint Commission on Rural Reconstruction (JCRR). After the GMD's defeat in the civil war, this commission acted as a shadow ministry of agriculture in Taiwan, contributing greatly to land reform and rural modernization and, moreover, launching one of the most sophisticated and best documented experimental family planning programs of the twentieth century in Taichung in 1963.[101] The experience and legacy of the rural reconstruction experiments of the pre-1949 era were thereby transferred to Taiwan and incorporated into official GMD policy-making for rural transformation there.

LESSONS OF WIDESPREAD EXPERIMENTATION DURING CHINA'S REPUBLICAN ERA

From the perspective of the widespread experimental programs in Republican China, it might be stated that the Communists merely joined the strong trend of experimentation that had gained momentum since the May Fourth era. The Communists, however, learned from these other experimental efforts only for tactical reasons and were determined to redirect rural experimentation toward their revolutionary goals. From the Communist point of view, the experiments of the Deweyans, liberal reformers, and NGOs had failed because they ignored the issue of political power and tried to work from within the inimical political environment.[102] The reformists never had the authority to transform their experimental projects into a general operational program for a larger jurisdiction. Even if individual non-Communist experiments appeared to work and were widely judged successful, they remained isolated and confined to small areas. The novel policy instruments generated in such places could never be spread systematically due to the reformists' lack of political authority.

In the course of the 1940s, the Communists gained power to proceed in policy implementation from one experimental spot to the entire area they controlled and thereby obtained a crucial capacity that the reformists of the 1930s had never enjoyed. Communist leaders made it clear that they did not see any meaning in experiments unless the Communist Party was in control of the overall experimental process. Thus, although the Communists' unorthodox experimental terminology, as well as its individual policies dealing with land reform, rural education, and health care, may have been influenced by the non-Communist experience, the point-to-surface technique of controlled experimentation by way of sent-down cadre teams, mass mobilization, struggle sessions, and wave-like extensions to neighboring areas constitutes a thoroughly Maoist creation.

Mao held that effective social experimentation could not be carried out as "blind" trial and error but had to be a planned, controlled activity so as to obtain systematic knowledge about feasible novel ways to achieve the goals of the Communist Party. For the Communists, experimentation was about finding innovative policy *instruments*, not about defining the policy *objectives* which remained the exclusive domain of the party leadership. A revealing internal directive, dating from 1940, on one Communist "experimental county" in the Taihang Base Area (then under the leadership of Deng Xiaoping) frankly states that "this experimental county was not established for experimenting" per se but for becoming an exemplar that generates and demonstrates successful leadership methods and policies.[103] Cadres in charge of model experiments were allowed to try out various ways and means to realize the policy goals set by the CCP leadership. But they were not authorized to redefine policy objectives on their own, and their experiments were subject to termination, curtailment, or revision by higher-level party organs at any time.

In sum, experimentation has been a core feature of the Maoist approach to policy-making since revolutionary times. In drawing lessons from the non-Communist experimental programs of the Republican era, Communist leaders developed an extremely instrumentalist understanding of policy experimentation that was compatible with the principle of hierarchical party control.

Maoist Methods of Revolution and Post-Mao Reform

Taking the formative historical experience of CCP leaders and their methods of rule seriously, it becomes clear that experimenting with concurrent local policy alternatives in post-Mao China was not an issue of random choice by enlightened leaders. When searching for new policy approaches to facilitate economic modernization in the late 1970s, China's veteran leaders shared their knowledge and appreciation of the "experimental point" method. They redefined the main mission of the party (from achieving communism to achieving rapid economic growth) and reactivated a repertoire of policy experimentation that had been reduced to model emulation campaigns for most of the period between 1958 and 1978. Post-Mao veteran leaders thereby reverted to the experience of the 1946–53 period that they saw as the most successful and splendid period of controlled large-scale structural change and economic policy in the history of the Communist Party.

Deng Xiaoping and Chen Yun were the most prominent advocates for applying the point-to-surface technique to economic modernization, even though they came to differ substantially with regard to the speed and extent of change. From 1978 to 1992, Deng repeatedly characterized reform and opening as a "large-scale experiment" that could not be carried out with the help of textbook knowledge but instead required vigorous "experimenting in practice."[104] Chen Yun propagandized the "experimental point" technique as a way to carry out controlled and cautious policy innovation.[105] However, in contrast to Deng, Chen took a very sceptical stance toward the introduction of non-socialist special economic zones whose creation Deng Xiaoping justified as an "experiment," pointing to the pre-1949 Communist base areas as a precedent.[106] Deng was an impatient advocate of rapid economic growth. Contrary to the common perception, however, Deng personally never cited the gradualist slogan "crossing the river by groping for the stones" to describe the logic of reform. In actuality, this formula was introduced by Chen Yun in December 1980 as an antidote to what he saw as reform exuberance, and the slogan then became a popular characterization of the Chinese reform approach.[107]

In its 1981 resolution on party history, China's post-Mao leadership identified certain Maoist methods as lasting and indispensable elements of official doctrine. The point-to-surface technique was paraphrased, as in Mao's 1943 article on leadership methods, as the combination of guidance through concrete work on individual issues (*gebie zhidao*, 个别指导) with the making of general policy appeals (*yiban haozhao*, 一般号召).[108] In the 1980s and 1990s, individual party theoreticians made efforts to establish experimentation as an original Chinese contribution to Marxist theory and argued that "a scientific socialist viewpoint can be established only through social experiments."[109] Others identified experimental points as "social science laboratories" and as powerful scientific instruments for linking the processes of obtaining knowledge and implementing policy.[110] In 1992, the importance of experimentation was even inserted into the constitution of the Chinese Communist Party, stipulating that the entire party "must boldly experiment with new methods, . . . review new experience and solve new problems, and enrich and develop Marxism in practice."[111]

China's post-Mao leadership removed the point-to-surface technique of policy experimentation from its original mass campaign context and integrated it into the administrative and entrepreneurial-state context of the post-Mao period. The paramount objective of policy-making was radically redefined from a utopian qualitative goal (completing socialist transformation) into a worldly quantitative goal ("quadrupling China's GDP from 1980 to 2000"). Thus the context and the objectives of experimentation in the post-Mao era were fundamentally different from those of the Maoist mass mobilization approach.[112]

However, with respect to the central role of "model experiments" and "proceeding from point to surface" for policy generation and implementation, there was no systemic shift between the Mao and Deng eras. Though the approaches to policy experimentation differ in important individual features (the role of outside work teams, local cadres, and legislation), the overall continuities that can be observed in nine of the twelve typical steps of experiment-based policy formation are striking (see Table 3.1).

Drawing lessons from what went wrong in earlier decades, the post-Mao leadership accomplished an overall radical turn away from ideological fever and single models for emulation. Instead it acknowledged regional variation and promoted concurrent experiments and multiple models.[113] Locally produced institutional and policy innovations were taken up by reformist policy makers eager to bolster their political standing and to keep their rivals at bay by godfathering "model experiments" that demonstrated the success and superiority of their policy preferences. If the experiments went wrong in the eyes of their advocates, they typically were phased out and brought to a silent end by no longer giving them attention.[114] In the background interviews conducted for this study, Chinese officials in charge of "experimental point work" unanimously stated that failing experiments typically

Table 3.1

Establishing "Model Experiments":

A Comparison of the Approaches of the Mao and Deng Eras

		Maoist Mass Mobilization Approach ([1928]-1943–1976)	Dengist Administrative Approach (1979–)
Steps in establishing "model experiments"	1	Make thorough investigation of several locations	
	2	Select a location conducive to successful experimentation	
	3	Dispatch a cadre "work team"	*Rely on local cadres*
	4	Nurture new activists and cadres in the location	
	5	Regularly report to higher-level party organs	
Steps in "proceeding from point to surface"	6	Send in investigation teams from higher-level authorities	
	7	Confirm/revise/terminate local model experiments	
	8	Reassign original work teams and local activists to surrounding locations	*[No work teams used]*
	9	Promote local model leaders to leading provincial or national positions	
	10	Launch an emulation campaign and intervisitation program	
	11	Give speeches and issue documents to spread the model experience	
	12	*[Formal legislation rarely enacted, 1957–78]*	*Enact national regulation/legislation*

are not terminated in a clear-cut way by formal administrative decisions or documents. Instead, administrators read the subtle signals from above and tacitly stop working on those projects that are no longer supported by policy makers. Only in very rare cases did failing "models" come under public scrutiny, typically in the context of criminal or corruption investigations that did not implicate top policy makers but targeted local or corporate misconduct as the root cause of their failure.[115]

Decentralized experimentation facilitated "guerrilla-style policy-making" (this is how Roderick McFarquhar referred to it in his comments at the 2008 conference) and "government on a shoestring" (as Lily Tsai commented at the conference): a low-cost way of local problem-solving and policy generation that has constituted the only constructive option for under-equipped local governments from revolutionary times to the present and that has, at the same time, served as a convenient technique for the party center to avoid accountability for local policy failures while receiving recognition for economically successful policy innovations generated by local initiative.[116] In a paradoxical turn, China's experiment-based policy process has helped circumvent severe deficiencies in administrative integration, fiscal capacity, policy coherence, and political accountability, while allowing systemic adaptive capacity and national economic strength to be built up.

Clearly, Chinese-style experimentation must not be mistaken as the policy makers' rational response to the inefficiencies in the economic system or as an attempt at "scientific," "evidence-based" policy selection. At every stage, from setting policy objectives to selecting model experiments and identifying generalizable policy options, "proceeding from point to surface" has always been an intensely politicized process driven by competing interests, ideological frictions, personal rivalries, tactical opportunism, or ad-hoc compromises.

For policy makers who wanted to change how the economy was run, experimentation turned out to be a good way to deal with uncertainty (the inability to predict the precise impact of specific reforms in a rapidly changing economic context) and ambiguity (the ambivalence, vagueness or even confusion in the policy makers' thinking about their policy priorities). In such an often volatile policy-making context, the "experimental point" method helped to release broad-based policy entrepreneurship that contributed to economic innovation and expansion. Though this process also produced costly fake and failed "models" along the way, the costs of failed local experiments were clearly much less serious, at least from the perspective of national policy makers and the majority of the unaffected jurisdictions, than the costs attached to failed national reform legislation. Moreover, since experimentation mobilized local knowledge and problem-solving, it produced a wealth of previously unavailable information on the workings and the potential of the local economy.[117] Yet post-Mao experimentation did not stop with the search for individual models and policy options. Rather, it resulted in serial, and cumulatively radical, redefinitions of policy parameters for economic activity over time.

Conclusion

In the Chinese approach to policy-making, the "experimental point" and "point-to-surface" methodology enjoy a systematic significance. The pattern

of experimental governance that we find in China has distinctive foundations in the hierarchical party-state and differs from models of decentralization or federalism that are frequently applied to explain the dynamics
of central-local interactions in China's economic reform.[118] The findings
presented in this chapter support Elizabeth Perry's proposition that "certain
elements of China's revolutionary inheritance have actually furthered the
stunningly successful implementation of market reforms."[119] This paradox
can also be seen in the case of reform-era experimentation that has been
crucial in facilitating policy innovation, yet is rooted in Maoist techniques
of rule.

One of China's core strengths in reforming its economy has been its
distinctive process of central-local interaction in policy generation that
enjoys an entrenched legitimacy within the Communist Party and can be
put to work to address the shifting policy priorities of the post-Mao era.
Explanations that stress central-local factional machinations as the paramount driving force behind policy innovation do not appreciate the extent
and importance of local initiative in generating novel policy instruments
and in transforming the parameters and priorities of central policy makers.
Furthermore, the effectiveness of experimentation is not based on all-out
decentralization and spontaneous diffusion of policy innovations. China's
experiment-based policy-making requires the authority of a central leadership that encourages and protects broad-based local initiative and filters out
generalizable lessons but at the same time contains the centrifugal forces
that necessarily come up with this type of policy process.

Conceptual dichotomies such as centralization vs. decentralization, or
constitutional concepts such as federalism that suggest a stability of vertical
checks and balances that are not a given in China's polity, cannot capture the
oscillating dynamics of China's policy-making approach. It is *experimentation
under hierarchy*, i.e., the volatile, yet productive combination of decentralized
experimentation with ad-hoc central interference, resulting in selective
integration of local experiences into national policy-making that is the key
to understanding China's policy process.

In searching for the prerequisites for China's unexpectedly adaptive
authoritarianism over the last three decades, this distinctive policy process
may provide a more powerful explanation than static factors (such as the
initial economic structure or the state's enforcement capacity), explanations
that ignore the process of policy-making and policy implementation
(arguments based on quasi-natural economic liberalization and inevitable
convergence with market principles), or explanations that treat policy

experimentation merely as a derivative feature of factional rivalry. It is China's historically entrenched process of policy generation through local experiments and model demonstrations that provides a productive link between central and local initiative, thus allowing policy makers to move beyond policy deadlock in spite of myriad conflicts over strategy, ideology, and interests.

Endnotes

This contribution is an expanded and revised version of an analysis that was originally published under the title "From Local Experiments to National Policy: The Origins of China's Distinctive Policy Process," *The China Journal*, no. 59 (January 2008): 1–30. In rewriting the original analysis, the author benefited greatly from conference discussions in Trier (June 2007) and Harvard (July 2008) and from extensive comments given at different stages of the research by Nara Dillon, Joe Fewsmith, Roderick MacFarquhar, Barry Naughton, Elizabeth Perry, Lea Shih, Tia Thornton, Lily Tsai, Ezra Vogel, and Wang Shaoguang. Peter Kuhfus made a crucial contribution by sharing his profound knowledge of Sino-Soviet interactions and lending generous support to locate and scrutinize Russian-language sources. Nancy Hearst helped tremendously by providing precious Chinese sources from the Fung Library at Harvard's Fairbank Center.

1. Thomas G. Rawski, "Implications of China's Reform Experience," *The China Quarterly*, no. 144 (December 1995): 1150–1173; Gérard Roland, *Transition and Economics: Politics, Markets, and Firms* (Cambridge, MA: MIT Press, 2000), pp. 63–65; Justin Yifu Lin, Fang Cai, and Zhou Li, *The China Miracle: Development Strategy and Economic Reform* (Hong Kong: Chinese University Press, rvsd. ed., 2003), pp. 321–325; Sharun W. Mukand and Dani Rodrik, "In Search of the Holy Grail: Policy Convergence, Experimentation, and Economic Performance," *American Economic Review*, 95, no. 1 (2005): 374–383.

2. For analyses of the extensive experimentation undertaken in these policy areas, see Jae Ho Chung, *Central Control and Local Discretion in China: Leadership and Implementation During Post-Mao Decollectivization* (Oxford: Oxford University Press, 2000); David Zweig, *Internationalizing China: Domestic Interests and Global Linkages* (Ithaca, NY: Cornell University Press, 2002); Susan Young, *Private Business and Economic Reform in China* (Armonk, NY: M.E. Sharpe, 1995); Jean C. Oi and Han Chaohua, "China's Corporate Restructuring: A Multi-Step Process," in Jean Oi, ed., *Going Private in China: The Politics of Corporate Restructuring and System Reform in the PRC* (Stanford, CA: Walter H. Shorenstein Asia-Pacific Research Center and Washington, DC: Brookings Institution Press, forthcoming); Carl E. Walter and Fraser J.T. Howie, *Privatizing China: Inside China's Stock Markets* (Singapore: Wiley, 2nd ed., 2006).

3. On extended experimental regulation in this policy domain, see Charles D. Booth, "Drafting Bankruptcy Laws in Socialist Market Economies: Recent Developments in China and Vietnam," *Columbia Journal of Asian Law*, 18, no. 1 (Fall 2004): 93–147.

4. For a systematic analysis of the patterns, dynamics, and effects of post-Mao experimentation, see Sebastian Heilmann, "Policy Experimentation in China's Economic Rise," *Studies in Comparative International Development*, 43, no. 1 (Spring 2008): 1–26.

5. A radical critique of explanations based on experimentation is put forward by Wing Thye Woo, "The Real Reasons for China's Growth," *The China Journal*, no. 41 (January 1999): 115–137. His analysis, however, is focused on a deterministic interpretation of the *results* of economic transition (inevitable convergence with market economics) and underrates the importance of experimental *processes* that facilitate policy changes in the first place.

6. For an influential analysis along these lines, see Jeffrey Sachs, Wing Thye Woo, Stanley Fischer, and Gordon Hughes, "Structural Factors in the Economic Reforms of China, Eastern Europe and the Former Soviet Union," *Economic Policy*, 9, no. 18 (April 1994): 102–145.

7. Gabriella Montinola, Yingyi Qian, and Barry R. Weingast, "Federalism, Chinese Style: The Political Basis for Economic Success in China," *World Politics*, 48, no. 1 (October 1995): 50–81; Yuanzheng Cao, Yingyi Qian, and Barry R. Weingast, "From Federalism, Chinese Style to Privatization, Chinese Style," *Economics of Transition*, 7, no. 1 (March 1999): 103–131.

8. Hongbin Cai and Daniel Treisman, "Did Government Decentralization Cause China's Economic Miracle?" *World Politics*, 58, no. 4 (July 2006): 505–535.

9. The background interviews conducted for this study revealed that even senior officials in charge of designing and supervising "experimental point work" over the last three decades (cadres up to the vice-ministerial rank were among the interviewees) apparently are unaware of a historical trajectory behind reform-era experimentation and instead ascribe the emergence of the "experimental point method" to Deng Xiaoping and the pursuit of administrative pragmatism.

10. For Stalin's consistent radical rejection of spontaneous economic activity, decentralized administration, and policy-making, see Robert Himmer, "The Transition from War Communism to the New Economic Policy: An Analysis of Stalin's Views," *Russian Review*, 53, no. 4 (October 1994): 515–529. Although there is much evidence of enterprise- and *kolkhoz*-level experimental problem-solving in the Soviet Union during the Stalin era, local experimentation was not systematically embraced by national policy makers and planners. They grudgingly came to tolerate local extralegal practices as a necessary evil to plug the gaps in the economy, but they did not take them up as a positive impulse to reform the general workings of the system. For detailed evidence on the Stalin era, see Paul R. Gregory, *The Political Economy of Stalinism: Evidence from the Soviet Secret Archives* (Cambridge: Cambridge University Press, 2004).

11. For the Stakhanovite movement of labor model emulation, see Lewis H. Siegelbaum, *Stakhanovism and the Politics of Productivity in the USSR, 1935–1941* (Cambridge: Cambridge University Press, 1988).

12. D.A. Avksent'evskii, *Opytnye stantsii narkomprosa i raionirovanie R.S.F.S.R.* (Experimental Stations of the People's Commissariat for Enlightenment and Regionalization of the RSFSR) (Moskva: Otdel O.P.U. Glavsotsvosa, 1925); N.K.Z. Gosudarstvennyi Institut Opytnoi Agronomii (State Institute of Experimental Agronomy), *Sel'skokhoziaistvennoe opytnoe delo R.S.F.S.R. v 1917–1927 gg.* (Agricultural Experiment Institutions and Stations Work in the RSFSR, 1917–1927) (Leningrad: State Institute of Experimental Agronomy, 1928).

13. Cf. Darrell Lee Slider, "Social Experiments and Soviet Policy-Making," Ph.D. dissertation, Yale University, 1981, pp. 9–13. Slider makes it clear that local social and

economic experimentation assumed a more prominent role in Soviet policy-making only from the Brezhnev era and cross-regional dissemination or national adoption of policy options generated through experimentation was almost never undertaken.

14. Stephen C. Averill, *Revolution in the Highlands: China's Jinggangshan Base Area* (Lanham, MD: Rowman and Littlefield, 2006): 241–249; Yu Boliu (余伯流), *Zhongyang suqu shi* (中央苏区史) (A History of the Central Soviet Area) (Nanchang: Jiangxi renmin chubanshe, 2001), pp. 245–246, 252–253.

15. Jiang Boying (蒋伯英), *Deng Zihui yu Zhongguo nongcun biange* (邓子恢与中国农村变革) (Deng Zihui and the Transformation of the Chinese Countryside) (Fuzhou: Fujian renmin chubanshe, 2004), pp. 44–64, 210–225; Li Jianzhen (李坚真), "Deng Zihui tongzhi yu tugai shiyan" (邓子恢同志与土改实验) (Comrade Deng Zihui and Experiments in Land Reform), in *Huiyi Deng Zihui* (回忆邓子恢) (Remembering Deng Zihui) (Beijing: Renmin chubanshe, 1996), pp. 233–238.

16. See Frederick C. Teiwes and Warren Sun, eds., *The Politics of Agricultural Cooperativization in China: Mao, Deng Zihui, and the "High Tide" of 1955* (Armonk, NY: M.E. Sharpe, 1993), p. 7.

17. Ilpyong J. Kim, *The Politics of Chinese Communism: Kiangsi under the Soviets* (Berkeley: University of California Press, 1973), pp. 114–115, 146, 173–174.

18. On Xingguo, see "Suqu jiaoyu gongzuo de mofan: Xingguo" (苏区教育工作的模范: 兴国) (A Model for Educational Work in the Central Soviet: Xingguo), *Jiangxi jiaoyu* (江西教育) (Jiangxi Education), no. 10 (2004): 44. As recently as 2004, Xingguo was still presented to leading cadres of the CCP as a model of a mass-based work-style; see Qian Jiang (钱江) and Ren Jianghua (任江华), "Xingguo: Suqu ganbu hao zuofeng dai zhuan" (兴国: 苏区干部好作风代代传) (Xingguo: A Good Cadre Work Style for Generations), *Renmin ribao* (人民日报) (*People's Daily*, hereafter *RMRB*) (August 30, 2004): 4.

19. See "Wang Guanlan: Guanzhu 'sannong' diyi ren" (王观澜: 关注"三农" 第一人) (Wang Guanlan: A Pioneer in Paying Attention to the "Agriculture-Village-Farmer" Issue), *Dangshi zongheng* (党史纵横) (Over the Party History), no. 9 (2006): 15–20.

20. For archival documents dealing with the establishment and performance of the two "experimental counties," see *Taihang dangshi ziliao huibian, di san juan, 1940.1–1940.12* (太行党史资料汇编第三卷1940.1–1940.12) (Compilation of Material on Party History in Taihang, Vol. 3, January-December 1940) (Taiyuan: Shanxi renmin chubanshe, 1994), pp. 260–281, 513–515. A rather hazy explanation for why the term "experimental county" was used instead of the more orthodox term "model county" is given in the otherwise insightful memoir by Li Xuefeng, *Li Xuefeng huiyilu (shang): Taihang shinian* (李雪峰回忆录[上]: 太行十年) (The Memoirs of Li Xuefeng, Vol. 1: The Ten Taihang Years) (Beijing: Zhonggong dangshi chubanshe, 1998), pp. 105–108. For a comprehensive history of the Taihang Base Area that suggests its special importance as a formative experience for many major CCP policy makers, see David S.G. Goodman, *Social and Political Change in Revolutionary China: The Taihang Base Area in the War of Resistance to Japan, 1937–1945* (Lanham, MD: Rowman and Littlefield, 2000). An instructive review of this book, presenting additional data and insights, can be found by Odoric Y.K. Wou in *China Review International*, 9, no. 2 (Fall 2002): 320–343.

21. This argument is put forward by David S.G. Goodman, *Deng Xiaoping and the Chinese Revolution: A Political Biography* (London: Routledge, 1994), pp. 41–45, who points

to "interesting similarities [of policies tried out at Taihang] with the economic policies of the post-Cultural Revolution period."

22. Carl E. Dorris, "Peasant Mobilization in North China and the Origins of Yenan Communism," *The China Quarterly*, no. 68 (December 1976): 697, 698, 700; Yu Boliu, *Zhongyang suqu shi*, pp. 259–261.

23. Chung, *Central Control and Local Discretion*, p. 49.

24. For Chinese works ascribing the "experimental point" method to Mao Zedong, see Sun Tie (孙铁), ed., *Dangde zuzhi gongzuo cidian* (党的组织工作词典) (Dictionary of the Party's Organizational Work) (Beijing: Zhongguo zhanwang chubanshe, 1987), p. 128; Deng Zhaoming (邓兆明), "Shilun Mao Zedong de diaocha yanjiu lilun" (试论毛泽东的调查研究理论) (On Mao Zedong's Theory of Investigation and Research), in *Mao Zedong baizhounian jinian* (毛泽东百周年纪念) (Commemorating Mao Zedong's One Hundredth Birthday) (Beijing: Zhongyang wenxian chubanshe, 1994), 1: 196–197; see also Hu Xiangming (胡象明), "Difang zhengce zhixing: Moshi yu xiaoguo" (地方政策执行: 模式与效果) (Local Policy Implementation: Modes and Effects), *Jingji yanjiu cankao* (经济研究参考) (Reference Material for Economic Research), no. 6 (1996): 39–42.

25. Mao Zedong (毛泽东), "Guanyu lingdao fangfa ruogan wenti" (关于领导方法若干问题) (On Certain Issues of Leadership Methods), in *Mao Zedong xuanji, disanjuan* (毛泽东选集, 第三卷) (Selected Works of Mao Zedong, Vol. 3) (Beijing: Renmin chubanshe, 1966), p. 855.

26. See a selection of Mao statements on the function of "models" in *Mao Zedong zhuzuo zhuanti zhaibian* (毛泽东著作专题摘编) (Thematic Excerpts from Mao Zedong's Works) (Beijing: Zhongyang wenxian chubanshe, 2003), pp. 238–239, 325–336. CCP propaganda brochures introducing local cases of a "model experience" were widely distributed after 1945; see, for example, *Laodong huzhu de dianxing lizi he jingyan* (劳动互助的典型例子和经验) (Typical Examples and Experience of Mutual-Aid Labor) (n.p., 1945). See also the February 18, 1951 Politburo decision that Mao personally drafted, as given in *Mao Zedong xuanji, diwujuan* (毛泽东选集, 第五卷) (Selected Works of Mao Zedong, Vol. 5) (Beijing: Renmin chubanshe, 1977), pp. 34–38.

27. Mao Zedong, "Zhengce he jingyan de guanxi" (政策和经验的关系) (On the Relation between Policy and Experience), March 6, 1948, in *Mao Zedong wenji* (毛泽东文集) (Collected Works of Mao Zedong) (Beijing: Renmin chubanshe, 1993), 5: 74.

28. Mao's comments were first published in *RMRB*, March 24, 1948. A reprint of the comments is contained in a widely disseminated CCP brochure: Liu Shaoqi (刘少奇) et al., *Tugai zhengdang dianxing jingyan* (土改整党典型经验) (Typical Experiences in Land Reform and Party Rectification) (Hong Kong: Zhongguo chubanshe, 1948).

29. On the inconsistencies and tactical compromises that characterized the CCP's land reform policies in the 1940s, see Luo Pinghan (罗平汉), "'Wusi zhishi' ji qi 'bu chedixing' zai pingjia" ("五四指示"及其"不彻底性"再评价) (Reassessing the "May Fourth Directive" and Its "Lack of Thoroughness"), *Qiusuo* (求索) (Quest), no. 5 (2005): 172–175.

30. See the central party directive that was personally drafted by Mao: "Xin jiefangqu de tudi gaige yaodian" (新解放区的土地改革要点) (Essentials of Land Reform in the Newly Liberated Areas), February 15, 1948, in *Mao Zedong xuanji, disijuan* (毛泽东选集, 第四卷) (Selected Works of Mao Zedong, Vol.4) (Beijing: Renmin chubanshe, 1991), pp. 1283–1284.

31. Vivienne Shue, *Peasant China in Transition: The Dynamics of Development Toward Socialism, 1949–1956* (Berkeley: University of California Press, 1980), pp. 69, 322–323.

32. Donald J. Munro, *The Concept of Man in Contemporary China* (Ann Arbor: University of Michigan Press, 1977), pp. 148–157; Shue, *Peasant China in Transition*, p. 6.

33. Pauline B. Keating, *Two Revolutions: Village Reconstruction and the Cooperative Movement in Northern Shaanxi, 1934–1945* (Stanford, CA: Stanford University Press, 1997), pp. 239–240.

34. Cf. *Zhongguo tudi gaige shiliao xuanbian* (中国土地改革史料选编) (Selection of Historical Materials on Land Reform) (Beijing: Jiefangjun guofang daxue chubanshe, 1988), pp. 292–298; Li Jianzhen, "Deng Zihui."

35. Deng Xiaoping (邓小平), "Guanche zhixing Zhonggong zhongyang guanyu tugai yu zhengdang gongzuo de zhishi" (贯彻执行中共中央关于土改与整党工作的指示) (Carry Out the CCP Central Committee's Directive on the Work of Land Reform and Party Consolidation), June 6, 1948, in *Deng Xiaoping wenxuan, 1938–1965* (邓小平文选, 1938–1965) (Selected Works of Deng Xiaoping, 1938–1965) (Beijing: Renmin chubanshe, 1989), pp. 109–124. The document was endorsed by Mao Zedong and disseminated as a guideline to the entire party leadership in June 1948. For Chen Yun's applications of the point-to-surface method, see Yu Jianting (余建亭), *Chen Yun yu Dongbei de jiefang* (陈云与东北的解放) (Chen Yun and the Liberation of the Northeast) (Beijing: Zhongyang wenxian chubanshe, 1998), pp. 246–249.

36. *RMRB* (March 23, 1950): 2.

37. On experimental sites in Shandong see *RMRB* (August 30, 1950): 2; "Rao Shushi tongzhi guanyu Huadong tudi gaige gongzuo de baogao" (饶漱石同志关于华东土地改革工作的报告) (Comrade Rao Shushi's Report on Land Reform Work in East China), November 1950, in *Zhongguo tudi gaige shiliao xuanbian*, p. 696.

38. Based on Zhou Enlai's report to the Chinese People's Political Consultative Conference, as given in *RMRB* (November 3, 1951): 1.

39. For official definitions of "typical models" (*dianxing*, 典型) and their use in guiding general policy, see Chen Beiou (陳北鷗), *Renmin xuexi cidian* (人民学习词典) (Dictionary for Popular Learning) (Shanghai: Guangyi shuju, 1953), p. 182.

40. See Wang Ruoshui (王若水), "Qunzhong luxian he renshilun" (群众路线和认识论) (Mass Line and Epistemology), *RMRB* (September 20, 1959): 11.

41. Heilmann "From Local Experiments to National Policy," p. 11.

42. This is based on an electronic search of the digital archive of *RMRB* for 1946–53. From 1946 to 1948, the term *shidian* was not mentioned at all; from 1949 to 1950 it was used in twenty-one articles with a clear geographical concentration referring to the Northeast region that was designated by the party center to carry out experiments, especially in industrial reorganization. From 1951 to 1953, after Zhou Enlai used it, the term became fashionable and appeared in more than 1,000 articles dealing with all sorts of subjects from land reform to education and marriage regulation. According to available sources, Mao used the term *shidian* late in life and even then only rarely. For a prominent use of the term *shidian* by Mao, see "Dui Hubei shengwei guanyu zhubu shixian nongye jixiehua shexiang piyu" (对湖北省委关于逐步实现农业机械化设想批语) (Comments on the Hubei Provincial Party Committee's Tentative Plan for Step-by-Step Implementation of Agricultural Mechanization), February 19, 1966, in *Jianguo yilai Mao Zedong wengao* (建国以来毛泽东文稿) (Manuscripts by Mao Zedong

94 HEILMANN

since the Founding of the State) (Beijing: Zhongyang wenxian chubanshe, 1998), 12: 12–14.

43. The term "experimental point" is not contained in any of the major Soviet treatments on social experimentation that were published in the 1960s. For an influential example, see B. Ionas, "Ob ekonomicheskikh eksperimentakh" (On Economic Experiments), *Kommunist*, no. 9 (1962): 51–59. From the Brezhnev era, "ekonomicheskii eksperiment," "eksperimentirovanie" (experimentation), and "opytnaia proverka" (experimental/empirical examination) became the standard terms denoting official experimentation. Cf. Slider, "Social Experiments and Soviet Policy-Making," passim.

44. For massive criticism of policy experimentation in the 1960s, see Eugène Zaleski, *Planning Reforms in the Soviet Union, 1962–1966* (Chapel Hill: University of North Carolina Press, 1967), p. 140. A comprehensive overview of Soviet experiments with planning reform from the 1960s through the 1980s is given by David A. Dyker, *Restructuring the Soviet Economy* (London: Routledge, 1992). Peter Rutland, *The Politics of Economic Stagnation in the Soviet Union: The Role of Local Party Organs in Economic Management* (Cambridge: Cambridge University Press, 1993), argues that local experiments became a widespread feature of administrative practice under Brezhnev, even though they met with bureaucratic obstruction and legal criticism, were almost never rolled out, and did not help to break up the ossified planned economy.

45. Liu Zijiu (刘子久), "Lun 'shidian'" (论 "试点") (On "Experimental Points"), *Xuexi* (学习) (Learning), no. 10 (October 1953): 10–11.

46. Mao frequently referred to the point-to-surface method by way of metaphors, such as "dissecting the sparrow" (*jiepou maque*, 解剖麻雀, 1956) or "squatting on one point" (*dundian*, 蹲点, 1962). Cf. Wang Jin (王進) et al., eds., *Mao Zedong dacidian* (毛泽东大辞典) (Mao Zedong Dictionary) (Nanning: Guangxi renmin chubanshe, 1992), pp. 879–882. The point-to-surface method is stressed as a systematic component of the Chinese Communists' campaign style by Gordon A. Bennett, *Yundong: Mass Campaigns in Chinese Communist Leadership* (Berkeley: Center for Chinese Studies, University of California, 1976), p. 39. "Test points" (*shidian*) are characterized as one of sixteen core "Sinomarxist" problem-solving techniques by Harro von Senger, *Einführung in das chinesische Recht* (Introduction to Chinese Law) (Munich: C.H. Beck, 1994), pp. 278–279.

47. Vietnamese policy makers have made extensive use of the experimental point methodology since the 1980s to promote economic reform; cf. *National Ownership in an Emerging Partnership: Review of Technical Cooperation in Viet Nam* (Hanoi: UNDP, October 2000). To my knowledge, the Maoist origins of the Vietnamese approach to policy experimentation have not yet been the subject of Western research. Chinese involvement in Vietminh "experimental point work" is mentioned in *RMRB* (May 28, 1954 and June 30, 1954). For clues about Chinese involvement in Vietminh land reform, see Joseph J. Zasloff, *The Role of the Sanctuary in Insurgency: Communist China's Support to the Vietminh, 1946–1954* (Santa Monica, CA: RAND, 1967), pp. 43–48; Edwin E. Moise, *Land Reform in China and North Vietnam* (Chapel Hill: University of North Carolina Press, 1983), pp. 170–191; Qiang Zhai, *China and the Vietnam Wars, 1950–1975* (Chapel Hill: University of North Carolina Press, 2000), pp. 13–17, 38–42, 75–76.

48. Yang Luo (杨洛), "Lun shidian fangfa de renshilun yiyi" (论试点方法的认识论意义) (On the Epistemological Significance of the Experimental Point Method), *Zhexue yanjiu* (哲学研究) (Studies in Philosophy), no. 1 (1984): 1–2.

49. This slogan originated during the Yan'an era. See Wang Huide (王惠德), " 'Mozhe shizi guohe' de zaiyi" ("摸着石子过河"的再意) (Reconsidering "Crossing the River by Groping for the Stones"), *Fangfa* (方法) (Methods), no. 3 (1993): 17–18. See also Chen Xiankui (陈先奎), *Deng Xiaoping zhiguo lun* (邓小平治国论) (Deng's Theory of Managing State Affairs) (Beijing: Huaxia chubanshe, 1997), pp. 174–178.

50. On the far-reaching changes in policy-making brought about by the forceful dissemination of "planning consciousness" and new administrative institutions, see Ezra F. Vogel, *Canton Under Communism: Programs and Politics in a Provincial Capital, 1949–1968* (Cambridge, MA: Harvard University Press, 1980), pp. 127–133. For the impact of economic planning on the PRC's political institutions, see Bai Guiyi (白贵一), "Dui guodu shiqi woguo dangzheng guanxi yanbian de lishi kaocha" (对过渡时期我国党政关系演变的历史考察) (A Historical Investigation of the Evolution of Party-Government Relations in Our Country During the Transition Period), *Henan daxue xuebao (shekeban)* (河南大学学报) (社科版) (Journal of Henan University [Social Science Edition]), no. 5 (1998): 58–61.

51. On the gradual introduction of central planning in China, see Thomas G. Rawski, *China's Transition to Industrialism: Producer Goods and Economic Development in the Twentieth Century* (Ann Arbor: University of Michigan Press, 1980), pp. 29–48; on the role of "advanced units," see pp. 46–47.

52. Chung, *Central Control and Local Discretion*, pp. 31, 34–36, with carefully analyzed examples from the GLF and CR periods, demonstrates how hollow official decentralization slogans had become in actual policy implementation.

53. Cf. Frederick C. Teiwes and Warren Sun, *China's Road to Disaster: Mao, Central Politicians, and Provincial Leaders in the Unfolding of the Great Leap Forward, 1955–1959* (Armonk, NY: M.E. Sharpe, 1999); Alfred L. Chan, *Mao's Crusade: Politics and Policy Implementation in China's Great Leap Forward* (Oxford: Oxford University Press, 2001). Chen Yun made a prominent plea for cautious experimentation to promote full socialization of trade and industry at the Eighth CCP Congress; see *RMRB* (September 21, 1956): 1.

54. The story of these experiments and the tragic fate of the main protagonists is told by Gao Huamin (高化民), "1957: 'Baochan daohu' zai yaolan zhong bei e'sha" (1957: "包产到户"在摇篮中被扼杀) (1957: "Household-Based Production Quotas" Strangled in the Cradle), *Yanhuang chunqiu* (炎黄春秋) (China Through the Ages), no. 7 (2000): 14–19.

55. Roderick MacFarquhar and Michael Schoenhals, *Mao's Last Revolution* (Cambridge, MA: Belknap Press of Harvard University Press, 2006), ch. 2, use this concept that plays a key role in Ian Kershaw's *Hitler, 1889–1936: Hubris* (New York: Norton, 1999) to characterize the logic of leadership relations under Mao after 1957.

56. See, for example, the detailed report written by Deng Zihui (reprinted in *Zhongguo tudi gaige shiliao xuanbian*, pp. 292–298) which carefully analyzes the negative lessons of prior work and proposes new policy approaches based on these experiences.

57. *RMRB* (January 17, 1960): 7. For the sequence of "experimental points," "key points," "point-to-surface" expansion, and policy generalization during the People's Communes movement see Bennett, *Yundong*, pp. 55–56, who ascribes the reorganization of 125 million peasants into communes within less than four months (September through December 1958) to a combination of "outright pressures" with "intense salesmanship."

58. *RMRB* (July 14, 1981): 5.

59. Ke Qingshi (柯庆施), "Lun 'quanguo yipanqi'" (论"全国一盘棋"), *Hongqi* (红旗) (Red Flag), no. 4 (February 16, 1959): 9–12.

60. *RMRB* (April 5, 1965): 5; (January 28, 1966): 5.

61. For portrayals of decision-making surrounding the Daqing (大庆) and Dazhai (大寨) models, written from the standpoint of the post-Mao official interpretation of party history, see CCP Central Committee Documents Research Office (中共中央文献研究室) and Central Party Archives (中央档案官), eds., *Gongheguo zhongda juece he shijian shushi* (共和国重大决策和事件述实) (A Factual Review of Major Decisions and Events in the PRC) (Beijing: Renmin chubanshe, 2005), pp. 289–303.

62. For a detailed analysis of this case, which illustrates the disastrous role of ideologically charged, utopian fever in experimentation, see Zhang Weiliang (张伟良), "Xushui 'gongchanzhuyi' shiyan de shibai ji qi jiaoxun" (徐水 "共产主义" 试验的失败及其教训) (The Failure of the Xushui Experiment in "Communism" and Its Lessons), *Qinghua daxue xuebao* (清华大学学报) (Academic Journal of Qinghua University), no. 3 (1999): 42–47. An analogous case with even more disastrous human consequences is analyzed by Liang Zhiyuan (梁志远), "Haoxian nongye 'weixing' jingyan huiji guanxiu ji" (亳县农业 "卫星" 经验汇集官修记) (Recording the Official Drafting of the Compilation of Hao County's Agricultural "Sputnik" Experience), *Yanhuang chunqiu*, no. 1 (2003): 22–25.

63. Cf. Tang Tsou, Marc Blecher, and Mitch Meisner, "National Agricultural Policy: The Dazhai Model and Local Change in the Post-Mao Era," in Mark Selden and Victor D. Lippit, eds., *The Transition to Socialism in China* (Armonk, NY: M.E. Sharpe, 1982), pp. 266–299.

64. Munro, *The Concept of Man*, pp. 149–150.

65. Yang Luo, "Lun shidian fangfa," puts a lot of effort into finding references in Chinese translations of the Marxist-Leninist classics that might point to the usefulness of policy experiments. However, he comes to the conclusion that experimentation as an instrument for revolutionary transformation or policy-making was not raised in the works of Marx, Engels, Lenin, or Stalin and that the experimental point method really is "Comrade Mao Zedong's creation."

66. To my knowledge, the political use of experimentation is mentioned in the Chinese translations of Lenin's works only in the context of transforming capitalist economic and technical expertise into a resource that serves the proletariat. See *Liening quanji* (列宁全集) (The Complete Works of Lenin) (Beijing: Renmin chubanshe, 1958), 27: 386. Ji Weidong (季卫东), "Lun falü shixing de fansi jizhi" (论法律试行的反思机制) (On the Feedback Mechanism of Legal Experimentation), *Shehuixue yanjiu* (社会学研究) (Sociological Studies), no. 5 (1989): 83, points to this rather isolated reference that is not further developed in other works or directives by Lenin.

67. Cf. Himmer, "The Transition from War Communism."

68. Qu Qiubai, as quoted by Yuan Jingyu (袁景禹), "Qu Qiubai bixia de xin jingji zhengce" (瞿秋白笔下的新经济政策) (The NEP as Depicted by Qu Qiubai), *Shenyang jiaoyu xueyuan xuebao* (沈阳教育学院学报) (Journal of Shenyang Teachers' College), no. 4 (December 2002): 8–10.

69. Cf. Zhu Zhenxin (朱枕薪), *Laonong Eguo zhi kaocha* (劳农俄国之考察) (An Investigation Tour of Worker and Peasant Russia) (Shanghai: Shangwu yinshuguan, 1923); Zhang Yunfu (張雲伏), ed., *Eguo xin jingji zhengce* (俄国新经济政策) (Russia's

NEP) (Shanghai: Xin jianshe shudian, 1929); Duo Bu (Maurice Dobb), *Sulian de xin jingji zhengce* (苏联的新经济政策) (The Soviet Union's NEP) (Shanghai: Haiyan shudian, 1951); Makaluowa [Makarova] (马卡洛娃), *Sulian xin jingji zhengce cankao wenku* (苏联新经济政策参考文库) (Reference Texts on the Soviet Union's NEP) (Changchun: Dongbei caijing chubanshe, 1953).

70. On Lenin's conception of the NEP as a "transitional mixed system," see Maurice Dobb, *Soviet Economic Development Since 1917* (London: Routledge, 6th ed., 1966), pp. 144–148.

71. John Dewey, *Lectures in China, 1919–1920*, translated from the Chinese and edited by R.W. Clopton and T.-C. Ou (Honolulu: University Press of Hawai'i, 1973), pp. 248, 58, and 247, respectively.

72. Hu Shi states that Dewey preferred the term "experimentalism" (*shijianzhuyi*, 实验主义) to "pragmatism" (*shiyongzhuyi*, 实用主义) to characterize his school of thinking; see Tang Degang (唐德刚), comp., *Hu Shi koushu zizhuan* (胡适口述自传) (Hu Shi's Own Oral History) (Hefei: Anhui jiaoyu chubanshe, 1999), pp. 112–113. See also Gu Hongliang (顾红亮), *Shiyongzhuyi de wudu* (实用主义的误读) (The Misreading of Pragmatism) (Shanghai: Huadong shifan daxue chubanshe, 2000), p. 105.

73. Yu Yingshi (余英时), *Xiandai weiji yu sixiang renwu* (现代危机与思想人物) (Contemporary Crisis and [the Role] of Intellectuals) (Beijing: Sanlian shudian, 2005), pp. 160–165.

74. Sun Youzhong (孙有中), "Cong gailiangzhuyizhe dao Makesizhuyizhe: Mao Zedong zaoqi sixiang de zhuanbian" (从改良主义者到马克思主义者: 毛泽东早期思想的转变) (From Reformist to Marxist: The Transformation of Mao Zedong's Early-Period Thinking), *Tansuo* (探索) (Probe), no. 2 (2002): 7–9.

75. Quoted in Stuart R. Schram, "Mao Studies: Retrospect and Prospect," *The China Quarterly*, no. 97 (March 1984): 105–106. Analogies between Dewey's and Mao's epistemologies are also pointed to in John Bryan Starr, *Continuing the Revolution: The Political Thought of Mao* (Princeton, NJ: Princeton University Press, 1979), pp. 70–71.

76. Di Xu, *A Comparison of the Educational Ideas and Practices of John Dewey and Mao Zedong in China* (San Francisco: Mellen Research University Press, 1992), p. 73.

77. Ibid., p. 111, states that Mao attended a talk by Dewey in Shanghai in spring 1920; Li Rui (李锐), *Sanshisui yiqian de Mao Zedong* (三十岁以前的毛泽东) (Mao Before His Thirtieth Birthday) (Guangzhou: Guangdong renmin chubanshe, 1994), p. 322 (quoted from Sun Youzhong, "Cong gailiangzhuyizhe dao Makesizhuyizhe," p. 7), claims that Mao was present during a Dewey talk in Changsha in late October 1920.

78. *Duwei wu da jiangyan* (杜威五大讲演) (Dewey's Five Major Lectures) (Beijing: Chenbaoshe, 1920), pp. 125, 137–138, quoted in Gu Hongliang, *Shiyongzhuyi de wudu*, p. 102.

79. "Gongzuo fangfa liushitiao (cao'an)" (工作方法六十条[草案]) (Sixty Articles on Work Methods [Draft]), drafted by Mao in January 1958, in *Jianguo yilai Mao Zedong wengao* (建国以来毛泽东文稿) (Manuscripts of Mao Zedong since the Founding of the State) (Beijing: Zhongyang wenxian chubanshe, 1992), 7: 45–65. Method no. 13 states: "Unleash and mobilize the masses. Everything through experimentation."

80. Cf. Gu Hongliang, *Shiyongzhuyi de wudu*, pp. 101–120.

81. Chow Ts'e-tsung, *The May Fourth Movement: Intellectual Revolution in Modern China* (Cambridge, MA: Harvard University Press, 1960), p. 176. Sun Youzhong, "Cong

gailiangzhuyizhe dao Makesizhuyizhe," pp. 7–9, presents evidence indicating that Mao was a Dewey-style "reformist" up to 1920 and only in 1921 became a committed radical.

82. Dewey, *Lectures in China*, p. 13 (contained in the introduction by the editors).

83. Munro, *The Concept of Man*, pp. 135–136.

84. Liu Haiyan (刘海燕), "30 niandai guomin zhengfu tuixing xianzheng jianshe yuanyin tanxi" (30年代国民政府推行县政建设原因探析) (Some Findings on Why the Nationalist Government Carried Out County Administrative Reconstruction in the 1930s), *Minguo dang'an* (民国档案) (Archives of the Republican Period), no. 1 (2001): 80.

85. In a truly global diffusion of institutional innovation, the American system was inspired by the organization of German agricultural research that later also served as a model for Soviet experimental stations; cf. Mark R. Finlay, "The German Agricultural Experimental Stations and the Beginnings of American Agricultural Research," *Agricultural History*, 62, no. 2 (Spring 1988): 41–50.

86. Randall E. Stross, *The Stubborn Earth: American Agriculturalists on Chinese Soil, 1898– 1937* (Berkeley: University of California Press, 1986), pp. 123–124, 145, 185, quotes American advisors who complained about the "show and museum effect" of experimental station work that seemed to them to be a futile "attempt to rediscover common facts already known."

87. These terms were used, for example, in a May 1924 article published in the national journal *Nongxue* (农学) (Agricultural Studies); cf. Stross, *Stubborn Earth*, p. 258.

88. James Y.C. Yen, *The Mass Education Movement in China* (Shanghai: Commercial Press, 1925), pp. 17–18.

89. Cf. Guy S. Alitto, "Rural Reconstruction during the Nanking Decade: Confucian Collectivism in Shantung," *The China Quarterly*, no. 66 (June 1976): 213–246.

90. See Tan Chongwei (谭重威), "Xiangcun jianshe shiyanjia Qu Junong" (乡村建设实验家瞿菊农) (Qu Junong, an Experimenter in Rural Reconstruction), *Yanhuang chunqiu*, no. 8 (1998): 36–39.

91. For official CCP policy, see Liu Shaoqi (刘少奇), "Guanyu baiqu de dang yu qunzhong gongzuo" (关于白区的党与群众工作) (On Party and Mass Work in the White Areas), May 1937, *Liu Shaoqi xuanji, diyi juan* (刘少奇选集，第一卷) (Selected Works of Liu Shaoqi, Vol.1) (Beijing: Renmin chubanshe, 1981), pp. 61–64. For reports on CCP and NGO "double activists," or close personal interactions between NGO leaders, non-Communist experimental county heads, and CCP cadres (sometimes based on old alumni connections), see Zhi Xiongwei (支雄伟), Wang Xiaofeng (王晓凤), and Huang Hongjing (黄宏京), "Zhang Hanhui zai Dingzhou de suiyue" (张寒晖在定州的岁月) (Zhang Hanhui's Time in Ding District), *Dangshi bocai* (党史博采) (Extensive Collection of Party History), no. 12 (2002): 42–43; Shang Jinlin (商金林), "Jinian Sun Fuyuan xiansheng" (纪念孙伏园先生) (Commemorating Mr. Sun Fuyuan), *RMRB* (September 18, 1987): 8; Li Guozhong (李国忠), "Suweiai yundong, xiangcun jianshe yundong yu Zhongguo nongcun de shehui bianqian bijiao" (苏维埃运动、乡村建设运动与中国农村的社会变迁比较) (A Comparison of the Soviet Movement and the RRM in China's Rural Social Transformation), *Gannan shifan xueyuan xuebao* (赣南师范学院学报) (Academic Journal of Gannan Normal University), no. 5 (October 2002): 30.

92. Li Guozhong, "Suweiai yundong," pp. 28–32.

93. On Mao's talks with Liang Shuming in Yan'an, see Guy S. Alitto, *The Last Confucian: Liang Shu-ming and the Chinese Dilemma of Modernity* (Berkeley: University of California Press, 1986), pp. 283–292.

94. Cf. Charles W. Hayford, *To the People: James Yen and Village China* (New York: Columbia University Press, 1990), pp. 202–203, 213, 222–223. After assuming national power, the Communists officially distanced themselves from the MEM/RRM and other earlier reform movements and negated any influence coming from them. The key critique that had already been articulated by individual Communist ideologues in the 1930s was that the reformist approach taken by the MEM/RRM represented a futile attempt to delay the revolution that was seen by the Communists as inevitable for the transformation of rural society. For a detailed analysis of Communist criticism of the MEM/RRM, see Klaus Birk, *Die ländliche Aufbaubewegung in China, 1926–1948* (The Rural Reconstruction Movement in China, 1926–1948) (Bochum: Projekt Verlag, 1998), pp. 197–203. Starting in the 1980s, the contributions of James Yen and Liang Shuming to rural reform were officially acknowledged again in the CCP media; cf. Xinhuashe (新华社), "Liang Shuming zouwan jin bainian rensheng lücheng" (梁漱溟走完近百年人生旅程) (Liang Shuming Concludes the Almost Century-Long Journey of His Life), *RMRB* (July 8, 1988): 3.

95. Keating, *Two Revolutions*, p. 189, argues that many of the rural reforms initiated in the Communist base areas, in particular the cooperative movement, drew on models that had originally been sponsored by non-Communist reformers (including the GMD) and funded by Western missionary or philanthropic organizations.

96. Wang Xianming (王先明) and Li Weizhong (李伟中), "20 shiji 30 niandai de xianzheng jianshe yundong yu xiangcun shehui bianqian" (20世纪30年代的县政建设运动与乡村社会变迁) (The Movement for County Administrative Reconstruction in the 1930s and Rural Social Change), *Shixue yuekan* (史学月刊) (Journal of Historical Science), no. 4 (2003): 90–104.

97. For an explanation of the experimental county project from the perspective of a leading experimenter, see Hu Changqing (胡長清) [alias Hu Ciwei, 胡次威], "Shenmo jiaozuo shiyanxian?" (什么叫做实验县?) (What Do We Mean by Experimental County?), *Shidai gonglun* (时代公论) (Public Opinion of the Times), no. 140 (November 30, 1934): 7–15.

98. Liu Haiyan, "30 niandai," pp. 77–81.

99. Jia Shijian (贾世建), "Qianxi Nanjing guomin zhengfu de xianzheng shiyan" (浅析南京国民政府的县政实验) (A Sketch of the Nanjing Nationalist Government's Experiments in County Administration), *Tianzhong xuekan* (天中学刊) (Tianzhong Journal), no. 1 (2003): 84–87.

100. See *RMRB* (June 21, 1947): 1.

101. See Zhou Xiuhuan (周琇環), ed., *Nongfuhui shiliao* (农復会史料) (Material on the History of the JCRR) (Taipei: Guoshiguan, 1995). For experimental sites supported by the JCRR on the mainland in 1948–49, see Tan Chongwei, "Xiangcun jianshe shiyanjia Qu Junong." For JCRR-sponsored large-scale experimentation on Taiwan, see Ronald Freedman and John Y. Takeshita, *Family Planning in Taiwan: An Experiment in Social Change* (Princeton, NJ: Princeton University Press, 1969).

102. An astute analysis of why Deweyan reformers failed can be found in Barry Keenan, *The Dewey Experiment in China: Educational Reform and Political Power in the Early Republic* (Cambridge, MA: Harvard University Press, 1977).

103. *Taihang dangshi ziliao huibian*, 3: 260–262.

104. For important Deng statements on experimentation, see *Deng Xiaoping wenxuan, 1975–1982* (邓小平文选, 1975–1982) (Selected Works of Deng Xiaoping, 1975–1982) (Beijing: Renmin chubanshe, 1983), p. 140; *Deng Xiaoping wenxuan, disan juan* (邓小平文选, 第3卷) (Selected Works of Deng Xiaoping, Vol. 3) (Beijing: Renmin chubanshe, 1993), pp. 78, 130, 373.

105. For a collection of Chen Yun quotes regarding experimentation in economic policy-making, see Wang Jiayun (王家云), "Chen Yun jingji juece de shi da yuanze" (陈云经济决策的十大原则) (Ten Major Principles Pursued by Chen Yun in Economic Decision-Making), *Huaiyang shifan xueyuan xuebao* (淮阴师范学院报) (Journal of Huaiyang Normal College), no. 3 (1998): 33. Chen Yun had stressed the importance of prudent experimentation consistently since his time as chief economic policy maker in the Northeast prior to the founding of the PRC.

106. *Zhonghua renmin gongheguo jingji dashidian 1949.10–1987.1* (中华人民共和国经济大事典1949.10–1987.1) (A Dictionary of Major Economic Events in the PRC, October 1949–January 1987) (Changchun: Jilin renmin chubanshe, 1987), p. 453.

107. Belonging to the folklore of China experts, the "groping for the stones" formula is frequently, yet incorrectly, attributed to Deng Xiaoping, who apparently abstained from using it. This point is made by Chen Xiankui, *Deng Xiaoping zhiguo lun*, p. 177. Double-checking Deng's works, I found no reference to the "groping" formula. It clearly was Chen Yun's creation. See *Chen Yun wenxuan* (陈云文选) (Chen Yun's Selected Works) (Beijing: Renmin chubanshe, 1995), 3: 279.

108. CCP Central Committee Documents Research Office (中共中央文献研究室), ed., *Guanyu jianguo yilai dangde ruogan lishi wenti de jueyi zhushiben* (关于建国以来党的若干历史问题的决议注释本) (Annotated Edition of the Resolution on Certain Questions in the History of Our Party since the Founding of the State) (Beijing: Renmin chubanshe, 1985), p. 57.

109. Lei Meitian (雷美田), "Jianli Makesizhuyi shehui shiyan de xin guandian" (建立马克思主义社会试验的新观点) (Establishing a New Standpoint on Marxist Social Experimentation), *Nanjing zhengzhi xueyuan xuebao* (南京政治学院学报) (Journal of PLA Nanjing Institute of Politics), no. 6 (1994): 38–41.

110. Yang Luo, "Lun shidian fangfa," pp. 3, 5.

111. *Constitution of the Communist Party of China*, bilingual Chinese-English edition (Beijing: Foreign Languages Press, 2003), pp. 26–27. On the insertion of the experimentation paragraph in 1992, see the brief comments in *Zhongguo gongchandang lici dangzhang huibian (1921–2002)* (中国共产党历次党章汇编 [1921–2002]) (A Compilation of All Previous Constitutions of the CCP) (Beijing: Zhongguo fangzheng chubanshe, 2006), p. 389. The first post-Mao party constitution of 1982 did not mention experimentation, nor did any of the previous party constitutions.

112. On the causes and direction of the cognitive and belief changes that opened the path to economic reform, see the classic study by Dali L. Yang, *Calamity and Reform in China: State, Rural Society and Institutional Change since the Great Leap Famine* (Stanford, CA: Stanford University Press, 1996).

113. Chung, *Central Control and Local Discretion*, pp. 14, 43–44.

114. A number of instructive case studies on failed local experiments in administrative reform are contained in Fu Xiaosui (傅小随), *Zhongguo xingzheng tizhi gaige fenxi*

(中国行政体制改革分析) (Beijing: Guojia xingzheng xueyuan chubanshe, 1999), pp. 153–168.

115. For two celebrated economic models of the 1980s, Daqiu (大邱) (rural industrialization) and Shougang (首钢) (profit contracts in state industry) that fell from grace in the 1990s, see Cao Jian (曹健), "Daqiuzhuang xingshuai" (大邱庄兴衰) (The Rise and Fall of Daqiu Village), *Nanfeng chuang* (南风窗) (For the Public Good), no. 6 (2002): 50–52; Edward S. Steinfeld, *Forging Reform in China: The Fate of State-Owned Industry* (New York: Cambridge University Press, 1998), pp. 165–224.

116. I am indebted to Lily Tsai for raising these points forcefully during the conference at Harvard in July 2008.

117. In his comments on this paper, Barry Naughton emphasized the generalized information effects of experimentation. Seen from such a depoliticized systemic perspective, the aggregate informational advantages of broad-based experimentation clearly outweigh the potential injustices brought about by the uneven distribution of costs and benefits among different experimental sites. In experimental practice, however, political and legal conflicts are frequently caused by demands to compensate the losers from the experiments.

118. Cf. *East Asia Decentralizes: Making Local Government Work* (Washington, DC: World Bank, 2005); Yongnian Zheng, *De Facto Federalism in China: Reforms and Dynamics of Central-Local Relations* (Hackensack, NJ: World Scientific, 2007).

119. Elizabeth J. Perry, "Studying Chinese Politics: Farewell to Revolution?" *The China Journal*, no. 57 (January 2007): 6.

CHAPTER 4

Learning through Practice and Experimentation: The Financing of Rural Health Care

WANG SHAOGUANG

Adaptive capacity is essential for all human societies because they all face unique circumstances, genuine uncertainties, novel complexities, and conflicts of values and interests, whereas everyone, including policy makers and policy experts, operates under conditions of bounded rationality. The best they can do is first to diagnose and treat the most urgent issue and eventually find a satisfactory but not necessarily optimal solution by comparing different options identified through trial and error. For a country like China that has been undergoing rapid and multiple transitions, adaptive capacity is vital because it has to navigate through uncharted and dangerous waters, facing the risk of capsizing at any time.

Social scientists know little about adaptive capacity, but one thing is certain: learning is the basis for adaptive capacity.[1] Here learning means using the experiences and lessons about a policy or an institution at another time/place to adjust the policy or institution for this time/place. For the sake of discussion, I distinguish four learning models (see Table 4.1) by their location along two dimensions: the promoter of learning and the source of learning.

Promoters of learning can be divided into two major categories: policy makers and policy advocates. Policy makers have to diagnose the nature and severity of the problems facing them and seek the most effective methods to solve them, which requires learning. Especially in the event of policy failure and institutional failure, policy makers are more prone to act on impulse to draw inspiration from their own or others' past experiences.

Table 4.1:
Four Learning Models

Promoter of Learning	Source of Learning	
	Practice	Experiments
Policy makers	1	2
Policy advocates	3	4

In addition to policy makers, bureaucrats, policy experts, media practitioners, and social stakeholders are also likely to become promoters of learning.[2] In the event of sharing similar attitudes toward certain issues, these people may form a tangible or intangible "advocacy coalition" in a specific policy area. The advocacy coalition will learn through various means to seek evidence to support its position. Meanwhile, it will also persistently promote its learning results to policy makers to influence the direction of policy and institutional change.[3]

Sources of learning can also be divided into two categories: practice and experimentation. The former includes the past and present practical experiences and lessons drawn from different regions in the home country as well as foreign countries. The latter refers to controlled experiments conducted on a small scale to discover effective problem-solving tools. In human society, it is generally impossible to conduct experiments similar to those done in a laboratory. In some specific policy and institutional areas, however, it is possible to conduct controlled experiments at different observation points or at different time intervals at the same observation point. Experiments in which key policy or institutional parameters are controlled can help discover which policy and institutional options are desirable and feasible. As long as a system treats diverse experimentation as a path to learning, it must allow for failure. Otherwise, there is no incentive to attempt new practices or to conduct new experiments. Of course, practices and experiments cannot be completely separated. Different practices often become the basis for policy and institutional experiments.

Clearly, "experimentation under hierarchy" (Heilmann's term) is just one (model 2) of four learning models. The four models are by no means mutually exclusive. It is likely that a country will learn by using more than one model. The adaptive capacity of a system depends on whether it can learn by making full use of all models. Logically, a system with a strong adaptive capacity should possess the following features.

First, the system is arranged in such a way as to make policy makers sensitive to emergent problems, difficulties, and imbalances, and the policy makers are willing to take responsibility to respond to challenges.

Second, policy makers firmly believe that the best way to find a path to solve policy and institutional problems is to learn through practice and experimentation rather than simply to emulate foreign models or fashionable theories.

Third, while preserving political unity, the system allows for decentralized decision-making in as many areas as possible and thus creates an institutional condition for seeking different problem-solving methods through decentralized practices and experiments. In other words, the system fosters diverse sources of learning without sacrificing overall coordination.

Fourth, it allows or encourages decentralized horizontal diffusion of new things generated from practice and experimentation before carrying out centralized vertical diffusion, especially during the early stages of decision-making.

Based on the foregoing theoretical analysis, this chapter attempts to assess the adaptive capacity of China's political system. By using the technique of "dissecting a sparrow" (*jiepou maque*, 解剖麻雀), it closely examines the policy/institutional area of the rural health-financing system. China's rural health-financing system since 1949 has undergone four stages fraught with vicissitudes: (1) the rise of the cooperative medical system (hereafter CMS, 1949–68); (2) the universalization of the CMS (1969–78); (3) the decline of the traditional CMS (1979–85); and (4) exploration for new CMS models (1986–2010). The purpose of this chapter is not to assess the pros and cons of each health-financing scheme but to analyze how policy makers and policy advocates pursue learning through practice and experimentation to adjust policy tools and policy objectives so as to respond to the changing environment.

The Rise of the CMS

Before 1949, user-pay was the only health-financing option available in rural China, thus depriving the vast majority of farmers of opportunities for health care. Consequently, China's infant mortality rate was as high as 250 per thousand births[4] and average life expectancy was barely thirty-five years.[5]

Soon after the People's Republic was established, the new regime laid down health-care guidelines for "serving the workers, peasants, and soldiers."[6] Even during the Korean War, the new government made rapid progress in developing rural medical organizations. The number of county-level health institutions rose from 1,400 in 1949 to 2,123 by the end of 1952, covering over 90 percent of the country.[7] Despite progress in health-care provision, however, there was no significant change with respect to health financing. The user-pay system still dominated rural China prior to 1955.

In 1955, an all-round upsurge of cooperative transformation swept across rural China, which served as a catalyst for institutional innovation in rural health care. More specifically, mutual-aid cooperatives in production, capital, farm implements, and technology inspired farmers to expand the cooperative approach to the area of health financing. It is likely that "the rural cooperative medical movement might never have taken place without the agricultural cooperative movement."[8]

There has been disagreement in the literature as to where the earliest cooperative medical scheme emerged. Evidence shows that different forms of health-care financing cooperatives appeared almost simultaneously in 1955 in Shanxi,[9] Henan,[10] Jiangsu,[11] and Zhejiang.[12] Regardless, health-care financing cooperatives would have emerged during the all-round upsurge of rural cooperativization. But it is clear that this practice emerged from farmer initiative rather than from experts or decrees by policy makers.

Take Mishan village (米山乡), in Gaoping county (高平县), Shanxi, as an example. Gaoping county was a so-called "old liberation area" (*lao jiefangqu*, 老解放区) that had come under the control of the Communist Party in 1945. In 1953, three private drugstores and ten traditional Chinese medicine practitioners in Mishan village formed the county's first united cooperative clinic. In May 1955, during the heyday of cooperative transformation, the Mishan United Clinic was converted into a United Health-Care Station. Unlike a united clinic, the united health-care station was established and financed by three parties: the agricultural production cooperative, the farmers, and the doctors. For that reason, its funding came from three sources: public welfare funds contributed by the agricultural cooperative, "health-care fees" paid by the farmers, and medical proceeds (mainly charges for medicine). By paying an annual "health-care fee" of RMB 0.5, a farmer was entitled to receive preventive health-care services and was exempt from all fees (for registration, home visits, injections, etc.), except for drug charges.

Mishan's cooperative medical system soon attracted a great deal of government attention. Officials from the Ministry of Health and the provincial Department of Health who visited Mishan on several occasions to conduct field investigations concluded that Mishan had "established a reliable socialist organizational basis for providing preventive health care in the rural areas." With the approval of the State Council, the Ministry of Health began to disseminate information about the Mishan experience.[13] By 1957, China had more than 10,000 cooperative medical stations.[14]

The commune movement launched in the summer of 1958 provided a more robust institutional infrastructure for cooperative health financing. Article 18 of the general regulations for China's first people's commune — Chayashan Satellite People's Commune (Chayashan weixing renmin gongshe, 嵖岈山卫星人民公社), in Suiping county (遂平县), Henan — states:

> The commune shall adopt a cooperative medical system under which members shall pay annual fees based on household size and will not pay any additional charges when visiting a doctor. The commune hospital shall refer special patients it cannot treat to an appropriate hospital for further treatment and shall cover their travel and medical expenses. For the time being, no referrals will be made for geriatric diseases or for patients with chronic diseases. When the economy is strengthened, the commune will provide free health care.[15]

This was the first time that a "cooperative medical system" was mentioned in China. On September 13, 1958 *Health News (Jiankang bao, 健康报)* a newspaper under the Ministry of Health, published an article entitled "Let the Cooperative Medical Scheme Blossom Everywhere," stating, the scheme "represents a new medical system for the people and a Communist-type public welfare undertaking. It is convenient for the people and boosts production. Meanwhile, it can help implement prevention as the first principle and strengthen prevention and treatment. Thus, it should be vigorously promoted nationwide."[16]

By the end of September, at least 963 communes in Henan, accounting for over 70 percent of the communes provincewide, had set up a cooperative medical system.[17]

During the commune movement, Jishan county (稷山县), Shanxi, was held up as a "red banner of rural health." In January 1959, Sun village in this county began to implement a cooperative medical system whereby each member paid an annual health-care fee of 2 RMB and received free medical services. Any difference was to be subsidized by public welfare funds. Subsequently, this practice spread rapidly throughout the county.[18] In November 1959, the Ministry of Health submitted to the CCP Central Committee the "Report on the On-the-Spot National Meeting on Rural Health Care in Jishan County of Shanxi" and an appendix entitled "Opinions on Several Issues Pertaining to the People's Commune Health Services." The report states:

The People's Communes have two optional medical systems at the present time. One is a user-pay medical service on an individual basis; the other is a collective medical service for commune members. Those who attended the meetings unanimously considered it more appropriate to adopt the collective health-care system for commune members based on the present level of productivity and the people's understanding. . . .The collective health-care system has sometimes been referred to as a "collective health-care" approach or a "cooperative medical system."[19]

This was the first time that the phrase "cooperative medical system" was mentioned in a central government document. The Opinions advised:

A small number of economically affluent communes can continue to offer community-run free health care but we should not rush to spread this practice. In addition, some communes have adopted a user-pay health-care system; nor should we immediately change this. Instead, it should be gradually transformed into a collective health-care system based on the communes' level of economic development and the people's understanding.[20]

Nevertheless, due to the strong push from the CCP Central Committee and the direct intervention of Chairman Mao, the rural CMS grew rapidly. The proportion of production brigades (administrative villages) providing cooperative medical services increased from 10 percent in 1958 to 32 percent in 1960 and to 46 percent in 1962 (see Figure 4.1), according to Anhui Medical University School of Health Management, which has conducted long-term tracking of the rural cooperative medical system.

After 1962, the central government drastically readjusted its policy orientation, including its attitude toward the rural medical system. In August 1962, the Ministry of Health issued the "Opinions on Adjusting Rural Grassroots Health Organizations," criticizing "some communes for their disposition to provide free medical services." This document also states: "The medical institutions originally established and funded by communes or production brigades can be transformed into entities run by doctors in the event any difficulties are encountered in operating them on an as-is basis." After the transformation, those entities were supposed to provide user-pay medical services and to assume sole responsibility for their profits and losses.[21] With a drastic decline in collective investment, except for in a small number of affluent areas, most communes and brigades halted or suspended the cooperative medical scheme. Consequently, cooperative health-care coverage plunged into a downward spiral. By 1964, fewer than 30 percent of the communes and brigades still maintained a cooperative medical system.[22]

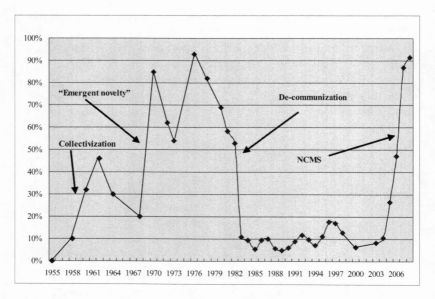

Figure 4.1:
Proportion of Villages Adopting the CMS (1955–2008)
Source: Author's databank.

Rural health conditions and the urban-rural disparity attracted Mao's attention in 1964–65. This turned out to be a period when the Chairman paid the most attention to health care. During those two years, he lashed out at the Ministry of Health no less than four times, the most famous of which is his June 26 directive (*liuerliu zhishi*, 六二六指示). In a conversation with his medical staff on June 26, 1965, Mao accused the Ministry of Health of working for only 15 percent of the population, namely, the urban residents, while leaving the peasants with few doctors and insufficient health services. He called for a "shifting [of] the focus of health work to the countryside."[23]

It has been widely believed that Mao's June 26 directive drew national attention to rural health care, thereby resulting in a quick restoration of the CMS that had ground to a standstill after 1962.[24] However, this is not the case. Although Mao paid unprecedented attention to rural health care in 1965, he focused on providing medical services for farmers and training medical practitioners for the rural areas by organizing mobile medical teams to be sent to the countryside. The mobile medical teams did not provide free medical services for farmers but rather "charged fees at reasonable rates."[25]

In other words, Mao's June 26 directive did not result in a dramatic change in rural health financing. In fact, the proportion of production brigades providing cooperative medical services declined further to 20 percent in 1968, lower than the level in 1964 (see Figure 4.1). The cooperative medical system did not become truly universal in rural China until after 1969.

Universalization of the CMS

In the summer 1968, reporters from *Wenhui Daily* (文汇报) conducted a field investigation of Jiangzhen commune (江镇公社), Chuansha county (川沙县), in Shanghai and published a report entitled "Gauging the Direction of the Revolution in Medical Education from the Growth of the 'Barefoot Doctors' in Jiangzhen Commune." Yao Wenyuan, then in charge of propaganda, referred the report to Mao. After Mao revised the report, it first appeared in *Red Flag* (*Hongqi*, 红旗) and then, on September 14, it was republished in the *People's Daily* (*Renmin ribao*, 人民日报).[26] Thereafter, the "barefoot doctors" became well known all over the world. However, the "barefoot doctors" addressed only the issue of basic rural medical services that were inexpensive and they did not solve the problem of health financing. Regardless of how inexpensive they were, medical services could not be universalized unless there was a sharing of risks.

One month after the "barefoot doctor" investigation report was published, Yao Wenyuan submitted another report to Mao about the CMS operated by Leyuan Commune (乐园公社), in Changyang county (长阳县), Hubei. Since 1966, Dujiacun brigade (杜家村大队) of Leyuan Commune had implemented a cooperative medical scheme whereby each farmer paid the cooperative a medical fee of 1 RMB per year and the production brigade contributed 0.5 RMB for each participant. Because the brigade clinic grew its own herbs to make herbal medicine, the costs for medical services were very low. Peasants paid only a 0.05 RMB registration fee each time they saw a doctor. The herbal medicine was provided free of charge. This system was enthusiastically embraced by the peasants. In 1967, the CMS was adopted by every brigade of Leyuan Commune.

After reading the "barefoot doctor" story in the *People's Daily* in mid-September 1968, Ni Bingwan (倪兵万), a staff member in the Medical Administration Section of the Health Bureau of Changyang county, deemed it worthwhile to disseminate information about Leyuan Commune's cooperative health-care experiences nationwide. After conducting a twenty-day field investigation of Leyuan Commune with two of his colleagues in early

October, Ni wrote an investigation report. The report highlighted the main benefits of the cooperative medical system, the most important of which was that it "resolved the difficulties facing poor and lower-middle peasants who cannot afford to see a doctor or buy medicine."

As soon as the *People's Daily* received the report, it held a symposium on the outskirts of Beijing to collect feedback from rural residents on the experiences of Leyuan Commune. The participants at the symposium reached a consensus that the CMS was a good way to overcome the difficulties of rural residents in seeing doctors and buying medicine, thus it would be worthwhile to spread the CMS nationwide. Referred by Yao Wenyuan and approved by Mao Zedong, on December 5, 1968 the *People's Daily* published an article entitled "The CMS Is Welcomed by Poor and Lower-Middle Peasants," together with an editor's note hailing "the CMS as a great revolution on the medical battlefront as it has overcome the difficulties facing rural residents who cannot afford to see a doctor or buy medicine."[27] Subsequently, the article was republished in all newspapers and periodicals nationwide. During the next eight years, Leyuan Commune received more than 50,000 visitors from all over the country seeking information on its experiences.[28]

To vigorously promote the cooperative medical system, the *People's Daily* began a special column entitled "Discussion on the Rural Medical System" and over the following eight years published some 107 articles in the column.[29] Local newspapers also published a multitude of articles aimed at introducing, discussing, and disseminating information about cooperative medical services and barefoot doctors. In addition, many books were published for the same purpose. Due to this powerful media campaign, after 1969 China saw an upsurge in the rejuvenation of the rural cooperative medical scheme. By 1976, the CMS had been adopted by 92.8 percent of production brigades nationwide and covered 85 percent of the rural population (see Figure 4.1).

A type of community-based health insurance, the CMS featured the following three characteristics. First, CMS expenses were shared by collectives (public welfare funds) as well as individuals (fees). Second, cooperative medical services were not legally required, but in the communes and brigades that adopted the system, participation was compulsory and user fees were deducted by the collective before distribution of income at year-end. Third, cooperative medical services relied on low-cost barefoot doctors who contributed to reducing medical costs to an affordable level by gathering, growing, harvesting, and making Chinese herbal medicines and by widely applying acupuncture.

Even during the most radical period of the Cultural Revolution, however, the Chinese government never imposed any nationwide CMS model. Instead, the cooperative medical scheme varied significantly by brigade, commune, county, and region. First, the risk-sharing pool could be run by a brigade, a commune, or both. A brigade-run system was most common. Second, the proportion of the contribution by the collective to the medical fund varied. It normally ranged from 30 percent to 90 percent of the fund. Only in a few cases were all medical costs covered by the collective; in most localities farmers were required to pay a fee, usually in the range of 1–3 RMB per person/year.[30] Third, there were large discrepancies in terms of benefits among participants in different brigades, communes, counties, and regions. Although a visit to the village clinic was almost always free, drugs could be free or co-paid (herbal medicines and acupuncture were normally provided free of charge), and referred hospital visits and hospitalization were mostly co-paid.[31]

It is worth noting that even during its heyday, the CMS never covered all communes and brigades nationwide because the government never required its implementation. Moreover, even in areas where it was adopted, the CMS did not proceed smoothly. During 1969–71, the CMS flourished despite the lack of a solid foundation. The proportion of rural areas adopting the CMS fell to 62 percent in 1972 and 54 percent in 1973 (see Figure 4.1). Subsequently, grassroots rural entities took the initiative in controlling costs, toughening procedures, strengthening management, and eliminating waste. Only after extensive experience had been accumulated in these areas did CMS coverage rebound to 92.8 percent of the brigades in the nation in 1976.[32]

In the 1970s, China was still a poor country but it managed to provide inexpensive and more or less equally accessible health care for most rural residents, even though the quality of medical services was not high.[33] The near-universal coverage facilitated significant improvements in health. Average life expectancy surged from 35 years before 1949 to 68 years in 1980, whereas the infant mortality rate fell from approximately 250 per thousand before 1949 to less than 34 per thousand in 1980.[34] China's health-care services became internationally recognized for their fairness and accessibility[35] and became a model for the World Health Organization to enhance the primary health-care movement globally.[36] The Nobel laureate economist Amartya Sen is by no means an uncritical admirer of Mao. However, he acknowledged that Mao's China enjoyed "a large and decisive lead over India" in terms of the health status of its people.[37]

A review of the evolution of rural medical services during the Mao era indicates that rural China started from scratch with few doctors and a small amount of drugs and ended up with a CMS characterized by low costs and wide coverage. In this process, inputs from the grassroots played a vital role.

The Decline of the Traditional CMS

When it was announced in August 1977 that the Cultural Revolution had officially ended, no one expected that the CMS would swiftly decline. Rather, the Constitution of 1978 called for its enhancement to safeguard the health rights of the people. In 1979, the Ministry of Health and four other ministries jointly released the first regulatory document, the Rural CMS Regulations (Trial). The Regulations defined the CMS as "a socialist medical system established by members of the People's Communes through collective force on a voluntary and mutual-aid basis." It further pointed out: "The Constitution prescribes that the country actively support and develop the CMS and tailor medical work to the needs of protecting the health of commune members and developing agricultural production."[38]

But by the first half of 1978 cracks were already emerging in the CMS. Document 37 issued by the CCP Central Committee on June 23, 1978 barred communes and brigades from "allocating and transferring human, financial, and material resources to conduct non-productive construction" and called for them to "cut non-productive expenditures."[39] Subsequently, some localities began to refer to cooperative health care as a system of "the poor eating the rich" and "adding to the burdens of the people." Consequently, the number of rural cooperative medical services drastically declined in the Northeast and disappeared entirely even from many economically strong brigades. As the cooperative medical services were closed, the barefoot doctors were either dismissed as non-productive personnel or contracted by brigade clinics to assume sole responsibility for profits or losses; in many brigades, it became too expensive for the peasants to see a doctor again.[40]

Similar problems were reported all over the country.[41] In 1980, for instance, "the cooperative medical services of many brigades were halted or ground to a standstill" in Henan province, leading to calls for urgent action to salvage them.[42]

Nationally, the proportion of brigades covered by the CMS fell from 92.8 percent in 1976 to 52.8 percent in 1982, a 40 percent drop in six years. During this period, some provincial governments (e.g., Heilongjiang, Jilin, Qinghai, and Fujian) enacted regulations aimed at "unswervingly promoting cooperative medical services," but the central leadership focused on implementing the household responsibility system and failed to take a stand on the CMS issue. The constitution of 1982 deleted any mention of the "cooperative medical system," and as a result of the abolition of the People's Communes in 1983, the rural CMS collapsed, with its coverage plunging to just 11 percent of China's villages (see Figure 4.1).

From the mid- through late 1980s, cooperative medical services still existed in suburban Shanghai and southern Jiangsu where the collective economy was well developed.[43] Elsewhere, however, such services were retained in only a few localities, such as Macheng county (麻城县) in Hubei and Zhaoyuan county (招远县) in Shandong.[44] With the end of the CMS, the vast majority of village clinics became privatized and the user-pay medical system was restored.

Why did the once booming CMS cease to exist after the reform? The most important reason was the change in the economic basis upon which the CMS operated. Only under the collective economy could funds for cooperative medical services (both public welfare funds and household fees) be withheld to ensure smooth financing. After the household responsibility system was implemented, the collective economy was very weak or even nonexistent in most villages, except in those regions where collective enterprises flourished. Therefore, it was no longer feasible in most localities to support cooperative medical services by withdrawing and retaining collective public welfare funds. The 40 percent decrease in CMS coverage as of 1983 when the People's Commune system was formally abolished is indicative of the importance of the collective economy to the CMS. In the 1980s, as cooperative medical services declined throughout most of the country, southern Jiangsu still retained more than 85 percent coverage, but this level could not be sustained in the 1990s when the collectively owned township and village enterprises there were restructured through "privatization." The experience in southern Jiangsu confirms that the collective economy was the backbone for the traditional CMS.

In addition, the term "barefoot doctors" was dropped and their nature changed. The Rural Cooperative Medical Regulations (Trial), ratified in 1979, stated that "barefoot doctors should work both as farmers and as doctors and participate in collective distribution" and they should "actively gather, grow, produce, and use Chinese herbal medicine and make full use of local sources of medicine to prevent and treat diseases." Only under such conditions could the CMS provide basic, low-cost medical services for farmers. As a result of the breakdown of the collective economy, however, most villages could not afford to pay the barefoot doctors reasonable salaries and had no alternative but to sell or contract the village clinics to individual doctors, offering as an incentive the possibility of making profits. Furthermore, it was no longer possible to collectively grow, gather, and produce Chinese herbal medicine after the land was contracted to individual households. Such changes increased the costs of health care. In early 1985, Minister of Health Chen Minzhang (陈敏章) officially announced that henceforth the term "barefoot doctor" would no longer be used.[45]

In much of the 1980s China's top leaders decided to let the rural CMS pursue its own course. Although they never expressly rejected the rural CMS, some health officials denounced the CMS as an offspring of the already repudiated Cultural Revolution and advocated dissolving it and contracting the village clinics to barefoot doctors. They asserted that this was an "inevitable trend" of development.[46] When the CMS collapsed, it was considered to be "great progress" and it was believed that "the user-pay medical system is here to stay for the foreseeable future in China."[47]

Doubts about the CMS led policy makers to ignore past experiences, which affected the formulation of rural health reform policies.[48] In the early 1980s, carefully worded official documents tried by every means to avoid using the phrase "CMS," replacing it with other terms such as "pooling of medical resources.[49] As the central leadership assumed an ambiguous attitude, most local officials were no longer interested in the system. In the words of one farmer, "With no push from the top and no action in the middle, the base simply fell apart."[50]

Exploring New Models for the CMS

That policy makers took an ambiguous stand on the CMS does not mean the public and private sectors stopped exploring suitable rural health-financing models. Debates continued in the mid-1980s regarding which financing system was appropriate for rural health care. One school of thought argued that China's rural health-financing system should adopt global trends of conventional health insurance; another school contended that China's unique CMS should be reinforced.[51] The central leadership remained equivocal.

In line with the new policy of invigorating the domestic economy and opening to the outside world, in September 1985 the CCP Central Committee issued the "Guidelines for Formulating the Seventh Five-Year Plan for the National Economy and Social Development," which called for exploring a variety of new social-security models. Subsequently, the Ministry of Health formulated the "Outline for Health Reform during the Seventh

Five-Year Plan Period," which stated that the rural health-care system should be gradually resurrected according to economic conditions and public willingness in each locality to adopt the CMS or another approach. The Outline underscored the necessity of actively exploring and developing a health-financing system suitable for the rural areas.[52]

The Ministry of Health leaned toward implementing a conventional health insurance system in the rural areas. In 1985 it endorsed the World Bank's proposal to establish a health insurance scheme in rural China and agreed to conduct a "China Rural Health Insurance Experiment" in Jianyang (简阳) and Meishan (眉山县) counties in Sichuan, with technical assistance from the RAND Corporation. To promote the experiment, the ministry organized an academic seminar on rural health insurance in Emei county (峨眉县), Sichuan, the purpose of which was to disseminate the message that it was imperative to implement a health insurance system in rural China.

The "China Rural Health Insurance Experiment" was the first controlled experiment in the area of rural health care. It was undertaken in two phases. During Phase 1, after twenty-six months of investigation and research in Jianyang and Meishan counties Chinese and American experts formed a task force to design rural health insurance schemes. In the early stage of Phase 2, the task force conducted pilot experiments in four administrative villages; in the later stage of Phase 2, the task force undertook experiments in twenty-six administrative villages. The controlled nature of the experiment was reflected in the testing of seven different insurance schemes in different administrative villages so as to examine their respective pros and cons and feasibility.

Compared with the traditional CMS, the "China Rural Health Insurance Experiment" was characterized by some distinctive features. First, risk-sharing was based on the township rather than the administrative village in order to enlarge the insurance pool and boost risk-bearing capabilities. Second, in the areas where the experiment was conducted, villagers participated in the health insurance scheme on a voluntary rather than a mandatory basis. But to avoid "moral hazard" and "adverse selection," the unit of participation was the household rather than the individual. Third, insurance premiums could be assumed by collectives or individual households, or shared by both. Fourth, focusing on catastrophic diseases, the insurance schemes covered more in-patient expenses and fewer out-patient expenses.[53] As we will see in the following paragraphs, the four features of this experiment influenced thinking on later rural health reform, even though this scheme was eventually rejected.

In addition to the experiment conducted by the Ministry of Health, there was a plethora of health insurance practices pursued in various parts of China in the late 1980s. Examples include a general health insurance program in Jinshan county (金山县) of Shanghai and in Jianli county (监利县) of Hubei; a preventive care insurance plan for mothers and children in Pengxi county (蓬溪县) of Sichuan; a maternal and child health insurance in Jinzhai county (金寨县) of Anhui, Jicheng county (冀城县) of Shanxi, and Shangshui county (晌水县) of Jiangsu; and a dental insurance scheme for elementary and middle-school students in Yuncheng county (运城县) of Shanxi.[54] Jintan county (金坛县) in Jiangsu experimented with both a general health insurance scheme and a single-item insurance scheme on a pilot basis.[55] Based on a survey of 62,571 peasants in twenty counties, in January 1988 the Rural Health-Care System Research Team of the Expert Committee on Health Policy and Management of the Ministry of Health recommended four rural health insurance schemes.[56] Subsequently, additional experiments were conducted in various localities.[57]

It is worth noting that many of the health insurance experiments still contained traces of the CMS even though some experts vigorously advocated that individuals participate at their own cost amid the "transition from the CMS to a rural health insurance system."[58] Under the health insurance scheme in Yuhang county (余杭县) in Zhejiang and Jintan county (金坛县) in Jiangsu, for example, more than 90 percent of the insurance costs were covered collectively, with only a symbolic amount of money paid by the individual participants.[59] These counties regarded the call to introduce "health insurance" as an opportunity to "add new content" in order to "enhance the vitality" of the CMS.[60] In addition, the CMS was retained in some areas, such as Guangji county (广济县) in Hubei, Changshu City (常熟市) and Taicang county (太仓县) of Jiangsu, Zhaoyuan county (招远) in Shandong, and the suburban counties of Shanghai.[61] But the user-pay medical system was implemented in the vast majority of the rural areas in China.

The diversity of practices makes it possible to explore the advantages and shortcomings of the different health-financing systems. In addition to the health insurance experiments mentioned above, in the mid-1980s academics began to carry out comparative studies of different health-financing systems. In 1987, working together with the Department of Medical Administration of the Ministry of Health, Anhui Medical University conducted a comparative study of the CMS and user-pay system by surveying some forty villages with matching conditions (per capita income, illiteracy rate, age composition, topography, and nationality factors) in Hubei, Shandong, and Beijing, half of which practiced the CMS and the other half a user-pay system. The survey found that the CMS was superior to the user-pay system according to fifteen out of nineteen indicators.[62] During 1988–90, the Ministry of Health set up a task force to study the feasibility and effectiveness of several rural health-financing systems using data collected from a sample survey of twenty counties in sixteen provinces. The study again confirmed the superiority of the CMS.[63] In addition to these nationwide surveys, there were numerous local surveys conducted at the regional, county, and township levels. Without exception, all the surveys reached the same conclusion: the CMS was superior to the user-pay system, and the vast majority of farmers favored the CMS.[64]

At the Fifty-Eighth World Health Assembly in 1986, the Chinese government pledged to "allow everyone entitlement to basic health care by 2000."[65] It was of course impossible to fulfill this pledge within fourteen years without changing the user-pay medical system for most rural residents. Research results showed unmistakably that only by restoring the CMS could China provide its farmers with adequate access to basic medical and preventive health services.

To solve the confusion, Professor Zhu Aorong (朱敖荣), who had long engaged in research on the rural medical system, rebutted point by point many of the arguments against the CMS and attributed its downfall to "health regulatory authorities censuring the CMS as a product of 'leftism' and using the propaganda machine to demonize it nationwide." Zhu used survey data to show that most rural residents supported the CMS, as he refuted the assertion that "the CMS has become outdated and health insurance represents the 'global trend.'" He strongly recommended that the central government re-establish cooperative health care as the basis of China's rural medical system.[66]

Facing the reality that over 90 percent of farmers had no medical security, others who worked on rural health problems gradually reached similar conclusions. First, the user-pay system not only deprived poor rural residents of access to basic health care but also led to poverty if the farmers were to become sick or seriously injured. Second, health insurance was not suitable for rural China because insurers were not interested due to the low profit margins, and farmers did not trust the insurers and blamed them for the complicated and incomprehensible red tape.[67]

Against this background, starting from the end of 1988, the central government repeatedly reiterated its pledge to realize universal rural health-care coverage by 2000 and to lay a solid foundation for universal health coverage by "restoring and improving the rural collective health financing system." By 1991, the central authorities were using such buzzwords as "cooperative medical system," "collective health financing," and "cooperative health insurance" in official documents.[68] The frequent use of the term "cooperative medical system" in central government documents put an end to the decade-long debate over the CMS. However, the vague terms "collective health financing" and "cooperative health insurance" suggest that the central policy makers still hesitated between the CMS and a health insurance system and hoped to find a way to combine them.

Nevertheless, the subtle change in the central government's attitude provided an opportunity for the CMS advocates. At the end of 1991, former health minister Qian Zhongxin (钱忠信) wrote a foreword, entitled "Rejuvenating the Cooperative Medical System," to a special issue of *China's Rural Health-Care Management*.[69] The journal also published an article written by Professor Zhu Aorong and his colleagues that stated, "On behalf of more than 900 million farmers, we sincerely and urgently request the ruling Communist Party and State Council leaders to pay as much attention to the CMS with respect to the birth, illness, old-age, and death of the 900 million farmers as they do to family planning, education, and science and technology, to make a decision and communicate it to political leaders at all levels, and concretely press ahead with the nationwide cooperative medical system." The article, pointing out that the CMS was "fundamentally different" from health insurance, recommended that in future policy statements "cooperative health insurance" be replaced by "cooperative medical system."[70] These scholars appealed directly to the top policy makers because they knew that the Ministry of Health officials had "overemphasized a lack of decision-making power and had taken a wait-and-see attitude."[71] Thus, restoring the CMS required more than a change of mind on the part of Ministry of Health officials — it required explicit support from the highest levels of the party-state.

To fix and restore the CMS as the foundation of the rural health-care system, the central government appropriated 20 million RMB to support an overhaul of rural cooperative medical services in 1991. In 1992 appropriations rose to 75 million RMB. Meanwhile, twenty-eight provinces and municipalities matched the central budgetary allocations with 2.5 billion RMB from local treasuries for the next two years. The government's capital infusion gave a shot in the arm to the rural CMS just as it was on the verge of extinction.[72] As a result, the CMS encountered a "minor spring" in 1992 (see Figure 4.1).

However, after Deng Xiaoping made his inspection tour of South China in 1992, the market-oriented reformers regained the upper hand. In September, the Ministry of Health recast the tone of the "Opinions on the Deepening of Health Reform" by stating: "In the rural areas, we should vigorously promote cooperative health insurance."[73] The point was driven home by the director-general of the Department of Health Policy and Legislation of the Ministry of Health when he stated: "Generally, China must follow the health insurance approach that has been adopted by more than one-hundred countries worldwide. Of course, our tactics will be different, but the basic strategy must be the same."[74] As a result, CMS coverage shrank drastically (see Figure 4.1).

In 1993, the pendulum swung once again, when the CCP Central Committee issued its "Decision on Several Issues in the Establishment of the Socialist Market Economic System," calling for developing and improving the rural CMS in lieu of "rural health insurance." In the same year, based on a nationwide investigation, the Office of Research under the State Council and the Ministry of Health submitted a research report entitled "Speeding up the Reform and Construction of the Rural Cooperative Medical System." The report set the objective of raising rural CMS coverage to 50 percent during the Ninth Five-Year Plan period (1996–2000) (national coverage was less than 10 percent at the time). But how would the problem of financing be resolved? The report recommended, "Setting up a mechanism to jointly raise funds from the state, collectives, and individuals." The crux of the issue was how the state would "make a joint investment." Would the government use its funding to support the CMS? The report did not elaborate on this.[75]

During the 1994–96 period, the Office of Research under the State Council and the Ministry of Health conducted a special survey of the CMS in fourteen counties of seven provinces, especially Kaifeng county (开封县) and Linzhou City (林州市) in Henan. At a National Workshop on the Rural CMS held in Linzhou in July 1996, State Councilor Peng Peiyun (彭佩云), in a bid to eliminate the ideological obstacles to cooperative health care, refuted various "erroneous notions."[76] Health Minister Chen Minzhang elaborated: "The central government now takes a very supportive position on developing and improving the CMS. The question is not whether to go ahead with the CMS but how to do it well. We should put developing and improving the CMS at the top of the agenda for rural health care." How? Chen Minzhang was fully aware that "financing is the focal and difficult problem in cooperative medical services." However, at this point the official guideline was to continue to follow a "user-paid, collective-subsidized, and government-guided and supported" approach.[77]

Subsequent to the workshop, local governments launched hundreds of pilot projects to promote the CMS. All of a sudden, the CMS was gaining momentum.[78] By the end of 1996, the proportion of administrative villages offering cooperative medical services had increased to 17.59 percent (the highest level since 1983), up 6.41 percent from the previous year (see Figure 4.1).

The CMS regained traction at this time. At a National Health Work Conference held in December 1996, policy makers reached a consensus that the key to strengthening rural health care was to develop and improve the rural CMS. After the meeting, the CCP Central Committee and the State Council issued the "Decisions on Health Reform and Development," making it clear that the state encouraged rural areas nationwide to establish and develop the rural CMS on a private-run/government-supported and voluntary participation basis, with funds raised mainly from farmers and subsidized by collectives. The role of government was merely to "support" such endeavors.[79]

From mid-1996 to mid-1997, the Chinese government took numerous initiatives to restore and develop cooperative medical services and it hoped to launch a new movement to rebuild the CMS. However, the results were disappointing. By the end of 1997, cooperative medical services covered only 17 percent of the nation's administrative villages, virtually no change from the previous year, and the proportion of rural residents participating in the cooperative medical scheme was merely 9.6 percent. The Second National Health Service Survey undertaken by the Ministry of Health in 1998 indicated that the proportion of rural residents participating in the cooperative medical scheme declined to 6.5 percent in 1998.[80]

The government's support for cooperative medical services after 1996–97 was beyond reproach. Why, then, was it so difficult to restore the CMS?

One reason is that although the central policy makers encouraged rebuilding the CMS, various central ministries enacted regulations barring any forced attempt to raise cooperative medical funds from farmers, thus pouring cold water on the emerging cooperative medical scheme. For this reason, even in Kaifeng and Linzhou, the two cities selected by the Office of Research under the State Council and the Ministry of Health for pilot programs, the cooperative medical scheme was halted.[81]

More importantly, restoration of the traditional CMS might not have been possible even with consistent government policy support because rural communities without a collective economy could no longer operate a CMS solely by collecting funds from farmers. However, the government failed to recognize this point at the time. In the 1990s, the government reaffirmed the importance of the CMS mainly because it had not depended on government funding. In statutes on cooperative health financing enacted prior to 1996, the central government repeatedly emphasized that "funds [were to be] raised mainly from farmers together with subsidies from collectives and policy support from governments at all levels." Actually, state budgetary allocations for rural cooperative medical services were meager (35 million RMB in 1999, or less than 0.5 RMB per capita).[82] The problem was that without financial support from the government it was virtually impossible to universalize cooperative medical services nationwide.

What shattered the illusion of restoring the CMS without government funding was a series of surveys and controlled experiments conducted in poverty-stricken regions (see Table 4.2). If the practice and experimentation conducted across rural China in the 1980s helped the government realize the necessity of rebuilding the CMS, then the practice and experimentation conducted in the 1990s led to the conclusion that the traditional CMS was fraught with grave deficiencies. The government had no alternative but to provide financial support; otherwise, it would never be able to realize its objective of "setting up various cooperative medical systems in most rural areas by 2000."

Interestingly, Tibet, adopting a different rural medical system, provided an illuminating example for the whole country. Prior to 1997, residents in the Tibet Autonomous Region enjoyed free health-care services subsidized by the central government and provided by public medical institutions. After 1997, using fiscal transfers from the central government, the Tibetan government set up a cooperative medical fund, subsidizing each farmer/ herdsman at the rate of 15–30 RMB per year if she/he took part in the CMS. The participants only had to contribute 10–20 RMB per person/per year. The county/township government and village organization would split the cost at a specific ratio for households that could not afford to pay the fee. This medical system covered the vast majority of the population in Tibet. The Tibetan experience showed that cooperative medical services could be universalized even in poverty-stricken areas as long as the government provided strong financial support.[83]

The foregoing experiments and the Tibetan experience point to the same conclusion: establishing and maintaining a rural CMS with extensive coverage requires financial support from the government. This completely

Table 4.2

Selected Rural Health-Care Experiment Projects, 1985–2005

Project	Organizer	Dates	Location	Key Findings
China Rural Health Insurance Experiment and Research	Ministry of Health (MOH), and RAND Corp.	1985–91	Jianyang and Meishan counties, Sichuan	Insurance premium rates set in the range of 1–2% of the per capita income of farmers, but difficult to collect insurance payments from the farmers
China Rural CMS Reform	State Council, MOH, WHO	1993–98	14 counties in 7 provinces	Government and collective financial support boosts farmers' enthusiasm to participate in cooperative medical schemes; otherwise such schemes cannot survive
Health Financing and Organization in China's Rural Poverty-Stricken Regions	China Health Economics Training and Research Network and Harvard University	1992–2000	114 counties in 14 provinces	In poverty-stricken areas, most households can only afford to pay less than 10 RMB per person per year for cooperative medical fees; infusion of government funds plays a significant role in implementation
CMS Reform and Development under Conditions of the Market Economy	MOH and United Nations Children's Fund	1999		Government funding is key to the sustainability of medical security for farmers
Strengthening Basic Health Services in China's Rural Poverty-Stricken Regions	Chinese government and World Bank	1998–2005	71 poor counties in 7 central and western provinces	Government funding is a prerequisite for cooperative medical schemes
Best CMS Practices in Rural China	Commission of Planning and Finance, MOH, WHO, and UNDP	2000–2002	Areas where the CMS was well established	Developing cooperative medical services is defined as "government behavior"

shattered the illusion that a CMS "funded primarily by individual farmers" could be established.

In the mid-1990s, a consensus emerged among rural health-care researchers: the government should assume, rather than deny or eschew, responsibility for funding the cooperative medical scheme. Otherwise, it was unlikely that the scheme could be universalized. However, this consensus was not immediately incorporated into government policy because the government was facing a serious financial crisis at the time: fiscal revenue as a percentage of GDP barely exceeded 10 percent and the proportion of central government fiscal revenue in GDP was merely 5 percent.[84] Even if the government had been willing to accept responsibility for the farmers' health security, it was unable to fund the scheme.

The tax-sharing reform introduced in 1994 swiftly reversed the decline in government extractive capacity. As shown in Figure 4.2, the Chinese government's fiscal revenue as a percentage of GDP rose to 16 percent by 2002, and the central government's fiscal revenue as a proportion of GDP rose to 9 percent. It was only at this time that the government had the fiscal capability to fund the rural cooperative medical scheme. Thus, the drastic change in the government's rural health-care policy at that time came as no surprise.

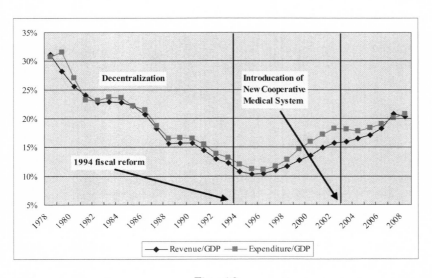

Figure 4.2:
Chinese Government Fiscal Revenue/Expenditures as a Percentage of GDP
Source: Author's databank.

In October 2002, the central government issued the "Decision on Further Boosting Rural Health-Care Work," expressly calling for "gradually establishing a new rural cooperative medical system," which, it was hoped, would "largely cover all rural residents by 2010." To realize this objective, the central government pledged that from 2003 on, its treasury would subsidize each farmer in the central and western provinces with 10 RMB per year for participation in the new cooperative medical scheme; local treasuries were expected to match the central government subsidy with no less than 10 RMB for each participant, and each participant was expected to contribute another 10 RMB to the scheme. In addition, assistance would be provided to poor rural residents who could not afford to pay the fee.[85]

In January 2003, the State Council forwarded the "Opinions of the Ministry of Health, the Ministry of Finance, and the Ministry of Agriculture on Setting up the New Rural Cooperative Medical System," calling on each province, autonomous region, and municipality directly under the central government to select at least two or three counties to implement the new cooperative medical scheme (hereafter NCMS) on a pilot basis and after gaining experience to expand the area of coverage. In the meantime, the State Council set up an Inter-Ministry NCMS Liaison Office (*xin nonghebu-jilianxi huiyi*, 新农合部际联席会议) chaired by Vice Premier Wu Yi (吴仪). Due to uneven regional economic and social development, the office first selected the provinces of Jilin (north), Zhejiang (east), Hubei (central), and Yunnan (west) to implement the NCMS on a pilot basis and subsequently expanded the experience nationwide. At that point, the development of China's rural cooperative health care entered a new stage.

Compared with the traditional CMS, the NCMS initially was characterized by the following:

First, it changed the nature of cooperative medical services: the NCMS was a government-led, mutual-aid/mutual-relief health-financing system that operated under the organization, guidance, and support of the government, whereas the traditional CMS had been mainly organized by village communities on their own.

Second, it boosted government financial support: the NCMS was funded by government-led multi-party financing and supported with annual budgetary appropriations from the central and local governments, whereas the traditional CMS had been funded mainly by fees paid by participants and subsidies provided by the collective economy at the village level (with the government having no responsibility for funding).

Third, it was designed mainly to tackle problems caused by catastrophic disease: the NCMS focused on addressing the problems facing farmers who had become poverty-stricken due to catastrophic disease, whereas the traditional CMS mainly dealt with common ailments and minor injuries.

Fourth, it enlarged the size of risk pooling: the unit of risk pooling under the NCMS was the county, whereas under the traditional CMS it was the village.

Fifth, it promoted the simultaneous establishment of a medical-assistance system by setting up special-purpose funds to provide medical assistance to poor rural households and the so-called "five-guarantee families."[86]

The above features of the NCMS represent a crystallization of the practices and experiments conducted over the past decade. Evidence revealed that with the end of support from the collective economy, the traditional CMS had become a tree without roots. If the government advocated a CMS but did not fund it, it was unlikely that it could be rebuilt on a large scale. Only government funding could sustain a cooperative medical scheme in the post-collectivist era.

The NCMS is of course imperfect and fraught with problems. Therefore, additional exploration has been conducted since its introduction. To ensure that the NCMS proceeds in a healthy way, since its inception the central government has established the principle of "truly benefiting the people, acting according to local conditions, coaching by example, and proceeding on a fail-safe path by conducting trials and summarizing experiences before going ahead with nationwide implementation."[87] A National NCMS Pilot Work Conference was held in September 2005. At the conference, based on progress up to that time, the central government decided to cover all of rural China with the NCMS by 2008, two years ahead of the original schedule. Meanwhile, the government subsidy for each NCMS participant was doubled from 20 RMB to 40 RMB.[88] At the National NCMS Work Conference held in February 2008, the government decided again to double the subsidy to 80 RMB per participant per year, effective in 2008.[89] By the end of 2009, the NCMS covered nearly all administrative villages in the country and 94 percent of rural households.[90] Thus, after nearly sixty years of development with a number of twists and turns, a cooperative health-care system finally reached an all-time high.

Conclusion

By tracing the evolution of China's rural health-financing system, we see how Chinese policy makers and policy advocates learn through practice and experimentation to respond to the changing environment by adjusting policy objectives and policy tools. Table 4.3 summarizes China's policy/institutional learning models.

Table 4.3
China's Policy/Institutional Learning Models

Promoters of Learning	Sources of Learning	
	Practice	Experiments
Policy makers	• Experiences of Mishan Village, Gaoping county, Shanxi (1955) • Experiences of Chayashan Satellite People's Commune, Suiping county, Henan (1958) • Experiences of Jishan county, Shanxi (1959) • Experiences of Leyuan Commune, Changyang county, Hubei (1968) • "China Rural CMS Reform" Project (1993–94) • "The Best CMS Practices in Rural China" Project (2000–2002)	• "China Rural Health Insurance Experiment and Research Project" (1985–90) • "China Rural CMS Reform Project" (1993–98)
Policy advocates	• Comparative study of the CMS and the user-pay system in Hubei, Shandong, and Beijing (1987) • Comparative study of the rural health-care system in 16 provinces (1988–90) • Numerous investigations and research on existing CMS programs (1985–2002) • First phase of the project on "Health Financing and Organization in China's Rural Poverty-Stricken Regions" (1992–96) • Tibetan experiences (1997–2002)	• Second phase of the project on "Health Financing and Organization in China's Rural Poverty-Stricken Regions" (1996–2000) • Project on "Strengthening Basic Health Services in China's Rural Poverty-Stricken Regions" (1998–2005)

Table 4.3 leads us to seven general observations:

First, during the past six decades, grassroots practices have always been the most important source of learning, transcending the divide between the Mao era and the post-Mao era. The earliest CMS models in the 1950s originated from grassroots practices instead of being designed by policy makers and experts. During the Cultural Revolution, it was widely believed that the famous models of the barefoot doctors in Chuansha county (Shanghai) and the CMS in Changyang county (Hubei) had been introduced by Chairman Mao. In fact, the models first emerged at the grassroots level before attracting the attention of the top leaders. Grassroots practices provided an inspiration for central policy makers and policy advocates and served as a driving force for policy/institutional innovations. In addition to drawing lessons from domestic practices, after the reform and opening to the outside world China also paid special attention to the experiences of other countries.[91]

Second, the bottom-up approach thrived because the Chinese political system allows and even encourages a diversity of practices. Even during the most radical period of the Cultural Revolution, the Chinese government never required implementation of a singular CMS model. In fact, CMS practices varied considerably by brigade, commune, county, and province. Moreover, even during its heyday the CMS never covered all brigades and communes in the country because the government never required nationwide implementation. The diversity of practices allowed decision makers to examine the advantages and shortcomings of the various health financing schemes.

Third, whereas there was virtually no experimentation during the 1949–76 period, controlled experimentation conducted within a narrow scope thereafter has become an important source of learning to identify viable policy objectives and effective policy tools. Such experimentation often requires using modern surveying and statistical techniques.

Fourth, prior to the 1980s, the promoters of learning were primarily policy makers who were highly sensitive to the needs and desires of ordinary Chinese and who were willing to take responsibility for responding to new challenges. Guided by the "mass line," they kept abreast of the latest developments by personally conducting periodic investigations at the grassroots levels or by reading public or internal reports submitted by health authorities and news agencies at various levels.

Fifth, after the 1980s, the promoters of learning began to include policy advocates (including central government agencies, local governments, international organizations, and domestic and foreign academic institutions), which played an increasingly important role in policy/institutional evolution. Sometimes different advocacy coalitions emerged to push different policy agendas. For example, a heated debate emerged in the 1980s over the CMS versus health insurance. This shows that China's political system has become increasingly open and inclusive.

Sixth, as the sources of learning have expanded from grassroots practices to systematic experimentation, and the promoters of learning have extended from policy makers to policy advocates, China's policy/institutional learning and adaptive potential has been further enhanced.

Seventh, when one contradiction is solved, new ones will inevitably arise, and, as a result, learning and adapting are an endless process. Compared with the 1980s and 1990s, the NCMS has many distinctive advantages, but it still faces a plethora of problems. Therefore, today exploration continues to be carried out in the area of rural health financing.

If the foregoing observations can be corroborated by dissecting other "sparrows" (other policy/institutional areas), we will gain a better understanding of China's political system. Heilmann reckons that China's "experimentation under hierarchy" is a "distinct mode of governance."[92] It endows the Chinese regime with extraordinary learning and adaptive capacity and enables it calmly to respond to all sorts of challenges under a radically changing environment. However, Heilmann's observation only involves one of the four learning models listed in Table 4.1. This chapter shows that China is well-versed not only in "experimentation under hierarchy," but also in other learning models as well. In other words, China's policy/institutional learning and adaptive capacity are far stronger than Heilmann suggests. For example, Heilmann asserts that "experimentation under hierarchy" has advantages in the economic policy area but does not help improve the provision of social and public goods. In particular, he cites basic health care as an example. This chapter indicates that this judgment is somewhat premature. China is fully capable of using various learning models to explore better ways of providing health care (and even an entire welfare system) to its citizens. On April 6, 2009, after three years of preparation and months of public consultation, China announced an outline for a comprehensive reform of its health-care system that pledged to extend some form of basic health insurance to 90 percent of the population by the end of 2011 and to provide "safe, effective, convenient, and affordable" basic health services to all citizens by 2020.[93] With five medical care schemes (that is, the New Rural Cooperative Medical Scheme, the Basic Medical Insurance for Urban Employees, the Basic Medical Insurance for Urban Residents, the Basic

Medical Insurance for Migrant Workers, and the Medical Assistance to Rural and Urban Residents) already in place,[94] covering 1.28 billion of the country's 1.32 billion people by the end of 2009,[95] China should have little difficulty in achieving its goals for 2011 and 2020.

Endnotes

1. Douglass C. North, *Institutions, Institutional Change and Economic Performance* (New York: Cambridge University Press, 1990), ch. 9.

2. David Dolowitz and David Marsh, "Who Learns What from Whom: A Review of the Policy Transfer Literature," *Political Studies*, 44, no. 2 (1996): 343–357.

3. Paul A. Sabatier and Hank C. Jenkins-Smith, eds., *Policy Change and Learning: An Advocacy Coalition Approach* (Boulder, CO: Westview, 1993).

4. Ka-Che Yip, "Health and Nationalist Reconstruction: Rural Health in Nationalist China, 1928–1937," *Modern Asian Studies*, 26, no. 2 (May 1992): 395–415.

5. Harry E. Seifert, "Life Tables for Chinese Farmers," *Milbank Memorial Fund Quarterly Bulletin*, 13, no. 3 (July 1935): 223–236.

6. Xu Jie (徐杰), "Dui woguo weisheng jingji zhengce de lishi huigu he sikao (shang)" (对我国卫生经济政策的历史回顾和思考 [上]) (A Historical Review and Reflections on China's Health Economic Policy [Part 1]), *Zhongguo weisheng jingji* (中国卫生经济) (Chinese Health Economics, hereafter *CHE*), no. 10 (1997): 7–8.

7. Yao Li (姚力), "Nongcun hezuo yiliao: Jingyan yu fansi" (农村合作医疗: 经验与反思) (Rural CMS: Experience and Introspection), 2007, at http://iccs.cass.cn/detail_cg.aspx?sid=267 (accessed July 7, 2010).

8. Zhang Zikuan (张自宽), Zhu Zihui (朱子会), Wang Shucheng (王书城), and Zhang Chaoyang (张朝阳), "Guanyu woguo nongcun hezuo yiliao baojian zhidu de huiguxing yanjiu" (关于我国农村合作医疗保健制度的回顾性研究) (A Retrospective Study of China's Rural CMS), *Zhongguo nongcun weisheng shiye guanli* (中国农村卫生事业管理) (China Rural Health Service Management, hereafter *CRHM*), no. 6 (1994): 4–9.

9. Yue Qianhou (岳谦厚) and He Puyan (贺蒲燕), "Shanxisheng Jishanxian nongcun gonggong weisheng shiye shuping 1949–1984 nian" (山西省稷山县农村公共卫生事业述评1949–1984年) (A Review and Commentary of Rural Public Health Care in Jishan County, Shanxi [1949–1984]). *Dangdai Zhongguo shi yanjiu* (当代中国史研究) (Studies of Contemporary Chinese History), no. 5 (September 2007): 62–69.

10. Song Binwen (宋斌文), "Woguo nongcun hezuo yiliao de guoqu xianzai he weilai" (我国农村合作医疗的过去、现在和未来) (The Past, Present, and Future of China's Rural CMS), *Yixue yu zhexue* (医学与哲学) (Medical Science and Philosophy), no. 3 (2004): 23–35.

11. Wang Qingyuan (王靖元) and Xu Debin (徐德斌), "Hezuo yiliao lishi huigu yu Ganyuxian shishi xinxing nongcun hezuo yiliao zhidu de zuofa" (合作医疗历史回顾与赣榆县实施新型农村合作医疗制度的做法) (A Historical Review of CMS and the Practice of Ganyu County in Setting Up a New Cooperative Medical Scheme), *Jiangsu weisheng baojian* (江苏卫生保健) (Jiangsu Health Care), no. 1 (2005): 11–12.

12. Qian Wenyan (钱文艳), "Jianguohou 30 nian Zhejiang nongcun hezuo yiliao zhidu de lishi kaocha" (建国后30年浙江农村合作医疗制度的历史考察) (A Historical Review of Zhejiang's Rural CMS for 30 Years after the Founding of New China), *Anhui nongye daxue xuebao (Shehui kexue ban)* (安徽农业大学学报) (社会科学版) (Journal of Anhui Agricultural University) (Social Science Edition), no. 6 (2006): 74–77.

13. Zhang Zikuan (张自宽), "Dui hezuo yiliao zaoqi lishi qingkuang de huigu" (对合作医疗早期历史情况的回顾) (A Recollection of the Early History of the CMS), *CHE*, no. 6 (1992): 21–23.

14. Xu Jie, "Dui woguo weisheng jingji zhengce de lishi huigu he sikao."

15. The general regulations, at http://hi.baidu.com/yh909106/blog/item/4861c32b4b3420f8e6cd40cb.html (accessed July 7, 2010) were drafted by the staff of *Red Flag* and provincial and local officials. When Mao Zedong saw the draft on August 7, 1958, he was overjoyed "as if he had found a precious treasure." On August 17 when an enlarged Politburo meeting was held at Beidaihe, he wrote a memo instructing "every comrade to discuss this document. It appears that this document can be distributed to provinces and counties for reference." On September 1, the General Regulations were published in *Red Flag* and became a template for setting up communes nationwide. See Shi Xiangshen (史向生), "Mao Zedong zai Henan de rizi li (毛泽东在河南的日子里) (Mao Zedong in Henan), *Xieshang luntan* (协商论坛) (Consultation Forum), no. 7 (2001): 41–46.

16. Li Decheng (李德成), "Zhongguo nongcun chuantong hezuo yiliao zhidu yanjiu zongshu" (中国农村传统合作医疗制度研究综述) (An Overview of China's Rural CMS), *Huadong ligong daxue xuebao (Shehui kexui ban)* (华东理工大学学报) (社会科学版) (Journal of East China University of Science and Technology) (Social Science Edition), no. 1 (2007): 19–24.

17. Cao Pu (曹普), "Gaige kaifangqian Zhongguo nongcun hezuo yiliao zhidu" (改革开放前中国农村合作医疗制度) (China's Rural CMS before the Reform and Opening to the Outside World), *Zhonggong dangshi ziliao* (中共党史资料) (Materials on CCP History), no. 3 (2006): 134–144.

18. Yue Qianhou and He Puyan. "Shanxisheng Jishanxian nongcun gonggong weisheng shiye shuping 1949–1985 nian."

19. Zhang Zikuan, "Dui hezuo yiliao zaoqi lishi qingkuang de huigu."

20. Ibid.

21. Xu Jie, "Dui woguo weisheng jingji zhengce de lishi huigu he sikao."

22. Cao Pu, "Gaige kaifangqian Zhongguo nongcun hezuo yiliao zhidu."

23. Yao Li (姚力), "Ba yiliao weisheng gongzuo de zhongdian fangdao nongcun qu: Mao Zedong '626' zhishi de lishi kaocha" (把医疗卫生工作的重点放到农村去: 毛泽东"六·二六"指示的历史考察) (Shift the Focus of Health Care to the Countryside: A Historical Perspective on Mao Zedong's June 26 Directive), *Dangdai Zhongguo shi yanjiu*, no. 3 (2007): 99–104.

24. Cao Pu, "Gaige kaifangqian Zhongguo nongcun hezuo yiliao zhidu"; Xia Xingzhen (夏杏珍), "Nongcun hezuo yiliao zhidu de lishi kaocha" (农村合作医疗制度的历史考察) (A Historical Review of the Rural CMS), *Dangdai Zhongguo shi yanjiu*, no. 5 (2003): 110–118.

25. Party Committee of the Ministry of Health (卫生部党组), "Guanyu chengshi zuzhi xunhui yiliaodui xia nongcun peihe shehuizhuyi jiaoyu yundong jinxing fangbing

zhibing gongzuo de baogao" (关于城市组织巡回医疗队下农村配合社会主义教育运动进行防病治病工作的报告) (Report on Organizing Mobile Medical Teams in the Cities to Send to the Countryside to Prevent and Treat Diseases amid the Socialist Education Movement), August 2, 1965, at http://news.xinhuanet.com/ziliao/2005-02/02/content_2539249.htm (accessed September 3, 2010).

26. Mao Zedong (毛泽东), "Dui weishengbu dangzu guanyu zuzhi chengshi gaoji yiwu renyuan xia nongcun he wei nongcun peiyang yisheng wenti de baogao de piyu" (对卫生部党组关于组织城市高级医务人员下农村和为农村培养医生问题的报告的批语) (Comment on the Party Committee Report of the Ministry of Health on the Problems of Organizing High-Level Urban Medical Persons Going to the Countryside and Training Rural Doctors), January 21, 1965, in *Jianguo yilai Mao Zedong wengao* (建国以来毛泽东文稿) (Mao Zedong's Manuscripts since the Founding of the PRC) (Beijing: Zhongyang wenxian chubanshe, 1996), 11: 318–319.

27. Revolutionary Committee of Changyang County, Hubei (湖北省长阳县革命委员会), "Women henzhuale sanjian dashi: Leyuan gongshe shixing hezuo yiliao zhidu de jingyan" (我们狠抓了三件大事: 乐园公社实行合作医疗制度的经验) (We Focused on Three Things: The Experience of Leyuan Commune in Implementing the CMS), *Renmin ribao* (人民日报) (People's Daily) (December 11, 1968).

28. Hu Zhendong (胡振栋), "Wuming yingxiong litui nongcun hezuo yiliao zouxiang quanguo" (无名英雄力推农村合作医疗走向全国) (Unknown Heroes Vigorously Promote Rural CMS Nationwide), *Jiuye yu baozhang* (就业与保障) (Employment and Security), no. 10 (2006): 19–22.

29. Cao Pu, "Gaige kaifangqian Zhongguo nongcun hezuo yiliao zhidu."

30. Fu Jianhui (傅建辉), "Cong jiti fuli dao shehui baozhang: Lun renmin gongshe yu jiating jingying shiqi de nongcun hezuo yiliao zhidu" (从集体福利到社会保障: 论人民公社与家庭经营时期的农村合作医疗制度) (From Collective Welfare to Social Security: On the Rural CMS during the People's Commune Period and Thereafter), *Guangxi shehui kexue* (广西社会科学) (Guangxi Social Sciences), no. 2 (2005): 167–169; Gu Jia'en (谷加恩), "Renmin gongshe shiqi nongcun hezuo yiliao shiye chenggong de yuanyin tanxi" (人民公社时期农村合作医疗事业成功的原因探析) (An Analysis of the Reasons for the Success of the Rural CMS during the People's Commune Period), *Wuhan zhiye jishu xueyuan xuebao* (武汉职业技术学院学报) (Journal of Wuhan Institute of Technology), no. 1 (2006): 28–31.

31. Liu Xingzhu and Cao Huaijie, "China's Cooperative Medical System: Its Historical Transformations and the Trend of Development," *Journal of Public Health Policy*, 13, no. 4 (Winter 1992): 501–511.

32. The areas not covered by the CMS were mainly border areas, minority nationality regions, alpine areas, old revolutionary base areas, fish-farming areas, and pastoral areas. Xia Xingzhen, "Nongcun hezuo yiliao zhidu de lishi kaocha."

33. World Bank, *Financing Health Care: Issues and Options for China* (Washington DC: World Bank, 1997).

34. David Blumenthal and William Hsiao, "Privatization and Its Discontents: The Evolving Chinese Health Care System," *New England Journal of Medicine*, 353, no. 11 (September 15, 2005): 1165–1170.

35. Kenneth W. Newell, ed., *Health by the People* (Geneva: WHO, 1975); V. Dukanovic and E.P. Mach, eds., *Alternative Approaches to Meeting Basic Health Needs in Developing*

Countries (Geneva: WHO, 1975); M. Stiefel and W.F. Wertheim, *Production, Equity and Participation in Rural China* (London: Zed Press, 1982); Dean T. Jamison et al., *China, the Health Sector* (Washington, DC: World Bank, 1984).

36. WHO, *Primary Health Care: Report of the International Conference on Primary Health Care, Alma-Ata, USSR, 6–12 September 1978* (Geneva: WHO, 1978).

37. Jean Drèze and Amartya Sen, *Hunger and Public Action* (Oxford: Clarendon Press, 1987), p. 205.

38. "Nongcun hezuo yiliao zhangcheng (Shixing cao'an)" (农村合作医疗章程) (试行草案) (The Rural CMS Regulations [Provisional Draft]), December 15, 1979, at http://www.bsyc.gov.cn/SQJS/ShowArticle.asp?ArticleID=427 (accessed July 7, 2010).

39. Wu Lixing (吴砾星), "Zhang Yanwu: Nongmin jianfu 'jixianfeng'" (章彦武: 农民减负"急先锋") (Zhang Yanwu: Pioneer in Reducing the Farmers' Burdens), *Nongmin ribao* (农民日报) (Peasants Daily) (May 27, 2006).

40. Zhang Zikuan (张自宽), "Nongcun hezuo yiliao yinggai kending yinggai tichang yinggai fazhan" (农村合作医疗应该肯定应该提倡应该发展) (The Rural CMS Should Be Affirmed, Promoted, and Developed), *CRHM*, no. 2 (1982): 31–33.

41. Fujiansheng weishengju (福建卫生局) (Fujian Health Administration), "Jianding buyi di banhao nongcun hezuo yiliao" (坚定不移地办好农村合作医疗) (Unswervingly Promote the Rural CMS), *Fujian yiyao zazhi* (福建医药杂志) (Fujian Medical Journal), no. 6 (1979): 1–2.

42. Fang Jian (房健), "Wei nongcun hezuo yiliao dasheng jihu" (为农村合作医疗大声疾呼) (Strongly Appeal for the Rural CMS). *Zhongyuan yikan* (中原医刊) (Central Medical Journal), no. 2 (1980): 2.

43. This judgment is based on the articles published in such magazines as *China Health Economics* (Zhongguo weisheng jingji, 中国卫生经济), *Journal of Shanghai Medical University* (Shanghai yike daxue xuebao, 上海医科大学学报), and *China Rural Health Service Management* (Zhongguo nongcun weisheng shiye guanli, 中国农村卫生事业管理).

44. Rural Economy Team of the China Health Economics Association (中国卫生经济学会农村经济组), "Nongcun de yiliao baojian xuqiu yu duice: Disanci quanguo nongcun weisheng jingji xueshu taolunhui zongshu (农村的医疗保健需求与对策: 第三次全国农村卫生经济学术讨论会综述) (Rural Health-Care Demand and Strategy: A Summary of the Third National Rural Health Economics Seminar), *CHE*, no. 1 (1986): 31–35.

45. Chen Fei (陈飞), Zhang Zikuan (张自宽), and Chang Hong'en (昌鸿恩), "'Chijiao yisheng' lailong qumai" ("赤脚医生"来龙去脉) (The Pedigree of Barefoot Doctors), *Jiankangbao* (健康报) (Health News) (November 9, 2007).

46. Li Decheng, "Zhongguo nongcun chuantong hezuo yiliao zhidu yanjiu zongshu."

47. Zhang Zikuan (张自宽), "Zhongguo de chuji weisheng baojian yao zou ziji de lu: 1985 nian 12 yue zai Guangdong Conghua shoujia PHC huiyishang de zongjie fayan" (中国的初级卫生保健要走自己的路: 1985年12月在广东从化首届PHC会议上的总结发言) (China's Primary Health Care Should Take Its Own Path: Summary Remarks at the First PHC Meeting in Conghua, Guangdong Province, December 1985), *CRHM*, no. 5 ([1985] 1993): 1–4; "Zai hezuo yiliao wenti shang ying chengqing sixiang tongyi renshi: 1987 nian 11 yue 19 ri zai quanguo chuji weisheng baojian hezuo zhongxin he nongcun weisheng shifanxian gongzuo huiyishang de zongjie jianghua" (在合作医疗问

题上应澄清思想统一认识: 1987年11月19日在全国初级卫生保健合作中心和农村卫生示范县工作会议上的总结讲话) (Clarify Thoughts and Unify Understanding with Regard to the Cooperative Medical System: Summary Remarks at the Meeting of Primary Medical Health Cooperative Centers and Model County for Rural Health, November 19, 1987), *CRHM*, no. 6 ([1987] 1992): 8–10.

48. Subcommittee of Medicine, Health, and Sports of the CPPCC National Committee (全国政协医药卫生体育委员会), "Guanyu nongcun weisheng gongzuo diaocha baogao" (关于农村卫生工作调查报告) (An Investigative Report on Rural Health Care), *Zhongguo weisheng zhiliang guanli* (中国卫生质量管理) (China Health Quality Management), Supplement 1 (1995): 7–10.

49. Cao Guoming (曹国明), "Dui woguo nongcun yiliao baojian zhidu mingcheng wenti de shangque" (对我国农村医疗保健制度名称问题的商榷) (A Discussion of the Name of China's Rural Health-Care System), *Zhongguo chuji weisheng baojian* (中国初级卫生保健, hereafter *CPH*), no. 10 (1993): 17–18.

50. Zhang Zikuan, "Zai hezuo yiliao wenti shang ying chengqing sixiang tongyi renshi."

51. Zhou Shouqi (周寿祺), "Hezuo yiliao yu jiankang baoxian de bijiao" (合作医疗与健康保险的比较) (A Comparison of the Cooperative Medical System and Health Insurance), *CRHM*, no. 12 (1987): 54–57.

52. Ministry of Health (卫生部) and the State Administration of Traditional Chinese Medicine (国家中医管理局), "'Qiwu'shiqi weisheng gaige tiyao" ("七五" 时期卫生改革提要) (The Outline for Health Reform during the Seventh Five-Year Plan Period), February 14, 1987, at http://www.zhongweiwang.org/health/html/2nd_page/zcfg/ncwswjhb/1951-2000-1-6.php (accessed July 7, 2010).

53. Shan Cretin, Albert P. Williams, and Jeffrey Sine, "China Rural Health Insurance Experiment: Final Report," *RAND Health Working Paper*, WR-411 (2006).

54. Commentator (本刊评论员), "Jiji tansuo he fazhan juyou Zhongguo tese de nongcun yiliao baojian zhidu" (积极探索和发展具有中国特色的农村医疗保健制度) (Actively Explore and Develop a Rural Health-Care System with Unique Chinese Characteristics), *CRHM*, no. 10 (1987): 2–5.

55. Jintan County Health Administration of Jiangsu Province (江苏省金坛县卫生局), "Dui shishi duozhong yiliao baojian zhidu de tansuo (对实施多种医疗保健制度的探索) (An Exploration of Diverse Health-Care Systems), *CRHM*, no. 9 (1987): 37–40.

56. Luo Yiqin (罗益勤), "Woguo nongcun shixing jiankang baoxian wenti de yanjiu" (我国农村实行健康保险问题的研究) (A Study of the Problems Facing Rural Health Insurance in China). *CPH*, no. 4 (1989): 2–7.

57. Li Xile (李希乐) and Shao Bingxiao (邵炳孝), "Cong hezuo yiliao yu yiliao baoxian de yitong kan woguo nongcun yiliao baojian zhidu gaige de celüe" (从合作医疗与医疗保险的异同看我国农村医疗保健制度改革的策略) (Assessing China's Rural Health-Care System Reform Policy Based on a Comparison of the CMS and Health Insurance), *CRHM*, no. 12 (1994): 1–3.

58. Hu Xintai (忽新泰) et al., "Weisheng baojian zhidu de gaige" (卫生保健制度的改革) (Health-Care System Reform), *CHE*, no. 10 (1987): 4–8.

59. Cheng Yunfei (程云飞) and Zhang Chengmo (张承模), "Qianlun 'fengxianxing' nongcun yiliao baoxian zhidu" (浅论 "风险型" 农村医疗保险制度) (An Analysis of a

"Risk-Oriented" Rural Health Insurance System), *Zhongguo weisheng shiye guanli* (中国卫生事业管理) (China Health Service Management), no. 5 (1987): 38–41.

60. Jintan County Health Administration, "Dui shishi duozhong yiliao baojian zhidu de tansuo."

61. Cai Shengga (才生嘎), "Wei jianli juyou Zhongguo tese de shehui yiliao baoxian zhidu er nuli" (为建立具有中国特色的社会医疗保险制度而努力) (Strive to Establish a Social Medical Insurance System with Chinese Characteristics), *CRHM*, no. 10 (1987): 5–6.

62. Research Group (系列研究课题组), "Nongcun hezuo yiliao baojian zhidu de xilie yanjiu" (农村合作医疗保健制度的系列研究) (Systematic Research on the Rural CMS), *CHE*, no. 4 (1988): 13–19.

63. Research Task Force of China's Rural Medical and Health-Care System (中国农村医疗保健制度研究课题组), *Zhongguo nongcun yiliao baojian zhidu yanjiu* (中国农村医疗保健制度研究) (A Study of China's Rural Health-Care System) (Shanghai: Shanghai kexue jishu chubanshe, 1991).

64. Zhou Shouqi, "Hezuo yiliao yu jiankang baoxian de bijiao." These surveys were published in journals such as *Chinese Health Economics* (*Zhongguo weisheng jingji*, 中国卫生经济), *China Primary Health Care* (*Zhongguo chuji weisheng baojian*, 中国初级卫生保健), *China Rural Health Service Management* (*Zhongguo nongcun weisheng shiye guanli*, 中国农村卫生事业管理), *China Hospital Management* (*Zhongguo yiyuan guanli*, 中国医院管理), and *China Village Doctors* (*Zhongguo xiangcun yisheng zazhi*, 中国乡村医生杂志).

65. Wu Yanming (吴雁鸣) et al., "Guanyu nongcun weisheng gaige de sikao: Yu weisheng juzhang tantao jige remen huati" (关于农村卫生改革的思考: 与卫生局长探讨几个热门话题) (Thoughts on Rural Health Reform: Discussing Hot Topics with Health Bureau Directors), *CRHM*, no. 7 (1988): 1–6.

66. Zhu Aorong (朱敖荣), "Hezuo yiliao: Dangqian nongcun weisheng gaige de guanjian" (合作医疗: 当前农村卫生改革的关键) (The Cooperative Medical System: The Key to Rural Health Reform), *CRHM*, no. 1 (1988): 51–54.

67. Many grassroots medical practitioners opposed replacing the CMS with health insurance. Miao Baoying (缪宝迎) and Wang Zhenhuan (王振环), "Danchun fengxianxing hezuo yiliao buyi tichang" (单纯风险型合作医疗不宜提倡) (A Pure Risk-Oriented CMS Should Not Be Promoted), *CPH*, no. 9 (1991): 9–10.

68. Li Peng (李鹏), "Guanyu guomin jingji he shehui fazhan shinian guihua he dibage wunian jihua gangyao de baogao" (关于国民经济和社会发展十年规划和第八个五年计划纲要的报告) (Report on the Outline of the Ten-Year Program and the Eighth Five-Year Plan for National Economic and Social Development), March 25, 1991, at http://www.sdpc.gov.cn/fzgh/ghwb/gjjh/P020070912638549139165.pdf (accessed July 7, 2010).

69. "Bianzhe an" (编者按) (Editor's Note), *CRHM*, no. 12 (1991): 1.

70. Zhu Aorong (朱敖荣), Wu Yanming (吴雁鸣), and Ye Yide (叶宜德), "Chongzhen hezuo yiliao baojian zhidu" (重振合作医疗保健制度) (Rejuvenating the CMS), *CRHM*, no. 12 (1991): 19–24.

71. Zhou Shouqi (周寿祺), "Zhongguo nongcun jiankang baozhang zhidu zongshu" (中国农村健康保障制度综述) (An Overview of China's Rural Health Security System), *Zhongguo yiyao guanli* (中国医药管理) (China Medical Management), no. 5 (1990): 5–8.

72. Bo Xianfeng (薄先锋) and Dong Jianzhen (董践真), "Huilaiba! Hezuo yiliao" (回来吧！合作医疗) (Come Back! CMS), *Zhongguo gaige* (中国改革) (China Reform), no. 2 (1993): 46–48.

73. Ministry of Health (卫生部), "Guanyu shenhua weisheng gaige de jidian yijian" (关于深化卫生改革的几点意见) (Opinions on the Deepening of Health Reform), September 23, 1992, at http://www.chinabaike.com/law/zy/bw/gw/wsb/1359988.html (accessed July 7, 2010).

74. Zhi Junbo (支峻波), "Shenhua weisheng gaige de fangxiang renwu yu zhengce" (深化卫生改革的方向、任务与政策) (The Direction, Task, and Policy of Deepening Health Reform), *Yixue lilun yu shijian* (医学理论与实践) (Medical Theory and Practice), no. 3 (1992): 1–4.

75. Yuan Mu (袁木) and Chen Minzhang (陈敏章), "Jiakuai nongcun hezuo yiliao baojian zhidu de gaige he jianshe" (加快农村合作医疗保健制度的改革和建设) (Speeding Up the Reform and Construction of the Rural CMS), *Renmin ribao* (July 2, 1994).

76. Peng Peiyun (彭佩云), "Zai quanguo nongcun hezuo yiliao jingyan jiaoliu huishang de jianghua" (在全国农村合作医疗经验交流会上的讲话) (Speech at the Nationwide Exchange on the Experience of the Cooperative Medical System), *CRHM*, no. 8 (1996): 1–2.

77. Chen Minzhang (陈敏章), "Guanche luoshi zhongyang guanyu fazhan he wanshan nongcun hezuo yiliao de zhongda juece: Zai quanguo nongcun hezuo yiliao jingyan jiaoliu huishang de jianghua" (贯彻落实中央关于发展和完善农村合作医疗的重大决策：在全国农村合作医疗经验交流会上的讲话) (Implementing the Key Decisions of the Central Government on Developing and Improving the Rural CMS: Speech at the Nationwide Exchange on the Experience of the CMS), *CRHM*, no. 8 (1996): 7–11.

78. Medical Administration Division, Ministry of Health (卫生部医政司), "Nongcun hezuo yiliao chuxianle lianghao fazhan shitou" (农村合作医疗出现了良好发展势头) (The Rural CMS Has Gained New Development Momentum), *CRHM*, no. 2 (1997): 13.

79. CPC Central Committee (中共中央) and State Council (国务院), "Guanyu weisheng gaige yu fazhan de jueding" (关于卫生改革与发展的决定) (Decision on Health Reform and Development), January 15, 1997, at http://www.china.com.cn/chinese/zhuanti/yg/933900.htm (accessed July 7, 2010).

80. Zhang Deyuan (张德元), "Zhongguo nongcun yiliao weisheng shiye de huigu yu sikao" (中国农村医疗卫生事业的回顾与思考) (A Review and Reflection on China's Rural Health Care), *Weisheng jingji yanjiu* (卫生经济研究) (Health Economics Studies), no. 1 (2005): 19–21.

81. Wang Shidong (汪时东) and Ye Yide (叶宜德), "Nongcun hezuo yiliao zhidu de huigu yu fazhan yanjiu" (农村合作医疗制度的回顾与发展研究) (A Review and Study of the Rural CMS), *CPH*, no. 4 (2004): 10–12.

82. Liu Yajing (刘雅静), "Woguo nongcun hezuo yiliao baozhang zhidu de lishi sikao ji zhengce jianyi" (我国农村合作医疗保障制度的历史思考及政策建议) (Historical Thoughts and Policy Recommendations for China's Rural CMS), *Shequ yixue zazhi* (社区医学杂志) (Community Medical Magazine), no. 6 (2004): 37–41.

83. Mao Zehe (毛泽禾), "Gonggu yu wanshan Xizang hezuo yiliao mianlin de wenti yu jiejue duice" (巩固与完善西藏合作医疗面临的问题与解决对策) (Problems and Solutions in Reinforcing and Improving the CMS in Tibet), *Xizang keji* (西藏科技) (Tibet Science and Technology), no. 8 (2002): 4–7.

84. Wang Shaoguang and Hu Angang, *The Chinese Economy in Crisis: State Capacity and Tax Reform* (Armonk, NY: M.E. Sharpe, 2001).

85. CPC Central Committee (中共中央) and State Council (国务院), "Guanyu jinyibu jiaqiang nongcun weisheng gongzuo de jueding" (关于进一步加强农村卫生工作的决定) (Decision on Further Boosting the Rural Health-Care Endeavor), October 19, 2002, at http://news.xinhuanet.com/newscenter/2002-10/29/content_612148.htm (accessed July 7, 2010). It is clearly not true that "rural health reform was only pushed to the top of the national policy agenda when the SARS epidemic in 2003 triggered massive public criticism," as suggested by Heilmann. See Sebastian Heilmann, "Policy Experimentation in China's Economic Rise," *Studies in Comparative International Development*, 43, no. 1 (2008): 1–26.

86. Zhu Qingsheng (朱庆生), "Jiji wentuo di tuijin Zhongguo xinxing nongcun hezuo yiliao zhidu jianshe" (积极稳妥地推进中国新型农村合作医疗制度建设) (Enthusiastically and Safely Promote the Construction of China's NCMS), September 17, 2004, at http://www.labournet.com.cn/28jie/0917–5.htm (accessed September 3, 2010). Some of these features have changed since 2004.

87. Ibid.

88. Wu Yi (吴仪), "Zai 2005 nian quanguo xinxing nongcun hezuo yiliao shidian gongzuo huiyishang de jianghua" (在2005年全国新型农村合作医疗试点工作会议上的讲话) (Speech at the 2005 National NCMS Pilot Work Conference), September 14, 2005, at http://www.gov.cn/ztzl/2006-02/18/content_203770.htm (accessed July 7, 2010).

89. Zhou Tingyu (周婷玉), "2008 nian woguo xin nonghe buzhu biaozhun fanfan fanwei kuoda" (2008年我国新农合补助标准翻番范围扩大) (China Doubles the Rate and Scope of Subsidies for the NCMS), February 15, 2008, at http://news.xinhuanet .com/newscenter/2008-02/15/content_7610807.htm (accessed July 7, 2010). The Chinese government announced in January 2009 that the government subsidy for each NCMS participant would increase to 120 RMB by 2011. "Guowuyuan tongguo yigai fang'an 3 niannei yuji touru 8500 yiyuan" (国务院通过医改方案 3年内预计投入 8500亿元) (The State Council Passes a Plan for Health Reform; Within Three Years It Is Planned That 850 Billion Yuan Will Be Invested), Xinhua Net, January 21, 2009, at http://news.xinhuanet.com/newscenter/2009-01/21/content_10698250.htm (accessed July 7, 2010).

90. National Bureau of Statistics, "Statistical Communiqué of the People's Republic of China on the 2009 National Economic and Social Development," February 25, 2010, at http://www.stats.gov.cn/english/newsandcomingevents/t20100226_402623115.htm (accessed July 7, 2010).

91. Zou Lixing (邹力行) and Meng Jianguo (孟建国), "Yinni Taiguo Feilubin nongcun jiankang baozhang zhidu ji dui women de qishi" (印尼、泰国、菲律宾农村健康保障制度及对我们的启示) (The Rural Health Security Systems of Indonesia, Thailand, and the Philippines and Their Implications), *CHE*, no. 8 (1995): 56–57; Yang Huifang (杨惠芳) and Chen Caigeng (陈才庚), "Moxige he Baxi de nongcun yiliao

baoxian zhidu ji qi dui Zhongguo jianli nongcun xinxing hezuo yiliao zhidu de jidian qishi" (墨西哥和巴西的农村医疗保险制度及其对中国建立农村新型合作医疗制度的几点启示) (The Rural Medical Insurance Systems of Mexico and Brazil and Their Implications for China's Establishment of the Rural NCMS), *Lading Meizhou yanjiu* (拉丁美洲研究) (Studies of Latin America), no. 5 (2004): 50–58.

92. Heilmann, "Policy Experimentation in China's Economic Rise."

93. Yuan Ye and Jiang Guocheng, "China Unveils Health Care Reform Guidelines," Xinhua News Agency, April 6, 2009, at http://news.xinhuanet.com/english/2009-04/06/content_11138643.htm (accessed July 7, 2010).

94. Shaoguang Wang, "China's Double Movement in Health Care," in Leo Panitch and Colin Leys, eds., *Social Register: Morbid Symptoms: Health under Capitalism* (Pontypool: Merlin, 2009), pp. 240–261.

95. National Bureau of Statistics, "Statistical Communiqué of the People's Republic of China on the 2009 National Economic and Social Development."

CHAPTER 5

Governing Civil Society: Adapting Revolutionary Methods to Serve Post-Communist Goals

NARA DILLON

One of the most noteworthy developments of the post-Mao era has been the rapid growth of a new sector of voluntary associations, non-profits, and other kinds of intermediate organizations. Over the last thirty years, this sector has grown to include private charities, recreational groups, advocacy organizations, trade associations, and scholarly groups, such as the Chinese Shakespeare Association. By 2003, more than 266,000 voluntary associations and non-profits were registered with the state, and the total number of state-sponsored, registered and unregistered organizations was estimated to exceed 8 million.[1] Clearly, this new arena for social interaction, service provision, and political participation has been enthusiastically embraced by millions of Chinese. Moreover, some of these organizations have managed to make an impact on the policy-making process in areas as diverse as economic policy, family planning, and environmental protection.[2]

Because most Communist regimes, including China, eliminated all non-governmental organizations not sponsored by the party-state, the rise of this new organizational sector represents an important form of regime change from the Maoist to the reform era. This gradual regime change has captured the attention of activists and scholars alike, eager to understand its significance and especially its potential for engendering further political reform. But if there is agreement that contemporary China has gradually moved away from an archetypical Communist regime over the last thirty years, there is much less agreement about the kind of regime toward which China is evolving.

Debates have emerged both within China and without over whether these new organizations comprise an incipient civil society. The shadow of 1989 has added urgency to this debate. Are China's voluntary associations becoming strong enough to push for further political reform, perhaps even something akin to the velvet revolutions of Eastern Europe in 1989 or the color revolutions in parts of the former Soviet Union in the 2000s? Or is China evolving into the limited pluralism of a more ordinary authoritarian regime, such as the kind of state corporatism once common in authoritarian Europe, Latin America, and the Middle East?[3]

Among the issues at stake in this debate is the fundamental question of how the new organizational sector should be conceptualized. The most commonly used term to describe it is "civil society." Although this popularity argues for its continued use, the concept has also provoked controversy. The concept was originally developed to analyze the rise of voluntary associations and informal groups independent from state authority in the West, which many consider a vital prerequisite for the political transformations that followed, especially democratization. As a result, many scholars argue that autonomy from the state is a defining characteristic of civil society.[4] Given this formulation, many question whether the concept travels well to other times and places. Since few, if any, of China's new voluntary associations and non-profits are truly autonomous from the state, characterizing them as a civil society seems premature. Indeed, many question whether China has ever had anything approaching a civil society.[5] Similar concerns about conceptual stretching have arisen over terms such as the public sphere and non-governmental organizations (NGOs).

Rather than reconceptualize civil society or these other terms, I will use the more neutral term "voluntary sector" to describe China's voluntary associations and non-profits, leaving their relationship to the state an open question. The voluntary sector lies between the state on the one hand and the private sector comprised of for-profit corporations on the other.[6] As for the organizations themselves, literal translations of Chinese terms for these organizations are not immediately recognizable in English, and their acronyms are even more confusing. To use more colloquial terms, I will refer to "social organizations" (*shehui tuanti*, 社会团体) and "popular organizations" (*minjian zuzhi*, 民间组织) as voluntary associations, and "non-governmental, non-commercial enterprises" (*minban feiqiye danwei*, 民办非企业单位) as non-profits.

Another key issue in the debate over the nature and direction of China's regime transition is the regulatory system governing the voluntary sector.

Issued in the wake of the 1989 Tiananmen Uprising, both the timing and the content of the new regulations clearly suggest that one of the Chinese Communist Party's (CCP's) goals is to prevent the voluntary sector from turning into a civil society, and ultimately a force for further political reform. Consequently, the effectiveness of the new administrative system established to supervise the voluntary sector has been viewed as an important indicator of state strength.

At this point, scrutiny of the new regulatory system has yielded contradictory assessments. On the one hand, when scholars examine the regulatory process, they come to the conclusion that the new bureaucracy is quite weak: it is understaffed, internally divided, and inconsistent. From this perspective, the new regulatory system has been only partially implemented and the goals of the new policy are far more ambitious than the capacity of the party-state to achieve them.[7] On the other hand, when scholars turn to evaluate the outcomes of this new policy, the overall assessment is that the new system is quite effective. The party-state has been able to promote favored sectors and organizations while constraining sectors and organizations that do not match its priorities.[8] Moreover, the vast majority of these new organizations have been careful to avoid challenging party rule, whether they are subject to regulation or not.[9] Some scholars reconcile this contradiction by arguing that these policies have stunted the healthy growth of the voluntary sector, which otherwise would have developed faster and stronger.

Although there is no doubt a great deal of truth to this counterfactual argument, it still leaves the existing contradiction between the weakness of the regulatory process and the effectiveness of the policy outcome unexplained. This contradiction helps fuel the debate over the future direction of the voluntary sector. The limits of the regulatory system give hope to those who see civil society beginning to form in China, whereas widespread compliance with, and even support of, CCP rule in the voluntary sector leads others to suspect that a more authoritarian voluntary sector is gradually being consolidated.

At this early point, the hypotheses advanced to account for the contradiction between China's voluntary sector regulatory process and the outcomes are tentative. One possibility is that the regulations are less important in achieving compliance from voluntary organizations than other factors, such as the political culture or the level of socio-economic development. Another possibility is that the current contradiction is simply a temporary phenomenon — a pause while these new organizations gather strength and direction

— that will eventually give way to a more openly confrontational relationship between state and society.[10] But I think we should not overlook a simpler, more straightforward hypothesis: perhaps we have misunderstood the nature of the regulatory process, and it is more effective than it appears. Perhaps the power of the Chinese state does not lie in its bureaucratic structure, but rather in the modes of governance that promote cooperation and inhibit defiance. From this perspective, we need to examine more than policy-making and institutional development to understand the balance of power between state and society — we also need to examine the implementation process.

If we temporarily set aside the larger debate about civil society to focus on explaining the seeming contradiction between process and outcome in China's regulation of the voluntary sector, cross-national comparisons to democratic pluralist and authoritarian-state corporatist regimes are not very useful. The cultural and socio-economic conditions in China and in the rest of the former Communist world are vastly different, not to mention other authoritarian regimes elsewhere. But if we shift from a comparative to a historical perspective, we can examine these various hypotheses under much more comparable cultural, political, and socio-economic conditions.

This chapter is composed of four parts. The first section examines the last historical period when China had a significant voluntary sector: the revolutionary period of the 1940s and 1950s, when both the Nationalist and Communist regimes struggled to control the unruly voluntary organizations during that time. The second part of the chapter compares contemporary Chinese policy toward the voluntary sector to these historical precedents, noting similarities to the earlier Nationalist approach to governing the voluntary sector. The third section compares contemporary implementation of these new policies to these historical precedents, this time drawing parallels to the revolutionary Communist approach to governing the voluntary sector. The final section returns to the question of regime change, sketching out the political implications of the hybrid mode of governance that has been developing in the post-Mao period.

Historical Comparisons: Regulating China's Voluntary Sector in the 1940s and 1950s

During the Republican period and into the early years of the Communist revolution, many Chinese cities boasted large and vibrant voluntary sectors. There are significant parallels in state-society relations between this

revolutionary period and the contemporary era. For example, the Nationalist regime (1928–49) tried to implement a comprehensive form of state
corporatism similar in many ways to the current system for business associations and labor unions. The peak of these efforts came during and after
World War II, when the Nationalist regime imposed emergency powers over
the voluntary sector, established a Ministry of Social Affairs, and enacted
a wide range of legislation to regulate and incorporate voluntary organizations.[11] In addition, Republican China's mixed economy has many parallels
to the contemporary period, with state-owned enterprises operating in private markets open to the world economy.

The Nationalists' approach to regulating the voluntary sector and incorporating key interest groups can be summarized as *legalistic*. The strategy was
premised on establishing a clear set of rules for establishing and operating
voluntary organizations. These laws and regulations established an institutional framework for ongoing party/state supervision of voluntary organizations' leadership, policies, and finances through the registration process
and ongoing reporting requirements.[12] The process was also *bureaucratic*: the
Ministry of Social Affairs was charged with organizing specialized divisions
to carry out this ongoing supervision and to enforce the laws and regulations when they were violated. In addition, the scope of these laws and
regulations was *comprehensive*, applying to all formal voluntary organizations
and establishing the state's power to define jurisdictions and to assess
needs.

Although this strategy toward regulating civil society may seem unexcep-
tional for a state corporatist regime like that of the Nationalists, the Nationalists' failure to control the voluntary sector during the Chinese Civil War
suggests how difficult effective regulation can be for a weak and divided
ruling party. The Communists and other labor activists were not only able to
undermine the Guomindang's (GMD's) control over the labor movement to
spark a major strike wave from 1946 to 1949, but even the official commercial and industrial associations rejected the economic controls that the
Nationalist regime tried to enforce in 1948.[13] Less dramatic than these political failures, the vast new regulatory process also failed to constrain the rapid
growth of private charities or exert much direction over their programs or
finances in the late 1940s. In important cities like Shanghai, registrations
were carried out and extensive reports were filed, but the GMD's regulatory
process made few if any changes in the operations of the city's voluntary
sector.[14]

At the most basic level, the profound failures of the GMD in the late 1940s caution us to not take the relative success of the CCP's contemporary regulatory process for granted. But the failures of the GMD also provide a rough test for some of our hypotheses about the contemporary regulatory system. First, they suggest that cultural arguments about the role of Confucianism or respect for authority in inhibiting the development of civil society may be overstated. Similarly, much lower levels of economic and social development during the 1940s did not constrain voluntary organizations and induce them to cooperate with the state. Instead, the GMD example suggests that when socio-economic and political conditions are deteriorating, voluntary associations, even those incorporated into the state, can change quickly and come out in opposition to the ruling party.

The failures of the GMD also suggest that we should look to the CCP's own revolutionary history for alternative approaches to managing the voluntary sector. Although the CCP was initially hostile to all voluntary organizations beyond its own mass organizations, the Second Sino-Japanese War led to new United Front policies that were much more moderate and supportive of private voluntary, even bourgeois, organizations. For more than fifteen years from 1937 to the early 1950s, the CCP followed its so-called "New Democracy" policy of seeking to cooperate with the voluntary sector.[15] Although this New Democracy policy was portrayed as transitional, the length of the transition and the ultimate fate of the voluntary sector were never made clear at the time, giving hope even to the leaders of middle-class and upper-class organizations, such as native-place associations and private charities, that they would find a place in New China.

The CCP's New Democracy policy toward the voluntary sector bore the mark of GMD influence, resulting in considerable continuity before and after the 1949 Communist takeover. The State Administrative Council issued its "Provisional Methods for Registering Voluntary Organizations" in 1950, banning all counter-revolutionary organizations and requiring all private organizations to register with the state and submit annual reports on personnel, activities, and finances.[16] Since private organizations had operated under similar (albeit more stringent) GMD regulations since 1929, many, if not most, welcomed the new regulations and immediately sought to register.[17]

The People's Republic of China (PRC) also created corporatist institutions similar in many ways to Nationalist precedents. In addition to establishing official labor unions and business federations and giving them reserved seats in the Chinese People's Political Consultative Conference and the local people's congresses, the CCP also tried to incorporate other kinds of voluntary associations and non-profits. In 1950 Song Qingling helped establish the People's Welfare League, a national federation of private charities, native place associations, and other organizations that provided public services. Similar to the Nationalists' Social Welfare Federation, the membership of the PRC's China People's Welfare League (*Zhongguo renmin jiuji hui*) consisted of organizations rather than individuals. In addition, it carried out most of the government supervision required under the 1950 regulations, such as reviewing annual reports, implementing policy changes, and policing its members.[18]

Although on paper these Communist policies and institutions seem to be less stringent versions of GMD policies, the reality is far more complicated. In many places, even cities with large voluntary sectors like Shanghai, registration was repeatedly delayed despite the entreaties of organizational leaders. Institutions like the Chinese People's Welfare League were established and their leaders were active, even enthusiastic about carrying out their responsibilities in governing the voluntary sector, but they were also overwhelmed by the scale of the task.

Despite the similarities in policies and institutions, the CCP's method of regulating the voluntary sector differed fundamentally from that of the GMD. Where the GMD approach was *legalistic,* the CCP strategy was *political.* The difference between legalistic and political approaches to governance is profound. For example, the GMD spent much of the Second Sino-Japanese War issuing a lengthy series of laws and regulations detailing all aspects of the voluntary sector and its relationship to the party-state. When the GMD returned to rule China's major cities in 1945, this elaborate legal infrastructure was already in place. In contrast, the CCP did not issue general guidelines on the New Democracy policy toward the voluntary sector until 1950, and even then only on a provisional basis.[19] Instead, speeches by party leaders, reports by cadres, work conferences, and short statements of principle developed for propaganda efforts defined the CCP's flexible and changing policy toward the voluntary sector. This flexible, political approach to policy-making created and exploited ambiguity — in many ways the opposite of the GMD legalistic effort to clarify and specify the rules of the game.

For example, the CCP's 1950 guidelines called for registering all voluntary organizations, just as the Nationalist government had required for decades. But under the Communists, this key step in the regulatory process was repeatedly postponed. Rather than a sign of the weakness of the new state, the failure to register voluntary organizations actually weakened the voluntary sector. One sign of the power of the ambiguity was that the surge in organizing activity that reached a crescendo in the late 1940s in Shanghai came to a complete halt in 1950, when the last new voluntary organization was founded, an orphanage in a Buddhist temple. Clearly, the GMD registration process was not as much of an obstacle to the growth of the voluntary sector as the CCP's lack of a registration process.[20]

More important than registration laws or corporatist institutions, mass campaigns were the key to Communist governance of the voluntary sector in the 1950s. A series of struggle campaigns against a succession of carefully selected targets eliminated potential sources of political opposition in the voluntary sector and at the same time fostered compliance from the surviving organizations. First targeting organizations with American connections during the Korean War, the CCP had little difficulty in mobilizing other voluntary associations and non-profits to drum up patriotic sentiment and anti-imperialist outrage to take over American-financed schools, hospitals, and orphanages.[21] The second major struggle campaign in the voluntary sector, the Campaign to Suppress Counter-Revolutionaries (*zhenya fandong yundong*, 镇压反动运动) overlapped with the anti-American campaign. This bloody campaign targeted organizations with connections to the GMD, organized crime, and religious groups perceived to be hostile to communism, such as the Yiguandao.[22]

The most important mass campaign related to the voluntary sector was a series of anti-corruption campaigns that began with the Three-Antis Movement (*sanfan yundong*, 三反运动) in 1952. By gradually targeting organizations accused of corruption, these campaigns eventually "reformed" all private voluntary associations and non-profits out of operation. The end-result was that only official, state-sponsored groups such as the official labor union and the Red Cross remained.[23] By the time the socialization campaign was launched in January 1956, there were few private organizations left to face revolutionary struggle, and those that did were hollow shells.[24]

The CCP managed to induce the voluntary sector to eliminate itself over the course of the early 1950s without provoking the kind of armed opposition that many other Communist revolutionaries faced after their revolutions. Clearly, formal laws and institutions cannot account for this kind of compliance and cooperation. Instead, we need to look to the CCP's campaign practices to find an explanation. One critical element of these campaigns was their *selectivity*. In each round, the majority of organizations was mobilized to struggle against a disliked minority, whether American missionaries or organized crime. The campaigns fostered solidarity within

impact of the various anti-campaigns

the majority, inhibiting the ability of the targeted organizations to make alliances and organize resistance. Furthermore, the campaigns created clear individual incentives to support state policy in order to avoid becoming future targets.[25] In addition to these political benefits, selectivity was also important for minimizing the administrative burden on the fledgling Communist party-state, which did not have sufficient staff to monitor the voluntary sector effectively, much less to dismantle it.

A second key ingredient to make struggle campaigns an effective means of governing the voluntary sector was their attack on the *legitimacy* of the target organizations. Whether aimed at the imperialistic attitudes of American missionaries, the cult practices of new religions like the Yiguandao, or charges of corruption against bourgeois philanthropists, the campaigns undermined these groups' often considerable social prestige well before they made any attempts to eliminate them. As a result, the campaigns severely limited the ability of these organizations to mobilize political support in their defense from the broader public.

Just as important in preventing collective resistance to CCP policies was the way in which the campaigns fostered *uncertainty*. The episodic nature of the mass campaigns, combined with little or no foreshadowing of future targets (and little information about the CCP's long-term plans for the voluntary sector) created considerable ambiguity. The lack of a legal basis or institutionalized process for these campaigns had a similar effect. As a result, participants in these campaigns had to learn the rules of the game from experience. Since the rules changed in each campaign, the survivors of earlier campaigns could not necessarily translate their hard-won lessons to new circumstances.

So although the CCP continued the legal and institutional infrastructure created by the GMD, it was the signature Communist struggle campaign that proved to be the most effective instrument for exerting political control over the voluntary sector. Selectivity, concerns about legitimacy, and uncertainty gave the thinly staffed new state bureaucracies of the early PRC considerable leverage over the large and well-established voluntary sector it had inherited from the Nationalist government. In contrast to this political strategy for governing the voluntary sector, the GMD's legalistic approach was comprehensive and bureaucratic, seeking to institutionalize and standardize state control over the entire sector. The result enhanced certainty for the voluntary associations and non-profits, giving them the ability to forge alliances and draw on support from the larger society when they encountered open conflict with the GMD in the late 1940s.

This kind of historical comparison of Chinese authoritarian and Communist regimes highlights a major difference that is often obscured in cross-national comparisons of regime-type: political vs. legalistic approaches to governance. Because most analyses of the voluntary sector's role in different kinds of political regimes developed first out of a comparison of authoritarian and democratic regimes, the analyses focus on the extent of state regulation as a key distinguishing feature. In other words, more regulation (and/or more effective enforcement) is considered more authoritarian, whereas less regulation (or less effective enforcement) is categorized as more democratic or pluralistic. This common-sense distinction obscures the fact that democratic and authoritarian regimes actually share an important characteristic: both define the relationship between the state and the voluntary sector in law. From this point of view, Communist regimes are distinctive not only for suppressing most of the voluntary sector, but also for adopting political strategies rather than legalistic approaches to governing the remaining vestiges of the voluntary sector after the revolution.

The Development of the PRC's Contemporary Policies toward the Voluntary Sector

When the CCP eased up on its political controls over society in the late 1970s and early 1980s, the minimal regulatory framework of the 1950s was still in place, even if elements of it, such as the regulations for religious groups and bourgeois organizations, had fallen into disuse during the Maoist period. After the rapid expansion of the voluntary sector under the old rules in the 1980s, the CCP gradually established a more comprehensive and more detailed regulatory system in the 1990s that bears striking parallels to the GMD's legalistic approach to voluntary-sector governance of the 1940s.

Early in the post-Mao reform period, people were slow to trust the new political freedoms they had been granted with the decisions to abandon class labels and struggle campaigns. Initially, few people stepped forward to revive old organizations or establish new ones. In the 1980s Deng Xiaoping reportedly personally met with surviving members of the Industrial and Commercial Federation to encourage them to revive the organization.[26] But as people saw that the rules of the game had changed, the number of new voluntary organizations quickly began to snowball in the mid-1980s.

The minimal regulatory framework inherited from the 1950s institutionalized the political hierarchy of the revolutionary period in China's new reform-era voluntary sector. At the top of the hierarchy are the official mass

Political hierarchy

organizations established and sponsored by the Communist party-state. The official youth league, trade unions, and women's federation have many of the privileges and official functions commonly found in Communist and state corporatist regimes. For example, the chairmen of the Communist Youth League and the All-China Federation of Trade Unions usually serve on the CCP Politburo, and their organizations have official roles in implementing state policy and providing services to their members. At the local levels, neighborhood groups such as residents' committees and village committees are simultaneously extensions of the local state and voluntary organizations important to local activists.

Next in the hierarchy come the official religious associations for the five sanctioned religions. Like their more privileged counterparts, these groups were officially established by the party-state to help the state regulate religious practice. But because religious groups are politically suspect, they are subject to far more state control than official mass organizations. For example, even temples, mosques, or churches that are members of the official religious associations have to register with the state Bureau of Religious Affairs.

Most new voluntary associations and non-profits in China's contemporary voluntary sector do not enjoy the privileges or protections of the official organizations established and sponsored by the Communist party-state, and therefore they rank lower in the political hierarchy of the voluntary sector. The bottom rung in this hierarchy is comprised of all the informal and illegal groups that are not registered with the state and have no legal status. Although estimates of the size of these groups are obviously difficult to hazard, most scholars agree that they vastly outnumber the upper ranks of the voluntary sector.[27]

The original 1950 regulations for voluntary organizations mandated that all voluntary associations and non-profit groups register with the state. The considerable gap between these minimal regulations from the New Democracy period and the new circumstances of the post-Mao reforms left considerable room for organizational entrepreneurs to operate. For example, the 1950 regulations mandated that national organizations register with the central Interior Ministry, which was abolished in a 1956 government reorganization drive. Similarly, since the procedures and standards for registration were not specified in the original regulations, wide variation in registration policies developed at the local and provincial levels. In practice, voluntary associations and non-profits registered with any government agency that would approve them.[28]

Even if the regulatory system inherited from the 1950s did not function as planned, it did serve to reestablish some of the key political divisions that helped the Communists splinter any potential political opposition from forming in the voluntary sector during the revolution. The stakes may no longer be as high, since the CCP now actively fosters the development of the voluntary sector rather than trying to suppress and eliminate it. But the legal and institutional divisions created by the registration system do inhibit cooperation across these lines. For example, faith-based non-profits that provide social services to people of different faiths must register with local governments as voluntary organizations and are prohibited from any kind of religious education. At the same time, temples or churches that provide services must register their programs with the official "Three-Self" religious associations and the Bureau of Religious Affairs and must limit their services only to members.[29]

The move toward a more legalistic governance strategy over the voluntary sector gathered momentum in the late 1980s. In 1987, the CCP established a drafting committee to revise the 1950 regulations and to tighten up this loose regulatory framework.[30] New regulations, issued in October 1989 in the wake of the Tiananmen Uprising, provided new tools to crack down on the voluntary sector.[31] The 1989 revisions updated the political ban included in the 1950 regulations: threats to national unity replaced counter-revolutionary crimes as the ultimate prohibition (Article 3). An extra layer of registration was added, creating a dual registration system. In addition to finding a sponsoring agency in the same field, voluntary associations also were required to register with the Ministry of Civil Affairs at the same level of the government hierarchy (Article 6–8). This dual registration process was an important step in creating a bureaucratic monitoring system within the Ministry of Civil Affairs. Finally, organizational monopolies were extended to all voluntary-sector organizations (not only the official mass organizations), with only one organization allowed in any one field and in any one political jurisdiction (Article 16).

Another round of policy changes toward the voluntary sector was launched in 1996, when Jiang Zemin convened the first meeting of the Politburo Standing Committee on NGOs.[32] This policy review contributed to the strategy announced at the CCP's 1997 Fifteenth National Congress aimed at reducing the government's administrative burden and streamlining the bureaucracy, known as the "Small Government, Big Society" (*xiao zhengfu, da shehui*, 小政府, 大社会) policy.[33] The goal of this new strategy was to shift many government functions to the voluntary sector, making the voluntary organizations an integral, even necessary, part of China's political future.

During the drafting process for the new regulations, disagreements emerged over the direction of voluntary-sector reform.[34] Officials in the Ministry of Civil Affairs pushed to end dual registration by eliminating the requirement that organizations must have the sponsorship of a line agency. They argued that this requirement imposed a heavy administrative burden that the line agencies were ill equipped to perform. The argument for streamlining the registration process was countered by the General Secretary of the State Council, Luo Gan, who asserted that the goal of the revision was to tighten control over the voluntary sector, not to loosen it.

As a result, the 1998 Voluntary Organization Registration and Management Regulations maintained the same structure of control, but provided much more clarity and specificity in definitions, procedures, and division of responsibilities between the sponsoring agencies and the Ministry of Civil Affairs. In particular, the new regulations clarified jurisdictional issues in maintaining organizational monopolies, such as prohibiting national and regional organizations from operating subsidiary branch organizations (Articles 19, 33). In addition, for the first time the regulations imposed minimum membership and financial standards, ensuring that without significant reform the small, financially weak organizations would lose their registration (Article 10). This provision stands out as the one major exception to the reform-era push toward defining the rules of the game more clearly and more specifically. Creating minimum standards for registration made the scope of the 1998 regulations more selective rather than more comprehensive.

In comparison to the regulations and institutions of the 1950s, however, these reform-era policies put much greater emphasis on using the law to define the rules of the game, as well as to institutionalize the increasing numbers and kinds of political controls. Corporatism has been revived and extended, and new bureaucracies have been created to monitor and regulate unincorporated organizations. The new reform-era policies toward the voluntary sector are not as thoroughly legalistic as those of the GMD in the 1940s, but they are clearly very different in nature and intent from the CCP's Maoist-era political strategies. Of course, the greatest change from the 1950s to the 1990s is the assumption underpinning these voluntary-sector strategies. In the 1950s, the ultimate goal was to eliminate the voluntary sector entirely, leaving only the continuation of revolutionary mass organizations. In the 1990s, the ultimate goal was to make the voluntary sector a

permanent partner with the state in order to relieve the state of its administrative burdens.

Implementing Voluntary-Sector Policy: Rectification Reviews

Although contemporary CCP policy may be much more legalistic,
implementation of these new policies is still very political. If anything, the
connections between the revolutionary period in the 1940s and 1950s and
the post-Mao reform period are more direct in terms of implementation
than in terms of policy-making. Although China's voluntary sector disappeared in the mid-1950s, revolutionary modes of governance continued in
the surviving official mass organizations. China's Leninist labor unions, for
example, were forced to toe the party line through major struggle campaigns
such as the Anti-Rightist Campaign and the Cultural Revolution.[35] Mass
campaigns are now relatively rare and do not feature the direct, personal
confrontations that made the struggle campaigns so effective in eliciting
compliance, but non-bureaucratic, revolutionary modes of governance are
still quite common.

For example, "rectification" (*qingli zhengdun*, 清理整顿) reviews have
been used to implement every major policy change in the voluntary sector in
the 1990s and 2000s.[36] The rectification review process is largely a reform-
era innovation that is used widely in many policy arenas besides the voluntary sector, from family planning to business regulation.[37] But the processes
of "cleaning up" (*qingli*, 清理) and "reforming" (*zhengdun*, 整顿) have been
central to mass campaigns since the revolutionary period. "Cleaning up"
entails purging people or organizations deemed incapable of complying
with state policy, whereas "reforming" involves changing organizations to
meet state standards.

Thus, these rectification reviews continue certain key campaign practices.
At the most basic level, they are episodic — defined by process rather
than institutional structure. These reviews typically begin by establishing
"leadership small groups" (*lingdao xiaozu*, 领导小组) under the direction of
the party secretary and the head of the government (or their deputies) and
mobilizing officials from all related party and government bureaucracies.[38]
Rectification reviews often feature propaganda work to publicize policy
changes among government officials, voluntary organization staff, and the
broader public. But the propaganda itself is very new. Contemporary propaganda efforts are more likely to be conducted by video conferencing and
press releases than by the public-address systems and the small groups of

the Maoist era. Moreover, contemporary propaganda slogans, such as the "Three Disconnects" (*san tuogou*, 三脱钩) and the "Five Linkages" (*wuge jiehe*, 五个结合), sound more like mottos written by accountants rather than revolutionaries.[39]

Rectification reviews often start with local test-runs to experiment with protocols and techniques.[40] Once the review process is honed, it is then carried out across the rest of the administrative jurisdiction in clearly delineated stages, each with deadlines and targets.[41] Finally, rectification reviews of the voluntary sector have outcomes similar to those of the 1950s mass campaigns: they result in the elimination of relatively large numbers of organizations.

The first major round of rectification reviews in the voluntary sector began in 1990 in the wake of the Tiananmen Uprising and the promulgation of the new registration regulations. Nationwide, between 1989 and 1992 an estimated 59 percent of China's voluntary associations lost their registration. The dual registration process was probably the biggest hurdle, since an estimated 41 percent of the organizations failed to re-apply for registration.[42] The average denial rate for applications was 30 percent, but it varied widely at the local levels, reaching as high as 51 percent in places like Chuansha county in Shanghai municipality.[43] Workers' and students' groups were targeted for elimination, and many other organizations failed to negotiate the dual registration process in the tense political climate following the Tiananmen protests.[44]

The second major round of rectification reviews implemented the 1998 revisions to the registration regulations in 1999–2000.[45] This time around, 26 percent of China's voluntary organizations had their registration revoked. Again, local variation was extreme. At the provincial level, 70 percent of Tianjin's organizations lost their registration, whereas the declines in Zhejiang and Hainan were only 9 percent and 5 percent respectively.[46] In addition to cracking down on qigong associations, this review also targeted religious groups and organizations with foreign connections.[47] The 1999–2000 rectification review not only reduced the size of the voluntary sector, it also changed its composition. Scholarly associations and trade associations became the predominant types of organizations because they were favored for their role in economic development.[48]

Although there were no major policy changes after the 1989 and 1998 regulations, rectification reviews became more common in the 2000s. One reason for the continued use of this method of control is that the policy changes in 1998 were so extensive. For example, many regions only began the process of registering non-profits in 2000–2001.[49] Another reason is that the method is being used to fine-tune government supervision of the voluntary sector by implementing smaller policy changes. For example, a push to disentangle the staff of voluntary associations and their sponsoring agencies began in 2004 and continues today.[50] Even though the issues at stake in the rectification reviews of the 2000s may be smaller, the purges continue. As a result, the reviews are becoming increasingly routine, although the timing, scope, and focus of each review continue to be ad-hoc decisions.

Over the course of the 1990s and 2000s, rectification reviews decisively shaped the development of the voluntary sector, significantly constraining its growth (see Table 5.1). The number of voluntary associations nationwide dropped sharply in the early 1990s, recovered to almost pre-1989 levels

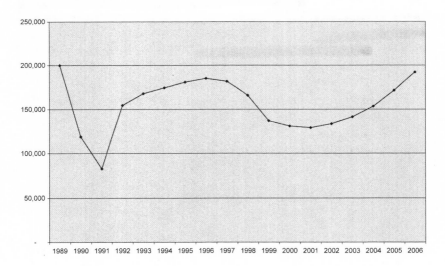

Figure 5.1:

Registered Voluntary Organizations in China, 1989–2006

Sources: Minzheng bu (民政部), ed., *Zhongguo minzheng tongji nianjian 2007* (中国民政统计年鉴2007) (China Civil Affairs Statistical Yearbook 2007) (Beijing: Zhongguo tongji chubanshe, 2007), p. 78; Wang Shaoguang (王绍光) and He Jianyu (何建宇), "Zhongguo de shetuan geming: Zhongguo renmin de jietuan bantu" (中国的社团革命: 中国人民的结团版图) (China's Associational Revolution: Associational Map of Chinese Citizens), *Zhejiang xuekan* (浙江学刊) (Zhejiang Academic Journal), no. 6 (2004): 72; Qiusha Ma, *Non-Governmental Organizations in Contemporary China: Paving the Way to Civil Society?* (New York: Routledge, 2006), p. 66.

in the late 1990s, only to plunge again after the second major round of rectification reviews thereafter.

Despite the increasingly specific regulations in 1989 and 1998 that seemingly limited local discretion, the rectification process still yields significant provincial and local variation. For example, in 2006 the number of voluntary associations in Fujian province was still 13 percent below its 1997 level, whereas Guangxi province's voluntary sector had grown by 66 percent (see Table 5.2). Although Fujian is wealthier, more heavily populated, and more closely integrated with the outside world, Guangxi now boasts a larger voluntary sector. Clearly, political factors are decisively important in shaping China's voluntary sector.

Rectification reviews are obviously not struggle campaigns, or even mass campaigns. They make no effort to mobilize voluntary associations against one another, or to mobilize the support of their members, clients, or the broader public. Yet, even though the reviews are top-down affairs, their impact on the voluntary sector is similar to that of the mass campaigns in several key respects.

First, rectification reviews are *selective*. This claim may seem surprising, given the nationwide reviews carried out in the 1990s. But even those two large-scale reviews only affected registered organizations, leaving the larger number of unregistered groups untouched. Although the exclusion of

[handwritten margin note: How reviews are similar to mass campaigns]

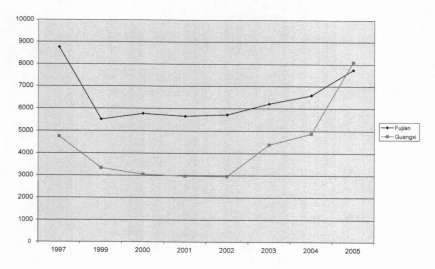

Figure 5.2:
Registered Voluntary Organizations in Fujian and Guangxi, 1987–2005

unregistered organizations was implicit in the way most of these reviews were conducted, in some cases this policy was made explicit. Ji'nan City, for example, instructed its reviewers to ignore the autonomously established non-profits when it began its 2001 review.[51] Another aspect of the selectivity of the review process is that it usually eliminates a minority of the organizations under review.[52] Careful targeting not only enhances the administrative capacity of the understaffed civil affairs' bureaucracy, it also limits the pool of potential resistance in the voluntary sector. As in the Maoist mass campaigns, the majority of organizations has a better chance of surviving the review process by complying with state policy (and seeking powerful patrons) than by banding together to resist change.

Second, rectification reviews are sensitive to the issue of *legitimacy*, even though the prestige of the voluntary sector seems much lower now than it was during the Republican period.[53] For example, the goals of the rectification reviews are often framed in terms of improving the "quality" of the voluntary sector by eliminating inactive and weak organizations.[54] Left unexplained is how these weak organizations affect other voluntary associations or non-profits, much less undermine the entire sector. (Or why unregistered groups do not have a similar effect.) Similarly, the organizations targeted for elimination are often discredited in the press. For example, a rectification review of non-profit kindergartens was recently launched in Xuancheng City of Anhui province.[55] The decision to eliminate unregistered kindergartens was framed as necessary to guarantee safety and educational standards, even though from the outside it is difficult to understand how a two-month paperwork review yields a better evaluation of the kindergartens' services than the parents' day-to-day experience. Furthermore, when challenged regarding specific decisions to revoke an organization's registration, government officials search for ways to bolster their credibility, such as turning to academics for support. For example, when the Ministry of Civil Affairs cancelled the registration of sixty-three innocuous national organizations, such as the Shakespeare Association and the French Cultural Studies Association, for failing to comply with government policy, the director of the NGO Research Center of Qinghua University endorsed the decision, arguing that it showed that government monitoring of the voluntary sector was improving.[56]

Third, rectification reviews create considerable *uncertainty* for the voluntary sector in ways similar to the uncertainty of the mass campaigns. The party-state can launch rectification reviews at any time, for any reason. As a result, these reviews cannot be anticipated, much less planned for.

Considerable discretion is left to the local levels, even in implementing national standards. This discretion not only allows well-connected organizations to emerge unscathed, but it also produces the kinds of local variation described above.[57] However, the most fundamental source of uncertainty in the rectification process is the wholesale suspension of registrations at the outset of the review. Rather than grandfather organizations established under previous regulations or provide a grace period to make the transition, rectification reviews require that organizations re-apply for registration. As a result, the legal status of all voluntary associations and non-profits is open to question by state authorities at any time.

Viewing the rectification process as an integral element in the PRC's reform-era strategy toward the voluntary sector — as important, or more important, than the regulations themselves — helps reconcile some of the contradictions in government policy. The increasing selectivity of the PRC's registration regulations during the reform period no longer seems at odds with the goal of increasing state political control over the voluntary sector. As long as potential threats are targeted, selectivity is a source of political control, rather than a measure of its failure. If selectivity leverages limited state capacity and inhibits collective resistance, the increasingly narrow focus on large organizations that cross state administrative jurisdictions is a more effective approach than trying to regulate all organizations. Similarly, the uncertainties generated by the review process help explain the apparent contradiction between the increasingly complex legal infrastructure for the voluntary sector and the uneven enforcement of those laws. Implementation of the laws is an important, or even more important, source of political control than the layers of oversight they establish.

Although rectification reviews are not mass campaigns, in the reform era the CCP has not forgotten how to mobilize real campaigns. So far, there has been one national mass campaign in the voluntary sector: the 1999 campaign against Falun Gong, a qigong organization that promotes health and spiritual practices. Falun Gong lost its registration in the rectification review process that began in 1996. In response, followers began petitioning and protesting to regain registration in 1998, culminating in a dramatic but peaceful show of force in front of Zhongnanhai in the spring of the following year. The government moved to ban the organization in July 1999 and mobilized a mass campaign against its members. Round-the-clock propaganda on television and mandatory political study sessions sought to convince the public that the organization was a dangerous cult that brainwashed its members to the point of ruining their health and even driving them to commit suicide. This public relations effort was accompanied by book-burning rituals to destroy the group's publications and videotapes, mass arrests of Falun Gong members, and purges of CCP members who practiced Falun Gong.[58] The selectivity of targeting a single organization, the effort to brand it as a cult to undermine its legitimacy, and the profound uncertainty the campaign created for Falun Gong members (and members of other qigong organizations as well) highlight the parallels between mass campaigns and the rectification process.

In both the rectification reviews and the campaign against Falun Gong, the CCP has eliminated the most destructive and destabilizing elements of the Maoist struggle campaigns and has adapted its revolutionary techniques for new conditions and purposes. As a result, strong elements of the kind of non-bureaucratic governance that made Mao famous (and infamous) persist into the reform era, and are applied to new institutional arenas like the voluntary sector.

Adaptative Regime Change and the Direction of China's Political Transition

Contemporary CCP policy toward the voluntary sector falls somewhere in between the GMD's legalistic approach and the political approach pursued by the party during the Maoist era. Policies are increasingly defined by regulation, but they are implemented by ad-hoc, non-bureaucratic mechanisms that amplify the power of the party-state. The core of this political approach to governance remains the same, even if the goals are no longer revolutionary: to exploit ambiguity as a strategic resource and source of power.

What are the implications of this semi-legalistic, semi-political approach to governance of the voluntary sector for the larger political transition underway in China? At the most basic level, it suggests that the current regime may be stronger and more effective than it appears. Certainly, the reform-era Chinese Communist regime has already survived longer than most authoritarian regimes (and longer than the Maoist regime). Although the CCP's longevity is shaped by many factors, it is striking that during the reform period, Falun Gong is the only voluntary association with national reach that has openly resisted government control. Despite the stubborn resistance of some Falun Gong adherents in China and extensive support from Falun Gong associations outside of China, it has proven to be no match for a mass campaign. The contrast with the widespread opposition from the voluntary sector to GMD rule in the late 1940s is instructive.

But if the contemporary Chinese Communist regime may be more resilient than it appears, the ultimate direction of the political transition underway is still quite obscure. Despite the inspiring examples of the velvet and color revolutions, these rectification reviews and mass campaigns should give pause to scholars and activists searching for the beginnings of an autonomous civil society in China. The relative autonomy that voluntary organizations experienced in the 1980s was revoked in the 1990s with little protest, and the weaknesses of the current regulatory system are often less liberating than they appear.

But the historical comparisons between pre-revolutionary, Maoist, and contemporary regulation of the voluntary sector suggest that *legalization* is as important a dimension of the state-society relationship as *autonomy*. Establishing clear rules of the game that are applied uniformly to all players limits the scope of authoritarian control — even if the rules of the game are themselves authoritarian. Legalization can reduce uncertainty and enhance the legitimacy of voluntary organizations, allowing them to grow, become more strongly institutionalized, and carry out their missions, limited as they may be.

Even if a democratic civil society does not appear to be on the horizon, this analysis suggests that another important form of regime change is underway in the incipient effort to define the legal relationship between the state and the voluntary sector. The political strategies used to enforce these laws may undermine their impact, but the fact that the state is defining at least some of the rules of the game is important. The transition toward legalization is obviously very incomplete, and its ultimate destination is unclear. But it has the potential to lead to more fundamental change.

This focus on legalization fits more closely with the demands for political reform expressed by many Chinese leaders of voluntary associations. Rather than demanding autonomy from the state, they much more commonly seek state patrons and the legal status provided by registration. The protests staged by Falun Gong in 1998–99 are the most vivid example of the value ordinary Chinese citizens place on the registration certificates issued by the Ministry of Civil Affairs. Rather than criticize these strategies as inherently conservative and likely to lead to government cooptation, we might better try to understand the conditions that make these strategies so prevalent, as well as the gains they might yield in exchange for accepting limits on autonomy. These limits may prove to be less constraining than the kind of uncertainty that revolutionary political techniques create.

The obvious limit of this approach to political reform is that legalization is not likely to lead to democratization or even liberalization in the same way that promoting the autonomy of the voluntary sector might.[59] But it can contribute to the development of the rule of law and impose limits on the arbitrary use of state power. Even if legalization of the voluntary sector leads to consolidation of an authoritarian form of limited pluralism, this kind of political reform still represents an important form of regime change that should not be ignored.

Endnotes

1. Minzheng bu (民政部), ed., *Zhongguo minzheng tongji nianjian 2007* (中国民政统计年鉴2007) (China Civil Affairs Statistical Yearbook 2007) (Beijing: Zhongguo tongji chubanshe, 2007), p. 6; Wang Shaoguang (王绍光) and He Jianyu (何建宇), "Zhongguo de shetuan geming: Zhongguo renmin de jietuan bantu" (中国的社团革命: 中国人民的结团版图) (China's Associational Revolution: Associational Map of Chinese Citizens), *Zhejiang xuekan* (浙江学刊) (Zhejiang Academic Journal), no. 6 (2004): 77.

2. Tony Saich, "Negotiating the State: The Development of Social Organizations in China," *The China Quarterly*, no. 161 (March 2000): 136–138; Joseph Fewsmith, "Chambers of Commerce in Wenzhou: Toward Civil Society?" in Zheng Yongnian and Joseph Fewsmith, eds., *China's Opening Society: The Non-State Sector and Governance* (NY: Routledge, 2008), pp. 177–179; Andrew C. Mertha, *China's Water Warriors: Citizen Action and Policy Change* (Ithaca, NY: Cornell University Press, 2008), pp. 2–3.

3. Fewsmith, "Chambers of Commerce in Wenzhou," pp. 182–183; Kenneth W. Foster, "Embedded within State Agencies: Business Associations in Yantai," *The China Journal*, no. 47 (January 2002): 41–65; Kenneth W. Foster, "Associations in the Embrace of an Authoritarian State: State Domination of Society," *Studies in Comparative International Development*, 35, no. 4 (December 2001): 84–109; Jonathan Unger and Anita Chan, "Corporatism in China: A Developmental State in an East Asian Context," in Barrett L. McCormick and Jonathan Unger, eds., *China After Socialism: In the Footsteps of Eastern Europe or East Asia?* (Armonk, NY: M.E. Sharpe, 1996), pp. 95–129; Anita Chan, "Revolution or Corporatism? Workers and Trade Unions in Post-Mao China" *The Australian Journal of Chinese Affairs*, no. 29 (January 1993): 31–61; Jude Howell, "New Directions in Civil Society: Organizing Around Marginal Interests," in Jude Howell, ed., *Governance in China* (Lanham, MD: Rowman and Littlefield, 2004), pp. 143–171; Baogang He, *The Democratic Implications of Civil Society in China* (New York: St. Martin's Press, 1997).

4. John Keane, *Civil Society: Old Images, New Visions* (Stanford, CA: Stanford University Press, 1998); Jean L. Cohen and Andrew Arato, *Civil Society and Political Theory* (Cambridge, MA: MIT Press, 1994).

5. William T. Rowe, *Hankow: Commerce and Society in a Chinese City, 1796–1889* (Stanford, CA: Stanford University Press, 1984); William T. Rowe, *Hankow: Conflict and Community in a Chinese City, 1796–1895* (Stanford, CA: Stanford University Press, 1989); Mary Backus Rankin, *Elite Activism and Political Transformation in China: Zhejiang Province, 1865–1911* (Stanford, CA: Stanford University Press, 1986); David Strand, *Rickshaw*

Beijing: City People and Politics in the 1920s (Berkeley: University of California Press, 1989); Philip C.C. Huang, "'Public Sphere'/'Civil Society' in China? The Third Realm between State and Society," *Modern China*, 19, no. 2 (1993): 216–240; Frederic Wakeman, Jr., "The Civil Society and Public Sphere Debate: Western Reflections on Chinese Political Culture," *Modern China*, 19, no. 2 (April 1993): 108–138.

6. The voluntary sector is also a vague concept, but it does have the advantage of distinguishing these organizations from the mass organizations of the Maoist period, for which there were many pressures to join. It is similar to Philip Huang's concept of the "Third Realm" in Chinese history and the comparative concept of the third sector. See Huang, "'Public Sphere'/'Civil Society' in China?" as well as Helmut K. Anheier and Wolfgang Seibel, eds., *The Third Sector: Comparative Studies of Nonprofit Organizations* (New York: Walter de Gruyter, 1990); Helmut K. Anheier and Jeremy Kendall, eds., *Third Sector Policy at the Crossroads: An International Nonprofit Analysis* (New York: Routledge, 2001); Samiul Hasan and Jenny Onyx, eds., *Comparative Third Sector Governance in Asia: Structure, Process and Political Economy* (New York: Springer, 2008).

7. Saich, "Negotiating the State"; Howell, "New Directions in Civil Society," pp. 143–171; Qiusha Ma, *Non-Governmental Organizations in Contemporary China: Paving the Way to Civil Society?* (New York: Routledge, 2006).

8. Ma, *Non-Governmental Organizations in Contemporary China*, p. 92.

9. Howell, "New Directions in Civil Society"; Ma, *Non-Governmental Organizations in Contemporary China*, pp. 74–75; Yiyi Lu, *Non-Governmental Organizations in China* (New York: Routledge, 2010).

10. Ma, *Non-Governmental Organizations in Contemporary China*, p. 77; Howell, "New Directions in Civil Society," pp. 161–162; Lu, *Non-Governmental Organizations in China*, pp. 129–137; Baogang He, *The Democratic Implications of Civil Society in China* (New York: St. Martin's Press, 1997); Andrew Watson, "Civil Society in a Transitional State: The Rise of Associations in China," in Jonathan Unger, ed., *Associations and the Chinese State* (New York: M.E. Sharpe, 2008).

11. Joseph Fewsmith, *Party, State and Local Elites in Republican China: Merchant Organizations and Politics in Shanghai, 1890–1930* (Honolulu: University of Hawai'i Press, 1985); Nara Dillon, "Paradox of the Welfare State: The Politics of Privilege in Revolutionary Shanghai," ms.

12. Shehui bu (社会部), *Shehui fagui huibian* (社会法规汇编) (Collection of Social Regulations) (Shanghai: Shehuibu Jinghuqu tepaiyuan banshichu, 1945).

13. Elizabeth J. Perry, *Shanghai on Strike: The Politics of Chinese Labor* (Stanford, CA: Stanford University Press, 1993); Suzanne Pepper, *Civil War in China: The Political Struggle 1945–1949* (Lanham MD: Rowman and Littlefield, 1978, 1999).

14. Zhou Yingshi (周应时), "Shanghaishi shehui jiuji shiye xiehui gaikuang" (上海市社会救济事业协会概况) (Summary of the Shanghai Municipal Social Relief Association), *Shehui yuekan* (社会月刊) (Social Monthly), 2, no. 2 (February 1947): 40–42; for examples of the reports, see Shanghai Municipal Archives (上海市档案馆) (hereafter SMA), no. Q115-16-2.

15. The change was most notable in the policy toward private charities, long considered a form of bourgeois exploitation. See, for example, Dong Biwu (董必武), "Zhu Zhongguo fulihui chengli ershi zhounian" (祝中国福利会成立二十周年) (On the Twentieth Anniversary of the Welfare Society), June 14, 1958, in *Dong Biwu xuanji*

(董必武选集) (Selected Works of Dong Biwu) (Beijing: Renmin chubanshe, 1985), pp. 474–476.

16. Gong'an bu zhengce falü yanjiushi (共安部政策法律研究室), ed., *Gong'an fagui huibian, 1950–1979* (公安法规汇编, 1950–1979) (Collection of Public Security Regulations, 1950–1979) (Beijing: Qunzhong chubanshe, 1980), pp. 465–468.

17. Shanghaishi shehui ju (上海市社会局), *Shanghaishi shehuiju fagui huibian* (上海市社会局法规汇编) (Collection of Regulations of the Social Office of Shanghai Municipality) (Shanghai: Shanghaishi shehuiju, 1930), 2: 79–81; Ma Yili (马伊里) and Liu Hanbang (刘汉榜), *Shanghai shehui tuanti gailan* (上海社会团体概览) (General Review of Voluntary Organizations in Shanghai) (Shanghai: Shanghai renmin chubanshe, 1993), p. 9.

18. SMA, no. B168-1-804; Ma Yili and Liu Hanbang, *Shanghai shehui tuanti gailan*, p. 9. The China People's Welfare League later evolved into the China Welfare Institute (*Zhongguo fuli hui*) mentioned in endnote 15 above.

19. Zhengwu yuan (政务院), *Shehui tuanti dengji zanxing banfa* (社会团体登记暂行办法) (Provisional Methods for Registering Voluntary Organizations) (Beijing, 1950).

20. Ma Yili and Liu Hanbang, *Shanghai shehui tuanti gailan*, p. 5; SMA, no. B168-1-796: 19.

21. Xinhua she (新华社) (New China News Agency) (January 19, 1951), (March 28, 1951), accessed in SMA, no. B168-1-804. For more detail on how these campaigns were conducted in Shanghai, see Nara Dillon, "New Democracy and the Demise of Private Charity in Shanghai," in Jeremy Brown and Paul G. Pickowicz, eds., *Dilemmas of Victory: The Early Years of the People's Republic of China* (Cambridge, MA: Harvard University Press, 2007), pp. 80–102.

22. Qian Lijun (钱丽君), "Shanghai jiefang chuqi de zhenya fangeming yundong" (上海解放初期的镇压反革命运动) (The Suppression of Counter-Revolutionaries Campaign during the Early Liberation of Shanghai), in Zhonggong Shanghai shiwei dang yanjiushi, Shanghaishi dang'an guan (中共上海市委党研究室, 上海市档案馆), eds., *Shanghai jiefang chuqi de shehui gaizao* (上海解放初期的社会改造) (Reform of Society during the Early Liberation of Shanghai) (Beijing: Zhonggong dangshi chubanshe, 1999), pp. 69–83.

23. Ma Yili and Liu Hanbang, *Shanghai shehui tuanti gailan*, pp. 9–10; SMA, no. B168-1-506.

24. SMA, no. B168-1-817.

25. For development of these campaign techniques, see Yung-fa Chen, *Making Revolution: The Communist Movement in Eastern and Central China 1937–1945* (Berkeley: University of California Press, 1986), pp. 181–182, 191; Lyman P. Van Slyke, *Enemies and Friends: The United Front in Chinese Communist History* (Stanford, CA: Stanford University Press, 1967), pp. 234–235.

26. Fewsmith, "Chambers of Commerce in Wenzhou," p. 175.

27. Wang Shaoguang and He Jianyu, "Zhongguo de shetuan geming," p. 77.

28. Ma, *Non-Governmental Organizations in Contemporary China*, p. 62.

29. Ibid., p. 71.

30. Lin Yimin (林翼民), "Minjian zuzhi guanli wushi nian" (民间组织管理五十年) (Fifty Years of Management of Civil Organizations), *Zhongguo minzheng* (中国民政) (Chinese Civil Affairs), no. 9 (1999): 44.

31. Guowuyuan fazhiju (国务院法制局), ed., *Zhonghua renmin gongheguo xin fagui huibian 1989* (中华人民共和国新法规汇编 1989) (New Regulations of the People's Republic of China 1989) (Beijing: Xinhua shudian, 1989).

32. Lin Yimin, "Minjian zuzhi guanli wushi nian," p. 45; Ma, *Non-Governmental Organizations in Contemporary China*, p. 63.

33. Lin Yimin, "Minjian zuzhi guanli wushi nian," p. 45; Saich, "Negotiating the State," pp. 127–182.

34. Saich, "Negotiating the State," pp. 130–131.

35. Paul Harper, "The Party and Unions in Communist China," *The China Quarterly*, no. 37 (January–March 1969): 84–119; Elizabeth J. Perry and Li Xun, *Proletarian Power: Shanghai in the Cultural Revolution* (Boulder, CO: Westview Press, 1997).

36. A more literal translation of *qingli zhengdun* (清理整顿) might be "clean out and reorganize."

37. The first use of the phrase *qingli zhengdun* (清理整顿) I have been able to find appears in a 1955 report on reducing the number of people enrolled in an unemployment relief program, although at that point it was more commonly the slightly longer form of *qingli he zhengdun* (清理和整顿). According to data gathered from searches in journal and newspaper databases, the popularity of the phrase began to pick up in the 1980s and then accelerated rapidly in the 1990s.

38. See, for example, Guizhou sheng difangzhi (贵州省地方志), ed., *Guizhou nianjian 1993* (贵州年鉴1993) (Guizhou Yearbook 1993) (Guiyang: Guizhou renmin chubanshe, 1993), p. 154; Qian Xiuyun (钱秀云), "Quansheng minban fei qiye danwei fucha dengji gongzuo qidong" (全省民办非企业单位复查登记工作启动) (Starting the Work of Rechecking the Registrations of Non-Profit Units in the Entire Province), *Anhui ribao* (安徽日报) (Anhui Daily) (November 11, 2000): A01; Kong Shaoqing (孔少青), "Jingyangxian licu minjian zuzhi guanli gongzuo" (泾阳县力促民间组织管理工作) (Promote Work in Jingyang County Based on the Management of Voluntary Organizations), *Zhongguo shehui bao* (中国社会报) (China Society News) (September 26, 2003).

39. Wang Xiuping (王秀萍), "Qieshi gaohao fucha dengji he qingli zhengdun" (切实搞好复查登记和清理政顿) (Earnestly Carry Out the Rechecking of the Registration and the Rectification), *Shanxi jingji ribao* (山西经济日报) (Shanxi Economic Daily) (March 29, 2001): 1; Hu Weihua (胡威华) and Xu Shuiquan (徐水泉), "Suzhou shetuan qingli zhengdun shixing 'san tuogou'" (苏州社团清理整顿实行三脱钩) (Cleaning Up and Reorganizing the Voluntary Organizations in Suzhou to Implement the Three Disconnects), *Zhongguo shehui bao* (December 1, 2004); Cai Weiwu (蔡违武), "Jiangxisheng shehui tuanti qingli zhengdun jin kou wuge jiehe" (江西省社会团体清理整顿紧扣五个结合) (Closely Rectify the Voluntary Organizations in Jiangxi Province to Realize the Five Linkages), *Shehui gongzuo* (社会工作) (Social Work), no. 2 (1998): 21.

40. Qian Xiuyun, "Quansheng minban fei qiye danwei fucha dengji gongzuo qidong," p. A01; Qi Hangjian (齐航建), "Shandong fucha dengji gongzuo zhaozhao chuxin" (山东复查登记工作招招出新) (Recheck the Registrations in Shandong to Clearly Weed Out the Old and Bring Forth the New), *Zhongguo shehui bao* (August 22, 2002).

41. Guan Zhonglin (关忠林), "Qingdao Chengyangqu jizhong qingli zhengdun minjian zuzhi" (青岛城阳区集中清理整顿民间组织) (Concentrate on the Rectification

of the Voluntary Organizations in Chengyang District of Qingdao), *Zhongguo shehui bao* (February 20, 2006): 6.

42. This is a rough estimate. The *Ministry of Civil Affairs Statistical Yearbook* reports conflicting data for this period. Wang Shaoguang and He Jianyu, "Zhongguo de shetuan geming," p. 72, estimate that 200,000 registered organizations existed in 1989, whereas Ma, *Non-Governmental Organizations in Contemporary China*, p. 66, reports that 118,691 organizations applied for re-registration in 1991, of which 89,969 were approved.

43. Chuanshaxian difangzhi (川沙县地方志), ed., *Chuansha nianjian 1992* (川沙年鉴 1992) (Chuansha Yearbook 1992) (Shanghai: Shanghai shehui kexueyuan chubanshe, 1992), p. 226.

44. Ma, *Non-Governmental Organizations in Contemporary China*, p. 70.

45. In some places, the review actually started in 1997, but then had to be redone to implement the 1998 policy changes.

46. Minzheng bu (民政部), ed., *Zhongguo minzheng tongji nianjian 1997* (中国民政统计年鉴 1997) (China Civil Affairs Statistical Yearbook 1997) (Beijing: Zhongguo tongji chubanshe, 1997), p. 252; Minzheng bu (民政部), ed., *Zhongguo minzheng tongji nianjian 2000* (中国民政统计年鉴 2000) (China Civil Affairs Statistical Yearbook 2000) (Beijing: Zhongguo tongji chubanshe, 2000), p. 134.

47. Tai'an nianjian bianjibu (泰安年鉴编辑部), ed., *Tai'an nianjian 1997* (泰安年鉴 1997) (Tai'an Yearbook 1997) (Ji'nan: Jilushe chuban, 1997), p. 172.

48. Wang Shaoguang and He Jianyu, "Zhongguo de shetuan geming," p. 73.

49. Qian Xiuyun, "Quansheng minban fei qiye danwei fucha dengji gongzuo qidong," p. A01; Wang Xiuping, "Qieshi gaohao fucha dengji he qingli zhengdun," p. 1; Shanghai-shi renmin zhengfu fazhan yanjiu zhongxin (上海市人民政府发展研究中心), *Shanghai jingji nianjian 2001* (上海经济年鉴 2001) (Shanghai Economic Yearbook 2001) (Shanghai: Shanghai jingji nianjianshe, 2001), p. 495; Zhou Lu (周鲁), "Ji'nanshi minban fei qiye danwei fucha dengji gongzuo quanmian zhankai" (济南市民办非企业单位复查登记工作全面展开) (The Work of Rechecking the Registration of Non-Profit Organizations in Ji'nan City Develops Comprehensively), *Zhongguo shehui bao* (April 7, 2001): 3.

50. Hu Weihua and Xu Shuiquan, "Suzhou shetuan qingli zhengdun shixing 'san tuogou'"; Li Ming (李明), "Wo sheng dui shehui tuanti jinxing qingli zhengdun" (我省对社会团体进行清理整顿) (Carrying Out Rectification of Voluntary Groups in Our Province), *Liaoning ribao* (辽宁日报) (March 8, 2008): 1.

51. Zhou Lu, "Ji'nanshi minban fei qiye danwei fucha dengji gongzuo quanmian zhankai," p. 3.

52. Chuanshaxian difangzhi, ed., *Chuansha nianjian 1992*, p. 226; Ma, *Non-Governmental Organizations in Contemporary China*, p. 87.

53. Legitimacy is very difficult to pin down, much less compare — so I make this claim with some hesitation. But the contemporary third sector has little history of providing services valued by the public or of successfully responding to major crises, as was the case during the Republican period. Furthermore, the reform-era voluntary sector is not yet a major route into the public arena for business and academic leaders as it was during the Republican period.

54. Minzheng bu (民政部), ed., *Zhongguo minzheng tongji nianjian 2005* (中国民政统计年鉴2005) (China Civil Affairs Statistical Yearbook 2005) (Beijing: Zhongguo tongji chubanshe, 2005), p. 14. For its use in a specific review, see, for example, Li Enhui (李恩惠), "Wo shi dui shehui tuanti jinxing qingli zhengdun" (我市对社会团体进行清理整顿) (Our City Carries Out Rectification of Voluntary Associations), *Benxi ribao* (本溪日报) (Benxi Daily) (March 13, 2008): 1.

55. Zhang Jingbo (张敬波), "Qingli zhengdun wuzheng youeryuan" (清理整顿无证幼儿园) (Carry Out Rectification of Unregistered Kindergartens), *Anhui ribao* (January 10, 2008): B1.

56. Ge Tao (葛涛),"Zhongguo shetuan da zhenghe" (中国社团大整合) (The Big Integration of Chinese Voluntary Organizations), *Zhongguo dushu bao* (中国读书报) (China Study Paper) (June 18, 2003).

57. Ma, *Non-Governmental Organizations in Contemporary China*, pp. 89–92.

58. Saich, "Negotiating the State," pp. 135–136; Elizabeth J. Perry, "Introduction," in *Challenging the Mandate of Heaven: Social Protest and State Power in China* (Armonk, NY: M.E. Sharpe, 2001), pp. xv–xx.

59. See, for example, Freedom House, "Freedom of Association under Threat: The New Authoritarians' Offensive Against Civil Society" (Washington, DC: Freedom House, 2008); Human Rights Watch, "Choking on Bureaucracy: State Curbs on Independent Civil Society Activism" (New York: Human Rights Watch, 2008).

CHAPTER 6

A Return to Populist Legality?
Historical Legacies and Legal Reform

BENJAMIN L. LIEBMAN

Introduction

Two story lines dominate appraisals of China's legal reforms. First, legal reforms and the party-state's embrace of legality as part of its contemporary ideology have been designed to distinguish China's reform-era leadership from its revolutionary predecessors, to facilitate economic development, and to bring China in line with international practice. Historical continuities, to the degree they exist, are largely manifest in problems that undermine the authority of law and legal institutions. Second, legal reforms have lagged behind economic reforms. The party-state has continued to view law primarily as a tool for achieving policy goals. Legal reforms have not imposed significant restraints on the party-state.

Both of these narratives are partly valid. To focus on these story lines, however, is to miss much of the complexity of China's legal development over the past three decades. The puzzle of Chinese legal reforms is not only how China has experienced record economic growth without robust protections for property rights,[1] but also why legal reforms have developed in ways that are unexpected and uncommon for a single-party authoritarian state.[2] The legacy of China's revolutionary legal practices is evident in continued party-state dominance of the legal system. But it is also reflected in the embrace of modern forms of populist legality. Likewise, although the party-state's approach to law is frequently instrumentalist, legal reforms have also encouraged and legitimized more robust and professional legal institutions and rights-based legal activism.

Two questions analyzed

This chapter analyzes the two questions that are the focus of this book in the context of the legal system. First, how have contemporary legal reforms influenced China's adaptive authoritarian model? Second, what role has China's revolutionary legal history played in shaping the development of the legal system since 1978? I address the first question by surveying three trends in the Chinese legal system: the state's instrumentalist approach to law, the importance of experimentation and flexibility, and tensions between trends toward professionalism and populism. The picture that emerges is of legal reforms that serve state interests in economic development, institutionalization, and legitimization, but also of a system in which innovations increasingly develop from the ground up, affect institutional relationships, and at times constrain state behavior.

To answer the second question, I examine links between China's legal practices during the revolutionary period and the early years of the People's Republic and the contemporary reforms. Historical practices are manifest in many of the problems that continue to undermine the Chinese legal system. Yet the historical legacy does not merely constrain contemporary legal development. Legal institutions, in particular the courts, have recently embraced aspects of revolutionary history, most notably populist legality, in new ways as they seek to increase their legitimacy within the party-state and with the public. Populism in the Chinese legal system refers to a range of forms of public expression, from public opinion created by the state-run media, to opinion in Internet forums, to collective action and individual protest by persons seeking redress of grievances. Populism also refers to efforts by legal institutions to seek public support by aligning outcomes with perceived dominant social norms or conceptions of popular morality or by making legal institutions more accessible. Many of these contemporary manifestations of populist legality have historical antecedents. Similarly, China's revolutionary legal history helps explain China's receptiveness to certain legal innovations. I conclude the chapter by discussing what linkages and discontinuities between historical and contemporary practices suggest about the sustainability of the Chinese legal reform model.

Adaptive Legality

How important has law been to China's creation of adaptive authoritarianism? Law is central to contemporary governance, both for the state, which now includes legality as part of its ideology, and for ordinary people, who increasingly articulate their interests in terms of legal rights. Yet China's thirty years of legal reforms present a paradox. Since 1978 China's legal system has developed perhaps faster than any legal system in history. The creation of new legal procedures has been an important part of the institutionalization process that has fostered regime resilience.[3] Nevertheless, this success has come despite the lack of robust legal institutions that Western theory often assumes are necessary for long-term growth.[4] Legal development is frequently characterized as lagging behind economic development. The experimentalist nature of policy implementation has been possible in part because existing laws and legal institutions do little to constrain officials at the local (or national) levels. Law has not, however, merely followed the economic reforms.[5] Three trends help to explain the role of law in reform-era governance and its contribution to regime resilience.

First, law during the reform period has primarily served as a tool for party policy, following, rather than leading, changes in policy. This instrumentalist approach to law continues to dominate. But legal reforms have evolved beyond the state's instrumentalist goals: reforms have also begun to regulate and impose limitations on state behavior and to foster law-based challenges to state action.

Scholarship on the role of law in China during the reform era often portrays legal development as constrained by China's authoritarian system.[6] This account is largely valid: much of the legal reform, in particular the creation of a legislative framework, focuses on facilitating already-established policy goals by searching for practical solutions to problems. During the first two decades of legal reforms the policy goal was primarily economic development; much law-making thus was directed to creating a legal framework for investors and other economic actors. More recently the creation of new laws focuses on broader goals, most notably addressing rising inequality.

Legal reforms have thus largely served to facilitate, rather than limit, the implementation of state policies. Law has been used to transform society,[7] and as a tool for the party-state to govern — a process Liang Zhiping (梁治平) refers to as the "functionalization of law."[8] Legal reforms largely reflect state interests rather than the rights and interests of individuals.[9] They have not been designed to impose significant limitations on the state.[10] Significant professionalization — ranging from better-trained judges to the development of specialized legislative staff — has not altered this approach to law.

Yet the legal system has not been a passive participant in the reform process. Legal reforms have created rules to regulate, regularize, and limit state conduct, as reflected in the development of administrative law.[11]

Flexibility continues, in written law and in practice, but it is also sometimes constrained. Legal institutions are not checks on party-state power, but detailed rules now exist dictating how administrative agencies should act — and what should happen when they do not act in accordance with the rules.[12] Enforcement of such norms is weak and there is little emphasis on procedural justice. Those seeking to use law to restrict the state must do so strategically and within the framework of party-state leadership. Nevertheless, law matters for the functioning of the state in a way that transcends the use of law as a tool for implementing state policy: legal rules provide a baseline against which state actions can be judged.

The state's approach to law has evolved along with changes in state policy. Law no longer merely facilitates economic development; increasingly, it is also used to regulate economic development. Laws in many important areas — from intellectual property to employment law to antitrust — have been adopted in advance of policy implementation, demonstrating that law is also being used to create new norms. Many laws are now the product of significant debate, both in the National People's Congress and, at times, in the media, rather than being exclusively the product of decisions by top party-state officials. This contrasts with the practice in the first two decades of legal reform when laws (and constitutional amendments) were often enacted only after policies had been both determined and implemented.[13] In addition, rather than serving solely to advance other policy goals, strengthening the legal system has become a key party policy.[14]

The second trend in legal reform has been an emphasis on experimentation, both formal and informal. Sebastian Heilmann has noted two manifestations of experimentalism in the legal system, through policy implementation ahead of legislation and via regulations and other legal norms that are classified as "experimental."[15] As in other areas of policy implementation, local authorities have been encouraged to legislate in advance of national regulations or laws, with a view to abstracting from local experience to the national level.[16] Local courts likewise are either explicitly or implicitly authorized to create new rules or to experiment with new procedures ahead of national laws or Supreme People's Court (SPC) interpretations. Even if not authorized to do so, courts often experiment by necessity when laws are absent or unclear.[17] Experimentation is not limited to the creation of formal laws or novel procedures: significant variance in enforcement may likewise reflect conscious experimentation.

As in other policy areas detailed by Heilmann, experiments in law-making and law implementation are used to inform the center,[18] albeit with the risk that experimentation will create opportunities for local protectionism. Experimentation has been particularly helpful in the legal system given the difficulties in rapidly creating a comprehensive legal framework.[19] Experimentation also permits legal authorities to maintain an ideological commitment to consistency in the legal system while at the same time permitting variation in practice.

Yet experimentation is not only used by local people's congresses or courts to fill in the gaps of unclear law, or to create new legal norms ahead of national regulations. Numerous experiments in law-making involve local authorities adopting rules that directly contradict existing law.[20] In Beijing, for example, regulations for Zhongguancun permit the formation of limited partnerships by individuals, even though the Partnership Law explicitly states that two or more individuals are required to form a limited partnership.[21] Similarly, Beijing regulations permit natural persons to be joint venture partners, despite explicit provisions in the Equity Joint-Venture Law that state that only legal persons can be partners. In adopting the provisions, Beijing authorities cited the need to "*dapo jinqu*," or break through the restricted areas.[22] Local courts similarly have directly violated established norms and law, ranging from awarding emotional damages ahead of SPC authorization (and later awarding emotional damages even in areas not authorized by the SPC) to invalidating provincial regulations that conflict with national laws (despite Chinese courts' lack of power of judicial review) to refusing to apply existing regulations because of courts' expectations that such provisions will soon be changed.[23] Courts have also experimented with mediation in administrative cases, despite the Administrative Litigation Law's explicit prohibition of mediation,[24] and with the use of juries in major criminal cases, despite the lack of a basis for doing so in the Criminal Procedure Law.[25] Such innovation is not limited to local authorities. In interpreting the Security Law, for example, the SPC explicitly contradicted the law in a number of key areas. The SPC interpretation was apparently made in consultation with other state actors and reflected the view that certain provisions in the law were incorrect. Instead of changing the law, the problems were addressed through the SPC interpretation.

Experimentation is also facilitating increased institutional competence. The Internet now helps to spread innovative rules and legal experiments, in particular those in the courts.[26] It is difficult to determine when local experiments are cleared with the higher authorities. Nevertheless, evidence from the courts suggests that judges increasingly look horizontally to other local courts, whereas they previously sought guidance from higher courts.

This suggests the possibility of innovative rules spreading with reduced use of the "point-to-surface" process that Heilmann describes.[27] Such experimentation remains subject to the shadow of hierarchy even if it is not directly guided by central authorities:[28] participants in the legal system are careful to navigate the boundaries of permissible experimentation, and central authorities retain the authority to terminate the experiments. Nevertheless, exercising this authority is increasingly difficult in the legal system, as new rules or practices may spread and generate public debate before higher authorities are able to intervene. In most cases, however, legal experimentation involves routine creation of new legal rules rather than challenges to state authority or interests. At the local level, experimentation is often possible because it aligns with local interests.[29]

Over time, this accretion of experimentation may lead to more robust legal institutions as courts develop both greater competence and confidence.[30] Experimentation is not only furthering policy implementation; it is also fostering professionalization and greater institutional competence within legal institutions. As a result, innovation in the legal system increasingly is influencing institutional dynamics. Yet there is also a risk that in the absence of transparency, accountability, or rules governing the principled devolution of authority such experimentation may exacerbate many of the problems that plague the Chinese legal system, including corruption and abuses of power. Experimentation may facilitate the development of new legal rules, but may also be an example of the arbitrary way in which law is often implemented in China.

Third, the legal system is characterized by tensions between trends toward professionalism and populism. The professionalization of legal actors and institutions is perhaps the single most significant accomplishment of China's legal reforms.[31] China has succeeded in improving training for judges, procurators, and lawyers, and in creating more formal legal procedures. Yet populism continues to play an important role in the Chinese legal system. Populist pressures have challenged the authority of legal institutions, but popular support is also being used as a potential source of legitimacy for legal institutions, both with the public and within the party-state.[32]

Tensions between populism and an emphasis on legal procedure date back to the Yan'an and Jiangxi Soviet periods, and I discuss this history in more detail below. Prior to 1978, these tensions were generally resolved in favor of populism. In contrast, the first two decades of legal reforms were characterized by attempts to minimize populist legality and shift toward professionalization and formality. Over the past decade, however, courts have faced two major sources of popular pressure: the media and the letters and visits system. Increased pressure on the courts has coincided with rising criticism of the courts for being inaccessible to ordinary people, for being corrupt or incompetent, and for failing to protect those left behind by the economic reforms. One response from the courts and other legal institutions has been to return to the revolutionary concept of "serving the people" as they react to a perceived lack of popular confidence and their weak position within the party-state. Court leaders have called on judges to better serve the people and to be proactive in response to disputes. In early 2009, for example, the president of the Henan Province High People's Court called on judges to take off their robes and put down their gavels, arguing that courts and judges are weak because they are removed from ordinary people.[33] The remarks provoked debate, with commentators arguing that ordinary people need fair courts, not a return to mass-line justice.[34] Nevertheless, the comments make clear that populism is once again central to the functioning of the Chinese legal system.

What do these three trends tell us about the role of law in the creation of China's adaptive authoritarian model? Adaptive authoritarianism has required the development of the legal system to facilitate policy implementation and to create rules by which the system functions. Creating rules of the game has helped to address the lack of predictability that is one side-effect of a governance model that stresses flexibility. Legal reforms have not imposed significant limits on state power and predictability is not yet a hallmark of the Chinese legal system. However, legal reforms have made radical departures from existing policy and law less likely.

The creation of a legal system that serves state interests has required permitting the legal system to develop in ways that appear at odds with the instrumentalist goals of the party-state. The party-state's rhetorical commitment to legality and emphasis on popular legal education have legitimized rights-based actions by individuals. This has been seen in a range of areas, including a number of efforts by academics and activists to use the Government Open Information Regulations to push for disclosure of information. In a similar example based on the Constitution, in December 2009 five law professors from Peking University Law School petitioned the Standing Committee of the National People's Congress, arguing that regulations governing demolition and relocation of urban households violated both the Constitution and the Property Law and thus required amendment.[35] Such strategic use of law demonstrates that law shapes state behavior even if it does not constrain it. Similarly, courts have accepted a widening range of rights-based claims from ordinary people. The term "court" in China has always referred to institutions that are very different from their Western counterparts. Nevertheless, judges and other participants in the legal system have increasing expectations regarding their own roles that are shaped both by practice in China and by understanding the roles like-named actors play in other legal systems.

The state's emphasis on flexibility and receptiveness to experimentation (as well as the difficulty central authorities face in monitoring low-level experimentation) increasingly is used strategically by individuals and groups to force the legal system to confront a wide range of legal grievances.[36] Ground-up experimentation and innovation primarily occur in areas outside of party concern, and areas of party concern remain broad. Hence, courts have innovated by creating new rules governing routine tort disputes and new doctrines governing contractual relationships. The state retains the ability to shut down innovation, as it did when, following a flurry of cases asserting claims under China's Constitution, it banned courts from accepting constitutional cases. Nevertheless, tolerance of such activism may be part of the party-state's success, as responsiveness (in particular by central authorities) enhances state legitimacy by sustaining the party-state's narrative that misconduct and malfeasance are products of wayward local officials, not institutional design.

The three trends highlight the flexibility that remains central to China's legal system. All legal systems must be flexible, and courts everywhere create new legal norms. But flexibility in China goes further. This flexibility is apparent not only in experimentation with new rules and procedures but also in the conscious abandonment of legal norms in order to address other interests. Flexibility has often been assumed to be a necessity brought about by the vagueness of many Chinese laws and the newness of many legal issues and institutions. The three trends demonstrate that although legal reforms are intended to create a legal system that is more rule-based and predictable, flexibility remains a key ideology underlying legal reform. Courts that yield to outside pressures from party leaders, the media, or individual petitioners are acting consistently with the design of the legal system — which demands that formal rules yield to policy goals. Ideological commitment to both flexibility and legality is an unusual combination, one that reflects both historical legacies and discontinuities. Yet it is this commitment to flexibility and legal rules that has allowed legal reforms to facilitate a range of policy goals, from economic development to social stability. Legal reforms may have failed to meet the aspirations of many in China and the West, but they have played an important role in constructing, implementing, and regularizing the flexibility that is a crucial aspect of adaptive authoritarianism.

Revolutionary Legacies and the Legal System

Descriptions of the impact of revolutionary history on China's post-1978 legal reforms often characterize the latter as a reaction to China's revolutionary and post-revolutionary experiences. This narrative comes from the party-state itself, which, beginning with the Third Plenum of the Eleventh Central Committee in 1978 and the trial of the Gang of Four in 1981, emphasized adherence to legality as a means of distinguishing China's new leadership from the excesses of the Cultural Revolution. According to this account, reform-era legal reforms have been much less influenced by revolutionary tradition than by a constant search for practical solutions. Most Chinese and Western scholarship adheres to this narrative.[37] Others have argued that legal reforms have largely consisted of ex-post legitimization of state policies already undertaken — and thus are neither tethered to revolutionary history nor are the result of conscious design.

Might revolutionary legal history explain some of the success of legal reform? This section surveys links between law in the revolutionary period and the early years of the PRC and the post-1978 legal reforms. Revolutionary legal experience continues to play an important role in shaping the evolution of the legal system today — including in ways that make the system receptive to reforms widely assumed to be transplants from Western liberal democracies. Revolutionary legal experience does not explain the "success" of legal reforms or suggest that the legal system developed as a result of explicit design, but it does help to elucidate both the complexity of such reforms and also their uniqueness.

Four related developments defined legal ideology from the revolutionary period through the mid-1950s. As discussed further below, these developments built upon China's legal traditions. First, tensions between an emphasis on legal procedures and revolutionary goals characterized debate over the role of law in the Jiangxi Soviet. Moderates within the party advocated an emphasis on legal procedures. But such voices lost out to critics of procedure and formality who advocated reliance on public sentiment as a basis for legal judgments. As Trygve Lötveit describes, by 1934 the approach to law in the Jiangxi Soviet shifted "from justice to Red terror."[38] The Jiangxi Soviet also created "mobile" courts, which were used for "enabling the

masses to express their opinions on judicial questions, and for arousing, or for releasing, mass sentiments at the trial."[39]

Second, similar efforts to make courts responsive to public views played out in more detail during the Yan'an period with the adoption of the Ma Xiwu adjudication method (*Ma Xiwu shenpan fangshi*, 马锡五审判方式). Some within the CCP had advocated institutionalization of the legal system along the Soviet model. But these attempts at professionalization and emphasis on creating legal procedures failed to address the rising social problems in the areas under CCP control.[40] Beginning in Yan'an in 1943, Ma Xiwu, then head of the Longdong District Court in the Shaan-Gan-Ning border area and later president of the region's high court and vice president of the SPC, rejected the emphasis on formality and expertise implicit in both Republican legal reforms and Western models. The goal of the Ma Xiwu method was the resolution of disputes through mediation.[41] Part of the appeal of the Ma Xiwu approach was its resonance with the traditional emphasis on informality and morality in dispute resolution.

Yet the emphasis on mediation did not mark a return to traditional forms of dispute resolution. The aim was not only to resolve disputes; it was also to transmit party ideology and policy, and in so doing to change and control society.[42] As Jiang Shigong (强世功) notes, the Ma Xiwu method became an instrument of state power and a tool for furthering party policies, not social justice; mediation became "a special kind of governmental art."[43] Resolving disputes did not simply require knowledge of law; it also required a full understanding of the situation that gave rise to the dispute. Ma Xiwu-style adjudication was characterized by roving tribunals and trials held "on the spot" in rural communities to obtain local knowledge about the dispute.[44] Resolving disputes successfully meant leaving all parties satisfied with the outcome, thus maintaining state authority in the eyes of the disputants.[45]

The Ma Xiwu method embodied core elements of CCP legal ideology. Law became inseparable from politics and was designed to advance party policy.[46] Law was practical and adaptable, not rigid or constraining. Legal institutions were neither independent nor specialized, and professionalism was explicitly rejected.[47] Written law yielded to actual experiences: a correct decision was one that met the emotions of the masses.[48]

Third, the party's approach to law was solidified a decade later during the 1952–53 Judicial Reform Movement. Led by Dong Biwu (董必武), the first head of the state's Political-Legal Committee (the precursor to the party's Central Political-Legal Committee), the movement focused on eliminating judicial personnel from prior to 1949 who continued to serve in office.[49]

They were replaced largely by "excellent personnel from the masses," including workers, peasants, women, and members of the military.[50] The Judicial Reform Movement was an explicit rejection of Western legality, including the concepts of professionalization and independence and the emphasis on procedure. Instead, the focus was on the class nature of law.[51] Popular views were important, reflecting the manifestation of mass-line ideology in law: legal norms should reflect popular views, but law should also be a tool for educating the masses and changing such views.

The Judicial Reform Movement did not make legal institutions irrelevant. As David Bachman shows, there was a significant volume of litigation in the courts during the 1950s, challenging the idea that legal institutions played only a marginal role during this period.[52] Significant attempts to reform legal institutions in the 1950s suggested that those advocating the creation of Soviet-style formal legal institutions did not completely lose out and that legal institutions could play a significant role within the party-state. The hopes of those advocating greater institutionalization, however, were soon dashed with the onset of the Anti-Rightist Campaign and the Cultural Revolution.

A fourth aspect of legal policy in the early years of the PRC was a significant emphasis on popular education concerning law. Legal education campaigns focused on the new land and marriage laws — which were crucial to Communist Party efforts to establish legitimacy. There were considerable efforts to publicize and encourage use of these laws as part of efforts to implement the policies of the new regime. There is also evidence of some surprise on the part of the state regarding the willingness of ordinary people to use the law, in particular when it came to divorce, resulting in modest retrenchment of state policy.[53]

China's revolutionary history is often blamed for many of the problems that the legal system faces today. For example, the influence of party political-legal committees is attributed to this revolutionary legacy,[54] as are the prevalence and legitimacy of intervention by party officials in court cases[55] and the party's continued instrumentalist view of law.[56] As Liang Zhiping notes, the state remains accustomed to intervening in matters of society and individuals without being limited by law — because the state remains strong and society continues to be fragmented.[57] Stability takes precedence over legality and courts remain weak players in the party-state structure, too often swayed by morality rather than law.[58] The revolutionary legacy helps explain what was until recently a lack of emphasis on profes-sional standards in the courts and procuratorates.[59] The informality of the

Ma Xiwu method is also blamed for corruption, because there are too few limits on judges' conduct.[60] And campaigns, rather than legal procedures, remain important mechanisms for enforcing law.[61]

Much of the progress in the Chinese legal system over the past thirty years is judged against the benchmark of the revolutionary period and the Cultural Revolution. Legal reform has primarily consisted of looking for overseas models, rather than looking to China's past. Party ideology remains important to the courts, evidenced in the recent emphasis on legal institutions' adherence to party leadership. Nevertheless, the revolutionary legacy is, in the eyes of many in the legal system, something to overcome.

But revolutionary history is not merely a constraint on an inevitable path toward Western-style rule of law. The legacy of revolutionary legality has contributed both to new problems in the Chinese legal system and to some unusual developments. Linkages between revolutionary history and contemporary developments provide insight into why the Chinese legal system has engaged in some reforms that are uncommon in more traditional authoritarian legal systems, including the embrace of legal aid and public hearings and education about law and individual rights. Such continuities also caution against those who see progress in the Chinese system as suggesting that legal reform in China will follow a traditional transitional path.

The clearest manifestation of the impact of revolutionary legal history is the embrace of populism by legal institutions. As noted above, contemporary legal populism encompasses two forms: legal institutions being influenced by public opinion and protest and legal institutions reaching out to serve and educate the masses. Legal populism is manifest in attempts to respond to pressures and in an emphasis on practical problem-solving. In contrast to the Cultural Revolution when legal institutions came under direct attack, contemporary legal populism channels popular views through the legal system.

Legal institutions are frequently swayed by populist pressures voiced in the media or through protests and petitioning. Numerous high-profile cases, including the Zhang Jinzhu case in the 1990s and the Liu Yong, BMW, She Xianglin, and Xu Ting cases in the 2000s, highlight the media's influence on the courts. The extensive steps courts have taken to constrain media access and coverage likewise reflect the emphasis of the courts to prevent such influence. The media can be a useful tool for weak parties confronting powerful local interests. Populist pressures, reflected or manufactured by the media, also lead to rapid and harsh punishment of criminal defendants and to courts that are careful to ensure that their decisions are in line with public opinion.[62]

Populist pressures are also evident in courts that adjust outcomes in response to petitioning and protesting.[63] Courts have reemphasized judges' obligation to placate and prevent petitioners, with courts aiming to eliminate petitioning entirely. Judges in many courts are now fined if cases they handle result in petitioning, even if the outcomes are substantively correct. Judges acknowledge that they change outcomes in response to petitioning or pay petitioners out of court to convince them to drop their complaints.

Judges facing populist pressures often take flexible approaches to legal rules, or ignore them altogether. China's courts are not unique in terms of being influenced by public opinion, but the impact of populist views of law is particularly strong in China because of the flexibility that characterizes many aspects of the legal system. The influence of popular opinion and individual protest on the legal system also demonstrates that in practice flexibility is not always attributable to corruption or judicial malfeasance. Courts that bend to accommodate the media or petitioners are not abandoning principle. They are doing exactly what their roles in the political-legal system require: adapting in a practical fashion to popular demands and ensuring that legal rules do not diverge too greatly from popular conceptions of right and wrong.

There was no Internet or commercialized media to pressure Ma Xiwu. Yet the existence and influence of petitioning reflects the persistence of the Ma Xiwu method and of a flexible approach to law that dates back to the Yan'an and Jiangxi periods: decisions are correct when they are accepted by the disputants. Similarly, courts' sensitivity to media pressures reflects the traditional position of the media as the eyes, ears, and mouthpiece of the party-state.

The legitimacy of reliance on public opinion was highlighted in a series of comments in 2008 by the new president of the SPC. Speaking about the trend whereby courts delay decisions in death penalty cases, Wang Shengjun (王胜俊) stated that courts should base decisions in capital cases on law, on the general public security situation, and on "the feelings of the masses."[64] These comments sparked online debate, with some praising the comments and others arguing that they reflected a return to pre-reform ideology and violated the principles of rule of law. One commentator, however, noted that the comments may also reflect a practical effort by the courts to increase their authority given their weak standing in the party-state and the widespread popular discontent with the courts.[65] In subsequent speeches Wang argued that courts should be subject to the "three supremes": the supremacy of the party, the supremacy of popular interest, and the supremacy of the constitution and law.[66] This phrase, originally used in a speech by Hu Jintao, has been the focus of education campaigns in the legal system since early 2008. In response, legal scholars again noted that Wang's list put law behind party and popular interests.[67]

Wang's comments, like the influence of the media and petitioning, demonstrate that judges today continue to be responsible for more than just applying the law. Judges are also responsible for meeting broader state goals, most notably social stability: in early 2010, a SPC spokesperson commented that maintaining social stability was the most important responsibility of local courts.[68] Judges continue to be evaluated in significant part based on the social effect of their work, not only on substantive correctness.

The influence of populist pressure highlights the differences between China's legal evolution and more conventional authoritarian legal systems. Court responsiveness to public opinion regarding the courts generally is not a characteristic associated with authoritarian regimes. The most important recent work on courts in authoritarian systems includes no discussion of the impact of populism or public opinion.[69] In China, however, populist pressure has become a key characteristic of the legal system over the past decade.

Populism may, however, also be a tool for legal institutions to promote their own authority and legitimacy. Having created a basic legal infrastructure to serve the interests of investment and economic development, legal officials in recent years have turned their attention to ensuring that the legal system also serves the interests of those left behind in China's social transformation and addresses the lack of public confidence in legal institutions. One manifestation of this trend has been emphasis on the concept of justice for the people (*sifa weimin*, 司法为民). The SPC re-introduced this phrase in 2003 following the Sixteenth Party Congress.[70] Noting that the concept *sifa weimin* was first adopted in the 1930s in the Jiangxi Soviet, then-SPC president Xiao Yang (肖扬) stated that the courts "want new representations of this good tradition" and should revitalize the tradition of the "people's judiciary."[71]

As explained by Xiao Yang, *sifa weimin* today means that the legal system should "serve the people," not private interests.[72] The recent emphasis on *sifa weimin* appears to be a reaction to arguments that legal reforms serve the interests of the economically and politically powerful. Within the contemporary *sifa weimin* movement are efforts to improve court accessibility by reducing filing fees, improving the handling of petitioners' grievances by making court leaders available to petitioners, increasing the emphasis on legal education, and maintaining social stability.[73] Courts should work to resolve social conflicts quickly and provide judicial assistance to those facing financial difficulties.[74] Law should not be passive: courts should be active in resolving disputes, making it easy for people to bring cases, including, if necessary, by bringing courts to the people.[75] In a return to the Ma Xiwu style, courts focus on accessibility for the public and on the combining of legal knowledge with knowledge of local situations.[76] Describing the approach of a court in rural Fujian, one scholar notes that anything that meets social needs is an acceptable method.[77] In Jiangxi province, judges have been compared to emergency medical workers, with responsibility to resolve social conflicts before they spread: one court requires that judges arrive in villages to mediate cases within one hour after a case or complaint is filed with the court.[78] *Sifa weimin* reflects an explicit departure from some of the formality that characterized earlier legal reform.[79]

Most aspects of the modern *sifa weimin* movement trace their roots to Ma Xiwu.[80] The term *sifa weimin* is now being used in new ways, including emphasizing fairness and equality before the law. Nevertheless, the link to the populist legacy of the 1940s and 1950s is clear. Commentators have criticized the reintroduction of the *sifa weimin* slogan, arguing that it conflicts with trends toward professionalization and respect for legal procedures. Yet the importance of *sifa weimin* is not merely to highlight tensions between revolutionary traditions and trends toward legalization and professionalization. The re-emphasis on justice for the people suggests that courts now see populism as a potential source of legitimacy with the public and the party.[81]

Renewed concern with popular opinion is also illustrated by the courts' emphasis on the concept of "decide the case and solve the problem" (*anjie shiliao*, 案结事了). The phrase means that courts should focus not only on deciding cases, but also on resolving all issues related to the case. The focus on problem-solving reflects the fact that in many cases court decisions do not "solve the problem" because litigants are unhappy or refuse to accept the decision. As a result, cases persist even after a decision is issued.

Beginning in 2007, then-president of the SPC Xiao Yang argued that courts should focus on resolving cases and solving problems so as to promote social harmony (*anjie shiliao, cujin hexie,* 案结事了促进和谐).[82] Courts should emphasize mediation and rapid resolution of cases and should work to ensure that litigants accept their decisions. As one commentator explained, *anjie shiliao* means courts should work to see that the "legal effects" and "social effects" of their decisions are united.[83] Likewise, court evaluation mechanisms should be adjusted to reward judges who are able not only to decide cases correctly but also to resolve related matters. As described by Wan Exiang (万鄂湘), vice president of the SPC, excessive attention to adjudication and emphasis on procedure have failed to resolve disputes or social contradictions; courts must take more pragmatic and involved approaches to solving problems.[84] Thus, for example, courts facing a party that refuses to go to court will not simply decide against the non-present party — because doing so might later result in petitioning and difficulties enforcing the decision. Instead, judges will seek out the party to try to obtain his or her view prior to issuing a decision.

The legacy of revolutionary legal ideology is also manifest in the resurgence of mediation in the 2000s, with the SPC now stating that all cases that can be resolved through mediation should be mediated.[85] The return to mediation reflects frustration with some of the problems of adjudication, most notably the courts' inability to enforce decisions and the perception that many litigants are dissatisfied with adjudicated cases. Re-emphasis on mediation is also consistent with attempts to build a "harmonious society" and to prevent letters and visits.[86] Like *anjie shiliao*, the return to mediation is a shift away from emphasis on adjudication and procedure. And courts are now mediating a wider range of cases: one recent commentary notes that mediation currently plays a role in all stages of a case, from case filing to enforcement. The percentage of first instance civil cases resolved through mediation or withdrawal of the lawsuit increased from 55 percent of nationwide cases in 2006[87] to 62 percent in 2009.[88] Whereas mediation was previously limited to civil cases, courts are now extending mediation to cover criminal and administrative cases as well.[89] Commentators have criticized this trend, arguing that it leads judges to coerce parties to settle[90] and that it also hinders the creation of new legal rules.[91] Lower court implementation of the "three supremes" has likewise focused on existing efforts to promote settlement,[92] make courts accessible,[93] prioritize cases touching on popular interests,[94] and coordinate decisions with local governments in order to maintain social stability.[95]

Wang Shengjun, who succeeded Xiao Yang as president of the SPC in 2008, has made it clear that emphasis on mediation and *anjie shiliao* are keys to implementing the mass line in the courts and to ensuring that China's courts are not unduly influenced by foreign models. Wang notes that implementing the "three supremes" in the courts requires the courts to focus on social realities and popular views, and the key is attention to *anjie shiliao*, mediation, and letters-and-visits work. Wang argues that "upholding the mass line" in the courts should be "placed on the same level" as professionalization of the courts.[96] Such efforts are central to ensuring that Chinese courts pursue their own development path, not one dictated by Western models. Wang also notes that Chinese courts must be vigilant against efforts by "hostile forces" to subvert the Chinese judicial system, stating that such forces seek to use the judicial system to Westernize and split the country.[97] Ma Xiwu is once again being celebrated. In January 2009 a local court in Gansu opened a "Ma Xiwu Exhibition Hall" to celebrate the Ma Xiwu method, and SPC President Wang wrote an inscription to mark the opening.[98] Wang also cites Ma Xiwu's example in his March 2009 Work Report to the NPC — the first time in recent years that Ma Xiwu has been mentioned.[99]

Despite the rhetorical emphasis on resisting foreign influence, the tradition of "justice for the people" and of mass-line ideology has also facilitated some innovative legal reforms. Much of the emphasis on *sifa weimin* has been in the courts. One of the most concrete examples of the concept in practice, however, has come from the Ministry of Justice. Since 1995 China has engaged in the widespread creation of legal-aid institutions.[100] Legal aid has been encouraged despite knowledge that the creation of a public interest bar has been an important catalyst for regime challenges elsewhere in Asia and in the color revolutions of the former Soviet bloc countries.[101] The embrace of legal aid is in part due to international influence and funding, as well as a belief that a modern legal system must include a legal-aid system.[102] Yet the development of legal aid was also a response to public perceptions that law was inaccessible to many and that the legal system served only those with power or influence. Boosting legal aid thus helps legal institutions, and in particular the Ministry of Justice, to position their own activities as serving the public. In parallel with the courts' embrace of *sifa weimin*, in recent years the Ministry of Justice has taken a series of steps designed to make legal-aid offices more responsive to public needs.[103]

Other legal institutions, most notably people's congresses and some administrative agencies, similarly portray their actions as being in line with popular opinion, or seek out popular input regarding policy.[104] Popular views are increasingly influential in law-making and rule-making, referred to as the process of open-door law-making (*kaimen lifa*, 开门立法). Such efforts are selective and often used strategically to advance particular agendas or in areas not central to party-state policy. For example, William Alford and Yuanyuan Shen note that the widespread debate surrounding the 2001 revisions to the Marriage Law was possible because of "[t]he state's indifference, if not condescension, toward women."[105] Nevertheless, experiments with public hearings and solicitation of public comments regarding draft legislation are striking for a system in which legislatures have only recently begun to be seen as fora where policies and rules are debated as well as enacted.

Many in China and the West describe the experiments as efforts to bring China into line with international practices.[106] Yet these experiments are facilitated by the strong ideological tradition of popular input into the legal system. Hearings serve not only to obtain popular input, but to facilitate the acceptance of new policies and for the state to obtain information about possible problems or contradictions. Hearings can be understood as a new manifestation of the mass line: input is sought to minimize problems and to improve the state's ability to implement its policies.[107] As with legal aid, international models have been important. But equally important has been the view that providing a limited mechanism for public input maintains social stability and boosts legitimacy, both for specific institutions and for the party-state. Understood as an expansion of long-established public feedback mechanisms, public hearings pose little threat of leading to broader calls for democratization.[108] Similarly, regulations on access to government information can be understood as a continuation of efforts to seek public input so that the state can gather information and address local malfeasance.

In the courts, populism is also being used to advance some reforms long advocated by liberal academics. Under the mantle of strengthening "judicial democracy," the SPC has instructed courts to become more open and accessible to the public.[109] The SPC has called on courts to strengthen communication with the public by proactively seeking public opinion, both directly and through the local people's congresses.[110] The Supreme Court also announced plans to make use of "special consultants," generally prominent experts or intellectuals, to critique court policies and to give voice to public criticism of the courts.[111] These steps have been criticized as shifts away from professionalism and the independence of judiciary and for focusing on making courts appear open rather than on improving court quality. But the SPC has also used "judicial democracy" to push local courts to make information on filings, hearings, and decisions publicly available.[112] Courts in a number of provinces have stated that they will put all court decisions online[113] and will stream trials over the Internet.[114] Reformers in China and Western observers have long advocated making court decisions publicly available and court proceedings more accessible. But doing so has proved difficult. Today such reforms are being implemented in the name of "judicial democracy" and "justice for the people."

Populist legality is also manifest in the continued use of legal education, or *pufa*, campaigns to educate about and induce compliance with new legal norms. Legal education campaigns remain important methods to pursue new policies.[115] Thus, for example, the enactment of the Birth Planning Law (more than twenty years after the creation of the one-child policy) is partially aimed at delivering the message that the state is serious about curbing some of the worst abuses in the birth planning system. Likewise, the Labor Contract Law and the Employment Promotion Law, both enacted in 2007, are used to send the message that the state is serious about cracking down on the worst workplace abuses (which are already illegal). The state continues to use legal education campaigns to emphasize policy goals, to educate ordinary people and officials about the law, and to induce local actors to change their conduct. In recent years some local courts have also returned to the use of public criminal trials as a means of public education.[116]

Yet the most important message of legal education campaigns since 1978 is the idea that law is being popularized. The primary goal of the *pufa* campaigns may be to deliver state ideology, not to increase understanding of law. Nevertheless, one message of the *pufa* campaigns is that law should be accessible to ordinary people. The *pufa* efforts encourage individuals to use law to protect their interests and have fostered the creation of a class of "barefoot lawyers" and legal experts in the countryside — persons without formal training who become local experts through self-study. Efforts to make it easier to pass the national bar exam, with the pass rate increasing from 7 to 20 percent over a short period, also suggest a reaction against a perceived overemphasis on developing an elite bar.[117]

Much of the re-emphasis on populist legality has come about in the past decade as Western-style legal reforms have encountered difficulties at the local levels. This return to popular legality is seen against the backdrop of increased instability, a perception that confidence in the legal system is declining, and the recognition that the first two decades of legal reform failed to address fundamental problems in the legal system. Critics of legal reforms argue that the legal system increasingly is becoming dominated by elites and that the emphasis on professionalization and formality results in a legal system that neither serves the interests of ordinary people nor tracks popular morality. Likewise, reforms are seen as focusing on the legal needs of major developed areas, thus ignoring regional differences. Understood against this backdrop, populism in the legal system serves not only to impose mass justice, but also to ensure that legal institutions do not ignore the interests of ordinary people. Put differently, problems in the legal system stem not only from continued party dominance but also from courts and other institutions straying too far from their tradition of relying on public input.

Parallels with the Ma Xiwu era should not be overstated. There is no sign that the project of law reform will be abandoned. Populism today affects the courts but has not led to the excesses of the revolutionary period or the Cultural Revolution. The contemporary embrace of legal populism also reflects attempts by Chinese leaders to reclaim the mantle of Confucian morality and leadership. Indeed, many of the trends described here have historical roots that go much deeper than the revolutionary period: concerns with the social effects of law (as opposed to doctrinal correctness), emphasis on mediation, attempts to reconcile law and popular morality, and efforts to deter potential petitioners all have historical antecedents in China that far precede Ma Xiwu. Such efforts were central to the role of the magistrate in imperial China. Likewise, as Eugenia Lean shows, Republican-era courts struggled to balance popular sentiment as they attempted to define their place in the context of modernization and reform.[118]

The degree to which "populist" views actually reflect the views of the public also should not be overstated — public opinion remains filtered and often refers to the views that party leaders have decided to embrace. Likewise, court efforts to appear responsive to popular opinion may be targeted more to party leaders than to the public. Contemporary and revolutionary populism also differ in important respects: revolutionary populism consisted in significant part of mass mobilization by the party. Populism today is rarely as broad-based. Yet the contemporary state also appears much less in control of populism, just as it is not fully in control of legal reforms.

Efforts to position the current work of the courts as consistent with revolutionary traditions may in significant part consist of using revolutionary language to pursue divergent and diffuse goals. The narrative of consistency with revolutionary legal tradition is being used to show court loyalty to party leadership and to rebuff calls for a Westernization of legal institutions. Such arguments may also protect courts from criticism and facilitate innovation. As other contributors to this volume show, the use of Maoist language for non-Maoist goals is not unique to the legal system. Such appeals may be particularly important in law, however, where reform efforts have often been understood as borrowing heavily from Western experience. Even if appeals to populist traditions are in significant part rhetorical, they may be important tools to emphasize the legal system's loyalty to the state and to legitimatize efforts to make the legal system more responsive to the grievances of ordinary people.

However, the historical links are clear: a re-emphasis on popular input and serving the people as a mechanism for resolving disputes and increasing the legitimacy of legal institutions and the party-state. Court leaders appear to believe that relying on formal legality is not a path to increase their authority. The courts' ability to increase their legitimacy with both the party-state and the public may depend on whether they can blend populist and professionalized justice. Whether they can do so may also determine whether the legal system can become a source of the party-state's legitimacy as well.

Conclusion

China's legal reforms have confounded those who argue that significant reform will necessarily give rise to political challenges to the state or that the party-state is not serious about such reforms other than as a tool for policy implementation. Legal reforms in many respects have exceeded even the most optimistic predictions made thirty years ago. Legal reforms have created a framework for facilitating economic development. But in some cases they have gone beyond the instrumental goals of the state: the legal system has become a vehicle for voicing individual rights and a forum for pressing for social change in discrete areas. Nevertheless, the likelihood of a direct political challenge to the state from legal institutions appears small. And although legal institutions play a more important and complex role today than they did in 1978, there has been no formal increase in their authority.

Historical continuities have played two discrete roles in contemporary legal reforms. First, revolutionary and pre-revolutionary history help to explain certain important elements in the contemporary legal system, in particular the emphasis on flexibility, informality, responsiveness to public opinion, and popular morality, and also a governance structure in which the formal powers of the courts are weak. Second, this history provides a narrative that has facilitated reform and innovation. Revolutionary history also impacts important discontinuities in the legal system: the emphasis on experimentation and flexibility and the willingness to adapt and correct mistakes are both products of governance mechanisms that, as Sebastian Heilmann shows, have a revolutionary pedigree.

To a significant degree the first two decades of reform were characterized by efforts to break with the past and to frame legal reform as being in line with international practices. More recently, the official narrative has shifted, with legal officials emphasizing fidelity to historical tradition, the uniqueness of China's own development model, and the need to avoid blind copying of the West. Yet one of the important reform-era developments is that the state no longer monopolizes how such narratives evolve or are used.

Historical continuities also help explain at least some of the ways in which China's legal reforms differ from those elsewhere. China has engaged in widespread study of foreign legal systems, and the desire to bring China in line with international practices is a major factor behind the legal reforms. The exceptionalism of China's legal reforms, however, comes from mixing foreign imports — from securities and antitrust law to legal aid to public hearings — into a system that continues to embrace flexibility and populism as core principles. Framing such imports as consistent with historical tradition is an important part of the mechanism of adaptation and conversion of Western imports to local dynamics. Legal reforms have been possible not only because of their practical usefulness for economic development or their role in bringing China into line with international practices, but also in some cases because of their fidelity to revolutionary tradition.

The key insight gained from recognizing historical continuities is that flexibility and populism are not historical artifacts; they continue to be key elements of contemporary legal ideology, which mixes increased commitment to the regularization that law brings with populist appeals and popular morality. Flexibility in both substantive law and procedure is needed not only to achieve the party-state's goals but also to ensure that law adjusts to local customs and demands. Adaptive authoritarianism demands that legal institutions continue to serve the policy goals of the state, often bending legal rules in the process. Permitting legal institutions to do this, however, also requires giving legal institutions room to develop, sometimes in surprising ways.

Most legal systems struggle to achieve a balance between professionalism and populism and between flexibility and adherence to legal rules. What appears different in China, however, is that courts that yield to popular input are not acting contrary to an idealized conception of their roles — they are doing exactly what they are supposed to do in the Chinese system. As a result, populism may present less of a problem to the authority of legal institutions in China, where responsiveness to public views (whether genuine or manufactured) remains a key aspect of the institutional obligations of courts.

It is common, in both China and the West, to observe that the Chinese legal system's embrace of both flexibility and populism is in tension with rule of law values.[119] Consistent application of the law and treating like cases alike is fundamental to most conceptions of the rule of law. China's success in legal and economic reforms, however, is partially due to ignoring what might be thought of as core legal values, even as law has become a key element of state ideology. The historical lineage of flexibility and populism, however, suggests that flexibility and populism may also provide a basis for legal institutions to strengthen their own legitimacy.

Tension between populism and professionalism is generally viewed as a problem undermining court legitimacy in China. Yet the embrace of populism may also be a vehicle for ensuring that courts have the space to continue to professionalize. Reliance on formality has failed to provide legitimacy. Court leaders now appear to recognize that they need to embrace populism if they are to succeed at professionalization. Legal principle is often assumed to be in tension with populist views of law; in China, however, building legitimacy for the legal system may require popular support.

Is this mixture of law, flexibility, and populism a sustainable model for continued evolution of the legal system? The tensions inherent in a return to or a continuation of populist legality may pose challenges that exceed those for the adaptive authoritarian model more generally. Legal institutions have shown a sophisticated ability to know when to innovate and when to yield to state interests of stability and development. Such a role may be sustainable so long as the legal system continues to play a supplementary role in regulating state and individual behavior, and not as a referee between state and citizen. One of the lessons of the reform experience is that those looking to the legal system as a base for constraining the party-state are likely to be disappointed. Nevertheless, the persistence of flexibility and populism as key ideological goals, while facilitating some reforms by legal institutions, also appears to raise fundamental questions about legal reforms: Can legal institutions' embrace of flexibility and populism provide a sustainable model for constructing legitimacy, both for such institutions and for the state?

Recognizing historical legal continuities helps illuminate fundamental questions about adaptive authoritarianism. If governance in China is not transitional, then what forms will China's legal institutions take in the future? Are there sustainable institutions that are neither associated with traditional authoritarian regimes nor are forerunners to Western legality? This question is being played out in the area of courts.

China's legal reforms cannot be dismissed as entirely instrumental. Yet the fact that a range of different actors are able to use law for purposes that at times are at odds with the instrumental goals of the state does not mean that China is transitioning to Western-style rule of law. China's legal reform experience is unique in its ability to mix foreign imports with Chinese tradition, and to recast many imported ideas to be in line with the ideological goals of the party. The challenge to sustainability may not be that embracing populism and flexibility undermines core rule of law principles but that ideological commitment to flexibility, populism, and legality risks creating expectations that cannot be met. China's courts appear to be on their way to assuming roles that are quite different from those with which we are familiar — both in Western states and in more traditional authoritarian regimes. If such a model proves sustainable it may be that the reasons for its success are rooted as much in China's pre-reform history as they are in events over the past thirty years.

Endnotes

1. Martin Shapiro, "Courts in Authoritarian Regimes," in Tom Ginsburg and Tamir Moustafa, eds., *Rule By Law: The Politics of Courts in Authoritarian Regimes* (Cambridge: Cambridge University Press, 2008), pp. 326–336. As Shapiro notes (p. 331), contemporary academic scholarship has undermined the "traditional development and rights story."

2. The role of courts and other legal institutions in authoritarian systems has only recently become a significant topic of academic discussion in law and political science. Tamir Moustafa and Tom Ginsburg, "Introduction: The Functions of Courts in Authoritarian Politics," in *Rule By Law: The Politics of Courts in Authoritarian Regimes*, pp. 1–22.

3. Andrew J. Nathan, "Authoritarian Resilience," *Journal of Democracy*, 14, no. 1 (January 2003): 6–17.

4. See, for example, Donald Clarke, Peter Murrell, and Susan Whiting, "The Role of Law in China's Economic Development," in Loren Brandt and Thomas Rawski, eds., *China's Great Economic Transformation* (Cambridge: Cambridge University Press, 2008), pp. 375–428.

5. Elsewhere I survey recent changes in the courts in detail. Benjamin L. Liebman, "China's Courts: Restricted Reform," *Columbia Journal of Asian Law*, 21, no. 1 (2007): 1–44. For an overview of changes in economic law, see Donald C. Clarke, "Legislating for a Market Economy in China," *The China Quarterly*, no. 191 (September 2007): 567–585.

6. See, for example, Stanley B. Lubman, *Bird in a Cage: Legal Reform in China after Mao* (Stanford, CA: Stanford University Press, 1999); Clarke, Murrell, and Whiting, "The Role of Law in China's Economic Development."

7. Liang Zhiping (梁治平), "Fazhi: Shehui zhuanxing shiqi de zhidu jianshe" (法制: 社会转型时期的制度建设) (Rule of Law: The Construction of a System in a Time of Social Transition), in Liang Zhiping (梁治平), ed., *Fazhi zai Zhongguo: Zhidu, huayu yu shijian* (法治在中国: 制度、话语与实践) (Rule of Law in China: Institutions, Discourse, and Practice) (Beijing: Zhongguo zhengfa daxue chubanshe, 2002), pp. 130–131.

8. Ibid., p. 140.

9. Yu Xingzhong (于兴中), "Jiefang, fazhan yu falü: Zou xiang hou xiandai de xiandai xing" (解放、发展与法律: 走向后现代的现代性) (Liberation, Development, and Law: Toward a Post-Modern Modernity), in Liang Zhiping (梁治平), ed., *Guojia, shichang, shehui: Dangdai Zhongguo de falü yu fazhan* (国家, 市场, 社会: 当代中国的法律与发展) (Nation, Market, and Society: Legal Development in Contemporary China) (Beijing: Zhongguo zhengfa daxue chubanshe, 2006), pp. 970–989. Liang Zhiping notes that the legal system is still characterized in significant part by a lack of public law or rights consciousness, both by those in power and by ordinary persons. Liang Zhiping (梁治平), *Fayi yu renqing* (法意与人情) (Legal Meaning and Personal Relationships) (Beijing: Zhongguo fazhi chubanshe, 2003), pp. 304–305.

10. Liang Zhiping, "Fazhi: Shehui zhuanxing shiqi," pp. 130–131.

11. Zhang Jianwei (张建伟), "'Bianfa moshi' yu zhengzhi wendingxing: Zhongguo jingyan ji qi falü jingjixue hanyi" ("变法模式" 与 政治稳定型: 中国经验及其法律经济学含义) (The "Reform Model" and Political Stability: The Chinese Experience and Its Legal and Economic Significance), *Zhongguo shehui kexue* (中国社会科学) (Social Sciences in China), no. 1 (2003): 143; Xie Hongfei (谢鸿飞), "Renmin de 'sifa' yu sifa de 'renmin'" (人民的"司法" 与 司法的"人民") (People's "Justice" and "the People" of Justice), at www.iolaw.org.cn/showarticle.asp?id=2291 (accessed March 3, 2009); Randall Peerenboom, "More Law, Less Courts: Legalized Governance, Judicialization and Dejudicialization in China," in Tom Ginsburg and Albert H.Y. Chen, eds., *Administrative Law and Governance in Asia: Comparative Perspectives* (London: Routledge, 2009), pp. 175–182.

12. Zuo Weimin (左卫民) and Zhou Changjun (周长军), *Bianqian yu gaige: Fayuan zhidu xiandaihua yanjiu* (变迁与改革: 法院制度现代化研究) (Change and Reform: A Study of Modernization of the Court System) (Beijing: Falü chubanshe, 2000).

13. Zhang Jianwei, "'Bianfa moshi' yu zhengzhi wendingxing," pp. 139–141.

14. Some have argued that the party is increasingly using the trappings of legality in its own procedures, as reflected by the creation of procedural rules governing the *shuanggui* detention system. Flora Sapio, "*Shuanggui* and Extralegal Detention in China," *China Information*, 22, no. 1 (2008): 7–37.

15. Sebastian Heilmann, "Policy Experimentation in China's Economic Rise," *Studies in Comparative International Development*, 43, no. 1 (2008): 6–9.

16. For a detailed study of this process in the context of air pollution regulation, see William P. Alford and Benjamin L. Liebman, "Clean Air, Clear Processes? The Struggle over Air Pollution Law in the People's Republic of China," *Hastings Law Journal*, 52, no. 3 (2000–2001): 703. For a general discussion, see Li Zhulan (李竹兰), "Lun guojia zonghe peitao gaige shiyanqu de lifa baozhang" (论国家 综合 配套改革试验区 的立法保障) (Discussion of the Legislative Protections in National Pilot Zones for Overall Reform), *Tianjin shifan daxue xuebao* (天津师范大学学报) (Journal of Tianjin Normal University), 192, no. 3 (2007): 15–19.

17. For a discussion of experimentation in the courts, see Benjamin L. Liebman, "Judges Becoming Judges? Judicial Innovation in China," paper presented at the European China Law Studies Association meeting, Hamburg, August 30–September 1, 2007.

18. Zhang Jianwei, "'Bianfa moshi' yu zhengzhi wendingxing," p. 141.

19. Ibid., p. 145.

20. As Donald Clarke explains, rules that are recognized as being inappropriate often are simply ignored rather than changed. Clarke, "Legislating for a Market Economy in China," pp. 567–585.

21. "Youxian hehuo guanli banfa" (有限合伙管理办法) (Measures for the Management of Limited Partnerships), adopted on February 13, 2001, *Zhongguancun xinwen wang,* at http://news.newzgc.com/html/2007/5900.htm (accessed March 8, 2009).

22. Yu Jingbo (于晶波), "Zhongguancun kaiqi 'xinhezi yundong' yunxu waiqi yu geren hezi" (中关村开启"新合资运动" 允许外企与个人合资) (Zhongguancun to Open "New Joint-Venture Campaign" to Allow Foreign Enterprises to Enter into Joint Ventures with Individuals), *Zhongguo xinwen wang,* March 25, 2004, at http://news.qq .com/a/20040325/000198.htm (accessed March 8, 2009).

23. I discuss these examples in more detail in Liebman, "Judges Becoming Judges?"

24. Such mediation is generally referred to as being *xietiao* (coordination) or *hejie* (reconciliation) rather than the more formal *tiaojie* (mediation). Ni Xuan (倪萱) and Zhang Jing (张静), "Wuhan dapo xingzheng anjian shenli jinqu lu geng kuan" (武汉打破行政案件审理禁区路更宽) (Wuhan Breaks Through the Restricted Area in Hearing Administrative Cases, the Road Is Wider), *Wuhan fayuan wang,* February 1, 2008, at http:// whfy.chinacourt.org/public/detail.php?id=3854 (accessed March 3, 2009).

25. In June 2009 the High People's Court of Henan province began to experiment with a "jury system" in major criminal cases in six municipalities. Under the experiment, jurors — selected from a pool of both ordinary people and people's congress representatives — submit their non-binding opinions regarding guilt and sentences to the courts in cases that have a "serious social impact," that have received public attention, or that may affect social stability. Chen Haifa (陈海发) and Ji Tianfu (冀天福), "Henan quansheng fayuan renmin peishentuan shidian gongzuo xianchanghui zai Kaifeng zhaokai" (河南全省法院人民陪审团试点工作现场会在开封召开) (The On-the-Spot Meeting on Experimentation in People's Jury Work of All Courts in Henan Province Opens in Kaifeng), *Zhongguo fayuan wang,* March 26, 2010, at http://www.chinacourt.org/html/ article/201003/26/401240.shtml (accessed March 30, 2010). Deng Hongyang (邓红阳), "Henan ni quanmian tuixing 'renmin peishentuan' zhidu" (河南拟全面推行"人民陪审团"制度) (Henan Drafts a Plan to Implement Comprehensively the "People's Jury" System), *Fazhi ribao* (法制日报) (Legal Daily), March 26, 2010, at http://npc.people .com.cn/GB/71673/11227704.html (accessed April 14, 2010). Commentators have criticized the experiment for lacking a legal basis in the Criminal Procedure Law, for its use in appeals rather than in first instance trials, and for the fact that defendants have no right to refuse the involvement of jurors. Wang Jiancheng (汪建成), "Feilü feima de 'Henan peishentuan' gaige dangshenxing" (非驴非马的"河南陪审团"改革当慎行) (The "Henan People's Jury System" Reform, Which Resembles Nothing on Earth, Should be Implemented Carefully), *Beida falü wang,* at http://article.chinalawinfo.com/ Article_Detail.asp?ArticleID=49885 (accessed April 14, 2010).

26. Benjamin L. Liebman and Tim Wu, "China's Network Justice," *Chicago Journal of International Law,* 8, no. 1 (2007): 257–321.

27. Sebastian Heilmann, "From Local Experiments to National Policy: The Origins of China's Distinctive Policy Process," *The China Journal,* no. 59 (2008): 2.

28. Ibid., pp. 5, 7.

29. Liebman and Wu, "China's Network Justice," pp. 294–301.

30. Ibid.

31. Arguments regarding professionalization are not only a reflection of efforts to strengthen legal institutions. As William Alford shows, lawyers have used calls for professionalism as a tool to restrict competition from non-lawyers. William P. Alford, "'Second Lawyers,' First Principles: Lawyers, Rice-Roots Legal Workers, and the Battle Over Legal Professionalism in China," in William P. Alford, Kenneth Winston, and William C. Kirby, eds., *Prospects for the Professions in China* (London: Routledge, 2011).

32. Ma Mingfeng (马明峰), "Yucheng fayuan sixiang cuoshi caliang sifa weimin chuangkou" (虞城法院四项措施擦亮司法为民窗口) (Yucheng Court's Four Measures Brighten the Window of Justice for the People), *Henan fayuan wang*, October 25, 2005, at http://hnfy.chinacourt.org/public/detail.php?id=66954 (accessed March 9, 2009).

33. Su Yongtong (苏永通), "Bu an 'fali' chupai de gaoyuan yuanzhang" (不按"法理" 出牌的高院院长) (A High Court President Does Not Play by "Legal Principle"), *Nanfang zhoumo*, February 19, 2009, at http://www.360doc.com/content/09/0222/08/72265_2611813.shtml (accessed July 8, 2010).

34. Qiu Feng (秋风) "Jiandu faguan, zhixu sifa huigui benxing" (监督法官, 只需司法回归本性) (To Supervise Judges Only Requires That the Judiciary Return to Its Basic Nature), *Nanfang dushi bao*, February 2, 2009, at http://opinion.nfdaily.cn/content/2009-02/02/content_4872731.htm (accessed July 8, 2010).

35. "Shangshu renda jianyi xiugai 'chaiqian tiaoli,' wu jiaoshou toulu 'huxian' dongji" (上书人大建议修改 "拆迁条例" 五教授透露 "护宪" 动机) (Five Professors Petition the NPC to Amend the "Regulations on Demolition and Relocation" and Reveal That Their Motive Is to Protect the Constitution), *Renmin wang*, January 6, 2010, at http://gd.people.com.cn/GB/123946/10716060.html (accessed April 14, 2010). The Legislative Affairs Office of the State Council responded quickly to the petition and to public debate regarding the regulations, releasing new draft regulations for public comment in January 2010. Chen Fei (陈菲) and Cui Qingxin (崔清新), "'Xin chaiqian tiaoli' zheng minyi, shouci xianding gonggong liyi fanwei" ("新拆迁条例" 征民意首次限定公共利益范围) (Public Comments Are Solicited Regarding the Draft of the "New Regulations on Demolition and Relocation," for the First Time the Scope of "Public Interest" Is Restricted), *Xinhua wang*, January 28, 2010, at http://news.xinhuanet.com/legal/2010-01/28/content_12894935.htm (accessed April 14, 2010).

36. It is not only rights activists who strategically use legal rhetoric to support their claims; such legal arguments are also used by disloyal agents of the state to justify actions, such as the taking of state property for personal use.

37. See, for example, Chi Haiping (池海平), "Sifa gaige yundong dui woguo xianxing sifa tizhi gaige de qishi" (司法改革运动对我国现行司法体制改革的启示) (The Implications of the Judicial Reform Movement for the Current Reform of the Judicial System in Our Nation), *Lilun yuekan* (理论月刊) (Theory Monthly), no. 6 (2004): 92–96. Chi argues that the 1952–53 Judicial Reform Movement was the most important event in the construction of China's legal system — and should be studied so as to ensure its mistakes are not repeated. Likewise, Mustafa and Ginsburg argue that the legal system has been used to build legitimacy and to distinguish China's reform-era leaders from those of the past. Mustafa and Ginsburg, "Introduction," p. 12.

38. Trygve Lötveit, *Chinese Communism 1931–1934: Experience in Civil Government* (London: Curzon Press, 2nd ed., 1979), p. 139.

39. Ibid., p. 127.

40. Wang Jide (王吉德) and Liu Jin'e (刘金娥), "Shaan-Gan-Ning bianqu gaodeng fayuan jigou shezhi ji qi zhineng de yanbian" (陕甘宁边区高等法院机构设置及其职能的演变) (The Design of the Shaanxi-Gansu-Ningxia Border Region High Court Structure and the Evolution of Its Functions), *Shaanxi dang'an* (陕西档案) (Shaanxi Archives), no. 2 (2007): 34–38.

41. Hou Xinyi (侯欣一), "Shaan-Gan-Ning bianqu renmin tiaojie zhidu yanjiu" (陕甘宁边区人民调解制度研究) (Research on the People's Mediation System in the Shaanxi-Gansu-Ningxia Border Region), *Zhongguo faxue* (中国法学) (China Legal Science), no. 4 (2007): 104.

42. Ibid., p. 105.

43. Jiang Shigong (强世功), "Quanli de zuzhi wangluo yu falü de zhilihua: Ma Xiwu shenpan fangshi yu Zhongguo falü de xin chuantong" (权利的组织网络与法律的治理化: 马锡五审判方式与中国法律的新传统) (The Organizational Nexus of Power and Governance by Law: The Ma Xiwu Adjudication Method and the New Legal Tradition in China), *Beida falü pinglun* (北大法律评论) (Peking University Law Review), no. 3 (2000): 1–61, at http://wen.org.cn/modules/article/view.article.php?article=1118 (accessed July 27, 2010). For an additional summary of the Ma Xiwu method, see Fan Yu (范愉), "Jianlun Ma Xiwu shenpan fangshi: Yizhong minshi susong moshi de xingcheng ji qi lishi mingyun" (简论马锡五审判方式：一种民事诉讼模式的形成及其历史命运) (Brief Discussion of the Ma Xiwu Adjudication Method: The Formation and Historical Destiny of a Civil Litigation Model), *Zhongguo minshang falü wang*, April 20, 2003, at http://www.civillaw.com.cn/Article/default.asp?id=9639 (accessed March 3, 2009).

44. Shao-chuan Leng, *Justice in Communist China: A Survey of the Judicial System of the Chinese People's Republic* (Dobbs Ferry, NY: Oceana Publications, 1967), p. 15; Stanley Lubman, "Introduction to Judicial Work in T'ai-hang," *Chinese Law and Government*, 6, no. 3 (Fall 1973): 4; Simon Roberts and Michael Palmer, *Dispute Processes: ADR and the Primary Forms of Decision Making* (Cambridge: Cambridge University Press, 2005), pp. 22–23. Ai Shaorun (艾绍润), *Ma Xiwu shenpan fangshi* (马锡五审判方式) (The Ma Xiwu Adjudication Method) (Xi'an: Shaanxi renmin chubanshe, 2007), pp. 48–56.

45. Hou Xinyi, "Shaan-Gan-Ning bianqu renmin tiaojie zhidu yanjiu," p. 108.

46. Jiang Shigong, "Quanli de zuzhi wangluo yu falü de zhilihua," pp. 1–61; Leng, *Justice in Communist China*, pp. 12, 29.

47. Jiang Shigong, "Quanli de zuzhi wangluo yu falü de zhilihua," p. 56.

48. Ibid., pp. 1–61.

49. Ibid., p. 41. Although they made up only about 6,000 of the 28,000 judicial personnel at the time, they were concentrated in the major cities and were often responsible for dispute resolution. Zhang Min (张憨), "Shilun 1952 nian sifa gaige yundong" (试论1952年司法改革运动) (Discussion of the Judicial Reform Movement of 1952), *Falü shiyong* (法律适用) (National Judges College Law Journal), no. 8 (2004): 55–58.

50. Ibid., p. 55.

51. Ibid., p. 56; Huang Wenyi (黄文艺), "1952–1953 nian sifa gaige yundong yanjiu" (1952–1953 年司法改革运动研究) (Studies on the 1952–1953 Judicial Reform Movement), *Jiangxi shehui kexue* (江西社会科学) (Jiangxi Social Sciences), no. 4 (2004):

37–42. There was, however, also an emphasis on legal education as new personnel were needed to replace those removed from office.

52. David Bachman, "Aspects of an Institutionalizing Political System: China, 1958–1965," *The China Quarterly*, no. 188 (2006): 933–958.

53. For a comprehensive study of the impact of the Marriage Law, see Neil J. Diamant, *Revolutionizing the Family: Politics, Love, and Divorce in Urban and Rural China* (Berkeley: University of California Press, 2000).

54. Chi Haiping, "Sifa gaige yundong," pp. 92–96.

55. As Jiang Shigong notes, although the relationship between the state and individuals has changed in China since the 1980s, law is "not yet separate from its political mother." Jiang Shigong (强世功), *Fazhi yu zhili: Guojia zhuanxing zhong de falü* (法制与治理: 国家转型中的法律) (Law and Governance: Law Amidst State Transition) (Beijing: Zhongguo zhengfa daxue chubanshe, 2003).

56. Chen Jianfu, *Chinese Law: Context and Transformation* (Leiden: Martinus Nijhoff, 2008), p. 52.

57. Liang Zhiping, "Fazhi: Shehui zhuanxing shiqi," pp. 130–131. Liang also notes, however, that such problems cannot be blamed entirely on communism: they also are a legacy of traditional culture.

58. Fan Yu, "Jianlun Ma Xiwu shenpan fangshi."

59. Not until 1983 did the Organic Law of the People's Courts call for judges to have expertise, and even then the law did not define expertise. The 1995 Judges Law was the first to provide specific requirements for serving as judges. Beginning in 2002 new judges and procurators were required to hold undergraduate degrees (not necessarily in law) and to pass the national bar exam. Zhang Min, "Shilun 1952 nian sifa gaige yundong," p. 58.

60. Fan Yu, "Jianlun Ma Xiwu shenpan fangshi." The Ma Xiwu method remains important in certain substantive areas, including marriage and debt cases, and in the countryside. Not everyone agrees that the Ma Xiwu method is the source of problems: there are those who contend that this approach is far more realistic than transplanting law from the West (or from Beijing) to the countryside. As Zhao Xiaoli notes, although legal reforms in the 1980s were designed to formalize legal procedures and move away from the Ma Xiwu style, in practice courts at the local level found doing so difficult. They were underfunded and remained "embedded in . . . a network of power relations [with] the local Party Committees and government." Zhao Xiaoli, "The Two Faces of the People's Tribunals in Rural China," *Perspectives*, 3, no. 4 (March 31, 2002), at http://www.oycf .org/oycfold/httpdocs/Perspectives2/16_033102/two_faces.htm (accessed March 8, 2009).

61. Wang Jianxun (王建勋), "'Yundong shi zhifa' beili fazhi jingshen" ("运动式执法" 背离法制精神) ("Campaign-Style Law Implementation" Deviates from the Spirit of the Rule of Law), *Nanfang dushi bao*, October 26, 2008, at http://www.nanfangdaily .com.cn/spqy/200810260040.asp (accessed July 8, 2010).

62. I discuss specific cases and court reactions to such pressures elsewhere. Benjamin L. Liebman, "Watchdog or Demagogue": The Media in the Chinese Legal System," *Columbia Law Review*, 105, no. 1 (January 2005), pp. 1–157; Liebman and Wu, "China's Network Justice." Public pressure does not always lead to outcomes in line with public opinion: in some high-profile criminal cases, most notably the Wang Binyu and Yang Jia cases, the authorities appeared to go out of their way to make it clear that public

sympathy for the defendants would not sway the courts. Such responses also suggest that courts do not have the final say in high-profile controversial cases.

63. Benjamin L. Liebman, "A Populist Threat to China's Courts?" in Mary Gallagher and Margaret Woo, eds., *Chinese Justice: Civil Dispute Resolution in Post-Reform China* (Cambridge: Cambridge University Press, forthcoming 2011).

64. Qin Xudong (秦旭东), "Zuigao fayuan yuanzhang tan sixing yiju yinfa zhengyi" (最高法院院长谈死刑依据引发争议) (The Discussion of the President of the Supreme People's Court on the Basis for Capital Punishment Stirs Up Controversy), *Caijing wang*, April 11, 2008, at http://www.caijing.com.cn/20080411/56061.shtml (accessed March 3, 2009).

65. Ibid.

66. Wang Shengjun (王胜俊), "Gaoju qizhi yu shiju jin nuli kaichuang renmin fayuan gongzuo xin jumian" (高举旗帜与时俱进努力开创人民法院工作新局面) (Hold the Flag High and Keep Pace with the Times to Kick Off a New Phase in Court Work), *Zhongguo fayuan wang*, August 7, 2008, at http://www.chinacourt.org/public/detail.php?id=316078 (accessed March 3, 2009).

67. He Weifang (贺卫方), "'Sange zhishang' shei zhishang?" ("三个至上" 谁致上？) (Which Is Supreme among the "Three Supremes"?), August 27, 2008, at http://blog.sina.com.cn/s/blog_488663200100atga.html (accessed March 3, 2009).

68. "Zuigao renmin fayuan bangongting fuzhuren, xinwen fayanren Wang Shaonan zuoke Xinhua wang, jiedu zuigao renmin fayuan gongzuo baogao" (最高人民法院办公厅副主任、新闻发言人王少南做客新华网,解读最高人民法院工作报告) (Wang Shaonan, the Spokesperson and Deputy Director of the General Office of the Supreme People's Court, Is a Guest at Xinhua Net and Interprets the Supreme Court's Work Report), *Zuigao renmin fayuan wang*, March 13, 2010, at http://www.court.gov.cn/xwzx/jdjd/zxft/201003/t20100313_2952.htm (accessed April 26, 2010).

69. See generally Mustafa and Ginsburg, "Introduction."

70. See "Zuigao renmin fayuan 'Guanyu luoshi 23 xiang sifa weimin juti cuoshi de zhidao yijian'" (最高人民法院 "关于落实 23 项司法为民具体措施的指导意见") (Guiding Opinion of the Supreme People's Court "On 23 Specific Measures for Implementing Justice for the People"), issued on December 2, 2003, *Xinhua wang*, at http://news.xinhuanet.com/legal/2003-12/03/content_1211777_1.htm (accessed April 26, 2010); Xie Hongfei, "Renmin de 'sifa' yu sifa de 'renmin.'"

71. Mao Jianjun (毛建军), "Zhongguo shouxi dafaguan Xiao Yang: Sifa weimin bushi jiandan kouhao" (中国首席大法官肖扬: 司法为民不是简单口号) (Chinese Chief Justice Xiao Yang: Justice for the People Is not a Simple Slogan), *Zhongguo xinwen wang*, September 20, 2003, at http://www.chinanews.com.cn/n/2003-09-20/26/348871.html (accessed March 3, 2009).

72. Ibid.

73. Ma Mingfeng, "Yucheng fayuan sixiang cuoshi caliang sifa weimin chuangkou."

74. Liu Shunbin (刘顺斌), "Shilun xiandai sifa linian yu sifa weimin de guanxi" (试论现代司法理念与司法为民的关系) (The Relationship between Modern Judicial Concepts and Justice for the People), *Dongfang fayan*, August 24, 2005, at http://www.dffy.com/faxuejieti/zh/200508/20050824070820.htm (accessed March 3, 2009).

75. Ibid.

76. For an insightful study of this new approach in one court in Fujian, see Yu Zhong (喻中), "Lun 'Lixin shenpan fangshi'" (论 "里心审判方式") (Discussing the "Lixin Adjudication Method"), *Qinghua faxue* (清华法学) (Tsinghua Law Journal), no. 11 (April 2007): 161–188. Among the courts' other efforts are helping litigants draft litigation-related documents, focusing on mediation, and being flexible regarding procedural requirements. In some areas, however, the Ma Xiwu system has persisted throughout the reform era — although it has received renewed attention in recent years.

77. Ibid.

78. Huang Hui (黄辉), "Fuzhou 'zhongdian faguan' yige dianhua jiudao 'jizhen' anjian li deng ke diao" (抚州 "钟点法官" 一个电话就到 "急诊" 案件立等可调) ("Hour" Judges in Fuzhou Will Arrive Immediately After One Phone Call in Emergency Cases), *Fazhi ribao*, April 6, 2010, at http://www.legalinfo.gov.cn/index/content/2010-04/07/content_2106012.htm?node=7863 (accessed April 7, 2010).

79. Xie Hongfei, "Renmin de 'sifa' yu sifa de 'renmin.'"

80. Wang Jide and Liu Jin'e, "Shaan-Gan-Ning bianqu gaodeng fayuan jigou shezhi ji qi zhineng de yanbian."

81. Ma Mingfeng, "Yucheng fayuan sixiang cuoshi caliang sifa weimin chuangkou"; "Zuigao renmin fayuan 'Guanyu luoshi 23 xiang sifa weimin juti cuoshi de zhidao yijian.'"

82. Yi Zhongfa (易忠法), "Lun 'anjie shiliao'" (论 "案结事了") (Discussing "Deciding the Case and Solving the Problem"), *Fazhi yu shehui* (Legal System and Society), no. 2 (2008): 194–195.

83. Ibid.

84. "Wan Exiang: 'Tiaopan jiehe' zui zhuyao qiangdiao 'anjie shiliao'" (万鄂湘: "调判结合" 最主要强调 "案结事了") (Wan Exiang: The Most Important Thing in "Unifying Mediation and Adjudication" Is "Deciding the Case and Solving the Problem"), *Renmin wang*, March 7, 2007, at http://news.sina.com.cn/c/2007-03-07/101112452959.shtml (accessed July 8, 2010).

85. Yi Zhongfa, "Lun 'anjie shiliao.'"

86. Xia Min (夏敏), "Anjie shiliao: Yige bu qingsong de shenpan keti" (案结事了: 一个不轻松的审判课题) (Deciding Cases and Solving the Problem: A Not Insignificant Adjudication Research Topic), *Zhongguo shenpan xinwen yuekan* (中国审判新闻月刊) (China Trial), no. 2 (2007): 12–16.

87. Zhongguo falü nianjian bianweihui (中国法律年鉴编委会), *2007 Zhongguo falü nianjian*) (2007 中国法律年鉴) (2007 Law Yearbook of China) (Beijing: Falü chubanshe, 2007), p. 1066.

88. Wang Shengjun (王胜俊), "Zuigao renmin fayuan gongzuo baogao" (最高人民法院工作报告) (Work Report of the Supreme People's Court), *Xinhua wang*, March 11, 2010, at http://news.sina.com.cn/c/2010-03-18/100119890014.shtml (accessed July 7, 2010).

89. "Wan Exiang: 'Tiaopan jiehe.'"

90. Wang Liming (王利明), "Tiaojie ying chongfen shanzhong dangshiren ziyuan yuanze" (调解应充分善重当事人自愿原则) (Mediation Should Fully Respect the Principle of Voluntariness for Litigants), *Beida falü wang*, at http://article.chinalawinfo.com/Article_Detail.asp?ArticleID=35220 (accessed April 1, 2010).

91. Xia Min (夏敏), "Tiaojie bing bu biran anjie shiliao" (调解并不必然案结事了) (Mediation Does Not Mean That the Case Has Been Decided and the Problem Has Been Solved), *Beida falü wang*, 2009, at http://article.chinalawinfo.com/Article_Detail .asp?ArticleID=49153 (accessed April 1, 2010).

92. "Zhongshi jianxin 'sange zhishang' zhidao sixiang, nuli kaichuang renmin fayuan gongzuo de xin jumian" (忠实践行 "三个至上" 指导思想努力开创人民法院工作 的新局面) (Fully Implement the Guiding Thought of the "Three Supremes" Resolutely to Kick Off a New Phase of Work of the People's Courts), *Jiange xian zhengfa wang*, December 1, 2008, at http://www.jgzfw.gov.cn/newsdisp.asp?id=4280 (accessed March 9, 2009); Ming Yiting (民一庭), "Huanggang minshi shenpan gongzuo renzhen guanche luoshi 'sange zhishang' zhidao sixiang" (黄冈民事审判工作认真贯彻落实 "三个至 上" 指导思想) (Huanggang Civil Adjudication Work Conscientiously and Thoroughly Implements the Guiding Thought of the "Three Supremes"), *Huanggang fayuan wang*, September 3, 2008, at http://www.hgzjfy.gov.cn/Article/ShowArticle.asp?ArticleID=93 (accessed March 9, 2009).

93. Ibid.

94. These include labor disputes, and cases concerning back pay, traffic accidents, and claims for support. Wang Qinqi (王勤淇), "Jianxing 'sange zhishang' luoshi sifa weimin" (践行"三个至上"落实司法为民) (Carrying Out the "Three Supremes" in Order to Implement Justice for the People), *Shanxi fayuan wang*, August 12, 2008, at http://www .sxfyw.gov.cn/funonews.asp?id=10282 (accessed March 9, 2009).

95. Zheng Yangfan (郑扬帆), Zhu Guilong (朱桂龙), and Yang Guodi (杨国地), "Xianfayuan jianxing 'sange zhishang' lüxing shenpan zhineng" (县法院践行" 三个至 上" 履行审判职能) (County Court Implements "Three Supremes" to Fulfill Its Adjudication Duties), *Meizhou ribao* (湄洲日报) (Meizhou Daily), November 10, 2008, at http:// www.xianyou.gov.cn/gov/news/bumen/webinfo/2008/11/10/1226023910705758 .htm (accessed March 9, 2009); Cao Shouye (曹守晔), "'Shequ faguan' shi 'Ma Xiwu shenpan fangshi' de jicheng he fayang" ("社区法官" 是 "马锡五审判方式" 的继承和 发扬) (The "Community Judge" Is the Descendant and Developer of the "Ma Xiwu Adjudication Method"), *Xinhua wang*, March 16, 2009, at http://news.xinhuanet.com/ legal/2009-03/16/content_11017957.htm (accessed July 8, 2010).

96. Wang Shengjun, "Gaoju qizhi yushi jujing nuli kaichuang renmin fayuan gongzuo xin jumian"; Wang Yinsheng (王银胜), "Qunzhong guannian he qunzhong ganqing shi renmin fayuan jiaqiang he gaijin gongzuo de yuan dongli" (群众观念和群众感情是 人民法院加强和改进工作的源动力) (The People's Feelings and Emotions Are the Origins of the Motivations for the Courts to Strengthen and Improve Their Work), *Zhongguo fayuan wang*, October 21, 2008, at http://www.chinacourt.org/public/detail .php?id=326302 (accessed March 9, 2009); Liu Xiaopeng (刘晓鹏), "Wang Shengjun: Fayuan yao jianli changtong de minyi goutong he biaoda jizhi" (王胜俊: 法院要建立畅 通的民意沟通和表达机制) (Wang Shengjun: The Courts Should Have a Smooth System for People to Communicate and Express Their Opinions), *Zhongguo fayuan wang*, June 23, 2008, at http://www.chinacourt.org/public/detail.php?id=308564 (accessed March 9, 2009).

97. In a return to revolutionary-era language, Wang argues that foreign forces will "use every and any means possible" to negate the Chinese legal system and "intervene in

contradictions among our people." He states that the judicial area is one of the "most important ideological areas" in which "our nation and foreign forces compete." Wang Shengjun (王胜俊), "Zai quanguo gaoji fayuan yuanzhang huiyishang de jianghua" (在全国高级法院院长会议上的讲话) (Speech at the National Conference for High Court Presidents), *Renmin fayuan bao*, December 22, 2008, at http://news.xinhuanet.com/legal/2008-12/22/content_10541536.htm (accessed July 27, 2010).

98. Wang Ye (王烨), "Ma Xiwu shenpan fangshi zhanting zai Gansu luocheng" (马锡五审判方式展厅在甘肃落成) (The Exhibition Hall of the Ma Xiwu Adjudication Method Opens in Gansu), *Zuigao renmin fayuan wangzhan*, January 22, 2009, at http://rmfyb.chinacourt.org/public/detail.php?id=125377 (accessed July 27, 2010).

99. Wang Shengjun (王胜俊), "Zuigao renmin fayuan gongzuo baogao" (最高人民法院工作报告) (Supreme People's Court Work Report), March 10, 2009, at http://www.gov.cn/2009lh/content_1261101.htm (accessed April 1, 2010).

100. One report puts the total number of government legal-aid offices at 3,081 — up from 0 in 1995. Li Hongbo (李红勃), "Falü yuanzhu zai Zhongguo: Lishi, xianzhuang yu weilai" (法律援助在中国: 历史、现状与未来) (Legal Aid in China: History, Current Situation, and the Future), *Zhongguo renquan*, no. 1 (2008): 48–51. Legal-aid lawyers reported handling 546,000 cases in 2008, up from 318,514 in 2006. Zhongguo falü nianjian bianweihui, *2007 Zhongguo falü nianjian*, p. 246; Zhongguo falü nianjian bianweihui (中国法律年鉴编委会), *2009 Zhongguo falü nianjian* (2009 中国法律年鉴) (2009 Law Yearbook of China) (Beijing: Falü chubanshe, 2009), p. 250.

101. Halliday and Liu make a similar point in their study of defense lawyers in China: the Ministry of Justice has facilitated networking among defense lawyers, resulting in the development of a nascent professional identity and activist lawyering. Terence C. Halliday and Sida Liu, "Birth of a Liberal Movement? Looking Through a One-Way Mirror at Lawyers' Defence of Criminal Defendants in China," in Terence C. Halliday, Lucien Karpik, and Malcolm M. Feeley, eds., *Fighting for Political Freedom: Comparative Studies of the Legal Complex and Political Liberalism* (Portland, OR: Hart Publishing, 2007), pp. 65–108.

102. The strong state role in legal aid may also be an attempt to pre-empt the development of a robust non-state public interest bar. But the Ministry of Justice has also permitted, if not entirely embraced, the development of non-state public interest lawyering.

103. For example, in 2007 the Ministry of Justice called on legal-aid institutions to "get close to the masses and serve society." In response, legal-aid offices expanded their use of telephone hotlines, online consulting, and the delivery of legal aid in villages, factories, and prisons. Zhongguo falü nianjian bianweihui (中国法律年鉴编委会), *2008 Zhongguo falü nianjian* (2008 中国法律年鉴) (2008 Law Yearbook of China) (Beijing: Falü chubanshe, 2008), pp. 281–282; Sun Chunying (孙春英) and Yu Nayang (于呐洋), "Sifabu jueding zai quanguo kaizhan 'falü yuanzhu bianmin fuwu' zhuti huodong" (司法部决定在全国开展"法律援助便民服务"主题活动) (The Ministry of Justice Decides to Hold Nationwide Activities on the Topic of "Making Legal-Aid Services Convenient for the Public"), *Sifabu wangzhan*, May 31, 2009, at http://www.legalinfo.gov.cn/moj/2008rdgz/2009-05/31/content_1097278.htm (accessed April 20, 2010).

104. For a discussion of provincial hearings, see He Cong (何聪) and Chen Jie (陈杰), "Jujiao 'kaimen lifa': Rang gongzhong cong yuantou canyu zhengfu lifa" (聚焦

"开门立法": 让公众从源头参与政府立法) (Focusing on "Open-Door Legislating": Allow Public Participation from the Start in Government Legislating), *Renmin ribao* (人民日报) (People's Daily), September 20, 2005, at http://news.xinhuanet.com/politics/2005-09/20/content_3516998.htm (accessed April 24, 2010); Song Bin (宋斌) and Cai Min (蔡敏), "Kaimen lifa: Zhongguo gongzhong kaishi quanmian canyu zhiding lifa jihua" (开门立法: 中国公众开始全面参与制定立法计划) (Open-Door Legislating: The Chinese Public Begins to Participate Fully in Formulating the Legislative Plan), *Xinhua wang*, September 23, 2005, at http://news.xinhuanet.com/legal/2005-09/23/content_3532066.htm (accessed March 9, 2009); Jiang Houliang (江厚良), "Geshui qizhengdian tingzhenghui de pobing yiyi" (个税起征点听证会的破冰意义) (The Icebreaking Significance of the Hearing on Tax Thresholds), *Guangzhou ribao* (广州日报) (Guangzhou Daily), August 30, 2005, at http://news.xinhuanet.com/legal/2005-08/30/content_3421427.htm (accessed July 27, 2010). Although most of the experiments with increased public input have been at the provincial or local levels, the National People's Congress has also solicited views for selected legislation — most notably the Marriage Law and the Property Law.

105. William P. Alford and Yuanyuan Shen, "Have You Eaten? Have You Divorced? Debating the Meaning of Freedom in Marriage in China," in William C. Kirby, ed., *Realms of Freedom in Modern China* (Stanford, CA: Stanford University Press, 2004), p. 261.

106. For examples see Feng Ying (冯英), "Xingzheng lifa tingzheng de minzhu jiazhi ji zhidu baozhang" (行政立法听证的民主价值及制度保障) (The Democratic Value and Systemic Guarantees of Administrative and Legislative Hearings), *Guoji guanxi xueyuan xuebao* (国际关系学院学报) (Journal of the Institute of International Relations), no. 2 (2006): 73–76; Peerenboom, "More Law, Less Courts," p. 6; Yang Haikun (杨海坤), "Guanyu xingzheng tingzheng zhidu ruogan wenti de yantao" (关于行政听证制度若干问题的研讨) (Discussion Concerning Some Issues Regarding the System of Administrative Hearings), *Jiangsu shehui kexue* (江苏社会科学) (Social Science in Jiangsu), no. 1 (1998): 74–81; Liang Jian (梁剑), "Touxi woguo tingzheng zhidu de xianzheng jiazhi huigui" (透析我国听证制度的宪政价值回归) (Careful Analysis of the Return of Constitutional Value in Our Nation's Hearings System), *Dongyue luncong* (东岳论丛) (Dongyue Tribune), no. 6 (November 2005): 193–195. Others, however, describe the hearings as mere showpieces designed to provide an illusion of popular influence in a system that remains authoritarian. Wang Faqing (王法庆), "Gongzhong canyu difang lifa de tantao" (公众参与地方立法的探讨) (Discussion of Public Participation in Local Law-Making), *Falü jiaoyu wang*, March 23, 2007, at http://www.china-lawedu.com/news/21606/138/2007/3/li8685775513237002784-0.htm (accessed March 3, 2009); Feng Ying (冯英), "Cong 'tingzheng xiu' dao 'tingzheng hui'" (从"听证秀"到"听证会") (From "Show Hearings" to "Hearings"), *Zhongguo shehui daokan* (中国社会导刊) (China Society Periodical), no. 8 (2005): 42–44.

107. Ji Weidong (季卫东), "Falü bianzuan de shixing: Zai shishi yu guifan zhijian de fansi jizhi" (法律编纂的试行: 在事实与规范之间的反思机制) (The Legal Codification of Experiments: The Process for Reflecting between Facts and Norms), *Zhongguo falü wang*, 2000, at http://article.chinalawinfo.com/article/user/article_display.asp?ArticleID=28644 (accessed March 3, 2009). Ji Weidong describes this process as "propaganda in the guise of soliciting feedback."

108. The limited nature of the experiments is highlighted by some of the strong criticism of such efforts within China. Zhao Jing'an (赵京安), "'Kaimen lifa': Zhuhai lifa tingzhenghui yiwai zao 'leng yu'" ("开门立法": 珠海立法听证会意外遭"冷遇") ("Open-Door Legislating": Zhuhai Legislative Hearing Unexpectedly Encounters "Cold Treatment"), *Xinhua wang*, September 14, 2005, at http://news.xinhuanet.com/legal/2005-09/14/content_3486821.htm (accessed March 3, 2009). Legislatures and administrative agencies have been criticized for selectively using hearings, and for selectively publicizing the fact hearings are held. Some commentators have noted that there is no mechanism or requirement for responses to public input, and little room for interest or expert groups. Wang Faqing, "Gongzhong canyu difang lifa de tantao."

109. Chen Baocheng (陈宝成), "Xinyilun fayuan gaige shouchang sifa minzhuhua" (新一轮法院改革首倡司法民主化) (The New Wave of Court Reform First Calls for Democratization of the Judiciary), *Fenghuang zixun*, March 31, 2009, at http://news.ifeng.com/mainland/200903/0331_17_1084150.shtml (accessed April 1, 2010).

110. "Zuigao renmin fayuan guanyu jinyibu jiaqiang minyi goutong gongzuo de yijian" (最高人民法院关于进一步加强民意沟通工作的意见) (Opinion of the Supreme People's Court on the Work of Further Strengthening Communication with the Public), *Zhongguo fayuan wang*, April 14, 2009, at http://news.xinhuanet.com/legal/2009-04/14/content_11184305.htm (accessed April 1, 2010).

111. "Zuigao renmin fayuan teyao zixunyuan gongzuo tiaoli" (最高人民法院特邀咨询员工作条例) (Working Regulations for Special Consultants in the Supreme People's Court), May 26, 2009, *Zuigao renmin fayuan wang*, at http://www.court.gov.cn/qwfb/sfwj/jd/201002/t20100224_1923.htm (accessed April 1, 2010).

112. "Zuigaofa chutai 'Guanyu sifa gongkai de liuxiang guiding'" (最高法出台"关于司法公开的六项规定") (The Supreme People's Court Releases "Six Regulations Regarding Judicial Openness"), *Zhongguo xinwen wang*, December 23, 2009, at http://finance.baidu.com/2009-12-23/122136317.html (accessed April 1, 2010).

113. "Henan sanji fayuan caipan wenshu shangwang: 'Gexing guanyuan' zhutui sifa xinxi gongkai" (河南三级法院裁判文书上网: "个性官员"助推司法信息公开) (Decisions by Three Levels of Courts in Henan are Put on the Internet: A "Unique Official" Promotes Open Judicial Information), *Zhengyi wang*, January 12, 2010, at http://www.jcrb.com/zhuanti/fzzt/lpsh/wl/201001/t20100112_300854.html (accessed April 20, 2010).

114. "Lianghui guancha: Zhongguo jinyibu tuijin sifa gongkai" (两会观察: 中国进一步推进司法公开) (Observations from the Two Meetings: China Further Promotes Judicial Openness), *Xinhua wang*, March 13, 2010, at http://news.xinhuanet.com/politics/2010-03/13/content_13163362_1.htm (accessed April 1, 2010); "Henan fayuan tingshen shixian wangluo tongbu zhibo" (河南法院庭审实现网络同步直播) (Courts in Henan Will Broadcast Live Trials via the Internet), *Xinhua wang*, March 12, 2010, at http://www.xinhuanet.com/chinanews/2010-03/12/content_19230473.htm (accessed April 20, 2010).

115. The emphasis on legal education also reflects the fact that law itself has become an ideology. Zhang Jianwei, "'Bianfa moshi' yu zhengzhi wendingxing." The term *pufa* appears to be a reform-era creation.

116. Wang Jianxun (王建勋), "'Gongshen dahui' yanzhong beili fazhi jingshen" ("公审大会"严重背离法治精神) (Public Trial Meetings Severely Violate the Spirit of

the Rule of Law), *Fenghuang zixun*, March 16, 2009, at http://news.ifeng.com/opinion/200903/0316_23_1062388.shtml (accessed April 1, 2010); "Wenzhou gongshen gongpan dahui zhi fansi" (温州公审公判大会之反思) (Reflections on Public Trials in Wenzhou), *Zhejiang zhisheng*, May 26, 2009, at http://www.am810.cn/bencandy .php?fid=62&id=412 (accessed April 26, 2010). Public trials were common during the revolutionary period. Chen Duanhong (陈端洪), "Sifa yu minzhu: Zhongguo sifa minzhuhua ji qi pipan" (司法与民主: 中国司法民主化及其批判) (The Judiciary and Democracy: Judicial Democratization in China and Its Criticism), *Beida falü wang*, 2002, at http://article.chinalawinfo.com/Article_Detail.asp?ArticleID=2638 (accessed April 1, 2010).

117. The loosening of bar passage standards is also a practical reaction to the shortage of judges in many rural areas, in particular in western China. Another example of a re-emphasis on popular legality is the reintroduction of people's assessors to the courts. The Supreme People's Court has called for increased involvement of people's assessors in hearing cases in order to better take account of public views. According to the SPC, the number of people's assessors increased from 57,000 in 2008 to 77,000 in 2009, with assessors participating in 25 percent more cases in 2009 than in 2008. Wang Shengjun, "Zuigao renmin fayuan gongzuo baogao," March 11, 2010.

118. Eugenia Lean, *Public Passions: The Trial of Shi Jianqiao and the Rise of Popular Sympathy in Republican China* (Berkeley: University of California Press, 2007), pp. 106–140.

119. For example, I refer to the rising influence of petitioning on the courts as a "populist threat." Liebman, "Populist Threat."

CHAPTER 7

Sustaining and Contesting Revolutionary Legacies in Media and Ideology

YUEZHI ZHAO

On June 20, 2008, Chinese Communist Party (CCP) General Secretary Hu Jintao celebrated the sixtieth anniversary of the founding of the *People's Daily* (*Renmin ribao*, 人民日报) (hereafter *RMRB*) by visiting the paper's headquarters, delivering a speech to the staff, and chatting on its online "Strengthen the Nation Forum" (*Qiangguo luntan*, 强国论坛). The BBC reported that Hu stated that the Internet is an important channel for the party to "understand what citizens are feeling and [to] gather people's wisdom."[1] However, the BBC made no mention of Hu's speech to the paper's staff. Mr. Yundan Shuinuan (云淡水暖), a well-known netizen, also noted that the most significant aspect of Hu's visit was his online chat, but he spoke in a language radically different from that of the BBC. In his view, China's established print and broadcast media have been hijacked by the dominant power bloc of bureaucratic, business, and intellectual elites. By going online, Hu demonstrated that his leadership has taken online public opinion as a source of support for party policies.[2] Other neo-Maoist netizens, perhaps to the horror of liberal intellectuals, went further to celebrate the victory of "network democracy" (*wangluo minzhu*, 网络民主) as a digital-age version of Maoist "mass democracy" (*da minzhu*, 大民主): as yesterday's "big-character posters" evolved into today's Internet postings, they have brought back the "four great freedoms" (speak out freely, air views freely, hold great debates, and big-character posters) of the Cultural Revolution (hereafter CR) era, engendering "a cultural revolution in new form"[3] to fulfill the goals of the Communist revolution. According to those netizens who tried to give Hu's visit their own political spin, the Internet, the most participatory and grassroots-oriented sector of the Chinese public communication system, has emerged as a potential new frontier for re-establishing the organic linkages between the central CCP leadership and the grassroots and for renewing the revolutionary project of socialism.

The *RMRB*'s own reports of Hu's visit differ from the BBC's liberal democratic language on the one hand and from the left-leaning netizens' radical re-appropriation of the Maoist discourse on the other. Although Hu addressed "netizen friends" (*wangmin pengyou*, 网民朋友), his term of reference for the Chinese public remained "the masses of people" (*renmin qunzhong*, 人民群众), a standard Maoist term. Thus, instead of seeing Hu's online debut as the BBC-implied awakening to the notion of citizenship in a liberal democratic polity, it appears more as a digital-age re-articulation of the CCP's revolutionary hegemony, especially its "mass-line" mode of political communication (from the masses, to the masses). Furthermore, and contrary to the neo-Maoist populist spin, in his speech to the *RMRB* staff, Hu stressed that the news media must uphold "the party principles" (*dangxing yuanze*, 党性原则) and "a correct orientation to public opinion" (*zhengque yulun daoxiang*, 正确舆论导向).[4] Finally, and no less significant, the *RMRB* embellished the headline of its report on Hu's visit with the phrase "Cordial Care, Tremendous Inspiration" (*qinqie de guanhuai, juda de guwu*, 亲切的关怀, 巨大的鼓舞), language that is characteristic of the Maoist discourse of establishing an emotive affinity between the party leaders and propaganda workers.[5] Another *RMRB* report effectively extends this affinity to those in the media and propaganda across the country, represented by fourteen individual and collective voices, with one attributed quote describing Hu's as "the most perfect, most profound, and most comprehensive speech about how to conduct news propaganda work well in the country's thirty years of reform and opening."[6] In all these ways, the *RMRB* continues with the Leninist notion of the newspaper as the party's collective propagandist, agitator, and organizer in the digital age.

That Hu asserted CCP leadership over the media at a crucial juncture in its propaganda endeavors during the eventful year of 2008 — after confronting the Western media over the riots in Tibet in March and mobilizing for the Wenchuan earthquake relief in May and before staging the Beijing Olympics in August — and that he did so by visiting the *RMRB* not only underscores the CCP's continuing emphasis on media and ideology but also extends its long-established method to exercise leadership in this area. Mao's preoccupation with ideological work and his close involvement in journalism during the revolutionary era, from publishing periodicals to penning editorials and providing calligraphy for the *RMRB*'s own masthead, are well known. He took ideological struggles to a new height by stating famously at the Tenth Plenum of the CCP's Eighth National Congress in September 1962 that if anyone wants to overthrow a government, he/she must first manufacture public opinion (*zao yulun*, 造輿论). The CCP's "Decision on the Great Proletariat Cultural Revolution," passed on August 8, 1966, invoked Mao's idea of launching the CR as a means to fight against "bourgeois ideological influence" and "capitalist restoration."[7] Although Deng Xiaoping shifted the CCP's priorities to economic growth, as early as January 1980 he rebuilt the bureaucratic authority of the CCP in the aftermath of the CR by reaffirming the Leninist principle of media control — "party newspapers and journals must unconditionally propagate the party's positions."[8] Deng edited and commented on many *RMRB* editorials, including the decisive April 26, 1989 piece that played an instrumental role in inciting the students to launch more protests, which led to the June 4 crackdown. Attributing "bourgeois ideological liberalization" and the CCP leadership's lapse in media control as a cause for the 1989 uprising, and drawing a lesson from the downfall of the Soviet Union wherein media liberalization was believed to be a key contributing factor, Deng instructed the CCP leadership to pursue accelerated market reforms on the one hand and re-emphasize ideological work on the other. Thus, "from June 1989 onward, the Central Propaganda Department and the propaganda system once again began to play a prominent, guiding role in Chinese society."[9] "Seizing with both hands, both hands must be tough" (*liangshou yiqi zhua, liangshou douyaoying*, 两手一起抓, 两手都要硬) became the mantra of the post-1989 CCP leadership under Jiang Zemin, who in September 1996 inspected the *RMRB* and delivered a speech there.[10]

And yet, Hu's multifaceted interaction with the now multi-platform CCP central organ and different journalistic and netizen accounts of his visit reveal profound contradictions in the CCP's continuing invocation of its revolutionary legacy to sustain its rule. First, symbolized by the *RMRB*'s two faces today — its print version and its Internet forum and their respective representations of Hu's visit — there is long-standing tension between the CCP's Leninist organizational discipline and its Maoist populist legacies within the revolutionary tradition itself.[11] Second, the tension between CCP revolutionary hegemony and liberal democratic discourse — promoted by liberal intellectuals as "universal values" (*pushi jiazhi*, 普世价值) — has intensified after thirty years of media reform and ideological transformation. In fact, along with their eagerness to frame Hu's online debut as an endorsement of "mass democracy" in the Maoist populist tradition, neo-Maoist netizens were quick to accuse the "distortion" of Hu's speech by *Southern Weekend* (*Nanfang zhoumo*, 南方周末), which, in their eyes, is a voice of the "elites" and a hotbed of "bourgeois ideological liberalization."[12] As these netizens' juxtaposition of elite media power versus Internet-based grassroots popular will implies, the CCP faces a formidable challenge to sustain its hegemony in a deeply divided market society and polarized ideological field. Although it has suppressed both the "line struggle" (*luxian douzheng*, 路线斗争) narrative[13] and the "class struggle" discourse and the media are no longer seen as tools of these struggles, for China's neo-Maoist netizens the "line struggle" between socialism and capitalism is not over, and the "citizens" to whom the BBC report referred are class-divided. Therefore, there is not only a dynamic tension between the official and popular discourses on the CCP's revolutionary legacies, but also a profound question concerning the "means" and the "ends" of contemporary CCP power: although it may be true that the post-Mao CCP "rejects the goals but not all the methods of the Mao-era propaganda methodology,"[14] is it possible in the long run for the CCP to prolong its rule by drawing on the rhetoric and means of the Chinese revolution without either being forced to completely shed its revolutionary color or being propelled to fulfill the revolution's promises for an equal and just society?

With the above question in mind, this chapter first analyzes the continuing relevance of the CCP's revolutionary legacies in the realm of ideology, media structure, and practices during the reform era. I should clarify that I understand "revolution" broadly to encompass not only the 1949 Communist revolution, but also the 1966–76 CR as its radical aftermath. Moreover, because the CCP conceives its own revolution as part of the international communist movement, the Leninist tradition and relevant Soviet experience, including the lessons of the Soviet Union's collapse, are also discussed. Similarly, the term "media" covers the broad realm of official and less official mediated communication, from party organs to Internet Web sites, from news to entertainment. Then, drawing upon the tenor of the "third debate on reform" between 2005 and 2007, I discuss how popular Internet voices have revived the Maoist populist legacy and have articulated an unofficial discourse on socialism in a critique of the CCP's post-Mao reforms for betraying the goals of the Communist revolution, thus threatening ultimately to undermine CCP legitimacy. I highlight that the Internet, as the quintessential technology of globalization and market integration, has become an unofficial forum for the expression of socialist ideas and anti-capitalistic sentiments in contemporary China.

Re-Articulating the Terms of the CCP's Revolutionary Hegemony

As Vivienne Shue observes, a common assumption about reform-era China is that "the Chinese state's main claims to legitimacy rest in its economic achievements, in an improving standard of living, in 'growth' or 'development.'"[15] Bruce Gilley goes so far as to claim that the current Chinese regime "advocates nothing at all," with its legitimacy "based wholly on performance."[16] The Western liberal focus on the authoritarian dimensions of Chinese state power, together with a tendency to ignore official discourses, especially if they do not offer anything new from the liberal democratic perspective — for example, Hu's address to the *RMRB* staff, as opposed to his Internet debut — has further contributed to these claims.

Nevertheless, economic success alone is neither a necessary nor a sufficient condition for political legitimacy. Drawing on the long tradition of statecraft in imperial China and extending to the reform era, Shue distills three key components in the logic of state legitimation in China: truth, benevolence, and glory, that is, the possession of a special knowledge of transcendence, benevolent care for the common people, and glorification of the Chinese nation.[17] Shue's discussion underscores the continuity between imperial and contemporary China in the legitimation claims of the state. Within this context, it is crucial to emphasize that the CCP came to power by sinicizing the Western "truth" of Marxism and leading a social revolution, and it launched its reform program not only by proclaiming a new "truth criterion" to liberate itself from much of the ideological baggage of Mao — through "practice is the sole criterion of truth" — but also by promising to develop, rather than abandon, socialism, supposedly showing that socialism is the only path to truth, benevolence, and glory — as in the popular song, "Only Socialism Can Save China." In fact, an essential feature of the CCP-led pursuit of an alternative Chinese modernity "is revolutionary hegemony, or the primacy of culture and ideology, not just in legitimating the modern nation-state but also in constituting the basic and core components of the new socialist country."[18] Despite the reform era's shift of focus from ideological revolution to economic development, the CCP continues to derive at least part of its political and ideological legitimacy from its revolutionary hegemony and some kind of discourse on socialism.

Because "ideological considerations played a significant role in determining the acceptability of certain policies over others" in China,[19] continuous re-articulations of party ruling doctrines have been an integral part of the

CCP-led reform process. In addition to foregrounding nationalism — i.e., the pursuit of China's national dignity and glory in the modern world — as the central component of its ideological legitimation, the CCP initially stabilized and rationalized the ideological fields for the market reforms by imposing the "Four Cardinal Principles"— upholding the socialist road, the dictatorship of the proletariat, the leadership of the Communist Party, and Marxism–Leninism–Mao Zedong Thought — while justifying the adoption of capitalist means of development by devising concepts such as "the primary stage of socialism" and "socialism with Chinese characteristics." Following the 1989 crackdown, Deng glossed over the ideological contradictions from pursuing capitalist development in China with his "no-debate" decree — there should be no debate about the capitalist or socialist nature of the reforms — and the dictum that "development is the only hard truth" (*fazhan cai shi ying daoli*, 发展才是硬道理).[20]

Deng's developmental path inevitably created profound political, ideological, and social tensions, because the CCP, the self-proclaimed vanguard of the working class, had engendered a capitalist stratum and had laid off state enterprise workers en masse. Thus, by 2001 the Jiang Zemin leadership was compelled to address these contradictions by inventing the "three represents" thesis (*sange daibiao sixiang*, 三个代表思想) — that the CCP has always represented the developmental requirements of China's "advanced productive forces," the orientation of China's "advanced culture," and the fundamental interests of the majority of the Chinese people. Although the doctrine's real objective is to redefine the CCP from a working-class vanguard to a "party of all the people," it is significant that it continues to speak the language of "scientific socialism," with references to "advanced productive forces" and "advanced culture."

After coming to power, the Hu Jintao leadership tried to address the 1990s excesses of market-driven development through a combination of ideological and social policy initiatives. Showing more eagerness than Jiang Zemin to reconnect with the revolutionary tradition, immediately after he became CCP general secretary Hu inaugurated his leadership by visiting Xibaipo (西柏坡) in December 2002 and reiterated Mao's teachings there. In addition to launching a set of social welfare-oriented policies,[21] Hu's leadership articulated a series of new political doctrines and implemented an ideological campaign that aims to "preserve the advanced nature of Communist Party members." In 2003 the "scientific concept of development" (*kexue fazhan guan*, 科学发展观) — "sustainable development" in the language of "scientific socialism"— was propagated in the aftermath of the

SARS epidemic to correct the single-minded pursuit of economic growth at the cost of human development and environmental sustainability. In 2004, the leadership sought to strengthen the official ideology by initiating a "Basic Research and Construction Project in Marxism" as a means to fend off the impact of neoliberalism as the ideology of global capitalism and to prevent the outbreak of a Chinese version of the "color revolutions" that had engulfed Eastern Europe and the former Soviet republics. Hu's next speech, on September 19, 2004, is particularly significant in terms of its echoes of Mao's 1962 speech about the role of ideology in regime change:

> The ideological field has always been an important battleground in the fierce struggles between us and enemy forces (*didui shili*, 敌对势力). A problem on this front will lead to social chaos, even loss of regime power. In order to cause chaos in a society and overthrow a regime, enemy forces will usually start with breaking an opening in the ideological field by putting people's thoughts in disarray ... a very important reason from the disintegration of the Soviet Union and the collapse of the Communist Party there was Gorbachev's advocacy of "ideological pluralism" and the so-called "glasnost," along with the repudiation of Marxism as a guiding ideology, which resulted in the riotous flow of non-Marxist and anti-Marxist trends.[22]

Simultaneously, the leadership attempted to address the mounting social conflicts by articulating the slogan "constructing a socialist harmonious society" (*jianshe shehuizhuyi hexie shehui*, 建设社会主义和谐社会), a society, according to Hu, that should "feature democracy, the rule of law, equity, justice, sincerity, amity and vitality."[23] In late 2005 and early 2006, responding to the economic depression and social disintegration in the rural areas, the CCP recycled a key 1950s slogan of socialist idealism, that is, "constructing a new socialist countryside" (*jianshe shehuizhuyi xin nongcun*, 建设社会主义新农村). Then, in October 2006, the Sixth Plenum of the Sixteenth CCP National Congress passed a resolution advocating the establishment of a "socialist core value system" (*shehuizhuyi hexin jiazhi tixi*, 社会主义核心价值体系), that is, a set of basic values that will serve as a common ideological basis for the CCP to claim cultural leadership over Chinese society. According to official elaborations, this core value system encompasses "Marxism as the guiding thought, socialism with Chinese characteristics as the common ideal, patriotism as the core national spirit, reform and innovation as the core spirit of the times, and the socialist perspective on honor and shame."[24] To be sure, terms such as "Marxism" and "reform and innovation" remain as slippery as the CCP defines them to be, and "the socialist perspective on honor and shame," as concretized in Hu Jintao's "eight honors and eight shames" (*barong bachi*, 八荣八耻), prioritizes patriotism. However, the "eight honors" do include the revolutionary ethics of "serving the people" (*fuwu renmin*, 服务人民), "solidarity and mutual support" (*tuanjie huzhu*, 团结互助), and "hard struggle" (*jianku fendou*, 艰苦奋斗).[25] Epitomizing the CCP's reclaiming of revolutionary symbolism to justify its rule and as part of the propaganda fare leading to the PRC's sixtieth anniversary celebrations in 2009, CCTV's flagship news program *Joint News Broadcast* (*Xinwen lianbo*, 新闻联播) included a regular recounting of pre-1949 revolutionary events under the headline "red memories" (*hongse jiyi*, 红色记忆).

Thus, instead of bidding "farewell to revolution," the CCP, although embracing market reform, continues to selectively draw upon its revolutionary legacies to sustain its rule at both the normative and tactical levels.[26] In particular, the Hu Jintao leadership has distinguished itself by intensifying the re-appropriation of the CCP's revolutionary traditions and further stressing media and ideological work. Although the CCP's doctrines and slogans should not be taken at face value and their efficacy must be empirically analyzed, they should not be dismissed as completely empty expressions in its already overflowing ideological dustbin. As the economic and social contradictions of "socialism with Chinese characteristics" become more acute, the CCP is increasingly compelled to elaborate on its ruling ideology in a way that will still have some appeal to the vast majority of the population. Even if its ideology is "a living lie,"[27] it sets the basic terms of the CCP's hegemony over Chinese society and serves as a symbolic resource for social contestation. As Timothy Cheek has observed,

> While foreign observers and Chinese intellectuals alike scoff at these tortured formulations, they reflect the efforts of the still-ruling CCP to explain the massive changes of reform in terms that do not patently contradict Chinese Marxist-Leninist orthodoxy. If we utterly dismiss the slogans of the Party as "political rubbish" or mere window-dressing, we will miss the actual polices of China's leaders and, more so, fail to understand how the CCP maintains its public legitimacy without democracy.[28]

To stay in power, the CCP must continue to articulate and re-articulate its socialist pretensions. Otherwise, as I have already alluded to and as I will discuss further later in this chapter, communistic and socialist discourses threaten once again to become a powerful subversive ideology against party-led capitalist developments in China. Moreover, the very acts of elaborating and disseminating official doctrine — from Jiang's maneuvers to codify the "three represents" in the CCP constitution to Hu's imposition of successive ideological education campaigns for CCP members, journalists, and academics — are themselves essential dimensions in the exercise of power.

Retaining the Leninist Core in a Commercialized Media System: The "Party Principle" and Its Mutations

The maintenance of a Leninist disciplinary core in the media system during a process of rapid commercialization ensures the media system's continuing subordination to the CCP's ideological objectives. The central doctrine that underlies CCP domination over the media is the system's "party character," or the "party principle."[29] Deriving directly from Lenin's theory of the press, this principle lies at the heart of the CCP's Leninist roots and its core components that were articulated in the very first resolution that the CCP passed on July 31, 1921 at its founding congress. The resolution, which echoes the conditions laid out by Lenin for joining the Comintern, makes four points regarding propaganda: (1) Journals, dailies, books, and pamphlets must be run by the CCP central executive committee or the provisional executive committee; (2) Each locality may publish a trade-union journal, a daily, a weekly, a pamphlet, or a provisional newsletter as needed; (3) All central and local publications must be directly managed and edited by CCP members; (4) No central and local publications should publish articles opposing the CCP's principles, policies, and decisions.[30]

Whereas the first three points concern the structural control of the press, the last point focuses on its editorial principle.[31] However, it was not until the 1942 Rectification Campaign in Yan'an that this Leninist principle was sinified and fully entrenched, through what Patricia Stranahan describes as the "moulding" of the *Liberation Daily* (*Jiefang ribao*) (解放日报) (hereafter *LD*) from May 16, 1941 to March 27, 1947 as the quintessential CCP central organ. As a key dimension in the campaign, the *LD*, which had been under the control of the Internationalists led by Bo Gu and modeled after the Soviet Union's *Pravda* and China's own leading commercial dailies of the time, including *L'Impartial* (*Dagong bao*, 大公报), went through a thorough layout change (*gaiban*, 改版) under the guidance of Mao.[32] Instead of allowing news not relating directly to life in the Shaan-Gan-Ning Border Region — international news about World War II in Europe and the Soviet Union's battles against the Germans — to take precedence over news about the Border Region and the CCP's activities and policy directives in the paper's layout, reporting about the Border Region and the CCP's policies assumed priority and received front-page treatment. At the same time, as part of

Mao's campaign to promote the mass line and reform "the eight-legged essay" writing style — which for Mao demonstrated a gap between the CCP's ideological workers and the masses in the Border Region — writers were required to reach out to the masses and write in a more accessible style. Underlying this "layout" change, then, was a fundamental change in the paper's editorial principles. Most significantly, as Wang Shiwei's "Wild Lilies" essays, which were published in the LD in March 1942 and accused by the CCP leadership for elitism, became the target of the campaign and solidified Mao's determination to reform the LD so as to "strengthen its party nature and to reflect the [ideas] of the masses," the CCP made it clear that there was no room for independent and critical thinking in the CCP organ.[33]

Thereafter, the mouthpiece theory (houshe lun, 喉舌论) — a metaphor regarding the press first articulated by Marx in 1849 when he referred to the press as the "mouthpiece of the spirit of the people in sustaining its own freedom [in the struggle against the Prussian state],"[34] and then in China by Liang Qichao in his 1896 conceptualization of the press as an instrument of agitation for the reform movement[35] — found its fullest articulation in CCP press theory. The legacies of the LD's "layout change" are still entrenched not only in Chinese media theory, but also in media practice today, from the CCTV's practice of prioritizing national news and the activities of CCP leaders over international news, which typically appear in the last segment of its 7:00 pm prime-time news program, to the Chinese media industry's continuing use of the term "layout change" to refer to changes in a newspaper's or a broadcast channel's editorial priorities.[36] Significantly, and the source of profound tension in the CCP's claim to monopolize media power, historical invocations of the mouthpiece metaphor speak of the newspaper as the mouthpiece of the broad masses, of ordinary party members, as well as of the CCP and its leadership. For example, in one of the earlier usages of the term, the 1929 CCP journal Party Life (Dangde shenghuo, 党的生活) spoke of itself as "the mouthpiece of ordinary party members." During the LD's "layout change" during the Rectification Campaign, which had the self-proclaimed objective of molding the CCP and the masses into one, on different occasions the paper spoke of itself as being the mouthpiece of the masses and of the CCP, without acknowledging any potential tension. In its April 1, 1942 "Letter to Readers" which launched a "layout change," the paper charged itself with the duty of "reflecting the masses and becoming their mouthpiece." Then, in a September 22, 1942 editorial, the paper stated that "the newspaper is the party's mouthpiece, the mouthpiece of this massive collective."[37]

It is not only in the second sense that the mouthpiece metaphor remains in the evolution of CCP media theory and practices; more specific disciplinary principles were established and reaffirmed to enforce the "party principle." Here again, the CCP's Leninist roots cast a long shadow well into the post-1949 period. A 1953 decision regarding the power of a CCP organ to criticize the CCP committee to which it is affiliated is a landmark. That year, *Yishan Peasant News* (*Yishan nongmin bao*, 宜山农民报), a newspaper affiliated with the CCP Committee of Yishan Prefecture in Guangxi, published a criticism of the Yishan Prefecture CCP Committee. The Guangxi Propaganda Department referred the case to the CCP Central Propaganda Department. In its resolution, the Central Propaganda Department made reference to a similar decision made by the Soviet Communist Party in 1939 and deemed the newspaper's act a serious violation of the party's organizational and disciplinary principles. The resolution stated that although a newspaper editorial department should "not repeat the same mistake in the newspaper . . . it has no power to oppose the party committee. This is the principle that a party paper must adhere to in its relationship with a party committee."[38]

It is difficult to underestimate the enduring power of the "party principle" as concretized in the *LD* in 1942 and in this 1953 decision. Not surprisingly, in the aftermath of the Great Leap Forward and the CR, when the media found itself amplifying the CCP's mistakes, liberal media reformers reached back to Marx and the CCP's own press history by underscoring the notion of the newspaper as the mouthpiece of the masses and coining the term "people's principle" (*renmin xing*, 人民性), that is, the media should serve as the mouthpiece of "the people," as a supplementary or even an oppositional doctrine to the "party principle." Discussion of the "people principle," along with calls for liberalizing the CCP's press-control regime, surfaced during Hu Yaobang's tenure as CCP general secretary in the early 1980s and reached a high point around the time of the CCP's Thirteenth National Congress in 1987, when then CCP general secretary Zhao Ziyang signaled great openness in the media and called for a strengthened role of the media in "supervising" officials.[39] However, as already noted, Deng had reasserted the "party principle" as early as 1980. Even Hu Yaobang, widely regarded as the most liberal of all CCP leaders, did not hesitate to reaffirm the party mouthpiece theory in his well-known 1985 speech "On the Party's Journalistic Work." Although Hu Yaobang belabored to say that the CCP's mouthpieces are "naturally" also the mouthpieces of the government and the people, he proclaimed that "at the most fundamental level, that the party's journalism is the party's mouthpiece . . . is unshakable." Furthermore, he pointed out that it is "very incorrect" to discuss the CCP's journalistic work in the same way as the economic reforms and to grant it the same relative autonomy that other businesses enjoy. "No matter how they are to be reformed," Hu Yaobang concluded, "it is absolutely impossible to change the nature of party journalism in the slightest sense and to change its relationship with the party."[40]

Although Hu Yaobang lost power for being too soft on the ideological front, his point about the limits of media reform turned out to be prescient, underscoring a deep consensus among CCP leaders on the imperative of maintaining media control. Although the CCP accelerated market-oriented development of the media system beginning in the early 1990s, it still clings to the "party principle." A September 2001 editorial in the *Chinese Journalist* (*Zhongguo jizhe*, 中国记者), an authoritative publication of the Xinhua News Agency, articulates the following "four no changes" — the CCP's bottom line — in the market-oriented reform of the media system: "Whatever the changes, the [media's] nature as the party's and people's mouthpieces must not be changed; the party's control of the media must not be changed; the party's control of cadres must not be changed; and a correct orientation toward public opinion must not be changed." The article further states that the CCP must "always command major decision-making power, controlling power over capital allocation, the right of censorship over propaganda, and the right to appoint leading officials."[41] Echoing Hu Yaobang in 1985, a 2002 Xinhua report states: "Whatever the circumstances, the nature [of the media] as party mouthpiece cannot be changed."[42]

With the rapid expansion of market-oriented media outlets that are not strictly CCP organs, the "party principle" has mutated into two functional doctrines. First, there is the doctrine of "the party in control of the media" (*dang guan meiti*, 党管媒体). That is, whereas the first three principles of the 1921 CCP Resolution mandate that central and local CCP committees run (and by implication, control) publications, the post-1989 CCP makes a distinction between "run" (*ban*, 办) and "control" (*guan*, 管), accepting the CCP's withdrawal from directly running all media outlets, while still retaining its power to control the system's macro-structure and editorial orientation. Journalism scholar Chen Lidan describes this doctrine as a distinctive post-1989 articulation because such an expression "was obviously inappropriate" at the onset of the reform in 1978, "at a time of settling scores from the CR and righting wrongs." However, "after 1989, this expression gradually gained currency."[43] In fact, by 2004 the term "adhere to the principle of the party in control of the media" had found its way into the decision of the Fourth Plenum of the Sixteenth CCP National Congress on strengthening the CCP's governance capabilities.

The other plank of a mutated post-1989 "party principle" is the "correct orientation toward public opinion." This doctrine, articulated by Jiang Zemin in a series of speeches between 1994 and 1996, most notably in his September 26, 1996 speech at the *RMRB*, can be seen as a mutation of the fourth point of the CCP's 1921 Resolution. Rather than trying to suppress all dissenting voices — no longer an obtainable objective in a commercialized and digitalized media system with a cacophony of voices — this doctrine aims to ensure that whatever the CCP deems to be the "correct" voice will dominate public opinion, and as Jiang specified, party organs, news agencies, and broadcasting stations are to function as pillars in this mission.[44]

Securing the "Commanding Heights": Government Regulation and Ownership Structure

The engendering of a socialist state by a CCP-led revolution meant that party control and government regulation of the media system were one and the same at the founding of the PRC. The CCP was aware of the need to separate party and government functions over the media in the New China. In its propaganda guidelines of October 30, 1949, the CCP Central Propaganda Department and the Xinhua News Agency instructed CCP-owned and -run news outlets to stop issuing administrative orders in the name of the CCP. On November 1, 1949, the State General Administration of Press (SGAP) was established on instructions from the CCP Central Propaganda Department's Publishing Committee to function as the government's administrative organ over the press. On April 25, 1950, the SGAP turned the Xinhua News Agency into a state news agency. The CCP Central Broadcasting Bureau also shifted its jurisdiction to the SGAP.

However, these efforts proved short-lived. By September 1954, the SGAP had been dismantled, and it was not until 1987 that a new government agency, the State Administration for Press and Publications, was reestablished. Although in 1954 there was a Broadcasting Bureau within the State Council, in an April 27, 1963 decision the CCP Central Committee installed a party committee leadership system in it, and by December 1967, it once again officially became a CCP apparatus to follow the "party's unitary leadership" (*dangde yiyuanhua lingdao*, 党的一元化领导).[45] Although a 1977

CCP document returned administrative control of broadcasting to the State Council, it was not until 1982, with the establishment of the Ministry of Radio and Television, that a government broadcasting agency was stabilized. Today, even though a number of State Council organs and their local counterparts, including the State Administration of Radio, Film, and Television (SARFT), the General Administration for Press and Publications (GAPP), the State Council Press Office, the Ministry of Industry and Information Technology, the Ministry of Culture, as well as the quasi-official China Internet Network Information Center (CNNIC), are involved in regulating different sectors of China's rapidly expanding public communication system, these agencies are ultimately subject to the directives of the Central Propaganda Department. Rather than diminishing the CCP's power in media and ideology, the rapid expansion of the government's regulatory apparatuses and the adoption of standard Western regulatory approaches — a process that accelerated around the time of China's accession to the World Trade Organization (WTO) in 2001 — have strengthened the CCP's overall capacity to carry out its propaganda directions. In a most telling case in 2006, when certain grassroots leftist Web sites were deemed subversive for their independent reporting of workers' unrest, the Internet Propaganda Management Division of the Beijing Government Information Office simply closed them down, citing their violation of an Internet business regulation requiring Web sites of this type to have a registered initial capitalization of 10 million yuan.[46] Reflecting the CCP's strategic adoption of the "rights" discourse, the report of the Seventeenth CCP Congress proclaims four rights — right to know, right to participate, right to express, and right to supervision — as important in realizing "socialist democracy." However, as Chen Lidan puts it, these "four rights" remain hollow and subordinate to the reality of "the party in control of the media."[47] That is, regulatory regimes and a rights discourse have been deployed in such a way that they do not challenge the CCP's control of the media. Calls by liberal intellectuals for a "press law," which would entail legislative debates in the National People's Congress over constitutional guarantees of press freedom, for example, continue to be ignored in the post-1989 period.

Another area in which revolutionary legacies continue to cast a long shadow is media ownership. One of the key components of the reform process has been the phenomenal expansion of the private sector and the massive privatization of state-owned enterprises in the Chinese economy. A concurrent development has been a gradual entrenchment of private property rights in the Chinese Constitution, which was amended in early

2004 to protect private property. In March 2007, the National People's Congress (NPC) approved a highly controversial property rights law to consolidate private property relationships. However, apart from common political economy rationales — public ownership, for example, in the form of crown corporations that can also be found in a capitalist economy — the CCP's legacy in promoting public ownership and its professed commitment to socialism place an extra ideological limit on privatization in China. Although the neoliberal doctrine of privatization has had considerable influence in China, Lenin's New Economic Policy (NEP) in 1921 — a loosening up of the Bolshevik's war communism economic policy to encourage market-based private economic development in recognition of the fact that the Soviet Union did not yet have a fully developed capitalist economy — served as a reference point in Chinese debates on the introduction of the market and the private sector in the economy during the early stages of the reform. Later, just as Lenin could reassure those who hoped to work toward communism by declaring that the Bolsheviks retained control of "the commanding heights" of the economy — large-scale industry, foreign trade, banking, and transport — in the 1990s the CCP adopted the policy of "seizing the big and letting go of the small" (*zhuada fangxiao*, 抓大放小) in state enterprise reform and claimed in the 1997 report of the Fifteenth National Congress that as long as the state controls important industries and key sectors, i.e., the "commanding heights" of the national economy, a certain reduction in the weight of the state sector "won't affect the socialist nature of our country."[48] Although the report does not directly invoke Lenin's policy, that it is widely known in the CCP and that the term "commanding heights" (*mingmai*, 命脉) was explicitly used are indicative of the historical linkage. Not only has CCP policy of "seizing the big and letting go of the small" been rather consistent since the mid-1990s, but this has ensured the improved profitability of the state sector and the continued fusion of business and government functions in the state sector.[49] The state sector was further strengthened as a result of the state's economic stimulus policies in response to the 2008–9 global financial crisis.

Given the post-1989 doctrine of "seizing with both hands," the field of media and ideology can be seen as one of the CCP's "commanding heights" in the broad Chinese political economy. Although the CCP promotes media commercialization, it continues to restrict private capital in this sector, let alone privatizing existing party-state media outlets. Here Lenin's theory about the difference between bourgeois "formal" press freedom and that of

Soviet or proletarian "substantive" press freedom based on the expropria-
tion of press ownership by the big capitalists cast a long shadow. The CCP's
initial class-based understanding of the nature of the press and its history of
dealing with private media are also relevant. In its August 8, 1948, "Measures
for Dealing with Domestic and Foreign Press and News Agencies in the
Liberated Cities," the CCP Central Committee states: "Newspapers, periodicals, and news agencies are the instruments of certain classes, political
parties, and social organizations to carry out class struggles, not business
enterprises. Therefore, in general, the policy for private industrial and commercial enterprises is not applicable to private newspapers, periodicals, and
news agencies."[50] Although exceptions were made, socialist transformation
was soon implemented in the remaining private media outlets. The CCP has
not only historically defined public ownership — which was then equated
with party-state ownership and direct control — as the foundation for
"socialist press freedom," but also has waged a protracted battle against
the emergence of privately owned newspapers as a hallmark of "bourgeois
liberalization" during both the Maoist and reform eras.[51]

At the same time, as the reform process deepens, the concept of private
ownership in the media has assumed new dimensions. In an era of com-
modified media development, Web forums and blogospheres, private
capitalists, rather than political essayists, have become a social force with
both the motivation and required capital to operate print and broadcast
media outlets. However, if profit-making is the primary motive, then private
capital participation can be either in the form of sole proprietary ownership
or in "private-public partnerships" in which a private company acquires
the operational rights of a state-owned media outlet or equity shares in the
business operations of a state-controlled media outlet.

As the CCP cultivates the media's entertainment function and accommodates private capital's profit-making rather than speech-making imperative,
it has developed a complex and differentiated policy regime regarding
private-capital participation in the media and cultural industries. Following
China's WTO accession in 2001, official media policies explicitly embraced
private capital as a junior partner in the media and cultural industries, while
reaffirming areas in which foreign and domestic private capital are prohibited. Full ownership of news and broadcasting outlets and the production
and distribution of news and informational content are deemed "sacred"
and continue to be monopolized by the party-state. Meanwhile, full or partial ownership in the peripheral areas of the media and culture industries,
including the production of film, television entertainment, and advertising

and audiovisual distribution, has been opened up to domestic private and foreign capital. In this way, the CCP retains strategic control over the media system and its ideological orientation, but no longer monopolizes production and distribution, especially in entertainment-, lifestyle-, and business-oriented media outlets.

Although the media are now recognized as both opinion organs and business enterprises, CCP officials remain wary of private capital because there is no guarantee that private news outlets will not turn against the CCP and support opposition forces, especially during times of political crisis.[52] Given that even the CCP-controlled news outlets ended up advocating "bourgeois liberalization" in 1989, this consideration is perhaps warranted. Furthermore, just as the CCP continues to be compelled to sustain the idea of socialism as a more just and equitable social order vis-à-vis capitalism, there continues to be an ideological barrier for sanctioning private media ownership despite the intellectual influence of liberal press theory, which equates a free press with a privately owned press. Media ownership by private capital undermines the conceptual and institutional foundations of the Chinese socialist state: it means the acceptance of a news outlet as first and foremost a private profit-making business, contrary to the CCP's Leninist definition of press freedom as being first and foremost freedom from capitalist control. "He who opens up the press to the bourgeoisie, he who does not understand that we are marching toward socialism in great strides" — Lenin cursed in 1917.[53] Although Lenin opened up this sector to private operators after the NEP in 1921 and more than 400 small presses and publications emerged, he "rejected the idea of granting freedom of speech and press to other Socialist parties"[54] during the NEP. Moreover, Lenin put great emphasis on supervision of private media outlets "so as to ensure the socialist nature of public opinion."[55] In any case, this sector was quickly eliminated by Stalin after 1925.[56] With the lessons of the Soviet Union's collapse in hindsight, there is probably real fear that acceptance of private news media ownership may indeed be one more step toward "capitalist restoration" both in theory and in practice. Apart from considerations derived from the bare authoritarian logic of sustaining its rule, this is not a step any CCP leader, still claiming to be heir to the Communist revolution and to the building of socialism, can take easily. This is a fact that theorists of globalization such as Aihwa Ong, in failing to take the history of Chinese socialism seriously and to differentiate the right-wing authoritarian states in Malaysia and Indonesia and the CCP-led Chinese state in their respective applications of neoliberalism, have ignored.[57]

Although allowing business and lifestyle publications, as well as entertainment content providers and distributors to operate as independent businesses, the CCP is attempting to capitalize its core media outlets and to build them into conglomerates. In the printing media field, for example, the GAPP in February 2009 announced that for-profit press and publishing entities would be decoupled from the government institutions with which they were affiliated and would be transformed into separate companies by 2010 and that the GAPP would no longer place restrictions on them in terms of ISBN numbers, publication licenses, and content. At the same time, the CCP hopes to nurture "six or seven internationally-recognized press and publication companies that are domestic leaders, each with assets and sales of over 10 billion yuan."[58] Furthermore, the CCP has used media conglomeration and capitalization through the stock market to assert its proprietary control of media institutions. For example, the press conglomerates built around CCP organs are said to be "affiliated" with CCP propaganda departments. In broadcasting, the CCP Propaganda Department traditionally assumes ideological leadership, whereas the SARFT and its local counterparts claim "administrative affiliation" with broadcasting operations, exercising power of de facto ownership. However, as a result of conglomeration, in some cases the CCP Propaganda Department has claimed a proprietary relation with broadcasting operations, and the role of the SARFT and its local counterparts has been limited to that of government regulator. In December 2007, the Propaganda Department of the Shanghai CCP Committee assumed stock ownership of the *Liberation Daily* press group (*Jiefang ribao baoye jituan*, 解放日报报业集团), which controls the Shanghai CCP organ *Liberation Daily* and its subsidiaries.[59] This marked an acknowledgment that the CCP's Propaganda Department has become "the boss of a company listed on the stock market."[60]

Revolutionary Legacies in Propaganda Management and Media Practices

First, the CCP has strengthened the role of the Propaganda Department as a proactive organizer of everyday propaganda, not only by forbidding certain topics and suppressing dissenting views, but also outlining specific requirements for news coverage on certain important topics — for example, front-page or lead-item treatment. Second, the CCP is strengthening the role of official news at both the national (i.e., Xinhua "general copy" [*tonggao*, 通稿], a practice started in Yan'an and institutionalized at the onset of the PRC to ensure the "correctness and responsible nature" of government news)[61] and local levels (written by provincial or municipal party organs). In an era of proliferating media outlets, such a measure has been especially important in providing the desired news framing. Third, there has been a renewed attempt to shape the ideological orientation of Chinese journalists, as exemplified by the 2003–4 "three-course education" (*sanxiang jiaoyu*, 三项教育) campaign to educate journalists in the CCP's "three represents" theory, in "Marxist press theory," and in "professional ethics." Fourth, the CCP has renovated its traditional *nomenklatura* system of personnel management by stepping up the training of propaganda officials and media managers through the deployment of the "revolving door" strategy. For example, at central-level media outlets, senior editorial managers are sent to take year-long "role play" (*guazhi*, 挂职) assignments in county-level CCP committees so as to get an insider's view of the work of local officials. Echoing Mao's 1959 teaching that newspapers must be run by those with a high level of political consciousness (*zhengzhijia banbao*, 政治家办报), in his June 2008 speech at the *RMRB* Hu Jintao stressed the importance of cadre training to "ensure that the power of leadership of the news and propaganda work is firmly grasped by individuals who are loyal to Marxism, to the party, and to the people."[62]

At the level of macro-managing propaganda, the handling by the Hu Jintao leadership of the SARS epidemic in 2003 provides an archetypical illustration of the CCP's instrumental uses of Maoist campaign methods during a major crisis. Initially, officials forced the media to cover-up the news about the SARS outbreak. However, this strategy backfired and provoked a political crisis as the news blackout "hampered the spread of information and efforts to curtail the disease."[63] It also sparked the spread of rumors through word of mouth and mobile phones, and finally led Dr. Jiang Yanyong to expose the epidemic to the international media. Consequently, the leadership not only allowed the media to report on the SARS crisis but it also turned the fight against SARS into a Maoist mass mobilization campaign.[64] During the process, the leadership retained tight control of *how* the crisis would be reported, including with respect to details regarding the scope of the epidemic and the number of cases. In particular, the "SARS party line" emphasized the leadership's care for the people and the sacrifice of CCP members, physicians, and ordinary people alike, with the patriotic theme of building national solidarity in a "people's war" against a common enemy. This more proactive propaganda approach was largely successful.[65]

The leadership quickly drew a lesson. Thus, the CCP Central Committee's 2004 "Decision on Strengthening the Construction of the Party's Governance Capabilities" explicitly states the need to "strengthen the ability to guide public opinion and assume preemptive power in public opinion work."[66] This ability was in full play during the media's reporting of the May 12, 2008 Wenchuan earthquake and its all-out mobilization for earthquake relief along the themes of the CCP's indispensable and benevolent leadership, the affinity among the party, the army, and the people, the words and deeds of Wen Jiabao as the "people's premier" in the tradition of Zhou Enlai, the vanguard role of CCP members, and the celebration of an unyielding national spirit during times of adversity. In his speech at the *RMRB*, Hu Jintao not only celebrated the media's achievements during the earthquake relief efforts but also called for a summation of this successful experience and its institutionalization over the long term.[67]

Finally, continuities in two reporting genres can be noted at the level of everyday journalistic practices. On the side of positive reporting, role-model reporting (both individual role models and model working experiences), one of the media reporting genres that was already consciously deployed at the time of the Yan'an *Liberation Daily*'s reporting on the Great Production Drive (*dashengchan yundong*, 大生产运动),[68] continues to be adopted. Heroes from the Mao era have been selectively resurrected. New models are constantly being promoted. One important difference, however, is that unlike during previous eras, model figures no longer have to be perfect. Propaganda guidelines warn against promoting extreme behavior in model figures, for example, someone who works so hard that he/she never goes home for Chinese New Year or is sick but never takes a rest, because "the masses will feel it is impossible to copy such behavior and it is hard to relate to."[69] One extension of this genre is the organized lecture tour by heroes and models (*yingmo baogao tuan*, 英模报告团) who have emerged from major collective endeavors such as fighting against SARS or a major natural disaster. Another popularized and commercialized mutation is the media-sponsored pageantry that celebrates heroic individuals. For example, since 2002 CCTV has sponsored an annual pageantry of those who "move China" (*gandong Zhongguo*, 感动中国). These individuals, ranging from exemplary public servants to heroes from all walks of life, including the collective of the Long March soldiers from more than seventy years ago, are said to truly embody the "socialist core value system."[70]

On the side of critical reporting, the reform period has witnessed the mutation of the media's tradition of "criticism and self-criticism" into "public opinion supervision" (*yulun jiandu*, 舆论监督). Carrying out "criticism and self-criticism" (*piping yu ziwo piping*, 批评与自我批评) in the media is a manifestation of one of the CCP's "three great superior traditions" (the other two are "seeking truth from facts" and "the mass line"). As a reportorial genre, "criticism and self-criticism" — the publication of contained and constructive criticisms of the party's work in a specific area — originated during the CCP's early revolutionary period. It became more regularized after the Yan'an Rectification Campaign and was formally promoted in the CCP Central Committee's April 19, 1950, "Decision on Carrying Out Criticism and Self-Criticism in the Press." The parameters of this practice were first set out in a 1953 resolution on the *Yishan Peasant News* case and then more comprehensively in the July 17, 1954, CCP Central Committee "Decision on Improving the Work of Newspapers."[71] This tradition of specific criticism of concrete work was replaced by the "create criticism" and symbolic violence of the CR as ideological differences and fractional struggles within the CCP leadership intensified. However, the tradition was quickly resurrected in the early reform period once Deng re-established CCP Leninist discipline and forged a reform consensus. As the liberal discourse of the press as the "Fourth Estate" and a "watchdog" of the government began to gain influence in the early 1980s, the more Western-sounding notion of "public opinion supervision" gradually replaced the Maoist notion of "criticism and self-criticism." By 1987, "public opinion supervision," which implies relative media autonomy vis-à-vis the party-state, had been adopted in Zhao Ziyang's Thirteenth CCP National Congress report. Following the rise of CCTV's *Focus Interviews* (*Jiaodian fangtan*, 焦点访谈) as the exemplary "public opinion supervision" reporting genre in the mid-1990s, the notion of "criticism and self-criticism" disappeared from Chinese journalistic discourse, even though there are enduring continuities in the practice of critical reporting carried out under these two doctrines. Not only are there many inherent limitations to the media's role in "public opinion supervision," but also there is growing resistance from local officials. In the context of mounting social conflicts and intensified debates on the basic direction of the reform process, the role of the media in "public opinion supervision," including the critical edge of CCTV's *Focus Interviews* program, had declined by 2004.[72] That role-model reporting, which does not have a Western equivalent, continues in both theory and practice, whereas "criticism and self-criticism," which is analogous to the West's "watchdog" media, was replaced by "public opinion supervision" during the reform period is perhaps indicative of the CCP's ability both to keep its traditions and to modernize them. Even more telling is that even though the *Yishan Peasant News* dared to target the Yishan CCP Committee in 1953, it is difficult today for CCTV to make a county-level CCP committee the target of its "supervision."

Reclaiming the Revolution Online: Totalitarian Nostalgia or Socialist Resilience?

Geremie Barmé uses the term "totalitarian nostalgia" to characterize the renewal of the popularity of Mao in Chinese popular culture in the 1990s.[73] To conclude her analysis of the post-1989 rebirth and modernization of the Chinese "propaganda state," Anne-Marie Brady states, "party propagandists have succeeded in marketing dictatorship."[74] By paying attention to the endurance of revolutionary legacies in the Chinese media, ideology, and popular culture, these analysts have gone a long way in dispersing illusions about the imminent emergence of a liberal democratic polity in China. However, by focusing on the totalitarian or authoritarian dimensions of post-1989 Chinese media and ideology, these analysts also fail to grasp the agency of the Chinese population and their organic relationship with the revolutionary orthodoxy, in what Timothy Cheek refers to as the "Maoist orthopraxy," i.e., "what people do with what the state hands them."[75] Furthermore, these analysts not only overlook the complicated dynamics of congruence, compromise, and conflict between elite and popular voices, but also evade the issue of substance, that is, the continuing appeal of socialist values in contemporary China. Anti-Communist right-wing triumphalism and leftist cynicism on China — the latter captured by Slavoj Žižek's characterization of post-Mao China as "an ideal capitalist state" doing the dirty job of controlling workers for capital"[76] — paradoxically join hands and mutually reinforce each other to understand China. The cumulative effect has been to displace any substantive engagement with China's revolutionary legacies and socialism as a possible alternative.

As China's post-Mao reform reaches a critical juncture, the "battle for China's past"[77] — from modern Chinese history in general to the CCP's revolutionary history, but especially the history of the Mao era of "socialist construction," including the CR in particular — has assumed critical importance for understanding China's present and for shaping its future. With regard to China's modern history, in a 2006 article published by the *China Youth News' Freezing Point Weekly*, for example, Yuan Weishi's revisionist interpretation of the Boxer Rebellion of 1900 developed into a major censorship and anti-censorship saga between the CCP's censorship regime and liberal intellectuals.[78] That the CCP still keeps such a tight lid on publications concerning the CR further underscores the political significance of the battle over the meaning and significance of the CR. At the same time, because the economic reforms have created new forms of injustices and engendered profound social and spatial divisions in Chinese society, and because an essential part of the Marxist-Leninist and Maoist ideology is the value of socio-economic equality and justice and the notion of socialism as a more just and more equitable society, "[t]he fact that Marxism-Leninism is still used to legitimize political suppression is a double-edged sword for the Chinese authorities."[79] Although the CCP has abandoned the language of "line struggle" and "class struggle," contestation over its revolutionary legacies, along with the "capitalism versus socialism" debate, has been an integral part of China's thirty years of reform. That Deng had to impose a "no-debate" decree to push ahead with his post-1989 reforms is in itself telling.

On the one hand, once the CCP repudiates the CR and adopts capitalist means of development, revisionist social forces and ideological voices inevitably demand the "whole package" of Western liberal democratic capitalism — from further privatizing the state sector to establishing multi-party democracy. As part of this ideological agenda, liberal intellectuals continue to advocate press freedom, a "press law," and independent newspaper publishing (*kaifang baojin*, 开放报禁), which are key demands of the 2008 petition known as "Charter 08."[80] On the other hand, rather than try to "re-legitimate" itself through multi-party elections after it came to power, the CCP hangs on to its original source of revolutionary legitimization while aiming to enhance it by trying to "deliver the goods" and claiming to fulfill its promise of building a socialist society. Because the CCP "has not repudiated the Chinese revolution or socialist values, nor the summation of Mao Zedong thought,"[81] the socialist tradition has not only functioned "to a certain extent as an internal restraint on state reforms," compelling the CCP to at least "couch its announcement in a particular language designed to harmonize the policy transformation with its proclaimed social goals," but also has given "workers, peasants and other social collectivities some legitimate means to contest or negotiate the state's corrupt or inegalitarian marketization procedures."[82] By the mid-1990s, acutely felt injustices and inequalities resulting from capitalist developments, along with manifestations of persistent Western imperialism and racism against China, galvanized an unofficial revival of socialism as both a normative framework at the popular level (as opposed to a ruling ideology) and a language of resistance against CCP policies.[83] Instead of calling for regime change, some workers and farmers have called on the CCP to live up to its revolutionary mandate against foreign capitalists, private interests, and local authorities.[84]

Although China's print and broadcast media are required to promote the official doctrines of the day, CCP Leninist discipline and the market-based truths of advertising revenue and market-driven growth have subjected them to the interests of the country's dominant political, economic, and intellectual elite. Notwithstanding the leadership's calls for the media to be closer to the people, the gap between their role as the mouthpiece of the ruling elite and the mouthpiece of ordinary people seems to have never been so enormous. In broadcasting, CCTV, the monopolistic and excessively commercialized state television network, has come to symbolize the worst of what the CCP media system has become. On February 9, 2009, when CCTV's illegal fireworks display set a spectacular fire that burned a recently furnished 30-story building attached to CCTV's highly controversial new headquarters in Beijing, Chinese bloggers and netizens used the incident to vent their anger toward the CCP's most pervasive media outlet, whose iconic new headquarters had come to symbolize "the extravagant, arrogant, domineering and monopolist approach" that characterizes the powerful elite "who appear to lord it over ordinary people."[85] In the print sector, market-oriented outlets have long overtaken traditional CCP organs as the "new mainstream." In Beijing, prominent outlets include urban dailies such as *Beijing News* (*Xinjing bao*, 新京报) and current affairs and business journals such as *Economic Observer* (*Jingji guancha bao*, 经济观察报), *Finance* (*Caijing*, 财经), and *China Newsweekly* (*Zhongguo xinwen zhoukan*, 中国新闻周刊). In Guangdong, *Southern Weekend* (*Nanfang zhoumo*, 南方周末) and *Southern Metropolitan News* (*Nanfang dushi bao*, 南方都市报), both market-oriented subsidiaries of the provincial CCP organ *Southern Daily* (*Nanfang ribao*, 南方日报) and known for their exposure of corruption and crusade for citizenship rights, have been major liberal forums. In popular entertainment, although profit-oriented producers have found revolutionary subject matters popular with audiences, revisionist interpretations of revolutionary symbols have become common. Thus, in April 2004 the SARFT had to issue a special administrative order to tighten censorship over television adaptations of the "red classics" in an attempt to prevent the production of television dramas that "flirt with" revolutionary classics by exploiting their fame but making excessive changes that denigrate the CCP's revolutionary legacies and present a less-than-dignified treatment of revolutionary heroes.

Still, the CCP's own market-oriented reform policies provide fertile ground for the subversion of its revolution in media and ideology. For example, by early 2009, following the policy of allowing the transfer of land-use rights and thus the potential re-emergence of a "landlord" strata in the countryside, a book entitled *The Rooster Didn't Call Out at Midnight* (*Banye ji bujiao*, 半夜鸡不叫), published under the imprint of the authoritative CCP Central Documentation Press, managed to subvert the image of Zhou Papi (周扒皮), the most famous literary icon of the exploitative landlord class created by the revolutionary author Gao Yubao (高玉宝).[86] With the "rehabilitation" of Zhou Papi and his type in the media, the rationale for the CCP's historical land reform and the destruction of the landlord class was undermined, threatening to challenge the legitimacy of the CCP's land reform program, a pillar of the Communist revolution. Class struggle in the media seems never to have been so real. Moreover, contrary to the CCP's rhetoric of promoting Marxism and keeping the media in the hands of Marxists, the media industry's profit motive and the predominant liberal and even neoliberal sensibilities of many of its gatekeepers have combined to marginalize leftist ideas.[87]

Within this media ecology, it is the Internet, the freer, most participatory, and most grassroots-oriented segment of the Chinese communication system, that has emerged as the unofficial forum for expressing socialist ideas and defending the CCP's revolutionary legacies. Although there may not be much contention over the continuing relevance of the Maoist legacy by "influential people"[88] (i.e., the politically and intellectually dominant post-Mao reformist elite), that the Internet has given rise to a revived and unofficial leftist, or more appropriately a broad discursive formation that is critical of the excesses and negative consequences of the market reforms, is not something to be dismissed. In fact, the existence of an unofficial Internet discourse on socialism should be taken seriously precisely because there are no other more-established channels for the expression of leftist political sensibilities, and because unofficial leftist ideas, forums, and Web sites, like their right-wing counterparts, have a precarious existence in China's highly controlled Internet environment. Along with escalated popular struggles for social justice and freedom from excessive exploitation and social dislocation in what has been characterized as the Chinese version of Polanyi's societal counter-movement against the destructive effects of the imposition of market relations on society[89] — epitomized by the Internet appeals by the parents of enslaved child laborers in the Shanxi kilns in early 2007 — both "old" and "new" leftists have waged a protracted

discursive struggle for socialist renewal as a response to capitalist development. No longer having access to political power or the print and broadcast
media, they have resorted to Internet-based interventions on major political
economic developments to challenge post-Mao official and liberal intellectual interpretations of China's revolutionary past, including the CR. Old
revolutionaries, left-leaning intellectuals, and grassroots online critics of the
market reforms have mounted successive waves of criticism against the
further privatization of China's state-owned sector, the entrenchment of
private property rights in the legal system, and the dominance of Western-
style market economics. As they appeal to the CCP leadership to heed its
own professed socialist beliefs, a protracted debate on the future of China's
reform, known as "the third debate on the reform," engulfed the Chinese
media and cyberspace between late 2004 and 2007.[90]

As was the case in the revolutionary era, socialist and nationalist
discourses are closely intertwined. Starting from the emergence of the *China
Can Say No* (*Zhongguo keyi shuo bu*, 中国可以说不) genre in popular writing
in the mid-1990s and the nationalist outcries against the NATO bombing of
the Chinese embassy in Belgrade in 1999, the resurgence of nationalistic
discourses among the young and urban educated has gone hand in hand
with the grassroots rejuvenation of socialism as a normative political and
socio-economic discourse. By late spring 2008, as young Chinese netizens
established Anti-CNN.com and circulated their own videos on YouTube to
expose the Western media's coverage of the riots in Tibet and to condemn
their hypocrisy and outright racism, popular Chinese disillusionment with
the West, especially the Western media, reached a new high. As Lu Xinyu
argues, an internationalist orientation that links the emancipation of the
Chinese nation with the emancipation of all weak nations in the world, and
the pursuit of justice and equality in both domestic and international
relations rather than a statism centering solely on economic interest, is at the
heart of the legacy of twentieth-century Chinese nationalism. In Lu's view,
the fact that this latest Internet-enabled nationalist movement was spear-
headed by overseas Chinese students and scholars — the better-educated,
more affluent, and most globalized members of the Chinese nation — has
made the liberal dismissal of Chinese nationalism as a modern version of
the xenophobic Boxers less convincing.[91] Rather, "it is precisely when these
young overseas Chinese entered the Western world as individuals that
they started to question the 'universal values' derived from globalization and
marketization, values they had earnestly accepted during their education
inside China."[92] The U.S.-originated global financial crisis in 2008 further

boosted unofficial Chinese online discussions on socialism as an alternative to capitalism.

In short, the "party principle," officially sponsored nationalism, the Internet, and integration with the global capitalist economy — the very forces that the reform-era CCP and pro-market intellectual elite mobilized to propel China forward — seem to carry China, as it were, backward to the future by keeping alive China's revolutionary legacies and re-engendering various leftist discourses at the grassroots. For example, as official censorship, together with marketization and concerted marginalization efforts on the part of liberal and neoliberal intellectuals, left no space for leftist discourse in the mainstream media, the "old leftists" within the CCP — some of whom are already in their nineties — discovered the Internet, which had just taken off as a new medium at the turn of the new century. In this way, the "old leftists," defying the dictum that the Internet is a medium for young people, unwillingly coalesced with and strengthened a multiplicity of online popular leftist and anti-neoliberal discourses, which, unlike the "old leftists," never had had access to the print media. In 2003, when the editors of *Pursuit of Truth* (*Zhenli de zhuiqiu*, 真理的追求), an "old left" journal that was suspended after it voiced opposition to Jiang Zemin's "three represents" thesis in 2001, saw little hope of resuming the journal's publication, they collaborated with nearly one hundred retired CCP officials to launch the Web site "Mao Zedong Flag" (*Mao Zedong qizhi wang*, 毛泽东旗帜网, maoflag.net). This prompted a rapid alliance of existing leftist forums and became a major site for the circulation of online leftist discourses, threatening to turn leftist voices into a dominant tenor in Chinese Internet chat rooms.[93] Underscoring the double-edged nature of the appeal of the Hu Jintao leadership to Maoist legacies, the Web site not only derived its name from Hu's promise that "we must uphold the great flag of Mao Zedong Thought at whatever time and under whatever circumstances," but also featured this statement as its motto. Even the *RMRB*'s "Strengthen the Nation Forum," launched in 1999 in the aftermath of the NATO bombing of the Chinese embassy in Belgrade so that Chinese netizens could vent their nationalist anger against the United States in an officially contained cyberspace, has attracted left-leaning participants.[94]

Because the "old leftists" are retired revolutionaries and the founders of the Chinese socialist state, they function as living embodiments and speaking subjects of the Communist revolution, rather than as the empty symbols and caricatured images of the revolutionary legacies that the party-state relies upon for its continuing legitimacy. Their presence in a broad leftist

discursive formation thus is particularly significant.[95] At one level, they maintain a vigilance on mainstream print and broadcast media and carry on an
unofficial "line struggle" with liberal outlets by exposing their "bourgeois
ideological orientations." The leftist Web site *Utopia* (*Wu you zhi xiang,* 乌有
之乡, wyzxsx.com), for example, runs numerous articles, and even special
features, exposing publications from the *Southern Daily* group for "hijacking
China" with their capitalistic ideological orientations.[96] More importantly,
they threaten to serve as the basis for a hegemonic alliance among the
CCP central leadership, "new left" intellectuals who have elaborated the
theoretical foundations for socialist renewal and a reinvigorated concept of
"people's democracy,"[97] and China's lower social classes who have engaged
in various struggles against the negative consequences of the economic
reforms. Although the "old leftists and retired revolutionaries aren't going to
be around much longer,"[98] a small and vocal group of retired government
officials, led by individuals such as Ma Bin (马宾), a former advisor to the
State Council Development Research Center, continue to issue leftist-
inspired political appeals to the CCP leadership on the course of China's
ongoing reforms. Moreover, there are many middle-aged and, more significantly, young left-leaning netizens as well as working-class activists who use
the Internet to advance the ongoing workers' struggles.[99]

The Hu Jintao leadership's re-articulation of the socialist discourse has
coincided with the revival of unofficial socialist sensibilities. Moreover,
in the view of liberal legal scholar He Weifang (贺卫方), the leftists are
"rampant" (*changjue,* 猖獗)[100] online precisely because they hit the CCP's
"soft ribs" of continuing to cling to its revolutionary legacies for legitimacy
and are therefore empowered to utilize the socialist discourse to critique the
reform with moral authority.[101] However, the CCP's propaganda-control
regime continues to harass and shut down leftist Web sites. In July 2007,
even the "maoflag" Web site was temporarily shut down when it posted an
open letter by seventeen former high-level CCP officials and Marxist
academics accusing CCP policies of making a mockery of Marxism and
taking the country "down an evil road."[102] Clearly, the Web site's placement
of Hu's statement as its banner was no protection against state repression.
It is precisely against this background — and Mao's endorsement of the
"big-character posters" during the CR — that one must understand the
specific spinning by the neo-Maoist netizens on the political significance of
Hu Jintao's attention to popular online expression during his visit to the
RMRB.

Conclusion

Viewed from the vantage point of media and ideology, the CCP's revolutionary legacies are alive in multifaceted and conflicted forms — as institutional embodiments, especially the Leninist control structures, as the normative values of socialism and communism, as governmental techniques such as the Maoist campaign practices, as lived and living experiences and consciousnesses, and, finally, as objects of discursive contestation. As they are being selectively abandoned by the CCP and subverted by liberal ideological forces in the market-driven media system, they are also being kept alive selectively, not only by the CCP for its own purposes of legitimacy and domination, but also by resistant Chinese social agents, especially Internet voices with a concern for social justice, the long-term sustainability of China's reform process, and/or voices claiming to speak for the "masses," i.e., China's vast social forces in whose name the revolution was fought. More specifically, if the CCP has clung to the revolution's Leninist organizational and disciplinary legacies from above, China's leftist intellectual forces and subordinate social agents have rediscovered the more populist and normative dimensions of the revolutionary legacies and the socialist discourse in their attempts to subject both the power of the post-Mao party-state and the power of the market to societal needs. It is precisely in this sense I have argued that if "socialism is the subordination of market and state to the self-regulating society,"[103] then "perhaps not only the party's official socialist slogans per se, but also their reappropriation by various Chinese social forces and the unfolding societal processes of subordinating both state and market to the social needs of the working people, are what the struggle for socialism in China is about."[104]

To conclude, complementing analyses on how the post-Mao CCP has managed to selectively mobilize revolutionary methods without endorsing their goals in the reform process, I would like to make two points. First, it is important to make distinctions both between different dimensions of the revolutionary legacies and between their official and popular invocations. Second, although the CCP has gone a long way in selectively retaining its revolutionary legacies to sustain its rule during the thirty years of economic boom, it remains an open question whether it can separate the means from the ends in the long run. To be sure, just as one should not underestimate the repressive and rigid nature of the CCP's market authoritarianism, one should not exaggerate the significance, let alone idealize the democratic nature, of what has been described as an unfolding Internet-led "second cultural revolution" as a continuation of the 1949 revolution. However, there is no doubt that the continuing relevance of China's revolutionary legacies needs to be understood not only in the CCP's official discourses and governmental practices, but also in the dynamic relation of mutual appropriation and antagonistic tension with resurgent unofficial socialist discourses and ongoing social contestations.

Endnotes

1. Michael Bristow, "China's Leader Makes Live Webcast," June 20, 2008, at http://news.bbc.co.uk/1/hi/world/asia-pacific/7465224.stm (accessed June 21, 2008).

2. Yundan Shuinuan (云淡水暖), "Wangluo de liliang" (网络的力量) (The Strength of the Internet), June 20, 2008, at http://bbs1.people.com.cn/postDetail.do?id=86776403&boardId=2 (accessed June 24, 2008).

3. Wujiang shangxia er qiusuo (吾将上下而求索), "Wangluo minzhu kaiqile wenhua geming xin xingshi" (网络民主开启了文化革命新形式) (Internet Democracy Opens a New Situation for a Cultural Revolution), July 2, 2008, at http://www.wyzxsx.com/Article/Class22/200807/43710.html (accessed July 4, 2008).

4. Hu Jintao (胡锦涛), "Zai *Renmin ribao* she kaocha gongzuo shi de jianghua (2008 nian 6 yue 20 ri)" (在人民日报社考察工作时的讲话 [2008 年6月 20日]) (Speech during Investigation Work at the *People's Daily* Editorial Offices [June 20, 2008]), June 21, 2008, at http://politics.people.com.cn/GB/1024/7408514.html (accessed June 26, 2008).

5. "Qinqie de guanhuai, juda de guwu" (亲切的关怀，巨大的鼓舞) (Cordial Care, Tremendous Inspiration), June 20, 2008, *Renmin ribao*, at http://politics.people.com.cn/GB/1026/7409978.html (accessed July 10, 2010).

6. "Quanguo xuanchuan sixiang zhanxian renzhen xuexi Hu Jintao zhongyao jianghua" (全国宣传思想战线认真学习胡锦涛重要讲话) (The Entire Nation Seriously Studies Hu Jintao's Important Speech on Propaganda Thought), June 23, 2008, *Renmin wang*, at http://politics.people.com.cn/GB/8198/125283/125284/7411100.html (accessed July 10, 2010).

7. "Zhongguo gongchandang zhongyang weiyuanhui guanyu wuchan jieji wenhua dageming de jueding (1966 nian 8 yue 8 ri tongguo)" (中国共产党中央委员会关于无产阶级文化大革命的决定[1966年8月8日通过], Decision of the Chinese Communist Party Central Committee on the Great Proletarian Cultural Revolution [passed on August 8, 1966]), *Renmin ribao* (人民日报, People's Daily), August 9, 1968, p. 1. For an online version of the document, see "1968.8.9 *Zhonggong zhongyang guanyu wuchan jieji wenhua dageming de jueding*" (1966.8.9 中共中央关于无产阶级文化大革命的决定), at http://news.sina.com.cn/c/144490.html (accessed September 7, 2010).

8. Deng Xiaoping (邓小平), *Deng Xiaoping wenxuan, di er juan* (邓小平文选, 第二卷) (Selected Works of Deng Xiaoping, Vol. 2) (Beijing: Renmin chubanshe, 2001), p. 272, cited in Dai Yuanguang (戴元光), *Zhongguo chuanbo sixiang shi: Xian dangdai juan* (中国传播思想史: 现当代卷) (A History of Chinese Communication Thought: Modern and Contemporary Volume) (Shanghai: Shanghai jiaotong daxue chubanshe, 2005), p. 191.

9. Anne-Marie Brady, *Marketing Dictatorship: Propaganda and Thought Work in Contemporary China* (Lanham, MD: Rowman and Littlefield, 2008), p. 45; Yuezhi Zhao, *Communication in China: Political Economy, Power, and Conflict* (Lanham, MD: Rowman and Littlefield, 2008), ch. 1.

10. "Dang he guojia sidai lingdao ren yu *Renmin ribao*" (党和国家四代领导人与《人民日报》) (Four Generations of Party and Government Leaders and the *People's Daily*), June 27, 2008, *Renmin wang*, at http://politics.people.com.cn/GB/1025/7432965.html (accessed June 24, 2008).

11. Timothy Cheek has discussed the differences within the CCP in terms of "bureaucratic Maoism" and "faith Maoism." See his *Propaganda and Culture in Mao's China: Deng Tuo and the Intelligentsia* (Oxford: Clarendon Press, 1997).

12. Sima Nan (司马南), "Nanfang zhoumo qujie Hu Jintao jianghua" (南方周末曲解胡锦涛讲话) (*Southern Weekend* Distorts Hu Jintao's Speech), June 29, 2008, at http://www.wyzxsx.com/Article/Class22/200806/43492.html (accessed July 10, 2010).

13. Wang Hui, "Depoliticized Politics, From East to West," *New Left Review*, no. 41 (September-October 2006): 29–45.

14. Brady, *Marketing Dictatorship*, p. 70.

15. Vivenne Shue, "Legitimacy Crisis in China?" in Peter Hays Cries and Stanley Rosen, eds., *State and Society in 21st Century China: Crisis, Contention, and Legitimation* (London: RoutledgeCurzon, 2004), p. 28.

16. Bruce Gilley, *China's Democratic Future: How It Will Happen and Where It Will Lead* (New York: Columbia University Press, 2004), p. 33.

17. Shue, "Legitimacy Crisis in China?" p. 33.

18. Liu Kang, *Globalization and Cultural Trends in China* (Honolulu: University of Hawai'i Press, 2004), p. 50.

19. Kalpana Misra, *From Post-Maoism to Post-Marxism: The Erosion of Official Ideology in Deng's China* (New York: Routledge, 1998), p. 8.

20. This statement was made by Deng during his "southern tour" in 1992. See "Zai Wuchang, Shenzhen, Zhuhai, Shanghai dengdi de tanhua yaodian (shibari yiyue 1992 dao ershiyiri eryue 1992)" (在武昌、深圳、珠海、上海等地的谈话要点 [1992年1月18日–2月21日]) (Excerpts from Talks Given in Wuchang, Shenzhen, Zhuhai, Shanghai, and So Forth [January 18, 1992-February 21, 1992]), in *Deng Xiaoping wenxuan, disan juan* (邓小平文选, 第三卷) (Selected Works of Deng Xiaoping, Vol. 3) (Beijing: Renmin chubanshe, 1993), p. 377.

21. Some of these policies include: abolishing the agricultural taxes and tuition fees for compulsory education to relieve the burden on farmers, increasing transfer payments to poor provinces to close the staggering regional gap, and establishing social security and health-care benefits for the rural population. For a detailed description and analysis of these policies, see Wang Shaoguang (王绍光), "Da zhuanxing: 1980 niandai yilai Zhongguo de shuangxiang yundong" (大转型: 1980年代以来中国的双向运动) (The Great Transformation: Two-Way Movements in China since the 1980s.), *Zhongguo shehui kexue* (中国社会科学) (Chinese Social Science), no. 1 (2008), at http://www.chinaelections.org/newsinfo.asp?newsid=130012 (accessed July 10, 2010). According to Wang, some of these policies began as early as 1999.

22. Hu Jintao (胡锦涛), "Zai shiliujie sizhong quanhui disanci quanti huiyishang de jianghua" (在十六届四中全会第三次全体会议上的讲话) (Speech at the Third Full

Meeting of the Fourth Plenary Session of the Sixteenth Party Congress), at http://vip.bokee.com/20080414511775.html (accessed September 7, 2010).

23. "Hu: Harmonious Society Crucial for Progress," Xinhua, June 28, 2005, at www.chinadaily.com.cn/english/doc/2005-06/28/content_455332.htm (accessed August 1, 2005).

24. Zhang Lihua (张利华), "Lun Zhongguo shehuizhuyi hexin jiazhi tixi de neihe yu cengci" (论中国社会主义核心价值体系的内核与层次) (On the Crux and Level of the Core Values of Chinese Socialism), June 5, 2007, Renmin wang, at http://theory.people.com.cn/GB/49150/49152/5825094.html (accessed July 1, 2008).

25. The eight "honors" are: patriotism, serving the people, a scientific spirit, hard work, solidarity and mutual support, trustworthiness and honesty, abiding by the law, and hard struggle. The eight "shames" are the opposites.

26. Elizabeth J. Perry, "Studying Chinese Politics: Farewell to Revolution?" *The China Journal*, no. 57 (January 2007): 16.

27. Gilley, *China's Democratic Future*, p. 33.

28. Timothy Cheek, *Living with Reform: China Since 1989* (New York: Zed Books, 2006), p. 43.

29. Yuezhi Zhao, *Media, Market, and Democracy in China: Between the Party Line and the Bottom Line* (Urbana: University of Illinois Press, 1998), p. 19.

30. "Zhongguo gongchandang de diyige jueyi" (中国共产党的第一个决议) (The First Resolution of the Chinese Communist Party), in Journalism Research Institute of the Chinese Academy of Social Sciences (中国社会科学院新闻研究所), ed., *Zhongguo gongchandang xinwen gongzuo wenjian huibian (shang juan)* (中国共产党新闻工作文件汇编[上卷]) (Selected Documents on Chinese Communist Journalism Work [Vol. 1]) (Beijing: Xinhua chubanshe, 1980), p. 1.

31. Huang Dan (黄旦), "Dang zuzhi banbao yu 'shou gongye' gongzuo fangshi" (党组织办报与"手工业"工作方式) (Running Newspapers by the Party and Management of the "Handicraft Industry"), *Xinwen daxue* (新闻大学) (Journalism University), no. 3 (Fall 2004): 14.

32. Mao, in turn, formed his theory of the party press by drawing inspiration from CCP propagandist Deng Tuo's pioneering work in running *Resistance News* (*Xinwen zhanxian*, 新闻战线), the regional CCP organ of the Jin-Cha-Ji base area. See Cheek, *Propaganda and Culture in Mao's China*; and Patricia Stranahan, *Molding the Medium: The Chinese Communist Party and the* Liberation Daily (Armonk, NY: M.E. Sharpe, 1990), p. 31.

33. Stranahan, *Molding the Medium*, p. 30; Chen Lidan (陈力丹), *Makesizhuyi xinwenxue cidian* (马克思主义新闻学词典) (Dictionary on the Study of Marxist Journalism) (Beijing: Zhongguo guangbo dianshi chubanshe, 2002), pp. 80–81; pp. 252–253. See also, Li Bin (李彬), *Zhongguo xinwen shehui shi: Chatuban* (中国新闻社会史: 插图版) (A Social History of Chinese Journalism: With Illustrations) (Beijing: Qinghua daxue chubanshe, 2008), pp. 153–158.

34. Dai Yuanguang, *Zhongguo chuanbo sixiang shi*, p. 193.

35. Chen Lidan, *Makesizhuyi xinwenxue cidian*, p. 80.

36. Li Bin, *Zhongguo xinwen shehui shi*, p. 155.

37. Chen Lidan, *Makesizhuyi xinwenxue cidian*, p. 80.

38. Ibid., p. 79.

39. For more discussion, see Zhao, *Media, Market, and Democracy in China*, ch. 2.

40. Hu Yaobang (胡耀邦), "Guanyu dangde xinwen gongzuo" (关于党的新闻工作) (On Party Journalism Work), February 8, 1985, *Renmin wang*, at http://news .xinhuanet.com/ziliao/2005-02/07/content_2557568.htm (accessed July 10, 2010).

41. "Bawozhu shenhua gaige de lishi jiyu" (把握住深化改革的历史机遇) (Grasp the Historical Opportunity to Deepen Reform), *Zhongguo jizhe* (中国记者) (Chinese Journalist), no. 9 (2001): 1.

42. "Jiji zhudong shenru chuangxin, jiada lidu wenbu tuijin: Youguan bumen fuzeren tan jinyibu shenhua xinwen chuban guangbo yingshiye gaige" (积极主动深入创新加大力度稳步推进: 有关部门负责人谈进一步深化新闻出版广播影视业改革) (Enthusiastically Initiate Innovation, Intensify Dynamism, and Go Forward with Stable Steps: A Responsible Person Speaks on Deeply Reforming the Journalism, Broadcast, and Television Industries), January 15, 2002, *Renmin wang*, at www.people.com.cn/GB/ shizheng/19/20020115/648902.html (accessed January 15, 2002).

43. Chen Lidan (陈力丹), "Dangguan meiti de jiben tizhi" (党管媒体的基本体制) (The Basic System of the Party Controlling the Media), *Chuanbo yu shehui xuekan* (传播与社会学刊) (Communication and Society), no. 6 (2008): 20.

44. Jin Guanjun and Dai Yuanguang, *Zhongguo chuanbo sixiang shi*, p. 194.

45. For a chronology of these transformations, see "Zhongyang guangbo shiyeju jigou jianbiao" (中央广播事业局机构简表) (Simple Chart of the Structure of the Central Communication Industry), August 1, 2007, at http://www.sarft.gov.cn/ articles/2007/08/01/20070908231035250793.html (accessed February 20, 1999).

46. Zhao, *Communication in China*, pp. 58–59.

47. Chen Lidan, "Dangguan meiti de jiben tizhi," p. 20.

48. Jiang Zemin (江泽民), "Zai Zhongguo gongchandang di shiwuci quanguo daibiao dahuishang de baogao" (在中国共产党第十五次全国代表大会上的报告报告) (Report at the Fifteenth National Chinese Communist Party Congress), September 12, 1997, at http://news.xinhuanet.com/zhengfu/2004-04/29/content_1447509.htm (accessed February 25, 2009).

49. Wu Muluan (吴木栾), "Zouxiang guojia zibenzhuyi?" (走向国家资本主义?) (Toward State Capitalism?), *Ershiyi shiji* (二十一世纪) (Twenty-First Century), no. 110 (December 2008): 24–35.

50. Jin Guanjun and Dai Yuanguang, eds., *Zhongguo chuanbo sixiang shi*, p. 197.

51. Zhao, *Communication in China*, ch. 4.

52. Author's interview with a media regulator, July 2004.

53. Chen Lidan, *Makesizhuyi xinwenxue cidian*, p. 143.

54. M.K. Dziewanowski, *A History of Soviet Russia* (Englewood Cliffs, NJ: Prentice Hall, 3rd ed., 1989), p. 133.

55. Chen Lidan, *Makesizhuyi xinwenguan sixiang tixi* (马克思主义新闻观思想体系) (The Intellectual System of the Marxist Perspective on Journalism), (Beijing: Zhongguo renmin daxue chubanshe, 2006), p. 389.

56. Ibid., p. 441.

57. Yuezhi Zhao, "Neoliberal Strategies, Socialist Legacies: Communication and State Transformation in China," in Paula Chakravartty and Yuezhi Zhao, eds., *Global Communications: Toward a Transcultural Political Economy* (Lanham, MD: Rowman and Littlefield,

2008), p. 43. For Aihwa Ong's argument, see her book, *Neoliberalism as Exception: Mutations in Citizenship and Sovereignty* (Durham, NC: Duke University Press, 2006).

58. "Jingyingxing xinwen chuban danwei mingniandi quanbu zhuanzhi" (经营性新闻出版单位明年底全部转制) (At the End of Next Year the Operation of Journalism Units Will Be Completely Changed), February 13, 2009, *Zhongguo qingnian bao*, at http://zqb.cyol.com/content/2009-02/13/content_2538411.htm (accessed February 14, 2009).

59. Although this post-revolutionary Shanghai CCP organ inherited the name of the Yan'an *Liberation Daily*, there is no direct institutional linkage.

60. Chen Lidan, "Dangguan meiti de jiben tizhi," p. 20.

61. Jin Guanjun and Dai Yuanguang, eds., *Zhongguo chuanbo sixiang shi*, pp. 202–203.

62. Hu Jintao, "Zai *Renmin ribao* she kaocha gongzuo shi de jianghua."

63. Joseph Fewsmith, "China and the Politics of SARS," *Current History*, 102, no. 665 (September 2003): 250.

64. Perry, "Studying Chinese Politics," pp. 15–16.

65. Fewsmith, "China and the Politics of SARS," p. 254.

66. "Zhonggong zhongyang guanyu jiaqiang dangde zhizheng nengli jianshe de jueding" (中共中央关于加强党的执政能力建设的决定) (Decision of the Chinese Communist Central Committee on Strengthening the Construction of the Party's Governance Abilities), at www.china.org.cn/chinese/ 2004/Sep/668376.htm (accessed October 2, 2004).

67. Hu Jintao, "Zai *Renmin ribao* she kaocha gongzuo shi de jianghua."

68. Stranathan, *Molding the Medium*, p. 35; ch. 4.

69. Brady, *Marketing Dictatorship*, p. 76.

70. Zhang Lihua, "Lun Zhongguo shehuizhuyi hexin jiazhi tixi de neihe yu cengci."

71. Chen Lidan, *Makesizhuyi xinwenxue cidian*, pp. 90–91.

72. Yuezhi Zhao and Sun Wusan, "Public Opinion Supervision: Possibilities and Limits of the Media in Constraining Local Officials," in Elizabeth J. Perry and Merle Goldman, eds., *Grassroots Political Reform in Contemporary China* (Cambridge, MA: Harvard University Press, 2007), pp. 300–324.

73. Geremie Barmé, *In the Red: On Contemporary Chinese Culture* (New York: Columbia University Press, 1999).

74. Brady, *Marketing Dictatorship*, p. 202.

75. Cheek, *Living with Reform*, p. 46.

76. Slavoj Žižek, *Welcome to the Desert of the Real! Five Essays on September 11 and Related Dates* (London: Verso, 2002), pp. 146–147.

77. Mobo Gao, *The Battle for China's Past: Mao and the Cultural Revolution* (London: Pluto Press, 2008).

78. For details on the case, see Zhao, *Communication in China*, pp. 57–58.

79. Gao, *The Battle for China's Past*, p. 193.

80. "Dissent in China: The Year of Living Dissidently," *The Economist*, 390, no. 8614 (January 17, 2009): 42. If the CCP is drawing negative lessons from the legacy of East European communism, China's liberal opposition is drawing inspiration, thus the name "Charter 08," which was intended to recall "Charter 77," the human-rights manifesto circulated by dissidents in Czechoslovakia in 1977.

81. Wang, "Depoliticized Politics," p. 44.

82. Ibid., p. 45.

83. See, for example, Yu Jianrong (于建嵘), *Zhongguo gongren jieji zhuangkuang: Anyuan shilu* (中国工人阶级状况: 安源实录) (The Situation of the Worker Class in China: A Record of Anyuan) (Hong Kong: Mingjing chubanshe, 2006); Elizabeth J. Perry, "Crime, Corruption, and Contention," in Merle Goldman and Roderick MacFarquhar, eds., *The Paradox of China's Post-Mao Reforms* (Cambridge, MA: Harvard University Press, 1999), pp. 308–329; Ching Kwan Lee, "Pathways of Labour Insurgency," in Elizabeth J. Perry and Mark Selden, eds., *Chinese Society, 2nd Edition: Change, Conflict and Resistance* (New York: RoutledgeCurzon, 2003), pp. 71–91; Kevin J. O'Brien and Lianjiang Li, *Rightful Resistance in Rural China* (Cambridge: Cambridge University Press, 2006). To the extent that Falun Gong, the first Internet-enabled popular protest movement in post-Mao era, eventually embraced an explicit anti-Communist right-wing politics is an exception. See Yuezhi Zhao, "Falun Gong, Identity, and the Struggle over Meaning Inside and Outside China," in Nick Couldry and James Curran, eds., *Contesting Media Power: Alternative Media in a Networked World* (Lanham, MD: Rowman and Littlefield, 2003), pp. 209–223; see also, Shue, "Legitimacy Crisis in China?"

84. Perry, "Studying Chinese Politics"; David Harvey, *A Brief History of Neoliberalism* (New York: Oxford University Press, 2005), p. 150.

85. Wang Xiangwei, "Mainlanders See Inferno as Just Desserts for Domineering CCTV," February 16, 2009, *South China Morning Post*, at http://guanyu9.blogspot.com/2009/02/mainlanders-see-inferno-as-just-deserts.html (accessed July 10, 2010).

86. Generations of Chinese were educated by this autobiographical novel, which had been a school textbook. I provide this in response to a question posed by one of this chapter's reviewers, "How widely was Gao Yubao read, and who was paying attention?"

87. For more elaboration, see Zhao, *Communication in China*, chs. 1 and 2.

88. This is a term used by one of this chapter's reviewers to challenge my point about the existence of a "battle for China's past." However, the main thrust of my argument is precisely to challenge any elitist perspective on Chinese politics.

89. Wang Shaoguang, *Da zhuanxing*.

90. For detailed discussion of these developments, see Zhao, *Communication in China*, especially chs. 5–6, and conclusion.

91. The most influential attack on the March and April 2008 wave of nationalism was made by Wu Jiaxiang (吴稼祥) in a April 2, 2008, *China Youth News* article, entitled "Mincui yi kesou, dazhong jiu fashao" (民粹一咳嗽, 大众就发烧) (Populism Is a Cough, the People Get a Fever). "New left" scholar Han Yuhai (韩毓海) offered the most influential critique of Wu's argument in an article entitled "Huida: Lun mincuizhuyi wenti ji qita" (回答: 论民粹主义问题及其它) (Reply: On the Issue of Populism and Other Things), April 22, 2008, at http://www.wyzxsx.com/Article/Class16/200804/37162.html (accessed July 3, 2008). That Wu's article was carried by *China Youth News*, an official party organ, and that the paper eventually rejected Han's article, which was originally solicited by the paper to respond to Wu, is significant. Hu had to publish his article on the Internet.

92. Lu Xinyu (吕新雨), *Zhongguo minzuzhuyi de "nei" yu "wai"* (中国民族主义的"内"与"外") (The "Ins" and "Outs" of Chinese Nationalism), manuscript provided

by the author. Lu Xinyu's encounter with *Southern Weekend* parallels Han Yuhai's experience with *China Youth News*. Her article was initially solicited by *Southern Weekend*, but the paper eventually rejected it. Personal conversation, June 27, 2008, Vancouver.

93. Andy Yinan Hu, "Swimming against the Tide: Tracing and Locating Chinese Leftism Online," M.A. thesis, School of Communication, Simon Fraser University, 2006, pp. 87–88.

94. Ibid., pp. 132–135.

95. Ibid., p. 80.

96. For relevant articles, see http://www.wyzxsx.com/Article/Special/hanjiannandu/Index.html (accessed July 10, 2010).

97. For the most systematic English-language elaboration of the notion of "people's democracy" in the "new left" literature, see Lin Chun, *The Transformation of Chinese Socialism* (Durham, NC: Duke University Press, 2006).

98. This comment was made by one of the peer reviewers for this chapter.

99. For a detailed mapping of China's online leftist discursive formation and its generational and ideological make-up, see Hu, "Swimming against the Tide." For examples of worker activists/Internet bloggers in a concrete struggle against factory privatization, see Zhao, *Communication in China*, pp. 309–315.

100. I have no doubt that He Weifang exaggerates the power of his leftist opponents in order to dramatize his own positions. I am grateful to one of this chapter's reviewers for suggesting such a possibility.

101. Cited in Zhao, *Communication in China*, p. 340.

102. Mark Magnier, "China Party Accused of Ideological Drift," *Los Angeles Times* (July 18, 2007), at http://articles.latimes.com/2007/jul/18/world/fg-china18 (accessed July 10, 2010).

103. Michael Burawoy, "For a Sociological Marxism: The Complementary Convergence of Antonio Gramsci and Karl Polanyi," *Politics & Society*, 31, no. 2 (2003): 198.

104. Zhao, *Communication in China*, p. 343.

CHAPTER 8

Retrofitting the Steel Frame: From Mobilizing the Masses to Surveying the Public

PATRICIA M. THORNTON

For the past several decades, the study of contemporary Chinese politics has been dominated by the assumption that Mao's death marked the advent of a new era defined by a popular and elite rejection of Maoist mass politics, particularly those associated with the Cultural Revolution. In the now famed Third Plenum of the Eleventh Central Committee of December 1978, the scholarly consensus reads a fundamental break with the defining features of the Maoist past; others perceive a more gradual evolution from Maoist totalitarianism toward a more consultative, inclusive "soft authoritarianism." Both interpretations cite the more routinized collective decision-making and institutionalized politics of the post-Mao era as evidence of a largely successful transition to a post-revolutionary epoch, marked by the rise of a new generation of party technocrats. In contrast to the Maoist dictum that class struggle is the primary means of "continuing the revolution under the dictatorship of the proletariat," the Sixth Plenum resolution released in 2006 asserts that it is the goal of "social harmony," and not the perpetuation of class conflict, that resides at the core of "the intrinsic nature of socialism." The resolution's startling assertion that the attainment of a "harmonious society" has been at the core of the party's mission since the founding of the PRC[1] signals that the social revolutionary impetus of the CCP, at last and irrevocably, succumbed to the Thermidor.

Yet, notwithstanding the party's "thorough negation" of Cultural Revolution–era mass politics, the post-Mao leadership has by no means repudiated the project of party-engineered mass transformation. To the contrary, Deng Xiaoping's efforts to construct a "socialist spiritual civilization," Jiang's

Zemin's focus on the "comprehensive development of people" (*ren de quanmian fazhan*, 人的全面发展), and Hu Jintao's "socialist harmonious society" can be read as successive iterations of a longer-term agenda consonant with the party's Leninist roots.[2] In his 1902–3 pamphlet, *What Is to Be Done?* Lenin famously argues that the obligation and duty of the revolutionary party "consists in a *struggle against spontaneity*," because the spontaneous impulses of the masses result "precisely in the ideological enslavement of the workers by the bourgeoisie." Lenin's chief instruction to his elite "party of a new type" was to "*drag* the labor movement *away*" from its spontaneous tendencies, and to mold it from without. Tactically, Lenin's strategy involved developing print media, courting mass organizations, and "unifying local activities" to train the popular will continuously in the direction of social transformation, in effect substituting the revolutionary zeal of the Bolsheviks for the heterogeneous and scattered aims of the internally divided masses.[3]

As Mao himself stressed on several occasions, the success of this project rested upon the party's ability to "manufacture public opinion" (*zao yulun*, 造舆论)[4] by creating new publics, particularly through the development of new collective entities with shared economic interests.[5] Accordingly, early in its history the Chinese Communist Party (CCP) depended heavily on two interrelated practices in its efforts to successfully shape popular will: the so-called revolutionary "mass line" (*qunzhong luxian*, 群众路线), and its cultivation by a web of party-controlled "mass organizations" (*qunzhong zuzhi*, 群众组织),[6] both of which proved adaptable to the shifting agendas and needs of the party-state over time. Early on, grassroots activists were continually pressed by higher-ups to reinterpret preexisting social tensions as deep-rooted class-based conflicts that required the intercession and continuing oversight of the party. In the process, local cadres honed the particular skill of not only reframing a wide range of social issues in terms set by the party center, but also of building new collectives at the local level receptive and subservient to the will of the center.[7]

However, in the decades following the revolution, the party's own success at grassroots organizing proved a double-edged sword. The revolutionary masses, safely installed in any number of party- or state-sponsored mass organizations, were curiously apt at the articulation and pursuit of collective interests not in keeping with the "mass line" defined by the center. The restive potential of key mass institutions during the Mao era repeatedly took party leaders by surprise, for example, when the façade of a united proletariat was fractured by the 1957 strike wave in Shanghai, as described by

Elizabeth Perry, pitting state-organized trade unions, youth leagues, and temporary workers against one another in a virtual standstill that lasted several weeks.[8] Even more dramatic were the conflagrations of the Cultural Revolution a decade later, when mass organizations waged often violent attacks against each other, party committees, and even People's Liberation Army units, as they did during the 1967 Wuhan incident.[9] Even after Mao's demise and initiation of the Dengist reform program, representatives of official mass organizations, trade unions, and state-organized work-units marched to Tiananmen Square in 1989 to declare their support for the on-going student demonstrations that had been derided as "counter-revolutionary" in the state-run press. More recently, albeit perhaps less dramatically, leaders of state-created "work-units" occasionally mobilize disenfranchised workers to collectively resist the excessive demands of state and local authorities to remand taxes or fees, or to wrest other concessions from superordinate administrative units.[10]

With the erosion of the party's former bulwark of collective institutions during the reform era, alongside the party's reinvention of itself from a revolutionary to a ruling party, the CCP has likewise retooled its mission and mode of operation with respect to both the mass line and the mass organizations under its control. In 1987, with nearly a decade of economic reforms underway but little evidence of political liberalization, then-premier Zhao Ziyang revived the notion of the revolutionary-era "mass line," as a potential vehicle for a process of consultation between the masses and elites, that he termed "public opinion supervision":

> The basic principle for establishing a system of consultation and dialogue is to carry on the the fine tradition of "from the masses, to the masses," and to make public the activities of the leading bodies ... through all forms of modern mass media, to give scope to the supervisory role of public opinion [*yulun jiandu*, 舆论监督], to support the masses in criticism of shortcomings and mistakes in work, to oppose bureaucratism, and in general to combat all unhealthy tendencies.[11]

In fact, three years earlier, Zhao had established one of the reform era's first think-tanks, the Chinese Economic System Reform Research Institute (CESRRI), and authorized it to conduct a series of ambitious surveys of mass attitudes regarding the progress of the on-going market reform. Resistance to the collection of popular survey data was fierce during the initial stages of reform, arising from both ends of the Chinese political spectrum: remnants of former radical forces of the Cultural Revolution derided the practice of polling as "bourgeois pseudo-science"; and advocates of market reform cautioned against producing "papers full of superficial, empty points based on single facts" that might not convey the complexities of the "actual situation."[12] Publication of the results of the polls sparked a barrage of criticism from the party press as well, including one commentator who warned that although "popular opinion" can be said to reflect an enlightened form of the public interest, "mass opinion" can be swayed by "negative and unhealthy" tendencies interjected by minority factions, and mass opinion thus requires moderation by higher-level authorities.[13]

Despite the fall from grace of Zhao Ziyang and his reformist cohort during the 1989 Tiananmen demonstrations, "supervision by public opinion" has nonetheless emerged as a key concern in contemporary political discourse,[14] albeit in modified form, demonstrating both the persistence and the plasticity of the practice over time. Liberated from its original tether to the Mao-era political practice of mass criticism of those in positions of power, Zhao recommended that the concept of "public opinion supervision" had come to refer almost exclusively to the anchoring of political work more narrowly in the hands of the party's technocratic elite, particularly through the supervision of the media and its effects on popular views by the routinized surveillance and polling of public opinion. Likewise, the politicized use of the term "masses" (qunzhong, 群众) in party discourse, which connotes a disorganized and largely latent form of political power and expression, in contrast to the formal hierarchy of power represented by the "government" (zhengfu, 政府) or "leaders" (lingdao, 领导), has been eclipsed during the previous two decades by analyses of "society" (shehui, 社会), a less politically freighted term connoting self-disciplining publics governed by internal rules and logics of differentiation.[15] The contemporary media are replete with references to large-scale public opinion polls and, increasingly, market surveys, denoting strong majority support within Chinese society for a stunning array of elite proposals, including the Beijing Municipal Health Department's current methods of hospital management,[16] a variety of ambitious urban redevelopment projects in Tianjin,[17] and even vigorously enhanced public security efforts in Yangzhou during the hosting of the 2008 Olympic Games.[18]

Yet this apparent perpetuation of high levels of approval for the regime and its shifting policies can also be read as a contemporary artifact of the Maoist legacy of "manufacturing public opinion" through the elite-engineered constitution of particular publics and manipulation of the medium through which opinions are solicited and exchanged. A handful of critics have charged that the new practice of surveying Chinese public opinion gives undue weight to the preferences of the small but growing upwardly mobile urban middle classes at the expense of the underprivileged and underrepresented rural populations,[19] or the "floating population" of migrant laborers unofficially residing in China's cities.[20] However, perhaps equally important is the range of broader sociological effects that arise from the technocratic quantification of public opinion, and the types of responsive public(s) this process constructs. The product of a largely non-transparent process of calculation and aggregation, public opinion survey practices in reform-era China, as elsewhere in the world, reconfigure mass subjects as atomized individuals (generally consumers) with discrete preferences that can be measured and numerically expressed. In contrast to the earlier Mao-era model of mobilizing popular opinion, with its emphasis on the processes of creating collective economic interests and class consciousness, modern survey methods instead recast the process of public opinion formation as a highly constrained type of depoliticized choice-making on the part of respondents selecting from a limited list of pre-screened options. The numeric aggregation of individual choices as a composite of "majority will" serves to marginalize more radical or divergent views and to normalize moderate positions, prompting some to argue that public opinion polling creates an "artificial political environment which does not mimic the real dimensions of the public sphere," but instead "domesticates" public opinion by diminishing its intensity and radical propensities.[21] Alongside the widespread dismantling of the formal collective institutions within which Mao-era political and economic interests were conjoined and nurtured at the grassroots, the new market-friendly practice of "making" public opinion remains a chief resource for legitimating the party's rule and demonstrating popular support for its policies in a technologically advanced but depoliticized media environment.

Mobilizing the Masses

With respect to Western invocations of "public opinion," Mao repeatedly expressed an abiding skepticism, if not outright derision. The so-called 1949 "China White Paper" produced by the U.S. State Department under Dean Acheson invoked the specter of "informed and critical public opinion" to make the case that American diplomatic efforts toward the Communists were doomed to fail, to which Mao angrily responded:

> In considering public opinion, the Achesons have mixed up the public opinion [*yulun*, 輿论] of the reactionaries with that of the people. Toward the public opinion of the people, the Achesons [of the world] have no "responsiveness"

[*ganying*, 感应] whatsoever and are blind and deaf. For years they have turned a
deaf ear to the opposition voiced by the people of the United States, China and
the rest of the world to the reactionary foreign policy of the U.S. government.
What does Acheson mean by "informed and critical public opinion" [*you jianshide
he pipingxing de yulun*, 有见识的和批评性的舆论]? Nothing but the numerous
instruments of propaganda, such as the newspapers, news agencies, periodicals
and broadcasting stations which are controlled by the two reactionary parties in
the United States, the Republicans and the Democrats, and which specialize in the
manufacture of lies and threats against the people. Of these things Acheson says
rightly that the Communists "cannot endure and do not tolerate" them (nor do
the people). That is why we have closed down the imperialist offices of information, stopped the imperialist news agencies from distributing their dispatches to
the Chinese press and forbidden them the freedom to go on poisoning the souls
of the Chinese people on Chinese soil.[22]

Six years later, during the 1955 campaign to criticize leading CCP author
and intellectual Hu Feng, Mao elaborated on some of the same themes,
noting that he had heard complaints "unpleasant to the ear" (*hen nantingde*,
很难听的) that the CCP policed a "uniformity of public opinion," or "an
absence of public opinion" (*meiyou yulun*, 没有舆论), or "a suppression of
freedom" (*yazhi ziyou*, 压制自由). Mao retorted that, unlike in capitalist
countries "where under the dictatorship of the bourgeoisie, revolutionary
people are not allowed to do or say what they wish (*luan shuo, luan dong*, 乱说
乱动), but can only be [called] well-behaved" (*zhi jiao tamen guigui juju*, 只叫
他们规规矩矩), the opposite was true in the People's Republic, where the
dictatorship of the proletariat restricted the rights of the exploiting classes,
but accorded freedom to the revolutionary masses. Furthermore, in response
to Hu Feng's charge that, insofar as the "absolute majority" of his readers'
lives were being spent "within one organization or another" where they were
subject to a "coercive atmosphere" in which they could not express their
true opinions, Mao pointed out that prior to the advent of the party, the
fragmented state (*sansha zhuangtai*, 散沙状态) of the masses had facilitated
their exploitation by the ruling classes, and that it was only the party's arduous victory and continuing leadership that made possible this new unity of
opinion. Dissenting views among the revolutionary masses, Mao remarked,
would be reconciled by democratic means of persuasion, with the advanced
elements educating the backward ones until all contradictions were resolved.[23]
A chief method by which the party's "democratic persuasion" produced a
"unity of opinion" during the Mao era was through implementation of the
"mass line."

According to Mao's famed 1943 formulation, the "mass line" refers to an operational principle through which

> In all the practical work of our Party, all correct leadership is necessarily "from the masses, to the masses." This means: take the ideas [*yijian*, 意见] of the masses (scattered and unsystematic ideas) and concentrate them (through study turn them into concentrated and systematic ideas), then go to the masses and propagate and explain these ideas until the masses embrace them as their own, hold fast to them and translate them into action. . . . And so on, over and over again in an endless spiral, with the ideas becoming more correct, more vital [*shengdong*, 生动] and richer each time. Such is the Marxist theory of knowledge.[24]

In Liu Shaoqi's 1945 report at the Seventh Congress on revising the party constitution, he further elaborated upon the viewpoint (*guandian*, 观点) of the "mass line," noting: "The viewpoint of doing everything in the interests of people (*renmin qunzhong*, 人民群众), of holding oneself responsible to them, of believing in their self-emancipation and of learning from them constitutes our mass viewpoint, which is the viewpoint of the vanguard of the people."[25] In the 1956 revision of the party constitution, Deng Xiaoping reiterated Mao's classic formulation, adding the following observation:

> The masses are the creators of history. The people's fetters can only be by their own hands; the people's happy lives can only be made with their own hands. We begin from this truth and the fundamental method of our work is: the masses and the leaders join together, working together to walk the mass line, freely mobilize the people, with the leaders launching mass movements on a grand scale, gathering the wisdom and ideas of the people, and relying upon the power of the masses to implement the general and specific policies of the Party.[26]

With respect to these three formulations of the Mao-era "mass line," Roderick MacFarquhar identifies two central trends: one, a duty on the part of party cadres to engage in "selfless service" by assisting the people to liberate themselves; and, second, a "leadership method" that involves the Mao-era party in "studying, coordinating, and systematizing" mass views and then propagating the resulting formulations back to the masses and "popularizing them until the people accepted them as their own."[27] In practical terms, Mao's concept of the mass line is, according to Marc Blecher, a "way of resolving conflict by attempting to define or create collective agreement," that "assigns a vigorous role to leadership, but abjures leaders from acting in an elitist (or to use the Chinese terms, commandist or subjectivist) fashion."[28] Some disagree, arguing instead that implementation of the "mass line" in practice either amounted to a largely ritualistic and formalized appearance of mass democracy,[29] or it was used only as a mechanism of top-down control. For example, in his path-breaking book on political participation in Mao's China, James Townsend finds that the various "institutions designed to encourage mass participation began to decline in effectiveness in 1956," thereafter acting almost solely in an educative or propagandistic capacity. Although he acknowledges that the use of the mass line to supervise or control bureaucratic behavior was revived temporarily during the Cultural Revolution, by 1969, Townsend concludes "as in the past, the tension evoked by mass mobilization has been resolved in favor of elite control,"[30] and the mass line was little more than window-dressing for the autocratic exercise of party power. Likewise, in his work on the institutionalization of rural participation, John Burns notes the extension of a similar trend during the early reform era, with most rural mass associations exercising only "advisory" power over the party-state by 1982.[31] More recently, Tianjian Shi argues that although high levels of mobilization were indeed central to the Leninist program, mass participation was a selective process, shaped by the "elimination of the organizational bases for people to articulate their interests collectively, 'forced departicipation' of previously participatory groups, and political education." Although the mass line, in Shi's view, "cannot guarantee bureaucrats will listen to people," it did "provide a normative setting for individuals to contact officials of their work units," generally with respect to resource allocation.[32]

However, others have proposed that the Maoist state developed and institutionalized a broad range of mass-line practices designed to encourage communication between cadres, particularly at the lower rungs of officialdom, and the masses. As Sebastian Heilmann's work demonstrates, these included "squatting on a point" (*dundian*, 蹲点), social investigation (*shehui diaocha*, 社会调查), the "four togethers" (*sitong*, 四同), "on-the-spot conferences" (*xianchang hui*, 现场会议), and the dispatch of cadre work teams (*gongzuo dui*, 工作队) to local communities. These practices, although limited in scope, did bring into the public and official realms opinions and ideas that were not expressed through other available channels,[33] provided information about how central policies were being implemented in myriad local contexts, and encouraged policy experimentation.[34] Xu Yong has argued that this mode of close administrative infiltration of the grassroots — frequently mistaken for totalitarianism (*jiquanzhuyi huozhe quannengzhuyi*, 极权主义或者全能主义) — was in fact the product of historical necessity arising from a prolonged condition of internal and external military threat. Wartime mobilization through a dense web of party-established mass organizations, combined with the participatory decision-making of mass-line politics, produced a unique but highly resilient and adaptable hybrid form of democratic centralism at the grassroots of Chinese society that protected the unity of the majority under conditions of attack from internal and external enemies of the revolution.[35]

New research on the micropolitics of the land reform campaign, particularly as it was carried out in the revolutionary base areas, illustrates the key role of party-established grassroots mass organizations in implementing the mass line and in building a new type of rural governance. Li Lifeng's investigation of the mobilization of "speak bitterness" (*suku*, 诉苦) campaigns in the revolutionary base and liberated areas demonstrates how, by relying on mass-line methods to identify and cultivate both poor peasants and local activists, cadres were able to effectively uncover and reframe pre-existing grievances as class-based contradictions. By establishing mass organizations within which to support alliances between activist elements and poor and lower-middle peasants, the party gradually succeeded not only in encouraging activists to adopt the party's mass line, but also in publicly performing it through a series of emotionally charged political rituals that unleashed a groundswell of popular support to flow to the party in advance of the actual land reform campaign. The marriage of mass-line politics with the establishment of revolutionary mass organizations in the "speak bitterness" movement, in Li's view, fulfilled four key political functions: the mobilization of the masses, the gathering of reliable intelligence (*huoqu xinxi*, 获取信息) regarding local conditions, the construction of legitimacy in local communities, and the successful isolation of potential (and actual) opponents. Furthermore, the party's formal recognition of local mass organizations and public enactment of mass-line policies in areas under their control replaced the old elite power structures with a new activist elite that was loyal to the party line. That mass organization members were publicly identified by their participation during the campaign and that grievances congruent with the mass line were aired in public lent momentum to the mobilization of class conflict, as participants found it more difficult to reverse themselves later on. The highly public enactment of such practices, Li concludes, firmly entrenched both the norms and principles of the mass line and the social composition of grassroots mass organizations in local communities.[36] Likewise, Liu Yu finds that the practice of Mao-era mass-line politics generally helped participants justify internally their individual support for and compliance with the revolutionary political goals by legitimizing personal behavior as rational in a collective context.[37]

In his work on the wartime Guomindang (GMD) strongholds of Jiangsu, Anhui, and Hubei, Chen Yung-fa demonstrates how the party's deployment of mass-line tactics through a dense web of mass associations allowed CCP leaders to modulate both the pace and intensity of social polarization. Strategically ambiguous class labels like "basic masses" (*jiben qunzhong*, 基本群众) and "feudal forces" (*fengjian shili*, 封建势力) served to selectively downplay or diffuse the "chaos of class alignment" when social tensions were running high, thereby simultaneously minimizing active opposition from the old elite even as the party stoked the underlying class antagonisms.[38] For Tetsuya Kataoka, the Communist success rested heavily upon the party's ability to "reshuffle and reintegrate" preexisting organizations through a highly flexible repertoire of tactical cooperation and suppression in the pursuit of centrally designed aims. Therefore, Kataoka notes with respect to the mass line, "a clear distinction must be drawn between what came 'from the masses' and what the Party did 'to the masses.'" Masters at cultivating and coopting preexisting village social formations, he concludes that:

> The accomplishment of the Chinese Communists was in refining this native source of power and combining it with a thoroughly modern organization imposed from above. Thousands upon thousands of separate, isolated, and cellular units were tied to a frame of steel. It seems as though the cells would have gone wherever the frame would take them, e.g., the resistance, the civil war, the Great Leap Forward, etc. This was because of the basically apolitical nature of the cells at the bottom. Their units presupposed local interest in "defending homes and villages."[39]

In the wake of the Communist victory, new mass organizations of various types — including cooperatives, collectives, and communes in the countryside, and work-units in the cities — steadily displaced earlier forms of social organization and created new collectives around shared economic interests that were nonetheless dependent upon the central power of the post-revolutionary state, cementing what party theoreticians referred to as its basic "organizational line" with its "political line."[40] In the rural areas, the restriction and eventual suffocation of rural markets, the gradual but steady elimination of family-farming sideline occupations, and the continued calls from the center to develop "local self-reliance" all contributed to the decline of inter-village linkages and increased the atomization of local communities from the early 1950s onward.[41] In the urban areas, the segmentation of the labor force into work-units, alongside the institution of the household registration system, proved to be similarly effective tools for segmenting, controlling, and managing the urban population beneath a central state administration.[42] The party's administrative infiltration of grassroots institutions in the wartime base areas and during the early years of its rule thus established a uniquely resilient *guerrilla work-style* (*zuofeng*, 作风) for constructing public opinion, elements of which survive in the contemporary party-state.[43]

However, the *resilience* and *adaptability* of these institutions subsequently proved to be challenging to continued centralized control: even as the party's new grassroots forms of mass organization atomized social contacts, they created new bulwarks of solidarity for the articulation and expression of collective material interests that were not always in keeping with the centrally imposed mass line. Periodically throughout the Mao era, organized masses slipped out of the center's grasp to openly challenge party-state control when collective entitlements were threatened or withheld, particularly during periods when the center relaxed its coercive grip on society. During the six months between October 1956 and March 1957, as many as ten thousand large-scale strikes and demonstrations involving workers and students unfolded across the country; the incidence of petitioning in rural areas also skyrocketed. Seizing the opportunity afforded by the Hundred Flowers Campaign when Chairman Mao encouraged the airing of grievances hoping to pre-empt revolts like those in Hungary, workers displaced by the socialization of industry carried out more than 1,300 strikes in Shanghai alone. Although the official press placed the blame on the excessively bureaucratic work-style of managers and party cadres, in fact, workers' demands included higher wages, better welfare, permanent status, and guaranteed promotions.[44] In the rural areas, communization in 1958 served to militarize agricultural production during the Great Leap Forward; excessive labor demands and dire food shortages mobilized members of the work teams and production brigades to resist, sometimes violently, the local leaders.[45] Likewise, the Cultural Revolution–generated turmoil partly shaped the party's own clientelist networks inside the workplace, triggering struggles between the so-called "conservative" mass organizations that were largely comprised of members of the party organization, and "rebel" mass organizations that generally drew their membership from diverse groups of disadvantaged workers and intellectuals or those who previously had been persecuted by party members and leaders alike.[46] In late July and early August 1967, mobilized mass organizations raided army depots and barracks and staged pitched battles in nearly every province. Although soon thereafter Beijing attempted to stifle this grassroots radicalization, the ultra-leftist factions not only survived, but continued their destabilizing political activities for several years, propagating what came to be called "new trends of thought" (*xin sichao*, 新思潮) that were highly critical of the party and the former's emergence as an exploitative social class in post-revolutionary China.[47] In his research on grassroots political action in the mid-1970s, Heilmann finds that in some areas radical factions infiltrated and seized control of provincial branches of mass associations, threatening to overtake the party. In Shaanxi and Jiangsu, factions of radicals argued that "party leadership is leadership over the general political line ... and not organizational leadership," and they even attempted to revive earlier slogans: "Mass organizations take the place of the party!" (*qunzhong zuzhi lai daiti dang*, 群众组织来代替党!).[48]

In the foregoing cases, it was rarely the case that entire units or entire mass organizations banded together to resist state power. Most often, the unity of the mass organizations created and maintained by the party-state fractured from within, generally along the lines of preexisting inequalities among the masses. State- and party-created mass associations thus became lightening rods for organizing dissent not only by building new social networks of alliances among individuals, but also by drawing attention to how some of the deep underlying inequalities that characterized state socialism during the Mao era were refracted and perpetuated at the local level. Zhou Xueguang argues that one unintended consequence of the party-state's stunning success in organizing the masses at the grassroots is that the process created large numbers of individuals with similar grievances, thus easing the barriers for collective action. Furthermore, due to the powerful and overlapping linkages forged between the party-state and workplace organizations, otherwise disorganized and fragmented discontent tended to be funneled in the direction of the state.[49] Under such conditions, "mass-line" practices of grassroots leadership may have offered opportunities to air grievances and resolve conflicts about the logistics of production and cadre work-styles, but, particularly when managed by low-level cadres and managers, were inadequate for redressing long-standing structural injustices, the sources of which lay with the center itself.

From Activist Masses to Receptive Publics

The tumultuous violence of the Cultural Revolution period unquestionably marked a turning point in the practice of mass politics under Maoist rule. In early 1967, then-premier Zhou Enlai addressed a rally of more than 20,000 self-proclaimed revolutionary rebels, noting that whereas previous mass movements had involved a simultaneous movement from top to bottom and bottom to top that mimicked the traditional formulation of the "mass line," the Cultural Revolution, by contrast, was "essentially" a "movement from bottom to top,"[50] with intensely politicized masses directly challenging the primacy of the party. The resulting cycles of radicalization and retaliation during the decade-long struggle effectively paralyzed the party's ability to make effective use of two of the chief frameworks of grassroots politics, the mass line and mass organizations, through which it had shaped the mobilization efforts of the previous decades. Deeply factionalized grassroots mass organizations propagated competing mass lines, disarticulating the party's "organizational line" from its "political line" and thereby undermining the party's capacity to effect even a rough approximation of the "unity of opinion" that purportedly obtained in the early Mao era. In some cases, high levels of politicization spelled the effective demise of key mass associations, like the Communist Youth League, which could no longer sustain its functions beneath the weight of the internecine struggles.[51] It is therefore hardly surprising that, in the wake of Mao's demise, the emerging Dengist regime identified as its chief tasks a thorough repudiation of the Cultural Revolution and a sustained campaign to deradicalize and demobilize Chinese society from the grassroots, to be carried out in part by "manufacturing public opinion" in a manner conducive to these aims.

To this end, the Dengist state moved quickly to enforce a new post-Mao hegemony, but not without facing lingering resistance from elements inside and outside the party center: mass activism did not die quickly. The blistering attacks on the theoretical and operational bases of the Cultural Revolution delivered by supporters of the Dengist faction in 1979 were followed in 1980 by the ruthless suppression of the Democracy Wall movement and the outlawing of "big democracy" — the right of revolutionary people to engage in great debate and to post their views publicly through the medium of "big-character posters." Comprehensive rectification of party and state offices and mass organizations began in 1983 in order to weed out the "three kinds of people" on the left who continued to undermine party unity and social stability, and to identify a reliable "third echelon" of leaders untainted by the "ultra-leftism" of the Mao era. As the rectification plan was originally conceived, the first stage targeted leading party organs and the headquarters of army units. The second stage, beginning in the winter of 1984, extended the process to some 13.5 million prefectural- and county-level cadres housed largely in local party branches and grassroots mass organizations. With respect to these local branches and mass associations, the chief tasks were to "unify thought" (*tongyi sixiang*, 统一思想), "correct work-styles" (*zhengdun zuofeng*, 整顿作风), "strengthen discipline" (*jiaqiang jilu*, 加强纪录), and "clean up organizations" (*qingli zuzhi*, 清理组织).[52] In June 1984, the Central Commission for Guiding Party Rectification issued a circular mandating the complete elimination of the factionalism produced by the Cultural Revolution in grassroots mass organizations that had split organizations down the middle, with forces aligning up internally with both "rebel" and "conservative" factions. Yet, as Keith Forster points out in his research on Zhejiang, the identification and excision of the "three kinds of people" envisioned by the reformers at the center necessitated a delicate microsurgery at the grassroots that few local cadres had either the skill or the political will to perform. In lieu of deciding definitively for one local faction over the other, the solution was to admit that none were wholly without blame,[53] and to adjure future grassroots political activism not clearly spurred by the center. Rather than placing grassroots political mobilization around collectively shaped economic interests at the heart of the mass political practices, discussions of mass-line practices from the early reform period onward focused instead on the party as it served and responded to the perceived needs and interests of the masses.[54]

These practical measures were matched by new discursive polemics designed to unravel radical Maoism by first "seeking truth from facts" (*shishi qiushi*, 实事求是) and progressed to the argument that "practice is the sole criterion of truth" (*shijian shi jianyan zhenli de weiyi biaozhun*, 实践是检验真理的唯一标准) and a new emphasis on Mao's thought as a "scientific system." Following suit, methodological debates in the social sciences began to prod, and then to overturn, earlier critical models for social investigation in favor of more "scientific" approaches, linking the former to the excesses of the recent past. In 1986, Vice-Premier of the State Council Wan Li boldly asserted to the National Soft Science Symposium that when the party announced it no longer regarded "class struggle as the key link," it was time to "draw a clear line between political and academic questions." As the experience of the Cultural Revolution demonstrated, the Mao-era "mass line" could and should no longer serve as a guide for rational decision-making or for research in the "soft sciences" (*ruan kexue*, 软科学); new, more "scientific" approaches that were capable of offering analyses of society untainted by the ideological remnants of ultra-leftism were required.[55] In particular, the Mao-era model of social investigation based on an examination of "typical cases" (*dianxing diaocha*, 典型调查) came under attack as a vehicle of subjectivism that distorted researchers' attempts to capture and convey popular sentiment. As Chen Chongshan, a member of the Beijing News Study Association (*Beijing xinwen xuehui*, 北京新闻学会) that was established in the early 1980s, argued, a reliance on "representative" (*you daibiaoxingde*, 有代表性的) research subjects only captures the views of a select minority of respondents. During the Cultural Revolution's high tide of ultra-leftism,

> The subjective bias (*zhuguan suiyixing*, 主观随意性) inherent in this research method increased greatly, with researchers frequently using the standpoint of class analysis to draw a priori distinctions between "friends" and "enemies" [of the revolutionary classes], or to use political behavior as a yardstick to draw a priori distinctions to divide people into leftists, centrists, and rightists, using themselves as the core, taking those whose opinions follow their own to be leftists, comrades, and friends, and taking those with contrary views to be rightists, outsiders, and enemies. Data selection carried the same bias and broadcast their views on a grand scale, by attacking those whose opinions differed from their own and emphasizing the unanimity of public opinions, excluding voices that differ. For this reason, [such methods] cannot completely, comprehensively, and accurately reflect the popular will and will lead to policy mistakes and will breed tragedies like the Great Proletarian Cultural Revolution.[56]

Early and ardent advocates of replacing Mao-era practices of social research with more scientific and more objective random sampling methods were centered in the news and propaganda departments of the media. In 1981, An Gang, then associate director of the Beijing News Study Association and a member of the editorial board of *People's Daily*, published an article entitled "Study our Readers," in which he proposed that an empirical investigation of the reading public should be considered the rightful heir to the Maoist concept of the "mass line" in propaganda work: "Studying our readers is simply the solution to the problem of how we might make even better our services to the broad masses."[57] Shortly thereafter, the association established its own "Audience Research Group," which initiated Beijing's first large-scale audience surveys. The initial poll, undertaken by central party news media groups and a small number of official mass associations, polled randomly selected Beijing residents to ascertain their views with respect to the reliability of the official media and their relative levels of interest in the content. The city of Tianjin followed up with its own "thousand household investigation" (*qianhu diaocha*, 千户调查), publishing the results in a 1984 report recommending how to improve the quality of life for Tianjin City residents, a process that municipal officials repeated annually for the next nine years. In 1986, central department-level officials conducted a large-scale survey of mass views on economic reform during the Chinese New Year holiday season and reportedly found that 87 percent of the polled Beijing residents stated that "the reforms of the past few years are a success," and 88.7 percent felt that "although prices are rising, the quality of life is also rising."[58]

As the unsteady course of economic reforms continued during the 1980s, the party leadership increasingly called upon those engaged in propaganda and ideological work not only to "guide public opinion" during periods of difficulty throughout the reform process, but also to monitor the public reception of recent policy developments. In 1985 Premier Zhao Ziyang's think-tank, the CESRRI, was authorized by the State Council to conduct a series of large-scale national surveys to measure the impact of the reform policies. From February through November of that year, the new think-tank employed over 400 statisticians and researchers and tapped resources in twenty-one government educational and research units to produce 156 reports, all of which reassured elites that there was a high level of popular support for the Dengist urban reform program.[59] In the following year CESRRI conducted fourteen more large-scale social surveys to collect and quantify public opinion with respect to matters of national policy. By 1988, CESRRI's success had spawned the creation of fifteen new public opinion institutes in Beijing. Stanley Rosen notes that several of these new "semi-private" organizations were in fact established by individuals who had practical experience with the turbulent history of "mass-line" politics during the Maoist era. The ranks of the new think-tank founders included a former top Red Guard leader of Beijing's high-school students, as well as an activist who had risen to national prominence during the 1976 Tiananmen incident, both of whom had been imprisoned during the 1970s for their participation in the mass politics of the day.[60] Yet, despite such prior experience with the less-structured practices of Maoist mass-line politics, the new survey researchers claimed that their work revealed clear majority support for the policies of the center. Even as social tensions rose precipitously in the late 1980s, and again in the wake of the traumatic 1989 crackdown following the Tiananmen demonstrations, the *People's Daily* continued to reassure its readers that random surveys demonstrated that the vast majority of the Chinese public collectively held "an optimistic attitude toward the current situation, and future developments (*Dui dangqian xingshi he weilai fazhan chi leguan taidu,* 对当前形势和未来发展持乐观态度)."[61]

Who Is Being Represented?

The transition from the Maoist "mass-line" dialectical model of intense engagement at the grassroots level to the more mediated process of polling and managing public opinion has been cast in official discourse as a shift in favor of increased mass participation in politics. As one 1986 *People's Daily* article explains,

> When "leftist" guiding ideas held the dominant position, and especially during the "Great Cultural Revolution" when the principles of socialist democracy were wrecked and trampled on, there appeared a very strange phenomenon: anyone who put forward views on political issues or undertook any study or discussion on such issues was politically questionable, had to undergo screening, and was even struck to the ground. The Third Plenary Session of the Eleventh CCP Central Committee opened up a new era in building socialist democracy; politics regained its original meaning, from being an affair of a few politicians it turned into an affair of millions of people.[62]

Likewise, as Swabey argues, the connection between the Western liberal democratic concept of representation and that of the "representative sample" in quantitative social science research is hardly coincidental: "Plainly, such a conception of government is quantitative.... Once we conceive the whole (the state) as composed of the parts (citizens) which are formally distinct but without relative qualitative differences, we are applying the notion in its essentials."[63] More recently, the Sixth Plenum of the Fifteenth Central Committee in 2001 released the decision "On Strengthening and Improving the Building of Party Work-Styles," in which it was proposed, in part, "to expand democratic recommendations and the scope of public opinion surveys and democratic discussion, to improve methods, and to enhance the quality" (*kuoda minzhu tuijian, minyi ceyan he minzhu pingyi de fanwei, gaijin fangfa, tigao zhiliang,* 扩大民主推荐、民意测验和民主评议的范围, 改进方法, 提高质量) of the ranks of its cadres. The proposal has been repeated several times since with respect to the use of public opinion polls and other forms of information as a method for improving governance and intra-party decision-making,[64] all offered as evidence that the reform-era party has undertaken efforts to become more democratic and more inclusive than it was during the Mao period.

Yet the reconfiguration of Maoist "mass-line" politics into the technocratic engineering of public opinion through polling and media supervision arguably reflects not an increasing closeness of the elites to the masses under a gradual evolution toward representative liberal democracy, but a further distancing of the post-Mao state from a social realm increasingly defined as an object for surveillance, manipulation, and control. As Jürgen Habermas notes, polls and surveys are not expressions of democratic will but a substitute for it, since they curtail the discursive conditions necessary for the

development of opinions in the public realm, most prominently, rational
and democratic deliberation involving a "critically debating public."[65] Pierre
Bourdieu is even more skeptical, vigorously asserting that the construction
of public opinion by polling and survey instruments is itself an

> *artifact* whose function is to conceal the fact that the state of opinion at any given
> moment is a system of forces, of tensions, and that there is nothing more inade-
> quate than a percentage to represent the state of opinion . . . [the public opinion
> poll] creates the idea that a unanimous public opinion exists in order to legitimate
> a policy, and strengthen the relations of force upon which it is based or make it
> possible.[66]

According to Bourdieu, a public opinion survey represents a tightly constrained form of participation that frequently requires respondents to choose
among pre-formed responses to a framed question, a process from which
"there is every likelihood of creating pure artifact out of thin air. Opinions
are made to exist which did not pre-exist the question." In the oft-recorded
high rates of refusal and abstentionism among those targeted by pollsters,
Bourdieu reads not only a degree of popular skepticism concerning the act
of polling, but also a rejection of the implicit political philosophy of public
opinion polling, "which credits everyone with not only the right but also the
power to produce . . . a judgment" on any range of issues. On the basis of
his study of non-respondents, he concludes that their apparent indifference
to the pollster is a manifestation of their disenfranchisement within a
political system in which technical expertise and perceived competence are
equated with political power.[67]

Indeed, the shift from Mao-era "on-the-spot" social investigation to
large-scale random polling techniques reflects a shift in the orientation of
the post-Mao leadership toward the types of knowledge about society that
are considered useful to the state. Mao-era social investigations drew clear
distinctions between the use of statistics to explain natural phenomena and
the social sciences, deriding the latter as "a poison of the capitalist class"
(*zichan jieji de dusu*, 资产阶级的毒素). The root of the "poison" resided in
the Marxist critique of the notion of randomness in social, and particularly
economic, phenomena, the fundamental nature of which could only be fully
explained by historical materialism and the Marxist laws of political economy.[68] Social investigation based on random sampling methods might fail to
reflect accurately the class nature of a given society, thereby obscuring
exploitative relationships beneath a cloak of numeric equivalence, or pool
the responses of members of various classes together without regard for
their different positions in society. By contrast, Mao-era statistical surveys

tended to rely on "typical investigations," in which data are collected from cases selected to represent various social groups or classes, not unlike Western models of stratified non-random sampling, in order to highlight the contrasts, contradictions, and antagonisms among them and thereby arrive at a better description of how different class positions experience social issues.[69] The replacement of class-based analyses involving sustained on-site direct engagement with social subjects based on large-scale random sampling deliberately creates distance between the researcher and the subject or subjects under investigation that advocates argue may produce more "objective" results, but also dramatically depoliticizes the broader context within which social investigation occurs, and may just as easily conceal crucial differences within a respondent pool.

Popular skepticism in China regarding the nature of polling and resistance to the constrained participation it requires arose even before public opinion surveys were formally legitimated by Zhao Ziyang's 1987 call to allow public opinion supervision to supercede the role of the "mass line" in policy formulation. According to the coordinator of the Beijing News Study Association that conducted the first large-scale "audience survey" in 1982, as soon as the project team finalized its research plan, members of the editorial board of the *People's Daily* began receiving ominous phone calls reporting that someone was planning to undertake "a bourgeois public opinion poll" (*zichan jieji minyi ceyan*, 资产阶级民意测验). Other critics quickly pointed out that random sample polling was not how social investigation was historically conducted in the People's Republic, and in fact constituted "an attack on so-called 'class-based analysis'" (*diudiaole suowei "jieji fenxi fangfa*,*"* 丢掉了所谓"阶级分析方法). Another accused the group of "specializing in collecting rightist opinions" (*zhuanmen souji youpai yijian*, 专门搜集右派意见) to the detriment of the masses.[70] In 1985, similar large-scale "audience surveys" conducted by *China Youth* magazine and a 1988 poll by People's University came under a hail of criticism, with one department head deriding public opinion polls in general as "the pseudo-science of the capitalist class" (*zichan jieji de wei kexue*, 资产阶级的伪科学); one university-based researcher expressed his skepticism that in the political climate of the early reform period, respondents would not answer any questions honestly, throwing all the results into doubt.[71] One 1988 poll of scientific and technical personnel in Jilin purportedly received a "cold reception," with fully one-third of the respondents refusing to fill out the questionnaires. Several of these defiant non-respondents instead drew "a tiger's head and a snake's tail" (*hu tou she wei*, 虎头蛇尾) on the form, suggesting that despite a promising beginning, the process of opinion polling would likely come to no good end, perhaps because the information gleaned thereof would inevitably be bent to the will of the poll-takers. Some even took the opportunity of the survey to express their anger that repeated calls to improve the situation of intellectuals had once again amounted to nothing more than empty promises.[72]

More recently, the party has taken avidly to polling, encouraging its new local committees to engage in regular and routine surveys of its members and ordinary masses as part of a broader effort to build "inner-party democracy."[73] "Appraisal forms" (*pingyi biao*, 评议表) are now widely used to elicit popular views of the party's effectiveness in carrying out specific tasks: for example, in February 2010 the Shanghai Huangpu District Party Committee distributed a survey to its subordinate party branches asking local party members to assess the effectiveness of their own grassroots work. The assessed topics included various local committee efforts to "spur development, promote harmony, and advance the central work of the unit in question"; whether local party committees played a significant role in "serving the masses and rallying them"; and whether or not party members had had "heart-to-heart" talks within the last year. Possible responses ranged from a simple "yes/no" to a spectrum of four choices that extended from "greatly effective" to "no effect at all."[74] Perhaps even more daring, the new local party committee at Shanghai Zhongtan Hospital experimented in 2008 by distributing "democratic appraisal forms" to the entire hospital staff, asking them to rate their colleagues who were party members on six criteria: "dedication," "discipline," "exemplarity," "team spirit," "relations with the masses," and "organizational ability." Without discussing the results, the party committee proudly reported that the respondents had not replied "irresponsibly," falling prey to either the "good old boy" phenomenon *("lao haoren" xianxiang*, "老好人"现象), nor had those polled used the opportunity to vent their anger against their colleagues.[75] However, the final results were not publicly posted, nor does it appear that the 2008 experiment was repeated.

Although such efforts have been widely heralded within the party as a major and innovative step advancing the goal of inner-party democracy, the structure of such surveys tightly constrains the "democratic exchange of views" both within the party and between the party and the public to the times and topics of the party's own choosing. Legitimate issues for polling include general assessments of the party's ability to either achieve the goals that it has set for itself, or how adequately grassroots members may perform their vanguard role within local work-units and communities. Broader normative concerns regarding the party's role or agenda with respect to either state or society clearly remain off the table, at least for the foreseeable future, although it was precisely these more challenging moral questions — who should rule, how, and why — that were aired, at least sporadically, during the contentious and sometimes violent mass-line exchanges of the Mao era.[76]

As Zhong Yang has argued, central to the party's attempt to reconfigure the relationship between the masses and the official media during the reform era is the introduction of the depoliticized concept of a passive media "audience" (*shouzhong*, 受众) to replace the (potentially activist) "masses" in academic and media policy discourses.[77] Although both the mass-line–associated practices of the Mao era and the public opinion polling of today can provide central leaders with telling information about the degree and depth of social grievances and the quality of central policy implementation at the local levels, the embrace of polling in official discourse is indicative of an underlying post-Mao shift away from direct and potentially conflict-ridden engagement with the masses in favor of more mediated forms of indirect political representation. In this still-emerging discursive framework, the public opinion poll — with its ability to reduce profound social cleavages to broad aggregates — serves to mask socio-economic divisions and reduces complex political engagement to a simpler, more easily digested set of metrics. Through the new practice of polling, the reform-era public is more readily assembled as a legible aggregate subject that thinks and desires without contradiction and whose complex and shifting pluralities are largely overwritten in the search for monochromatic majorities in the construction of a "socialist harmonious society."

The End of the Mass Line?

Historically, one chief resource of the Mao-era party-state was its considerable power to mobilize mass participation and enlist the resources and energies of social forces to achieve ideological and practical ends. Yet with the onset of the market reform, the party-state's reinvention of the notion of participation has been largely divested of its ideological and political content and purged of references to the Mao-era class struggle that preceded and helped to shape it. Seen in this light, the governing practices that increasingly define the era of market reform represent an ambitious attempt to create new non-class forms of identity and more highly mediated forms of representation that disarticulate social conflict from the material relations of power.[78] Over the course of the reform era, the party-state has sought to appropriate and transform Mao-era methods of mobilization in order to generate a new politics that ultimately undoes the Leninist project of revolutionary engagement with the end of effecting social democracy,[79] even as it retains the Leninist method of overwriting the general will with that of the vanguard party leadership.

Ongoing market reforms continue to be mediated by existing class relations and political structures, and are carried out in no small part through the repertoire of elite governing practices and policy styles inherited from the Maoist era. Largely emptied of their ideological content by the post-Mao leadership, these practices have been reinvented as a form of technocratic "social engineering" that sometimes aims to alleviate, but more generally to displace and to conceal, the rising inequalities that result from marketization. Contemporary neoliberal forms of governance generally operate through a calculative logic that seeks to align the rational economic interests and limited political freedoms of the subjects in such a way that individuals are mobilized to participate voluntarily in their own self-regulation. Whereas the mass mobilizations of the Mao era aimed to impose a new socialist order and to rectify the cadre ranks, mobilization during the post-Mao era is no longer seen as an end in itself, but instead, when it is permitted, serves as a mechanism for achieving better — meaning, more efficient and more effective — technocratic policy outcomes. These notions of participation shape the contemporary practices of depoliticized governance that elide the contestation and antagonism that represent the core of direct democratic and mass participatory politics.

As I have argued, the transformation of these practices reflects deeper epistemological shifts that have important political consequences for the survival and adaptability of China's authoritarian regime. From the early Dengist rallying cry to "seek truth from facts," to the argument that "practice is the sole criterion of truth," party theoreticians deftly maneuvered the "criterion of practice" with the so-called "criterion of productive forces," thereby giving rationalizations based upon economic productivity an unprecedented degree of official "truth."[80] This deeper epistemological shift, which places economic production for the market at the center of the reform era project, is reflected in the turn away from the post-Mao era model of social investigation based on an examination of "typical cases" to the random survey methods now used for public opinion polling. In Mao's conception of scientific social investigation, notions of class and class struggle determined how "representative" cases were to be selected for study. When exemplary cases were uncovered, they were elevated as norms, propagating more widely the moral propositions they espoused through the "point-to-surface" (*you dian dao mian*, 由点到面) method lucidly described by Sebastian Heilmann,[81] with the goal of creating what Børge Bakken refers to as an "exemplary society" governed by social revolutionary ideals.[32] However, the post-Mao abandonment of "class struggle as the key link" and the apparent acceptance of the role of randomness in social and economic events have paved the way for new epistemologies of social knowledge and new "ways of seeing like a state"[83] that are more conducive to the logic of depoliticized politics associated with neoliberal globalization.[84]

This strategic top-down effort to depoliticize Chinese society during the reform era, beginning with the "thorough negation" of the Cultural Revolution, has proved key to the adaptive authoritarianism of the current regime by retying the tethers between the cellularized mass organizations at the grassroots to the steel frame of the party's policing of the mass line. Likewise, it can be argued that the successes of the Maoist party-state in organizing, mobilizing, and politicizing the grassroots ultimately proved its own undoing: revolutionary radicalism under state socialism attracted, condensed, and overdetermined the very sort of widespread social disaffection that Western-style market capitalism successfully deflects, disperses, and disengages from the institutions in which power inheres.[85] The PRC was by no means the only society to have experienced profound social turmoil during the 1960s, nor was it alone in adopting broad socio-political and economic reforms at the end of the 1970s that served to disperse, fragment, and redirect social tumult in its embrace of consumerism.[86] To a lesser extent, the Keynesian welfare arrangements of the capitalist West also served to mobilize and direct popular dissatisfaction against the institutions of the state, tendencies that the waves of privatization that originated under Reagan and Thatcher successfully defused and mitigated. As Wang Hui rightly notes, the periodic return of mass protest over the course of the 1980s, culminating in the 1989 Tiananmen demonstrations, represented the final series of great mass eruptions pressing for a more directly participatory form of political engagement that arguably has its origins in the Red Guard movements of the 1960s.[87] What is perhaps most remarkable is that the party-state was so successful in swiftly re-channeling the energies of the generation that gave birth to the Tiananmen protests in the direction of market-driven economic modernization.[88] As Bauman has noted regarding the transition from state socialism to consumer-driven market societies elsewhere, dissent, too, can indeed be successfully privatized, frequently melting away into a sea of suppressed anxieties, personal inadequacies, and longings that serve to lubricate the global machinery of capitalism.[89]

* The author wishes to thank the editors, Sebastian Heilmann and Elizabeth Perry, for their guidance, the two anonymous reviewers who provided comments, as well as the following individuals, all of whom contributed suggestions and advice: Federica Ferlanti, Karl Gerth, Bill Kirby, Roderick MacFarquhar, Barry Naughton, and Yuezhi Zhao. Earlier drafts of this paper were presented at two consecutive workshops, "Adaptive Authoritarianism: China's Party-State Resilience in Historical Perspective," at the University of Trier and Harvard University, respectively; and at a meeting of the "History/Media/Representation" working group organized by Matthew D. Johnson and James Reilly at the University of Oxford. The author is grateful for the generous comments and questions offered by participants at all three venues.

Endnotes

1. Alice L. Miller, "Hu Jintao and the Sixth Plenum," *China Leadership Monitor*, no. 20 (Winter 2007): 5–6.

2. Meisner observes that "At no time in the history of the People's Republic was there so great an emphasis on the Leninist character and leadership role of the Chinese Communist Party as during the reign of Deng Xiaoping." Maurice Meisner, *The Deng Xiaoping Era: An Inquiry into the Fate of Chinese Socialism, 1978–1994* (New York: Hill and Wang, 1996), p. 164.

3. Vladimir Ilyich Lenin, *What Is to Be Done?*, trans. Joe Fineberg and George Hanna (London: Penguin Books, 1988).

4. See, for example, "Dui zhongyang wenge xiaozu jianghua (yijiu liuqinian yiyue jiuri)" (对中央文革小组讲话) [一九六七年一月九日]) (Speech to the Central Cultural Revolution Small Group [January 9, 1967]), in *Mao Zedong sixiang wansui* (毛泽东思想万岁) (Long Live Mao Zedong Thought) (Hong Kong: Bowen shuju, 1967), p. 662; and records of Mao's remarks at the Eighth Plenum in October 1968, for example, Zhu Tingxun (祝庭勋), "Mao Zedong wei shenme xuan zhong Li Desheng" (毛泽东为什么选中李德生) (Why Did Mao Zedong Select Li Desheng?), *Wenshi bolan* (文史博览) (Culture and History Vision), no. 8 (2007): 26–27.

5. Marc Blecher, "The Contradictions of Grass-Roots Participation and Undemocratic Statism in Maoist China and Their Fate," in Brantly Womack, ed., *Contemporary Chinese Politics in Historical Perspective* (Cambridge: Cambridge University Press, 1991), pp. 153–179, esp. pp. 133–134.

6. By "mass organizations" here I refer not only to the party's own formal structures of representation at the local level, including labor unions, women's federations, and youth leagues, but more broadly to units of production, including work-units (*danwei*, 单位) and communes. The former have traditionally been listed as "administrative

work-units" (*xingzheng danwei*, 行政单位), whereas the others are considered "production work-units" (*qiye danwei*, 企业单位). However, it is clear that throughout the Mao era and beyond, the "mass line" was a central working principle for both.

7. Jack Gray notes that the practice of the mass line arose of dire necessity during the Civil War period in response to the broader question of "how to maximize the resources of the Liberated Areas in order to maintain their defence. Political, ideological, and cultural changes clustered around an economic nucleus ... the mass-line, in this, its first sweeping application, served economic purposes." Jack Gray, "The Two Roads: Alternative Strategies of Social Change and Economic Growth in China," in Stuart R. Schram and Marianne Bastid, eds., *Authority, Participation and Cultural Change in China: Essays by a European Study Group* (Cambridge: Cambridge University Press, 1973), p. 124.

8. Elizabeth J. Perry, "Shanghai's Strike Wave of 1957," *The China Quarterly*, no. 137 (March 1994): 1–27.

9. Dong Guoqiang (董国强), "1967 nian xiatian Nanjing 'daoxu' fengchao de taiqian muhou" (1967年夏天南京「倒许」风潮的台前幕后) (Nanjing in the Summer of 1967: Behind the Stage of the "Down with Xu" Campaign), *Ershiyi shiji wangluo ban* (二十一世纪网络版) (Twenty-First Century Internet Edition), no. 56 (November 2006), at http://news.ifeng.com/history/zhuanjialunshi/dongguoqiang/200907/0713_7314_1246746.shtml (accessed July 13, 2010); on the participation of mass organizations in the Cultural Revolution more generally, see Hong Yung Lee, *The Politics of the Chinese Cultural Revolution: A Case Study* (Berkeley: University of California Press, 1978); and Keith Forster, *Rebellion and Factionalism in a Chinese Province: Zhejiang, 1966–1976* (Armonk, NY: M.E. Sharpe, 1990).

10. Patricia M. Thornton, "Comrades and Collectives in Arms: Tax Resistance, Evasion, and Avoidance Strategies in Post-Mao China," in Peter Hays Gries and Stanley Rosen, eds., *State and Society in 21st Century China: Contention, Crisis and Legitimation* (New York: RoutledgeCurzon, 2004), pp. 87–104.

11. Zhao Ziyang, "Advance Along the Road of Socialism with Chinese Characteristics," report delivered at the 13th National Congress of the Communist Party of China on October 25, 1987," *Beijing Review*, 30, no. 45 (November 9–15, 1987), p. xix.

12. Hai Dong (海东) and He Bin (何斌), "Chen Chongshan he tade 'minyi ceyan'" (陈崇山和她的"民意测验") (Chen Chongshan and Her Public Opinion Test), *Xinwen jizhe* (新闻记者) (News Journalist), no. 2 (1989), at http://academic.mediachina.net/article.php?id=5840 (accessed July 13, 2010): 34–35; Wu Jinglian, "Preface to the Chinese Edition," trans. in Bruce L. Reynolds, ed., *Reform in China: Challenges & Choices: A Summary and Analysis of the CESSRI Survey* (Armonk, NY: M.E. Sharpe, 1987), p. xx.

13. See Stanley Rosen, "The Rise (and Fall) of Public Opinion in Post-Mao China," in Richard Baum, ed., *Reform and Reaction in Post-Mao China: The Road to Tiananmen* (New York: Routledge, 1991), pp. 64–72.

14. Yuezhi Zhao and Sun Wusan, "Public Opinion Supervision: Possibilities and Limits of the Media in Constraining Local Officials," in Elizabeth J. Perry and Merle Goldman, eds., *Grassroots Political Reform in Contemporary China* (Cambridge, MA: Harvard University Press, 2007), pp. 300–324.

15. Cong Riyun (丛日云), "Dangdai Zhongguo zhengzhi yujing zhong de 'qunzhong' gainian fenxi" (当代中国政治语境中的"群众"概念分析) (Analysis of the Context of the "Mass Line" in Contemporary China), *Zhengfa luntan* (政法论坛) (Tribune of Political Science and Law), no. 2 (2005): 15–25.

16. He Yong (何勇) and Wang Junping (王君平), "Minyi diaocha yaode shi qunzhong renke de 'manyi lu'" (民意调查要的是群众认可的"满意率") (What Public Opinion Polls Want Is Any "Rate of Satisfaction" among the Masses), *Renmin ribao* (人民日报) (People's Daily) (November 28, 2006).

17. Ao Teng (傲腾) and Chen Jie (陈杰), "Minxin gongchenghui minsheng — Tianjin shishi ershi xiang minxin gongcheng jishi" (民心工程惠民生—天津实施二十项民心工程纪实) (Report on the Twenty Projects to Benefit the People's Livelihood in Tianjin), *Renmin ribao* (July 25, 2008): 1, at http://unn.people.com.cn/GB/14748/7559944.html (accessed July 13, 2010).

18. Hu Liqiang (胡立强) and Yang Xiye (阳锡叶), "Minyi diaocha quan zhong zeng zhi 30%" (民意调查权重增至30%) (The Power of Public Opinion Polls Increases to 30%), *Renmin ribao* (February 26, 2008): 2.

19. Zhang Yong, "Public Opinion without Public? State Democracy, Middle-Class Consumerism, and Opinion Surveys in Post-Mao China," paper delivered at the 53rd Annual Conference of the International Communication Association, San Diego, May 23–27, 2002.

20. Wenfang Tang, *Public Opinion and Political Change in China* (Stanford, CA: Stanford University Press, 2005), p. 34.

21. Benjamin Ginsberg, *The Captive Public: How Mass Opinion Promotes State Power* (New York: Basic Books, 1986), esp. ch. 2; Susan Herbst, "Surveys in the Public Sphere: Applying Bourdieu's Critique of Opinion Polls," *International Journal of Public Opinion Research*, 4, no. 3 (1992): 220.

22. Mao Zedong, "Why Is It Necessary to Discuss the White Paper," August 28, 1949, in *Selected Works of Mao-Tse-tung, Volume IV* (Peking: Foreign Languages Press, 1961), p. 444.

23. Mao Zedong, "In Refutation of 'Uniformity of Public Opinion,'" May 24, 1955, in *Selected Works of Mao-Tse-tung, Volume V* (Peking: Foreign Languages Press, 1977), p. 172.

24. Mao Zedong, "Concerning Methods of Leadership," June 1, 1943, in *Selected Works of Mao Tse-tung, Volume III* (Peking: Foreign Languages Press, 1965), p. 119.

25. Liu Shaoqi, "On the Party," May 14, 1945, in *Selected Works of Liu Shaoqi, Volume I* (Beijing: Foreign Languages Press, 1984), p. 349.

26. Deng Xiaoping (邓小平) "Zhongguo renmin da tuanjie he shijie renmin da tuanjie" (中国人民大团结和世界人民大团结) (The Great Unity of the Chinese People and the Great Unity of the People of the World), *Zhonghua renmin gongheguo chengli shizhounian jinian wenji* (中华人民共和国成立十周年纪念文集) (Collection of Writings on the Tenth Anniversary of the Founding of the People's Republic of China) (Beijing: Renmin chubanshe, 1959), p. 64.

27. Roderick MacFarquhar, *The Origins of the Cultural Revolution, Volume 1: Contradictions Among the People* (New York: Columbia University Press, 1974), pp. 116–117.

28. Marc Blecher, "Consensual Politics in Rural Chinese Communities: The Mass Line in Theory and Practice," *Modern China*, 5, no. 1 (January 1979): 105, 122. See also Mitch Meisner, "Dazhai: The Mass Line in Practice," *Modern China*, 4, no. 1 (January 1978): 27–62; and Mark Selden, "The Yenan Legacy: The Mass Line," in A. Doak Barnett ed., *Chinese Communist Politics in Action* (Seattle: University of Washington Press, 1969), pp. 99–151.

29. See, for example, Martin King Whyte, *Small Groups and Political Rituals in China* (Berkeley: University of California Press, 1974) on the limited scope and highly constrained nature of participation in political study groups.

30. James R. Townsend, *Political Participation in Communist China* (Berkeley: University of California Press, new ed., 1969), pp. 142–143; for his assessment of the Cultural Revolution, see his "Preface to the Third Impression," p. xii.

31. John P. Burns, *Political Participation in Rural China* (Berkeley: University of California Press, 1988), pp. 83–85.

32. Tianjian Shi, *Political Participation in Beijing* (Cambridge, MA: Harvard University Press, 1997), pp. 269, 47.

33. Blecher, "The Contradictions of Grass-Roots Participation and Undemocratic Statism," pp. 153–179.

34. Sebastian Heilmann, "From Local Experiments to National Policy: The Origins of China's Distinctive Policy Process," *The China Journal*, no. 59 (2008): 1–30.

35. Xu Yong (徐勇), "'Xingzheng xiaxiang': Dongyuan renwu yu mingling: Xiandai guojia xiang xiangtu shehui shentou de xingzheng jizhi" ("行政下乡": 动员、任务与命令: 现代国家向乡土社会渗透的行政机制) (Administration of the Countryside, Mobilization, Mission, and Command: The Penetration of the Administrative Mechanism into Rural Society of the Modern State), *Huazhong shifan daxue xuebao* (华中师范大学学报) (Journal of Central China Normal University), no. 5 (2007): 2–9.

36. Li Lifeng (李里峰), "Tugai zhong de suku: Yizhong minzhong dongyuan jishu de weiguan fenxi) (土改中的诉苦: 一种民众动员技术的微观分析) (Complaints and Difficulties of Land Reform: A Micro Analysis of a Type of Technology to Mobilize the People), *Nanjing daxue xuebao (Renwen kexue, shehui kexue ban)* (南京大学学报 [人文科学社会科学版]) (Journal of Nanjing University [Philosophy, Humanities, and Social Sciences Edition), no. 5 (2007): 97–109.

37. Liu Yu, "From the Mass Line to the Mao Cult: The Production of Legitimate Dictatorship in Revolutionary China," Ph.D. dissertation, Columbia University, 2006. I am grateful to Elizabeth Perry for bringing this source to my attention.

38. Yung-fa Chen, *Making Revolution: The Communist Movement in Eastern and Central China, 1937–1945* (Berkeley: University of California Press, 1986). As Tsou Tang also notes, "The mass line was not a mere method of implementing class struggle and cannot be traced exclusively to this concept. In actuality, it also served as a balance to radical policies derived from the notion of class struggle … and led Mao to advocate increasingly moderate policies in many areas." See Tang Tsou, *The Cultural Revolution and Post-Mao Reforms: A Historical Perspective* (Chicago: University of Chicago Press, 1986), p. xliv.

39. Tetsuya Kataoka, *Resistance and Revolution in China: The Communists and the Second United Front* (Berkeley: University of California Press, 1974), p. 301.

40. The concepts of the "organizational line" and the "political line" were considered inextricably linked to the party's practice of the "mass line" in the period leading up to the Cultural Revolution. As one 1958 *Renmin ribao* editorial asserts, "Dajia dou zhidao, qunzhong luxian shi women dangde genben zhengzhi luxian he zuzhi luxian … dangde zuzhi luxian jiu yao baozhang dangde zuzhi he chengyuan neige gou miqie lianxi qunzhong wei shixian dangde zhengzhi luxian" (大家都知道, 群众路线是我们党的根本政治路线和组织路线 … 党的组织路线就要保障党的组织和成员那个密切联系群众为实现党的政治路线) (Everyone knows, the mass line is the basic political and organizational line of our party … the party organizational line is to guarantee the

organization and to unite closely with the members to realize the political line of the party). See "Qunzhong luxian shi women dangde genben luxian" (群众路线是我们党的根本路线) (The Mass Line Is the Fundamental Line of Our Party), *Renmin ribao* (December 11, 1958): 7; Du Li (杜李), *Qunzhong guandian yu qunzhong luxian* (群众观点与群众路线) (The Mass Viewpoint and the Mass Line) (Shanghai: Shanghai renmin chubanshe, 1955), esp. pp. 50–59.

41. See, for example, Vivienne Shue, "Emerging State-Society Relations in Rural China," in Jørgen Delman, Clemens Stubbe Ostergaard, and Flemming Christiansen, eds., *Remaking Peasant China: Problems of Rural Development and Institutions at the Start of the 1990s* (Aarhus: Aarhus University Press, 1990), p. 77; Pauline B. Keating, "Getting Peasants Organized: Village Organizations and the Party-State in the Shaan Gan Ning Border Region, 1934–1945," in Feng Chongyi and David S.G. Goodman, eds., *North China at War: The Social Ecology of Revolution, 1937–1945* (Lanham, MD: Rowman and Littlefield, 2000), pp. 25–58; Jean C. Oi, *State and Peasant in Contemporary China: The Political Economy of Village Government* (Berkeley: University of California Press, 1989), p. 230.

42. Xiaobo Lü and Elizabeth J. Perry, "The Changing Chinese Workplace in Historical and Comparative Perspective," in Lü and Perry, *Danwei: The Changing Chinese Workplace in Historical and Comparative Perspective* (Armonk, NY: M.E. Sharpe, 1997); Tiejun Cheng and Mark Selden, "The Origins and Social Consequences of China's *Hukou* System," *The China Quarterly*, no. 139 (September 1994): 644–668.

43. Gang Guo, "Organizational Involvement and Political Participation in China," *Comparative Political Studies*, 40, no. 4 (2007): 462.

44. Perry, "Shanghai's Strike Wave of 1957"; Shen Shiguang (沈士光),"Xiangqile 1956 nian" (想起了1956年) (Thinking about 1956), *Zhongguo gaige* (中国改革) (China Reform), no. 1 (2005): 74–75; Shen Shiguang "1956 nian weiji" (1956 年危机) (The Crisis of 1956), *Dangshi zongheng* (党史纵横) (Over the Party History), no. 4 (2005): 24–26.

45. Li Ruojian (李若建), "Dayuejin yu kunnan shiqi Zhongguo liangshi chanliang, xiaofei yu liutong" (大跃进与困难时期中国粮食产量、消费与流通) (Grain Output, Consumption and Circulation in China during the Great Leap Forward and the Hard Times), *Zhongshan daxue xuebao (Shehui kexue ban)* (中山大学学报[社会科学版]) (Journal of Sun Yatsen University [Social Science Edition]), no. 6 (2001): 123–132; see also scattered reports in Yang Jisheng (楊繼繩), *Mubei: Zhongguo liushi niandai da jihuang jishi* (墓碑: 中國六十年代大饑荒紀實) (Tombstone: The True Record of the Great Chinese Famine in the 1960s) (Hong Kong: Tiandi tushu, 2008).

46. Townsend, *Political Participation in China*; Charles Bettleheim, *Cultural Revolution and Industrial Organization in China: Changes in Management and the Division of Labor* (New York: Monthly Review Press, 1974).

47. Wang Shaoguang, "'New Trends of Thought' on the Cultural Revolution," *Journal of Contemporary China*, 8, no. 21 (1999): 197–217.

48. Sebastian Heilmann, "Turning Away from the Cultural Revolution: Political Grass-Roots Activism in the Mid-Seventies," Center for Pacific Asia Studies, Stockholm University, Occasional Paper 28 (September 1996), p. 8.

49. Xueguang Zhou, "Unorganized Interests and Collective Action in Communist China," *American Sociological Review*, 58, no. 1 (February 1993): 54–73.

50. *Keji zhanbao* (科技战报) (Science and Technology Battle Bulletin) (February 1, 1967), as cited in Tsou, *The Cultural Revolution and Post-Mao Reforms*, p. 82. Tsou dates the

meeting to January 25, 1967, although the footnote contains a typographical error that sources the publication to 1966.

51. On the suspension of the Communist Youth League and its organ, *Zhongguo qingnian* (中国青年) (China Youth) during the Cultural Revolution, see James R. Townsend, *The Revolutionization of Chinese Youth: A Study of Chungkuo Ch'ing-nien*, China Research Monograph No. 1 (Berkeley: Center for Chinese Studies, University of California, November 1967), esp. pp. 59–71.

52. Richard Baum, *Burying Mao: Chinese Politics in the Age of Deng Xiaoping* (Princeton, NJ: Princeton University Press, 1994), pp. 166–167.

53. Keith Forster, "Repudiation of the Cultural Revolution in China: The Case of Zhejiang," *Pacific Affairs*, 59, no. 1 (Spring 1986): 5–27.

54. See, for example, a 1996 *Renmin ribao* editorial, which cites a new iteration of the mass line based on the principle of seeking truth from facts, consistent with the 1981 *Guanyu jianguo yilai dangde ruogan lishi wenti de jueyi* (关于建国以来党的若干历史问题的决议) (Resolution on Several Questions in the History of Our Party Since the Founding of the State) that centers on four supposed mass assessments of party activity: "Does the party receive the endorsement (*yonghu*, 拥护) of the masses? Does the party receive the praise (*zancheng*, 赞成) of the masses? Does the party make the masses happy (*gaoxing*, 高兴)? Does the party have the agreement (*daying*, 答应) of the masses?" Huang Guojun (黄国均), Chen Zhihui (陈智慧), and Ren Dali (任大立), "Qunzhong luxian shi dangde shengming luxian" (群众路线是党的生命路线) (The Mass Line Is the Life Line of the Party), *Renmin ribao* (July 2, 1996): 9. By contrast, a 1958 *Renmin ribao* editorial bearing nearly the same title argues forcefully against the traditional view that concerted mass (political and economic) action constitutes "great disorder under heaven" (*tianxia daluan*, 天下打乱). "Qunzhong luxian shi dangde gongzuo de shengming luxian" (群众路线是党的工作的生命路线) (The Mass Line Is the Life Line of Party Work), *Renmin ribao* (December 26, 1958): 7.

55. Wan Li (万里), "Juece minzhuhua he kexuehua shi zhengzhi tizhi gaige de yizhong zhongyao keti: Zai quanguo ruan kexue yanjiu gongzuo zuotan huishang de jianghua" (决策民主化和科学化是政治体制改革的一个重要课题: 在全国软科学研究工作座谈会上的讲话) (Democratic and Scientific Decision Making Is an Important Topic of Political Reform: Speech at the National Soft Science Meeting), *Renmin ribao* (人民日报) (August 15, 1986): 1.

56. Chen Chongshan (陈崇山), "Zhongguo shouzhong yanjiu zhi huigu (shang)" (中国受众研究之回顾 [上] (Reflections on Research on the Chinese Audience [Part 1]), *Dangdai chuanbo* (当代传播) (Contemporary Communications), no. 1 (2001): 13.

57. As cited in ibid., p. 13.

58. Xi Zi (希子), "Minyi ceyan zai Zhongguo xingqi" (民意测验在中国兴起) (The Rise of Public Opinion Polls in China), *Guangjiao jing* (廣角鏡) (Wide Angle) (Hong Kong), no. 234 (March1992): 50–52, at http://sunzi1.lib.hku.hk/hkjo/article.jsp?book= 16&issue=160235 (accessed July 10, 2010).

59. Stanley Rosen and David Chu find some bias in the statistical results of the Reform Commission, which found in its survey on reactions to price reform high levels of public concern about inflation, a finding that happened to support the commission's own position at the time that the reform should continue, albeit at a slower rate. A group

of young researchers at the affiliated CESRRI instead found that popular support for price reform was high, and that the public wished the reform to speed up. See Stanley Rosen and David Chu, *Survey Research in the People's Republic of China* (Washington, DC: Office of Research, U.S. Information Agency, 1987), p. 7.

60. Rosen, "The Rise (and Fall) of Public Opinion," pp. 69–70. See also Catherine Keyser, *Professionalizing Research in Post-Mao China: The System Reform Institute and Policy Making* (Armonk, NY: M.E. Sharpe, 2003), esp. pp. 19–36.

61. "Guojia kewei daguimo chouyang diaocha biaoming sanbai duowan zhuanye rencai qianli dai fajue tamen poqie yaoqiu tongguo gaige fahui caizhi" (国家科委大规模抽样调查表明三百多万专业人才潜力待发掘他们迫切要求通过改革发挥才智) (An Optimistic View on Current Conditions and Future Development: The Science Commission Carries Out a Large-Scale Sample Survey, More Than Three Million Professionals Need to Explore Their Potential, They Urgently Request to Undergo Reform to Unleash Their Talent and Wisdom), *Renmin ribao* (May 25, 1988); Yu Changhong (于长洪) and Wang Jun (王军), "Shouci quanguo shehui renji guanxi xianzhuang chouyang diaocha biaoming, gongzhong dui dangqian xingshi he weilai fazhan te leguan taidu" (首次全国社会人际关系现状抽样调查表明, 公众对当前形势和未来发展持乐观态度) (The Results of the First National Sample Survey on the Current Situation for Interpersonal Relations; the Public Has a Very Optimistic Attitude about the Current Situation and Future Development), *Renmin ribao* (August 27, 1992).

62. Benbao pinglunyuan (本报评论员), "Zhengzhi wenti keyi taolun" (政治问题可以讨论) (Political Issues Can Be Discussed), *Renmin ribao* (August 30, 1986).

63. Marie Collins Swabey, "The Representative Sample: A Quantitative View," in Hanna Fenichel Pitkin, ed., *Representation* (New York: Atherton Press, 1969), p. 85.

64. "Zhonggong zhongyang guanyu jiaqiang he gaijin dangde zuofeng jianshe de jueding (2001 nian 9 yue 26 ri Zhongguo gongchandang dishiwujie zhongyang weiyuanhui diliuci quanti huiyi tongguo)" (中共中央关于加强和改进党的作风建设的决定 [2001年9月26日中国共产党第十五届中央委员会第六次全体会议通过]) (Resolution on Strengthening and Improving the Construction of the Party Work-Style [Passed at the Sixth Plenary Session of the Fifteenth Chinese Communist Central Committee on September 26, 2001]), *Renmin ribao* (October 8, 2001); "Zhongzubu caiqu cuoshi guanche luoshi shuwujie liuzhong quanhui jingshen, tuidong lingdao banzi he ganbu duiwu dangyuan duiwu zuofeng jianshe" (中组部采取措施贯彻落实十五届六中全会精神, 推动领导班子和干部队伍党员队伍作风建设) (The Party Organization Department Adopts Measures to Implement the Spirit of the Sixth Plenary Session of the Fifteenth Central Committee and to Promote Construction of the Work-Style of the Leadership Group and the Ranks of Cadres and Party Members), *Renmin ribao* (October 12, 2001); Jia Dechen (贾德臣), "Kuoda minzhu, wanshan banfa, tupo nandian jianquan yongren jizhi de zhongyao huanjie" (扩大民主, 完善办法, 突破难点, 健全用人机制的重要环节) (Expand Democracy, Perfect Methods, Break Through Difficulties, and Establish a Sound Employment Mechanism), *Renmin ribao* (February 13, 2003); "Tixian kexue fazhan guan yaoqiu, jianshe gao suzhi ganbu duiwu: Zhongyang zuzhibu yinfa shishi 'Tixian kexue fazhan guan yaoqiu de difang dangzheng lingdao banzi he lingdao ganbu zonghe kaohe pingjia shixing banfa'") (体现科学发展观要求, 建设高素质干部队伍: 中央组织部印发实施《体现科学发展观要求的地方党政领导班子和领导干部综合考核评价试行办法》) (Realize the Requirements of a Scientific View of Development,

Establish a High Quality Corps of Cadres: The Central Organization Department Issues Trial Procedures for Implementation to Local Leaders and Cadres to Reflect the Scientific Concept of Development), *Renmin ribao* (July 7, 2008).

65. Jürgen Habermas, *The Structural Transformation of the Public Sphere: An Inquiry into a Category of Bourgeois Society* (Cambridge, MA: MIT Press, 1995). Habermas's discussion of "the manufactured public sphere and nonpublic opinion" appears on pp. 219–221.

66. Pierre Bourdieu, "Public Opinion Does Not Exist," in Armand Mattelart and Seth Siegelaub, eds., *Communication and Class Struggle: An Anthology in 2 Volumes* (New York: International General, 1979), 1: 125.

67. Pierre Bourdieu, *Distinction: A Social Critique of the Judgement of Taste* (Cambridge, MA: Harvard University Press, 1984), pp. 398–413.

68. Zou Yiren (邹依仁), "Shilun tongjixue de xingzhi ji qi yu shuli tongjixue de guanxi" (试论统计学的性质及其与数理统计学的关系) (Dealing with the Nature of the Study of Statistics and Its Relationship to the Study of Mathematical Statistics), *Jingji yanjiu* (经济研究) (Economic Research), no. 1 (1980): 70.

69. S. Lee Travers, "Bias in Chinese Economic Statistics: The Case of the Typical Example Investigation," *The China Quarterly*, no. 91 (September 1982): 478–485.

70. Hai Dong and He Shu, "Chen Chongshan," p. 35.

71. Xi Zi, "Minyi ceyan zai Zhongguo," p. 66.

72. *Keji ribao* (科技日报) (Science and Technology Daily) (April 4, 1988), as cited in Rosen, "The Rise (and Fall) of Public Opinion," p. 75.

73. For a fuller description of the broader initiative, see Joseph Fewsmith, "Inner-Party Democracy: Development and Limitations," *China Leadership Monitor*, no. 31 (Winter 2010).

74. Zhonggong Huangpu quwei zuzhibu, (中共黄浦区委组织部), "Dangyuan dui Nanjing donglu shequ (jiedao) zonghe dangwei dang zhibu pingyi biao" (党员对南京东路社区 [街道] 综合党委 党支部评议表) (Comprehensive Appraisals by Party Members of the Committee and Party Branch of East Road District [Neighborhood] of Nanjing), February 5, 2010, at http://www.shlxhd.gov.cn/website/styleseven/Branch ActivityDetail/style/7/branchPartyId/40281f9214468ba701144882cffb00c3/branch ActivityId/bd01c1e926cc0f970126f3fc61e014b2;jsessionid=EB2E93F6BA0918020F33 DE7C0DF34E88 (accessed April 22, 2010).

75. Shanghaishi Zhongtan yiyuan dangzhibu (上海市中潭医院党支部), "Minzhu zhangxian zhengqi, gongdao zi zai renxin" (民主彰显正气、公道自在人心) (A Healthy Environment for the Manifestation of Democracy, A Fair Mind), December 29, 2008, at http://www.shlxhd.gov.cn/website/styleseven/BranchActivityDetail/style/7/ branchPartyId/40281f92169579f60116a3b514c408b4/wicket:pageMapName/wicket-1/branchActivityId/bd01c1e91e7e8a0c011e8037cee6049b (accessed July 2, 2010).

76. For example, some of the more dramatic public debates during the Cultural Revolution erupted over the party's "bloodline theory" (*xuetong lun*, 血统论), or the so-called "new trends of thought" (*xin sichao*, 新思潮) (described by Wang Shaoguang in "New Trends of Thought") both of which raised more pointed questions about the party's right to rule.

77. Zhang Yong, "From Masses to Audience: Changing Media Ideologies and Practices in Reform China," *Journalism Studies*, 1, no. 4 (November 1, 2000): 617–635.

78. Yiching Wu, "Rethinking 'Capitalist Restoration' in China," *Monthly Review*, 57, no. 6 (November 2005): 44–63.

79. On the role of contestation in deliberative democracy, see Nancy Fraser, "Rethinking the Public Sphere: A Contribution to the Critique of Actually Existing Democracy," *Social Text*, 8, no. 25/26 (1990): 56–80.

80. Michael Schoenhals, "The 1978 Truth Criterion Controversy," *The China Quarterly*, no. 126 (June 1991): 243–268.

81. Heilmann, "From Local Experiments to National Policy."

82. Børge Bakken, *The Exemplary Society: Human Improvement, Social Control, and the Dangers of Modernity in China* (New York: Oxford University Press, 2000).

83. James C. Scott, *Seeing Like a State: How Certain Schemes to Improve the Human Condition Have Failed* (New Haven, CT: Yale University Press, 1998).

84. Wang Hui, "Depoliticized Politics, From East to West," *New Left Review*, no. 41 (September-October 2006): 41.

85. Zygmunt Bauman, "Communism: A Post-Mortem," *PRAXIS International*, no. 3+4 (1991): 191.

86. For the shift from group-based forms of articulating public opinion to their wholesale replacement by quantitative public opinion polling in the United States, see the work by Susan Herbst, especially "On the Disappearance of Groups: 19th- and Early 20th-Century Conceptions of Public Opinion," in Theodore L. Glasser and Charles T. Salmon, eds., *Public Opinion and the Communication of Consent* (New York: Guilford Press, 1995), pp. 89–104; and Susan Herbst, *Numbered Voices: How Opinion Polling Has Shaped American Politics* (Chicago: University of Chicago Press, 1993).

87. Wang Hui, *China's New Order: Society, Politics, and Economy in Transition*, ed. Theodore Huters (Cambridge, MA: Harvard University Press, 2003).

88. I wish to thank Sebastian Heilmann for this insight.

89. Bauman, "Communism," p. 189.

CHAPTER 9

The Elusive Search for Effective Sub-County Governance

JOSEPH FEWSMITH

In June 2008 more than 10,000 people marched angrily on the party and government offices of Weng'an county in southwestern Guizhou province, burning the public security building and offices of the Chinese Communist Party (CCP). Protests and violent outbursts have become common in contemporary China, but the Weng'an riot was dramatic in its size and suddenness, and it is remarkably well-documented because the official press reversed course and made it into an object lesson. The various accounts that soon appeared made clear at least the outlines of the horrific governance that generated this paroxysm of local violence.[1]

Weng'an is a poor county with mineral resources, particularly phosphates, and with rivers that can be exploited for hydroelectric power. Local cadres, under pressure from above to speed up economic growth and, no doubt, motivated by their own greed, pushed hard to develop these resources. Doing so, however, required requisitioning large tracts of land and moving people off of it. As often happens in rural China, the local peasants did not feel that they had received adequate compensation and there had been several protests in the past. These protests were dealt with harshly by local public security officials as well as local gangsters. Local cadres had found cultivation of gangs useful for exploiting resources and maintaining "public order," just as local gangsters found colluding with public security and the local party organization to be profitable. Indeed, there was considerable overlap between the criminal gangs and the party organization. Under the rough order imposed by these forces, local resentments built up. In May 2008, a 16-year-old girl went out late at night with a politically connected youth and was found dead the next morning. Rape and murder were widely suspected, though officially denied. Failure to deal adequately with the case led to an explosion of anger and violent protest.[2]

The Weng'an case is an extreme example, but it nevertheless highlights features of contemporary China that are widespread. First, the case highlights the vertical structure of political power in China. Local cadres are not responsible to local citizens but to higher-ups; and those higher-up, for their own purposes, encouraged and pressured cadres in Weng'an to pursue growth at all costs. In order to achieve these ends, local officials turned naturally to local security forces and gangsters to contain social resistance — at least until such resistance burst out in a display of violence. The top-down pressure and the abusive use of power and coercion to meet goals may have been more extreme than in most places, but the situation of local officials being responsible only to their higher-ups reflects the basic political structure in China.

A recent, detailed case study of a poor county in northwest China dissects this structure, showing the degree to which power is personalized and concentrated. The party secretary is the core of the local power structure and the personnel system is the chief means of exercising control. When a cadre is to be selected, the local organization bureau will nominate a candidate, usually according to the "tone" set by the party secretary. Then the deputy party secretary with responsibility for that sector will approve the decision (or not), and the party secretary's conference will make the decision. In this county, the conference consists of the party secretary and the three deputy party secretaries. Once they have decided, the nomination is put to the Standing Committee of the local People's Congress for formal appointment. It is, however, the decision of the conference of the party secretary that has substantive meaning.[3] Although there is a civil service exam, it is a formality — only 10 percent of those who pass the exam are employed, so the exam cannot serve as a gateway to office.[4] The author concludes, "In fact, with respect to the selection, promotion, and use of cadres, the county government generated by the political reality of local society and the distribution of personnel and administrative resources has virtually no relationship to a modern civil service. . . ."[5]

The party secretary may be the center of the local political structure, but Li Changping, a former party secretary in Hubei province, makes clear the degree to which local party secretaries are "captured" by local interests. Having been appointed to his post in Qipan township in Jianli county, Li gathered some old classmates together to listen to their advice on how to be a good official. One classmate said that several party secretaries he knew had sincerely wanted to be good officials, but within a few months of assuming office, all of them had become what the peasants called "idiotic, mediocre, and corrupt officials." To consolidate power, the classmate continued, the party secretary had to protect the interests of the cadres at the same level and the leaders at higher levels "at the expense of the people."[6] This pursuit of the interests of local cadres drove the relentless expansion of local government as well as the institutionalized deceit of higher levels. As Li wrote in his famous letter to Premier Zhu Rongji, "Any newly appointed leader unable to withstand internal and external pressures needs to abuse his authority by putting some people on the government payroll." This "need" leads to the relentless expansion of the size and expense of local government. In 1990, Li said, Qipan township had 120 cadres; in 2000, when he addressed his letter to the premier, it had 340. In 1995, 70 percent of towns and townships had savings, but by 2000 some 90 percent had deficits of at least 4 million yuan.[7] These deficits were in the interests of local cadres who saw high-interest loans to towns and the township as a source of additional income.[8] Moreover, local authorities knowingly passed erroneous figures up to the higher levels. In 1999, Li writes, Jianli county's revenue was less than 180 million yuan, but it reported revenue in excess of 220 million yuan. Similarly, in 1999 the per capita income of the peasants in the county had *declined* by 800 yuan (a huge decline), but the official report declared that incomes had *increased* by 200 yuan.[9]

Li's description of conditions in Hubei is borne out by a study undertaken by the Central Party School during the same period. Using Hunan province as an example, the report states that the average indebtedness of towns or townships was 2–3 million yuan; village-level collectives had average debts of 100,000 yuan. Nationwide, there were some 38 million cadres, a ratio of one cadre for every thirty citizens. There were more than 600,000 cadres in *excess* of the authorized number (*bianzhi*, 编制) at the county level and above, and more than 2 million excess cadres at the town and township levels.[10]

In his path-breaking study of peasant resistance in Hunan, political scientist Yu Jianrong confirms the picture in these studies and concludes that the basic causes of cadre-peasant conflict are structural. The cadre-selection system made lower-level cadres "absolutely obedient" to higher levels, whether or not what was being asked of them conformed with national policies; the frequent transfer of cadres from outside the area rewarded short-term behavior; and the web of interests in local areas made it extremely difficult for problems to be exposed and rooted out.[11]

Differences in geography, economic structure, wealth, and historical-development patterns make it extremely difficult to generalize about China, but there is a great deal of consensus that local governments expanded rapidly in the 1990s, that the indebtedness of local governments grew dramatically, and that their relations with peasants in many parts of the country deteriorated, sometimes to a dangerous extent. For instance, Zhao Shukai, a researcher at the State Council Development Research Center, estimates that the number of employees in township governments approximately tripled between the mid-1980s and the mid-1990s. Despite repeated pressures from the central government, township governments would not reduce their payrolls, frequently resorting to various deceptions to hide the true numbers of employees. Even when the township governments could not pay their employees on time or had to go into debt to pay them, or both, they would not reduce the size of their payrolls. Obviously, there were benefits to the employees in terms of job security and extra-bureaucratic opportunities, so they would remain on the payrolls even if their salaries were not disbursed regularly. Township party secretaries also found it easier to keep such people on the payrolls than to deal with disgruntled laid-off cadres.[12]

According to a survey conducted by the Ministry of Agriculture, as of 1998 town and township governments had a total indebtedness of over 177 billion yuan, or an average of 4 million yuan per town and township — precisely Li Changping's estimate. In addition, village debts reached 418 billion yuan, an average of 210,000 yuan per village.[13]

As fiscal woes mounted at the township level, cadres increasingly became responsible for collecting their own salaries. As Zhao Shukai writes:[14]

> In many places, ensuring income not only is the responsibility of township and town leaders, but also the assignment for virtually all township and town personnel. We have found from our investigations that one common way employed by township and town leaders is to give township and town cadres the assignment of collecting taxes and fees in each and every village, and their collection performance is directly linked with these cadres' wages. Those who fail to fulfill their assignments not only receive no wages, but also have to raise the money to be delivered to the upper departments.

The combination of hierarchical control, frequent transfers, and dense social networks (among local elites), as Yu Jianrong suggests, places local government in conflict with the local citizenry. Such conflicts lie behind the tens of thousands of "mass incidents" in China today, including the Weng'an riot described above.

This structure of local politics comes directly out of the CCP's revolutionary experience, though it has roots in China's pre-revolutionary history. The revolution required both strict hierarchical control and entrusting great power in individual hands. This combination, as Perry and Heilmann argue in the Introduction to this volume, gave the party great flexibility, a tradition that lives on in the party's adaptability. But it is also a tradition that personalizes power, particularly at the local levels, and that leads to principal-agent problems, namely the abuse of power by local officials. As will be discussed below, the CCP has tried to restrain the behavior of local agents through a number of mechanisms, but to date it has refused to allow the institutionalization of mechanisms that would restrain the exercise of party power. Thus, when confronted with a continuation of mass incidents, which are an inevitable result of the power structure, and the possibility of checking party power by creating formal institutions, the party has consistently chosen to maintain its hierarchical and, in local terms, arbitrary power. Thus, the conflicts we see in contemporary China are rooted in a failure to build the local state in ways that are responsive both to vertical control and to the constituents being served. This failure is very much rooted in the thinness of late imperial rule on the one hand and the legacy of China's revolution on the other.

The Imperial Past

Perhaps the most significant political characteristic of the late imperial period was the thinness with which Chinese society was ruled. Even as the population quadrupled between 1650 and 1850 to approximately 400 million, the number of counties (the lowest official level of administration) remained constant, as did the number of officials — roughly 20,000 — governing the polity. By the late Qing, a county magistrate ruled an average of over 320,000 people.[15] The very wide areas that district magistrates were expected to govern raised real issues of governance. Taxes were difficult to collect, disputes difficult to adjudicate, and order difficult to maintain. Qing officials were aware of this problem, and as early as the seventeenth century Gu Yanwu suggested creating jurisdictions below the county level to extend bureaucratic control. Had China done so, it would have been following the pattern of other large imperial jurisdictions that at approximately the same time were extending their bureaucratic control downward. After all, the seventeenth century was the age of state-building in Europe as nations like France consolidated control over territory and built the bureaucracies that underlay their absolutist states.[16]

Philip Kuhn argues that China did not follow this route for at least three reasons. First, there were the traditional notions of Confucian frugality. States that raised taxes were considered bad states. Indeed, the Kangxi Emperor froze taxes and declared that they would not be raised. Second, county seats were the base of religious cults, which made the division of counties difficult. And most importantly, the bureaucracy opposed any efforts to dilute itself through expansion. As Kuhn puts it, "Nothing in the self image of literati-bureaucrats would have been consistent with a broad expansion of the civil service corps."[17]

Kuhn also argues that nineteenth-century proposals, particularly by Feng Guifen, to expand the participation of the non-office-holding literati in the selection of officials, both at high levels and in a proposed stratum of village-level officials, were soundly rejected by his contemporaries as dangerously corrupting the public interest. Feng's critics, firmly rooted in notions of Confucian hierarchy, argued that the public interest could best be discerned by an impartial elite appointed from above; selection from below — some sort of voting, even by a very limited electorate — would merely license the pursuit of private interest and factionalism, and there was enough of that already without giving it political legitimacy.[18]

Rejection of Feng's proposals to regularize the sub-county political elite and expand political participation hardly curtailed the growing influence of the sub-county social and economic elite. That elite was expanding in part because of the increasing commercialization of society since the late Ming. During the Qing, there was rapid growth in mercantile activity and organization, including the growth of native banks (*qianzhuang, yinhao*, 钱庄,银号), native place associations (*tongxianghui*, 同乡会), and guilds. This commercial growth increasingly brought the traditional scholar class together with the commercial elite. Although these two groups never totally merged, by the late nineteenth century there was considerable overlap between the two, particularly in the commercialized areas of the lower Yangzi River.[19]

This trend accelerated during and after the Taiping Rebellion as local society was organized by the local elite to defend against the rebels, as the local elite undertook rehabilitation projects of various sorts in the aftermath of the rebellion, and as the central government, financially drained by the struggle, retreated from local affairs.[20] As Rankin argues, extra-bureaucratic local elites increasingly took over public management functions in order to rehabilitate their areas in the aftermath of the Taiping Rebellion, and, as they did so, they inevitably jostled with officialdom for control of resources and local authority.[21] The promulgation of self-government regulations in 1908 marked public recognition of these trends as well as an effort to bring them back under state control.

This "public sphere," as Rankin calls the realm that grew up between officialdom and private activity, differed in important ways from the public sphere that Habermas argues developed in pre-revolutionary Europe. Habermas's public sphere is urban-based and composed of people willing to confront the state. Indeed, what defines the mature public sphere, in Habermas's view, is its ability to force the state to legitimate itself before the public; it is by its very nature a check on the power of the state.[22] In contrast, China's public sphere increasingly came into conflict with the traditional state, but it never saw itself as a check on the power of the state. After all, a major reason why societal elites eventually shifted their allegiance from the Qing was that they were mobilized on the basis of nationalism. At least rhetorically, social elites were not fighting state power but rather were objecting to a weak and corrupt power that could not defend China from external threats. Originally it was the *qingyi* (清议) ("pure talk") protests against the settlement of the Sino-French War that mobilized nationalist sentiments, and *qingyi* sentiments continued to grow, especially in the wake of the Sino-Japanese War, fueling the 1898 Reform Movement and then filtering into the constitutionalist movement of the first decade of the twentieth century.[23] But the nationalism that animated China's search for "wealth and power," as Benjamin Schwartz pointed out many years ago, sought a strong state more than a liberal state.[24]

Moreover, as Rankin argues, elite power emerged in the late Qing in the context of an authoritarian political structure that remained strong enough, at least until its very end, to prevent the emergence of autonomous organizations. As Rankin puts it, "It was possible for social organization to increase, for authority to shift from bureaucracy toward the elite, and for political opposition to develop under the centralized bureaucratic monarchy," but such organizations were never independent enough from the state or powerful enough to become a basis for the reorganization of politics. They never had the social or political wherewithal to withstand the power of the militarists who emerged, much less the Nationalists or Communists. Social elites ended up channeling their support to others, such as the reorganized Guomindang, rather than challenging the state.[25]

Although the early twentieth century witnessed the growth of autonomous and federalist movements, the overwhelming weight of Chinese thought, whether in the late Qing or Republican periods, was integrationalist. Separate interests did grow up in the late nineteenth century as the social elite began organizing, and interest groups emerged very vigorously in the Republican period as the business community, workers, women, and others began organizing. But the vocabulary of autonomous organization was notably weak. Liang Qichao talked in terms of "grouping" (*qun*, 群) and was the first to call for the formation of chambers of commerce, but Liang was hardly an interest-group theorist. On the contrary, Liang could never bring himself to say that the push and pull of *private* interest could ever generate the *public* interest.[26] Indeed, even warlords, who effectively fragmented China's polity in the 1910s and 1920s, argued that they were working to build a strong and united China (sooner or later).[27] Autonomous movements did not stand a chance against such sentiments.

State-Building in the Republican Period

The history of state-building during China's Republican era (1912–1949) remains controversial, but the continuity of efforts to restrict interest groups, assert the primacy of the state, and penetrate society (not always successfully) is remarkable. Shortly after the Revolution of 1911, Yuan Shikai began extending his military control in the lower Yangzi valley, which had been supportive of the revolutionaries. For instance, in Shanghai, Zheng Rucheng, one of Yuan's supporters, led his troops into the city to secure its loyalty to Beijing. Thus, when the Second Revolution broke out later that year, the revolutionary forces of Chen Qimei and Niu Yongjian were quickly routed.[28] At the same time, the Shanghai City Council in Chinese-ruled Shanghai, the most successful exercise in local self-government in modern Chinese history, was shut down as the northern warlords tightened their grip over the city.[29]

The tendency to centralize power and repress alternative political movements exemplified by Yuan Shikai was raised to new heights by the Guomindang (国民党) (GMD) as it reorganized into a Leninist form in 1924 and allied with the nascent Chinese Communist Party (*Gongchandang*, 共产党) (CCP) in the First United Front. As a revolutionary movement, the GMD identified with the public interest. Although it never exemplified the desire to revolutionize society that would characterize the CCP in its early years in power, it nevertheless was quite hostile to the expression of private interest outside its control. In 1929, the Nationalist government moved to bring the expression of business interests under its control by promulgating the Commercial and Industrial Trade Association Law and a new Chamber of Commerce Law.[30] These laws imposed a corporatist structure on the business community, much as similar laws brought labor unions and women's associations under state auspices.

Moreover, the GMD, like the CCP, was founded as a revolutionary party whose claim to legitimacy lay in a solipsistic claim to know the truth. Thus, the GMD identified itself as the embodiment of the national interest, and interests outside of, much less opposed to, the party were considered hostile or potentially hostile to the party-state. The GMD established itself as a tutelary party precisely to bring such interests into alignment with the party-state. It is not surprising that Nathan's look at the constitutions of the Republican era (as well as the PRC) reveals that they all asserted the primacy of state interests, and no judicial body then or since has been allowed to assert the legitimacy of organized private interests against the state.[31]

If the Nationalist party-state saw political power as monotonic and indivisible, it nevertheless had a difficult time extending its reach into local society. The need for revenue, the modernizing impulse of the government, and simply the strength of the government pushed its agents to penetrate more deeply into the society.[32] But this penetration appears to have been more one of political power than of modern state-building. By and large, tax systems were not regularized, the court system remained weak, and the role of intermediary associations was minimal (and minimized).[33]

Prasenjit Duara argues, on the basis of evidence from North China, that the expansion of the state in the 1920s and 1930s did not reflect an increasing professionalization of the bureaucracy and corresponding efficiency of administrative rule. On the contrary, informal structures of power, particularly brokers of various sorts, grew at least as quickly as the formal state. The formal state could neither carry out its functions without these informal structures of power nor encompass these informal organizations within the formal bureaucracy. Financial exactions on local society grew, but the state's proportion of revenue did not expand. Duara calls this process "state involution," and notes that it not only marked the ineffectiveness of state-building but actually constituted an obstacle to state-building.[34] Local society felt the burden of an increasingly demanding state, but it did not reap the benefits of bureaucratic efficiency. Nor did the central state benefit because local bureaucrats became parasitical on both the state apparatus and local society.

The Local State under the CCP

In contrast to the Nationalists' limited efforts (or capacity) to penetrate society and build sub-county government, the CCP extended its control deep, revolutionizing every aspect of life in the newly established PRC.[35] Land reform in the countryside and the Thought Reform Campaign of 1951, the Three-Anti and Five-Anti Movements of 1951 and 1952, respectively, in the cities — all against the emotional background of the Korean War — allowed the CCP to remake socio-economic-political life at the local levels in ways not previously imaginable.[36] The implementation of the state purchase and sale of grain system under the planned economy, imposed in 1953, enabled the state to extract resources at an unprecedented rate. In the 1930s, total government revenues, including at the central, provincial, and local levels, amounted to 5 to 7 percent of GNP, but the political control and mobilizational efforts of the CCP raised this figure to 30 percent.[37] Such penetration of sub-county society was unprecedented in Chinese history.

As the CCP burrowed deeply into Chinese society, it sought to remake it in its own image.[38] Perhaps the most lasting feature that emerged out of this revolutionary effort was the hierarchical political order centered on the personnel appointment system. Built on the Leninist principle of "democratic centralism," the appointment system, as suggested at the beginning of this chapter, means that decisions about who to promote are decided by a very small number of people at one or two levels above those being considered for promotion. The very small number of people involved, the strict secrecy maintained, and the last-minute revelation of personnel decisions had an organizational logic. More extensive consultations, a more open decision-making process, or even earlier revelation of personnel decisions risked expanding the scope of conflict within the party. Personnel decisions thus required centralization and party discipline.[39]

This system made hitting "hard targets" a relatively simple matter, whether with regard to family planning or GDP figures. The annual cadre evaluation, which awards points in different categories, made it relatively easy for lower-level cadres to understand the priorities of the higher levels, just as it simplified and facilitated the job of the higher levels to evaluate the performance of lower-level cadres (taking into account the inevitable "slippage" between what the evaluations said and what the reality on the ground was). It meant that when the regime decided that economic growth was the primary task, then the same mobilizational system that had previously been employed for class struggle was used for economic construction. The cadre evaluation system was critically supplemented by tax policies that allowed lower levels to retain a quota over tax revenues (as well as to build up extra-budgetary revenues), which provided material incentives paralleling the cadre evaluation system.[40] Such measures allowed the cadre system to adapt remarkably quickly and successfully to the regime's new priorities, something other Leninist systems were unable to do.

The tightness of control over personnel decisions and the limited scope of hard targets, however, opened the system to abuse. If promotion depended on the decisions of one person (the so-called "number-one person" (*yibashou*, 一把手) or, perhaps, two or three people, cultivating personal relations became necessary for promotion. For the patron, the cultivation of such personal relations had obvious political — and often material — benefits; the patron could count on the loyalty of subordinates, making the achievements of political targets easier. For the client, cultivating patronage provided a route to promotion; if the patron was promoted, the client had hopes of following him up the political ladder. Thus, this tight vertical control had the serious downside of exploding into networks of personalistic ties that threatened to undermine party legitimacy at the local levels and political control at the higher levels.

Similarly, if generating GDP numbers was the chief criterion (other than personal relations) for promotion, then cadres could do many things — such as building "image" projects, ignoring negative externalities (such as the local environment), raising funds from peasants, seizing peasant land and providing inadequate compensation, and even reporting incorrect figures (as Li Changping's account, cited above, suggests) — that boosted these numbers and ignored the resultant social problems. The popular saying, "numbers produce cadres, and cadres produce numbers" (*shuzi chu ganbu, ganbu chu shuzi*, 数字出干部, 干部出数字), speaks volumes about the operation of local government, at least in many parts of the country.

These structural issues lie behind the problems of finance and social order described at the beginning of this chapter. As has become clear over the past decade, peasants and local cadres are engaged in competition over local economic resources, whether increased taxes or land appropriation. Peasants objected to increased taxes, especially as they become aware of central regulations forbidding taxation in excess of 5 percent of their income (taxes were frequently 30–40 percent of income).[41] Increasingly, peasants organized and waged "rightful resistance" to excessive taxation.[42] They also petitioned higher levels, including Beijing, in the hopes that their concerns might be heard. Such protests mounted quickly in the 1990s, and Beijing finally responded in 2006 by eliminating all agricultural taxes and fees. This provided considerable relief for millions of peasants, but also created new problems. On the one hand, without revenue, local governments faced a fiscal crisis and sometimes turned to dubious methods, such as requisitioning land for development, that provoked violent outbursts. On the other hand, faced with a lack of income, some areas simply stopped building public works.

The central government is well aware of these problems, though often uncertain of how to resolve them. Over the last three decades, and particularly since the 1990s, China has carried out a variety of reforms of the party system, the state system, and the way in which local governments relate to (or are supposed to relate to) citizens. Some of these reforms have been undertaken by the central government, some have been supported by the central government, some have emerged from the local crises and have attracted the attention of the central government, and some have been carried out at the local levels. No reforms, however, ever seem to be the product of a single level of government; the rule of thumb appears to be that three levels of government must agree for any reform to proceed. The hierarchical nature of China's authoritarian system is visible everywhere.

Technocracy and "State-Building"

Following the Cultural Revolution, there was wide agreement within the Dengist coalition that it was necessary to restore and, indeed, to improve upon the "good" traditions of the CCP, particularly with regard to restoring "normal inner-party life" and normalizing the promotion process in order to eliminate (or reduce) factionalism within the party.[43] The need to institute a regularized retirement system, as aging cadres returned to power following the Cultural Revolution, further rationalized the cadre system, and the promotion of technocrats who fit the bill as "younger and better educated" dramatically changed the profile of China's political elite.[44]

Hong Yong Lee, who traced this process in the 1980s, believed that the promotion of technocrats would reduce the role of ideology as well as pave the way for bureaucratization and limitations on the way power is used at the highest levels. As in early modern Europe, the creation of professional bureaucracies would rationalize the state.[45] Changes in the composition of China's cadre ranks have certainly "normalized" China's bureaucracy to a great extent (and made it more competent), but, as Xu Xianglin points out, this is not so much a process of a bureaucratic apparatus gradually transforming the political system as it is a process of the political elite deciding on new goals and remaking the cadre ranks accordingly. Technocrats remain dependent, and political goals continue to be decisive.[46] The creation of a younger, better-educated, and more professional cadre force goes a long way in explaining the survival and adaptability of the CCP, but it has not led to the creation of a professional, rule-bound civil service distinct from the party.[47] On the contrary, there is more discussion in recent years on the importance of the party dominating state institutions than there was in the past and the party-state has been further consolidated.

Moreover, to the extent that the remaking of the cadre force has generated more professional governance, these changes are confined to the central level and some of the more prosperous, east coast localities (particularly urban areas). Much of the interior, including especially the poorer areas of the central and western parts of the country, continue to be governed by informal political networks in which power relations are far more important than bureaucratic rules. It is precisely these power relations, built on the basis of the personal relations that the hierarchical personnel appointment system indirectly promotes, that are the source of abuse that promotes contention within the party, the alienation of common party members, and, most notably, clashes with citizens.

It was not until the 1990s as social protests began to mount that the CCP began to focus on reforming the cadre system. New regulations on cadre promotion were promulgated on a trial basis in 1995 and confirmed with minor changes in 2002.[48] These regulations attempt to dilute the authority of local party secretaries by opening up the cadre promotion system. The promotion process, as specified by the regulations, consists of "democratic recommendation" (*minzhu tuijian*, 民主推荐), investigation (*kaocha*, 考察), preparation (*yunniang*, 酝酿), discussion and decision (*taolun jueding*, 讨论决定), and appointment (*renzhi*, 任职). This process apparently involves more people in a procedurally more open process, supposedly making it more difficult for the "number one" leader to make personnel decisions arbitrarily.

Unfortunately, the regulations failed to achieve their objective. As subsequent studies have shown, the new regulations could not break up the tightly held decision-making process. Prior to meetings of the Standing Committee, which was supposed to democratically recommend candidates for promotion, there was to be a party secretary's conference at which the decision would be made (as described in the study of a poor northwest county mentioned above). The Standing Committee would then simply ratify the decision of the *yibashou*, reversing the relation between the party secretary and the Standing Committee that the regulations had hoped to promote. "Only looking up" (*weishangzhuyi*, 唯上主义) was a psychology and practice deeply embedded in local politics.[49]

Moreover, local authorities always possess more information about their particular circumstances than higher-level authorities, so even though the regulations were intended to increase higher-level control over cadre promotions, localities used the advantages of information asymmetries to negate the intent of the regulations.[50] How this could be done was explained by one cadre who was convicted of selling offices (it is not explained how he was exposed, but the odds of being caught in such a scheme appear to be quite low). For him, the imposition of formal procedures presented no obstacle to blatantly illegal activity. As he put it:[51]

> Every time prior to the verification of cadres I would hold a secretaries' office meeting to set a "tone." I would use the age, work experience, educational background, experience, and rank of those who had given me gifts to set a standard and demarcate a scope. I absolutely would not name anyone's name, but would let the Organization Bureau go "find people" within the "scope" I had demarcated. After they had found them, we could proceed according to the procedures. On the surface, the rationale was clear and the procedures lawful, but in reality, this was using individuals to draw the lines and using individuals to define the scope. I used this method to reward all those who had given me gifts.

Indeed, the promulgation of these regulations may have exacerbated the situation. Prior to these regulations, those who hoped to be promoted only needed to cultivate a very limited number of people. But with more people, at least formally, involved in the process, those who sought promotion found it necessary to curry favor with more people. And that cost money. So if they were successful in being promoted, they certainly aimed to get their investments back![52]

At the same time that the government has been trying, with limited success, to address problems in the cadre promotion system, it has been taking steps that might lead to better governance and state-building at the local levels. In 2007, the State Council undertook the first national survey of how well law was being used for administrative purposes (*yifa xingzheng*, 依法行政) at the municipal and county levels. On the positive side, the survey found that 90 percent of China's municipalities and counties have established leading organs for administration by law, and in 2006 over 2.2 million person-days were spent in training, suggesting considerable resources devoted to emphasizing law. On the negative side, it found that only 30 percent of people believed that their areas had "limited government."[53]

In 2004 the government set the goal of a "service government" and began emphasizing the need to provide public goods. In September 2007, the government tried to reduce that scope of arbitrary power of local governments by eliminating 186 items that required approval. In order to reduce the number of administrative disputes, the State Council approved regulations governing appeals of administrative decisions. Zhejiang province even abolished the category of "soliciting business and attracting investment" (*zhaoshang yinzi*, 招商引资) on their cadre evaluation form. These and other steps, taken in the name of generating a "harmonious society," may contribute to state-building at the local level. In order to judge the likelihood of success it is useful to look at some examples of reform to see what sorts of conditions seem to promote success.

Conditions for Institutional Innovation

The central state seems aware that reliance on new regulations, no matter how well designed, is insufficient to resolve issues of local governance. That is why it has both proposed solutions to local issues and encouraged, up to a point, the emergence of local experimentation that at least has the promise of reducing social tensions and may, perhaps, contribute to local state-building. The types of changes China's local government has witnessed in recent years span the spectrum from social change spawning new institutional arrangements to local crises demanding government response to a proactive search for solutions by the central government.

The question is whether these innovations in local government can be institutionalized and whether they will result in the construction of a more professional bureaucratic apparatus at the sub-county level. Much is changing in China, so it is no doubt too early to reach firm conclusions, but an examination of cases suggests the importance of several variables. Perhaps the most important variable is the importance of the private (or non-state) economy; areas with stronger private economies are better able to build "public spheres," though even this conclusion, as we shall see, needs to be advanced carefully. Second, the condition of financial resources is critical; the more the local state needs to "ask" for resources, the more it is likely to include the public in the decision-making process. Third, crisis is a stimulus for innovation. In areas where the political and economic order are reasonably stable, there is no compelling reason to reform, and the status quo generally prevails. Extreme crises, like that in Weng'an, however, are not likely to generate reform. Fourth, political entrepreneurship is a critical, even if poorly understood, variable. There are many people at the local level who, either out of idealism or a desire to build their own reputations, are willing to undertake political innovations. Political innovations are invariably risky, and not everyone who opens up an area of political reform is rewarded with promotion. The risk factor makes the fifth variable, support from above, important, even though it is often difficult to evaluate from the outside. Few innovations have occurred, much less been sustained, in areas where there is no political support from at least the county level, if not higher. Finally, and most difficult to evaluate, is the role of public support. Reforms that not only win over the local population, as measured by a decline in political contestation including petitions to higher levels, and particularly those that have become well known throughout China appear to have a greater chance of surviving and deepening. Nevertheless, wide publicity can also expose the reforms to political backlash.

What follows is a quick tour of four instances of institutional innovation, two in the wealthy east coast province of Zhejiang and two in poor inland areas, Chongqing municipality and northern Sichuan province. Certainly the relative wealth of these areas affects both the problems faced by local government as well as the responses to local issues. A contrast of these innovations helps illuminate the factors that support or inhibit reform.

SOCIAL CHANGE AND INSTITUTIONAL INNOVATION: WENZHOU CHAMBERS OF COMMERCE

The importance of the private economy in promoting local innovation is best illustrated by the case of Wenzhou, the area in southern Zhejiang province that pioneered the development of the household enterprise. Because Wenzhou is located far from major transportation routes and is in a "front line" area likely to be embroiled in any conflict that might break out between Taiwan and the mainland, the Wenzhou-ese were largely left on their own. With little state investment, the local state was relatively weak. Moreover, with a strong sense of their uniqueness (the Wenzhou dialect being perhaps the most difficult for outsiders to learn) and a tradition of sojourning in quest of economic improvement, the Wenzhou-ese relied on their Wenzhou connections and their own willingness to take risks to build the local economy around individual and family enterprises. Even during the Cultural Revolution, Wenzhou-ese were known to travel throughout China buying and selling.

The rapid development of the private economy in Wenzhou also had a negative side. Wenzhou products developed a reputation for being of poor quality, often pretending to be something they were not. The problem became so serious that it threatened to undermine Wenzhou's economic development. In 1987, 5,000 pairs of Wenzhou-made shoes were burned in Hangzhou in a protest against their poor quality. But the protest was not carried out by angry residents of Hangzhou but rather by the authorities of Lucheng District, the district in Wenzhou where the shoe trade is concentrated. Following this demonstration of government displeasure, the Lucheng District government organized the Shoe Industry Rectification Office (*Luchengqu xieye zhengdun bangongshi*, 鹿城区鞋业整顿办公室) which then organized the Lucheng District Shoe Industry Association (*Luchengqu xieye xiehui*, 鹿城区鞋业协会) that all shoe manufacturers were required to join. This government-organized trade association then worked with leading shoe manufacturers to establish industry standards — embodied in the Management Regulations on the Rectification of the Quality of the Lucheng District Shoe Industry and the Provisional Regulations on After-Sales Service in the Shoe Industry. Manufacturers who did not comply with the new regulations were shut down.[54]

From that beginning, Wenzhou established over 100 chambers of commerce and trade associations. Even if the creation of chambers of commerce and trade associations was originally a top-down process encouraged, respectively, by the Federation of Industry and Commerce and the Economic and Trade Bureau, they have come to express the interests of their members (or, at least, leading members) and have developed quasi-democratic leadership. Nevertheless, there has been remarkably little "spillover" from their particular interests in industry to broader interests in governance. For instance, in 2003 Wenzhou launched an "efficiency revolution," which, at first glance, seemed to respond to business complaints about the inefficiency of city government. It turns out, however, that the campaign was launched in response to higher-level calls to increase the openness and effectiveness of local government and the results were limited at best.[55] Government officials did not disagree. In a survey of 49 Wenzhou officials, only one thought the efficiency revolution had achieved obvious results; the majority (39) responded that "there were results, but they are not obvious," whereas 9 reported that there simply had been no results.[56]

Similarly, government response to proposals raised by the local people's congress has been poor. Although government departments report a high degree of satisfaction with their responses — often running between 80 percent and 90 percent — a closer look reveals that the people's congress raises precisely the same proposals year after year, indicating that the delegates are not satisfied at all by the response to the original proposal.[57]

Moreover, efforts to limit the approvals that bureaucrats write personally
(*pishi*, 批示), a traditional way to avoid transparency and sometimes to
engage in corrupt behavior, have not been very successful. Despite
Wenzhou government's repeated stress on reforming this system, the same
survey of 49 government officials found that only 2 (4.1 percent) felt the
results of this reform were "very good," whereas 17 (34.7 percent) found
them to be "comparatively good," 20 (40.8 percent) said they were "OK,"
and 4 (8.2 percent) concluded that they were "not good."[58] In a survey of
entrepreneurs who were asked to grade the performance of the government, one entrepreneur replied "40 percent." He deducted points both for
the government not doing much to support economic development and for
interfering inappropriately in business operations. Another business leader
was even harsher, giving the Wenzhou government a score of only 20
percent. He criticized the government for its poor efficiency, the complexity
of personal relationships, the privatization of public goods, low investment
in education, and the old-fashioned thinking still dominating government
officials.[59]

   In some ways the development of chambers of commerce in Wenzhou
seems to be a harbinger of broad-scale change in socio-political relations at
the local level, but as can be seen by the absence of a spillover effect, local
government, precisely because it is embedded within a hierarchical political
organization, is able to resist the professionalization that would seem to be
a logical response to a burgeoning market economy. Indeed, the strength of
the political organization is such that the very legitimacy of the chambers of
commerce depends on the local party-state extending recognition.

PARTICIPATORY BUDGET-MAKING: CAN LOCAL PEOPLE'S CONGRESSES
SUPERVISE LOCAL GOVERNMENTS?

About two hours up the road from Wenzhou lies the county-level city
of Wenling, administratively subordinate to Taizhou municipality. Like
Wenzhou, Wenling's economy is based on private ownership, though the
Taizhou area pioneered the stock cooperative system (*gufen hezuo zhi*, 股份
合作制) rather than the family-based enterprises that characterize the
Wenzhou economy. Beginning in 1998, Wenling began to implement a
system of "democratic consultation meetings" (*minzhu kentanhui*, 民主恳谈
会), during which citizens at the village and township levels can voice
their concerns over public policy issues such as contemplation of new
construction.[60]

Beginning in 2005, this reform took another step forward when Xinhe township (one of eleven townships in Wenling) combined the form of a democratic consultation meeting with the proceedings of the local people's congress. At first, the people's congress would review the township budget, representing an unprecedented opening up of the budgeting process, as local people's congresses generally approve budgets without viewing any line items or holding discussions. The following year, the process was expanded to include the organization of committees to review budget priorities in the areas of agriculture, industry and commerce, and society. These committees then reported to the people's congress, making suggestions about budget allocations. In the second year, the budgetary figures supplied by the township government were more detailed.[61]

This promising experiment almost came to an end the following year when a new party secretary was appointed. By then, however, Wenling had earned a national reputation for its pioneering reform and sufficient pressure was put on the new party secretary, both by academics and by a member of the Standing Committee of the National People's Congress, to resurrect the system. Still, this experience highlighted the fragility of many of China's reform experiments — they are often tied to the interests or enthusiasm of one person and can wither whenever that person moves on. Nevertheless, in this case the experiment was resurrected and, over the next couple of years, it was expanded. It is now undertaken in five townships in Wenling.

As promising as this and similar experiments in participatory budget-making are, they have no influence over cadre evaluation or over the selection and promotion of township cadres. In other words, there is a real question whether this sort of reform can force local cadres to be responsible to local citizens (even such a highly select group of citizens who populate the local people's congresses) and can regularize the operations of sub-county governments.

PROMOTING INNER-PARTY DEMOCRACY

There has been much talk in recent years about promoting inner-party democracy. This discussion has to do with the concentration of power in the hands of local party secretaries (the focal point of the 1995–2002 rules on the selection and promotion of cadres) as well as the unwillingness of the party to contemplate broader democratic reforms. Pingchang county in northern Sichuan province has pioneered this reform with support from higher-level authorities and local reform-minded officials. As early as 2001, Pingchang carried out an experiment with "public recommendation and direct elections" (*gongtui zhixuan*, 公推直选), which the journal *Liaowang dongfang* (瞭望东方) lauded as the first such experiment in the history of the CCP. In 2002, Bazhong City, which oversees Pingchang and two other counties, transferred Liu Qianxiang to Pingchang as the new party secretary. Liu quickly decided to continue this experiment as well as to carry out a controversial redistricting in order to consolidate functions and reduce the number of cadres.[62]

Such public recommendations and direct elections differ dramatically from past practices. The recommendation of candidates took place at a meeting of all party members of a given township or town. Representatives of the public were allowed to attend and participate in the selection of candidates, though the non-party people could not exceed 30 percent of the number of party members in the area (unfortunately, the materials available do not say how these representatives were chosen; perhaps they were the heads of the various "small groups" [*xiaozu*, 小组] in the villages). Potential candidates were required to give speeches and answer questions, after which everyone voted by means of a secret ballot. This produced a pool of potential candidates whose qualifications were checked by the election commission. Afterward, there was another vote, again by secret ballot, that generated a list of formal candidates. It was required that there be two candidates for party secretary as well as more candidates for deputy party secretary.

Voting took place in separate rounds, and only party members could vote (though representatives of the public were allowed to stay and observe the procedures). The first round was for party secretary, and the loser in that election would then join the pool of candidates for deputy party secretary. The second round of voting was for deputy party secretary. Most townships have three deputy party secretaries, so there would be at least four candidates. Again, any candidates who failed in this round of voting were allowed to compete for a position on the party committee. Unfortunately, the available materials do not make it clear whether there were more candidates than positions for committee members; there may have been the temptation to have an equal number of candidates and positions at this level so that egos would not be overly bruised. But even if that were the case, all candidates had to go through a public selection process, deliver campaign speeches, and be voted on by the entire body of party members.[63]

The Pingchang reform was promising in that it tried to address the issue of local party secretaries being responsible only to those above; indeed, its claim to fame was that its version of inner-party democracy amounted to a reinterpretation of the old Leninist principle of "the party controls the cadres" (*dang guan ganbu*, 党管干部), and, alas, this was its undoing. Higher-levels criticized Pingchang for violating the principle of "the party controls the cadres," and the experiment was rolled back.

INNOVATION IN A VERY POOR PLACE

One finds a different dynamic in Maliu township of Chongqing Municipality, which illustrates the importance of the financial balance of power in determining bargaining relationships. In this poor township, declining revenues in the wake of the 1994 tax reform meant that local cadres could not carry out public works (or derive income from such projects) without going to the peasants for funding. Cadres resorted to strong measures, particularly in 1997 and 1998 when they pressed for payments of back fines that had been levied but never collected. This extra pressure provoked strong reactions from the peasants, including repeated submissions of petitions to the higher authorities. In 1999, when peasants learned that they were being pressed for money to build a better office building for the township government, they responded by surrounding the township offices and not allowing the cadres to leave.[64]

Higher-level authorities would not allow cadres in Maliu township to use force, but the transfer of cadres opened up new possibilities. One Li Hongbin, appointed party secretary in 1998, adopted new methods to restore order. First, he required local cadres to talk with local families to understand the peasants' point of view. Second, he extensively involved the peasants in the decision-making process. For instance, four villages on the far side of the river that divided the township wanted a bridge built, but Li insisted that everyone who supported the project sign a form confirming his or her agreement. Third, and most critical, Li established a committee for the construction of the bridge and included four non-cadre residents, one from each of the four villages, to handle the finances. The tendency of cadres to derive benefits from any public works projects was, of course, the crux of peasant-cadre tensions in Maliu township. By establishing a procedure that assured peasants that no cadre could benefit materially from this project, Li was able to slowly win the trust of the peasants.

The critical points in this case are first that it took a crisis in peasant-cadre relations to reach a breakthrough to manage a public works project, and second that the poor financial shape of the township increased the peasants' leverage. The sad part of this case is that this new equilibrium lasted only a short while. With the abolition of the agricultural tax, revenue for Maliu township dried up and the township became completely dependent financially on Kai county, of which Maliu is a part, and thus no longer sought funds for public works projects from the peasants. The balance of power shifted once again, and cadres turned their attention from their constituents (the peasants) to their superiors. The opening of public accountability proved to be brief, and one can hardly speak of the emergence of any sort of civil society or bureaucratized (as opposed to party) government at the township level.[65]

Conclusion

Looking at the local state over the past century and a half, it is apparent that the failure of the late imperial government to extend the scope of the bureaucracy downward as the population grew meant that sub-county governance was necessarily based on a certain degree of outsourcing of government functions both to "private" institutions, such as lineages, which incorporated important public functions, and to putatively public functionaries, including clerks and runners, who were paid from private funds "squeezed" in return for services.[66] As local society was mobilized in the fight against the Taipings and in the effort to reconstruct local order in the aftermath of the rebellion, the public sphere expanded and incorporated functions normally considered important by the central bureaucracy. The local elite was also mobilized on the basis of nationalism, as the inability of the Qing to defend the country undermined the local elites' confidence in the competence of the dynasty and brought calls to include the newly mobilized local elite in the governance of the nation. The dynasty, feeling threatened by the newly mobilized elite, reacted defensively, creating yet greater doubt and suspicion on the part of the local elite. When a newly assertive central government tried to recentralize authority in the first decade of the twentieth century, the local elites defected. They may not have wanted a revolution (certainly not a social revolution), but the revolutionary movement seemed to promise the ouster of the incompetent and corrupt rulers and, perhaps, the establishment of a constitutional order in which the local elite would be prominent actors.

But the Revolution of 1911 revealed the weakness of the emergent public sphere. There was no tradition of building the public interest on the basis of contending private interests, and certainly the local elite were unable to stand up to the strength of the militarists who came to dominate Chinese society. Yet another revolution, that of the Nationalists in 1927–28, brought new elite actors to compete at the sub-county level. These new elites sometimes compromised with the extant elite, sometimes competed with them, and sometimes drove the local elite to the cities to avoid banditry or demands by local strongmen. Space at the sub-county level was crowded with more competitors, but state-building was partial at best. Rather, state involution in many parts of China meant that more and more people were being supported by taxes but local governments were neither fulfilling the tasks assigned from above nor providing services to those below.

The Communist revolution in 1949 brought unprecedented penetration of local society, even as it closed any semblance of a public sphere. The new revolutionary rule focused on mobilization, both to consolidate a new political order and to transfer resources from the countryside to the city as the party focused on the creation of a capital-intensive industrial structure. Out of this came a new party-state in which lower levels were responsible to higher levels. Path dependence made the central features of this order difficult to change, even though reform showed that it could be put to new uses. Indeed, with the inauguration of reform the CCP demonstrated that a hierarchical, authoritarian structure, long conditioned to pursue centrally decided tasks, could be revamped with younger, better-educated cadres and given incentives — both political and material — to pursue economic growth. Over time, and perhaps with the lessening of ideological campaigns, local political networks grew, serving their own interests as much as those of higher levels. The result is that the same structures that proved remarkably adaptable to the task of economic reform also provided incentives for local cadres to work for their own interests, competing with local residents over scarce economic resources. This is a competition that cadres routinely win and that the citizens protest, sometimes violently. It is this predatory tendency that erodes the legitimacy of local government and has led government leaders to refocus on the building of sub-county government.

As new local elites emerged with the growth of the economy, and as associations once again began playing a significant role in local society, the possibility of building responsive state structures, incorporating a role for the public sphere, seems possible. There are, however, still significant obstacles. One is that despite the diversification of socio-economic life, political rhetoric remains integrative. There is no legitimate political discourse that sees the public interest as emerging from contestation among private interests, and there is no basis in contemporary China for the public sphere to demand that the state legitimate itself through public approval (in the Habermasian sense).

Even more important are the ruling structures of the CCP, which are designed to make lower-level cadres responsive to higher-level cadres. Changing the logic of the political system to make local-level cadres responsible to the constituents whom they serve is not simply an incremental reform, analogous to growing out of the plan, but rather it challenges the very logic of the system. This contradiction is most apparent in the case of the Pingchang reforms, which seemed to provide a way of thinking about modifying the logic of the system. Unfortunately, higher levels deemed it too much of a challenge. Perhaps the Pingchang approach can be revived in the future, but the reversal of this approach reflects the caution of higher levels and the resistance such reforms face at local levels. The type of budget supervision pursued in Wenling perhaps offers a more feasible path of reform, at least in part because it does not challenge the local party. However, many areas do not have the funds necessary to carry out this type of reform (funds are necessary to host longer and more frequent sessions of the local people's congress), and local officials understandably resist reforms that curtail their freedom of action. Local cadres have revealed enormous talent to achieve the economic goals set by higher levels, but they have been highly resistant to reforms that will curtail their authority, make local government more responsive to citizens, and diminish the principal-agent problem facing the center. The personalization of political power at the local level has given the local state great adaptability, but it has often set the interests of local officials against those of local citizens. The result is that good governance at the sub-county level so far has proven elusive.

Endnotes

1. Ding Buzhi (丁卜之), "Weng'an 'bu'an' de xiancheng" (瓮安不安的县城) (Weng'an, An "Unsafe" County Seat), July 10, 2008, *Nanfang zhoumo wang*, at http://www .infzm.com/content/14365 (accessed July 15, 2010); and Wang Weibo (王维博), "Fengbao yanzhong de Weng'an guanyuan" (风暴眼中的瓮安官员) (Weng'an Officials in the Eye of the Storm), *Zhongguo xinwen zhoukan* (July 14, 2008): 34–37.

2. Joseph Fewsmith, "An 'Anger-Venting' Mass Incident Catches the Attention of China's Leadership," *China Leadership Monitor*, no. 26 (Fall 2008), at http://www.hoover .org/publications/clm/issues/China_Leadership_Monitor_No_26.html (accessed July 13, 2010).

3. Zhou Qingzhi (周庆智), *Zhongguo xianji xingzheng jiegou ji qi yunxing: Dui W xian de shehuixue kaocha* (中国县级行政结构及其运行: 对 W 县的社会学考察) (The

Structure and Operation of China's County-Level Administration: A Sociological Investigation of County W) (Guizhou: Guizhou renmin chubanshe, 2004), p. 109.

4. Ibid., p. 108.

5. Ibid., p. 115.

6. Li Changping (李昌平), *Wo xiang zongli shuo shihua* (我向总理说实话) (I Spoke the Truth to the Premier) (Beijing: Guangming ribao chubanshe, 2002), p. 10.

7. Ibid., p. 5.

8. Ibid., p. 2.

9. Ibid., p. 3.

10. Zhonggong zhongyang zuzhibu ketizu (中共中央组织部课题组), ed., *Zhongguo diaocha baogao (2000–2001): Xin xingshixia renmin neibu maodun yanjiu* (中国调查报告 [2000–2001]: 新形式下人民内部矛盾研究) (China Investigation Report [2000–2001]: A Study of Contradictions Among the People under the New Conditions) (Beijing: Zhongyang bianyi chubanshe, 2001), p. 85.

11. Yu Jianrong (于建嵘), "Nongmin you zuzhi kangzheng ji qi zhengzhi fengxian: Hunan sheng H xian diaocha" (农民有组织抗争及其政治风险: 湖南省 H 县调查) (Organized Struggles by Peasants and Their Political Risks: An Investigation of H County in Hunan), *Zhanlüe yu guanli* (战略与管理) (Strategy and Management), no. 3 (2003): 12.

12. Zhao Shukai (赵树凯), "Xiangcun zhili: Zuzhi he chongtu" (乡村治理: 组织和冲突) (Rural Governance: Organization and Conflict), *Zhanlüe yu guanli*, no. 6 (2003): 1–8. See also, Jean C. Oi and Zhao Shukai, "Fiscal Crisis in China's Townships: Causes and Consequences," in Elizabeth J. Perry and Merle Goldman, eds., *Grassroots Political Reform in Contemporary China* (Cambridge, MA: Harvard University Press, 2007), pp. 75–96.

13. Li Bing (黎兵) et al., eds., *Quxiao nongyeshui hou nongcun gongzuo jizhi biange yantao* (取消农业税后农村工作机制变革研讨) (An Exploration of the Change in the Village Work Mechanism since the Abolition of the Agricultural Tax) (Chengdu: Sichuan Academy of Social Sciences and Meishan Municipal Government, 2006), p. 156.

14. Zhao Shukai, "Xiangcun zhili," p. 3.

15. Keith R. Schoppa, "The Political Creativity of Late Imperial China," paper presented at the project on China's Rise in Historical Perspective, University of Virginia, April 24, 2009.

16. Thomas Ertman, *Birth of the Leviathan: Building States and Regimes in Medieval and Early Modern Europe* (Cambridge: Cambridge University Press, 1997).

17. Philip A. Kuhn outlines these three reasons in his *Origins of the Modern Chinese State* (Stanford, CA: Stanford University Press, 2002), p. 23.

18. Ibid., pp. 66–73.

19. Mary Backus Rankin, *Elite Activism and Political Transformation in China: Zhejiang Province, 1865–1911* (Stanford, CA: Stanford University Press, 1986).

20. Philip A. Kuhn, *Rebellion and Its Enemies in Late Imperial China: Militarization and Social Structure, 1796–1864* (Cambridge, MA: Harvard University Press, 1970).

21. Rankin, *Elite Activism and Political Transformation in China.*

22. Jürgen Habermas, *The Structural Transformation of the Public Sphere: An Inquiry into a Category of Bourgeois Society* (Cambridge, MA: MIT Press, 1989).

23. Mary Backus Rankin, "'Public Opinion' and Political Power: *Qingyi* in Late Nineteenth Century China,' *Journal of Asian Studies*, 43, no. 3 (May 1982): 453–484.

24. Benjamin Schwartz, *In Search of Wealth and Power: Yen Fu and the West* (Cambridge, MA: Belknap Press of Harvard University Press, 1964).

25. Rankin, *Elite Activism and Social Transformation in China*, pp. 306–307.

26. Chang Hao, *Liang Ch'i-ch'ao and Intellectual Transition in China, 1890–1907* (Cambridge, MA: Harvard University Press, 1971); and Andrew J. Nathan, *Chinese Democracy* (New York: Knopf, 1985).

27. Diana Lary, *Region and Nation: The Kwangsi Clique in Chinese Politics, 1925–1937* (Cambridge: Cambridge University Press, 1974).

28. Pan Gongzhan (潘公展), *Chen Qimei* (陈其美) (Taipei: Shengli chuban gongsi, 1954), pp. 58–59.

29. Mark Elvin, "The Gentry Democracy in Chinese Shanghai, 1905–14," in Jack Gray, ed., *Modern China's Search for a Political Form* (London: Oxford University Press, 1969), pp. 41–65.

30. Lifayuan bianyichu (立法院编译处), ed., *Zhonghua minguo fagui huibian* (中华民国法规汇编) (A Compendium of Laws and Regulations of the Republic of China) (Shanghai: Zhonghua shuju, 9 vols., 1934), 3: 567–570 and 6: 187–197.

31. Nathan, *Chinese Democracy*.

32. Philip Kuhn, "Local Self-Government under the Republic: Problems of Control, Autonomy, and Mobilization," in Frederick Wakeman, Jr. and Carolyn Grant, eds., *Conflict and Control in Late Imperial China* (Berkeley: University of California Press, 1975), pp. 257–298.

33. Elizabeth Remick argues that some counties were more successful than others in state-building. Interestingly, she finds that state-building was most successful (among the four counties she studies) in Kaiping county, Guangdong, which was outside the reach of the Guomindang state. See Elizabeth J. Remick, *Building Local States: China During the Republican and Post-Mao Eras* (Cambridge, MA: Asia Center, Harvard University, 2004). See also Shen Yansheng (沈延生), "Nongzheng de xingshuai yu chongjian" (农政的兴衰与重建) (The Rise, Fall, and Reconstruction of Rural Politics), *Zhanlüe yu guanli*, no. 6 (1998): 1–34.

34. Prasenjit Duara, *Culture, Power, and the State: Rural North China, 1900–1942* (Stanford, CA: Stanford University Press, 1988), pp. 74–77.

35. Yang Kuisong (杨奎松), "Jianguo chuqi zhonggong ganbu renyong zhengce zhi kaocha: Jiantan 1950 niandai fan 'difang zhuyi' de youlai" (建国初期中共干部任用政策之考察: 兼谈1950年代反 "地方主义" 的由来) (An Investigation into the CCP's Cadre Policy in the Early Years of the PRC: Also a Discussion of the Origins of Opposition to "Localism"), in Huadong shifan daxue Zhongguo dangdai shi yanjiu zhongxin (华东师范大学中国当代史研究中心), ed., *Zhongguo dangdai shi yanjiu (diyi ji)* (中国当代史研究 [第一辑]) (Contemporary History of China [Vol. 1]) (Beijing: Jiuzhou chubanshe, 2009), pp. 3–39.

36. Ezra Vogel, *Canton under Communism: Programs and Politics in a Provincial Capital, 1949–1968* (Cambridge, MA: Harvard University Press, 1969); Kenneth Lieberthal, *Revolution and Tradition in Tientsin, 1949–1952* (Stanford, CA: Stanford University Press, 1980); and James Z. Gao, *The Communist Takeover of Hangzhou: The Transformation of City and Cadre, 1949–1954* (Honolulu: University of Hawai'i Press, 2004).

37. Nicholas R. Lardy, "Economic Recovery and the 1st Five-Year Plan," in Roderick MacFarquhar and John K. Fairbank, eds., *The Cambridge History of China*, vol. 14: *The*

People's Republic, Part I: The Emergence of Revolutionary China, 1949–1965 (Cambridge: Cambridge University Press, 1987), p. 151.

38. On Leninist organization, see Kenneth Jowitt, *The Leninist Response to National Dependency* (Berkeley: Institute of International Studies, University of California, 1978). On the formation of the CCP cadre system, see Yang Kuisong, "Jianguo chuqi zhonggong ganbu renyong zhengce zhi kaocha."

39. Xu Xianglin (徐湘林), "Dang guan ganbu tizhixia de jiceng minzhu shi gaige" (党管干部体制下的基层民主试改革) (Democratic Grassroots Reforms under the Structure of the Party Controlling Cadres), *Zhejiang xuebao* (浙江学报) (Zhejiang Academic Journal), no. 1 (2004): 106–112.

40. On the importance of the financial system for stimulating economic growth, see Jean C. Oi, *Rural China Takes Off: Institutional Foundations of Economic Reform* (Berkeley: University of California Press, 1999).

41. Thomas P. Bernstein and Xiaobo Lü, *Taxation without Representation in Contemporary Rural China* (Cambridge: Cambridge University Press, 2003).

42. Kevin J. O'Brien and Lianjiang Li, *Rightful Resistance in Rural China* (New York: Cambridge University Press, 2006).

43. Joseph Fewsmith, "Elite Politics," in Merle Goldman and Roderick MacFarquhar, eds., *The Paradox of China's Post-Mao Reforms* (Cambridge, MA: Harvard University Press, 1999), pp. 47–75.

44. Melanie Manion, *Retirement of Revolutionaries in China: Public Policies, Social Norms, Private Interests* (Princeton, NJ: Princeton University Press, 1993).

45. Hong Yung Lee, *From Revolutionary Cadres to Party Technocrats in Socialist China* (Berkeley: University of California Press, 1991).

46. Xu Xianglin, "Hou Mao shidai de jingying zhuanhuan he yifuxing jishu guanliao de xingqi" (后毛时代的精英转换和依附性技术管僚的兴起) (Elite Change in the Post-Mao Period and the Rise of Dependent Technocrats), *Zhanlüe yu guanli*, no. 6 (2001): 65–76.

47. The idea of creating a civil service was outlined in Zhao Ziyang's report to the Thirteenth Central Committee in 1987, but the Tiananmen events soon ended whatever efforts had been made in this direction.

48. "Dangzheng lingdao ganbu xuanba renyong gongzuo tiaoli" (党政领导干部选拔任用工作条例) (Regulations on the Selection and Appointment of Party and Government Leading Cadres), *Renmin ribao* (人民日报) (People's Daily) (July 23, 2002): 1.

49. Tian Yu (田雨), "Dangzheng lingdao ganbu xuanba renyong tizhi jianjinshi gaige" (党政领导干部选拔任用体制渐进试改革) (The Incremental Reform of the Party and State Cadre Promotion System), in Xu Xianglin, ed., *Jianjin zhengzhi gaige zhong de zhengdang, zhengfu, yu shehui* (渐进政治改革中的政党, 政府, 与社会) (Party, Government, and Society in the Chinese Incremental Reform) (Beijing: Zhongxin chubanshe, 2004), pp. 108–124.

50. Guo Peng, "Asymmetrical Information, Suboptimal Strategies, and Institutional Performance: The Paradox of the 1995 Regulations of China's Official Promotion System," Ph.D. dissertation, Boston University, 2004.

51. Wen Shengtang (文盛堂), "2003 nian de fanfubai douzheng" (2003 年的反腐败斗争) (The Struggle Against Corruption in 2003), in Ru Xin (汝信), Lu Xueyi (陆学艺),

and Li Peilin (李培林), eds., *2004 nian: Zhongguo shehui xingshi fenxi yu yuce* (2004年: 中国社会形势分析与预测) (2004: Analysis and Forecast of the Situation in Chinese Society) (Beijing: Shehui kexue wenxian chubanshe, 2004), p. 162.

52. Guo Peng, "Asymmetrical Information, Suboptimal Strategies, and Institutional Performance."

53. Wu Jing (吴兢) and Huang Qingchang (黄庆畅), "Zhongguo jiceng yifa xingzheng zhuangkuang quhao, zhifa zhiliang rengxu tigao" (中国基层依法行政状况趋好, 执法制量仍需提高) (The Trend in Grassroots Legal Administration Is Good; The Quality of Upholding the Law Needs to Be Raised), *Renmin ribao* (August 25, 2007).

54. Chen Shengyong (陈剩勇), Wang Jinjun (汪锦军), and Ma Bin (马斌), *Zuzhihua, zizhu zhili yu minzhu: Zhejiang Wenzhou minjian shanghui yanjiu* (组织化, 自主治理与民主: 浙江温州民间商会研究) (Organizing, Self-Governance, and Democracy: Research on Unofficial Chambers of Commerce in Wenzhou, Zhejiang) (Beijing: Zhongguo shehui kexue chubanshe, 2004), p. 38.

55. Yu Jianxing (郁建兴) et al., *Minjian shanghui yu difang zhengfu: Jiyu Zhejiang sheng Wenzhou shi de yanjiu* (民间商会与地方政府: 基于浙江省温州市的研究) (Unofficial Chambers of Commerce and Local Government: Based on Research in Wenzhou City of Zhejiang Province) (Beijing: Jingji kexue chubanshe, 2006), pp. 117–119, 136.

56. Ibid., p. 132.

57. Ibid., p. 131.

58. Ibid., p. 133. Three others stated they did not know, and three did not respond.

59. Ibid., p. 131.

60. Joseph Fewsmith, "Taizhou Area Explores Ways to Improve Local Governance," *China Leadership Monitor*, no. 15 (Summer 2005), at http://www.hoover.org/publications/clm/issues/2903596.html (accessed July 13, 2010).

61. Joseph Fewsmith, "Exercising the Power of the Purse?" *China Leadership Monitor*, no. 19 (Fall 2006), at http://www.hoover.org/publications/clm/issues/4469936.html (accessed July 13, 2010).

62. Joseph Fewsmith, "A New Upsurge in Political Reform? — Maybe," *China Leadership Monitor*, no. 24 (Spring 2008), at http://www.hoover.org/publications/clm/issues/16611021.html (accessed July 13, 2010).

63. Ibid.

64. Joseph Fewsmith, "What Happened in Maliu Township?" *China Leadership Monitor*, no. 25 (Summer 2008), at http://www.hoover.org/publications/clm/issues/20102784.html (accessed July 13, 2010).

65. Ibid.

66. On clerks and runners, see Bradly W. Reed, *Talons and Teeth: County Clerks and Runners in the Qing Dynasty* (Stanford, CA: Stanford University Press, 2000).

CHAPTER 10

Central-Local Dynamics: Historical Continuities and Institutional Resilience

JAE HO CHUNG

Maintaining stability and ensuring survival are the principal goals of any political regime. China is no exception, regardless if its rulers were emperors, generalissimos, or general secretaries. History has repeatedly witnessed so many failed states around the world changing their names or even totally disappearing from the map.[1] Given this, the restoration of China as a global player, if not a hegemonic competitor, seems all the more remarkable. What has enabled China to avoid the fate of so many of the socialist dictatorial regimes, like the Soviet Union and Romania? How has China managed to shield itself from threats of demise or collapse?[2] What constitutes the recipe for its political resilience?

Fatal threats to the "mandate of heaven" (*tianming*, 天命) and dynastic collapses were familiar themes to the rulers of the Chinese empire throughout history. In most cases, the key recipe for a dynastic collapse involved some combination of eruption of peasant rebellions, the rise of local strongmen, and foreign aggression. As the cases of the Qing dynasty and the Republican era vividly demonstrate, the Taiping and Nian rebellions, the rise of provincial armies and later of regional warlords, and the Western and Japanese encroachment since the Opium War jointly contributed to their respective demise.[3] All these historic episodes took place as spatial competitions in that alternative forces sought to obtain geographical bases of opposition to the imperial court or the central government in power. This is precisely where the crucial importance of central-local dynamics comes into play.

Many of China's eye-catching accomplishments with transitional reforms since the late 1970s have been widely attributed to successful decentralization

— downward delegation of decision-making authority from the central to local governments — accompanied by de-ideologization and marketization. Although some may disagree regarding the extent to which the post-Mao decentralization measures actually brought about these economic successes, it is difficult to dispute their impact on transforming the norms and procedures of governing localities in post-Mao China.[4] In fact, over the last two decades many studies have suggested that the post-Mao decentralization measures were so extensive in scope that the localities became sufficiently powerful to defy Beijing on a number of occasions.[5]

Despite forewarnings about the possible collapse or even territorial disintegration of China, particularly due to the rise of regionalism, provincialism, and localism, Beijing still seems to command quite effectively and confidently. It may be that the "reports of China's death have in fact been greatly exaggerated," as John Fitzgerald aptly notes.[6] How do we explain the resilience of the power of Beijing to rule the localities? The answer lies in the remarkable adaptability of the People's Republic (the Chinese Communist Party in particular) to changing environments and new challenges. More specifically, the resilience can be attributed to: (1) the Chinese Communist Party leaders' lingering memories of, if not preoccupation with, China's centrifugal traditions; and (2) their adaptive ability to revive and renovate old rules and institutions to cope with the new challenges generated by a wide range of decentralization measures during the reform era.

The remainder of this chapter consists of three sections. The first discusses the revolutionary legacy of encouraging local initiatives and the temporary suspension of the tradition of centrifugality in Maoist China, and contrasts these with the revived trends of localism during the post-Mao era. The second section examines the elements, both perceptual and institutional, of resilient authoritarianism in the People's Republic that have enabled Beijing to rein in local assertiveness and defiance effectively. The mechanisms and linkages of such resilience can be traced back to both traditional China and the revolutionary period under the rule of the Chinese Communist Party (CCP).[7] The chapter concludes with some observations about future possibilities in the evolution of central-local dynamics in China.

Revolutionary Legacies, Suspended Tradition, and the Reform Factor

Chinese history is replete with dynastic cycles of unification and disintegration over a period of more than two millennia. Few dynasties managed to last longer than 300 years before giving way to a conflict-ridden interregnum followed by a new mandate of heaven. As Owen Lattimore observes, "[O]ld China was a decentralized country in which every province had a life of its own."[8] Some even go so far as to note that the total number of years under a disintegrated China may easily outnumber those under a unified China.[9] The centrifugal tradition has long been an integral part of Chinese history, waiting to resurface whenever conditions become ripe. Therefore, there are no special reasons to believe that the People's Republic is either immune or invulnerable to the chronic possibility of territorial division and disintegration, although it clearly commands stronger power over the localities than any of its imperial predecessors.[10]

LEGACIES OF THE REVOLUTIONARY ERA

Many Chinese still feel nostalgic about the pre-1949 years of revolutionary struggle and they often derive both pride and inspiration from those difficult years. Although it is true that some of the key administrative styles and organizational principles of the People's Republic originated during this period of extreme hardship, it is also important to note that the political circumstances of this period were both special and unique, if not extraordinary. Therefore, applying these principles to the more normal circumstances of the post-1949 years was not a simple matter.

Let us first look at the experiences of the Jiangxi Soviet (1931–34). During this brief period, the E-Yu-Wan Soviet government had a highly decentralized decision-making structure whereby most policies, with the exception of military-related policies, were decided by county-level authorities. Given the special geopolitical circumstances of the Jiangxi Soviet, the provincial level was almost irrelevant and, consequently, Mao had a profound interest in managing the townships. Agrarian policy varied considerably among the different counties and townships. Naturally, the policy styles of decentralized experimentation, mass participation, and two-way communication (i.e., democratic centralism) grew out of these unique environments.[11] Romantic and innovative as they may seem, these experiences were not easily adaptable to the enormously expanded environment of the People's Republic after 1949.

A similar assessment can be provided for the experiences during the years of the base areas. During much of the Yan'an era, the Communist leaders did not focus on the whole country in its entirety. Initially, they worked in a small, geographically remote, and inaccessible area in Shaanxi province.

Although the size of the region under Communist control expanded over the years, even that was widely disconnected by the areas ruled separately by the Guomindang forces, regional warlords, and the Japanese army. Therefore, until the mid-1940s CCP leaders focused on garnering mass support at the grassroots levels. Central-local relations received relatively scant attention.[12]

The famous tenet of "implementing according to local conditions" (*yindi zhiyi*, 因地制宜) was developed during the years of the base areas but, again, this period was more special than normal from the perspective of central-local relations. Having to carry out a geographically disconnected revolution in widely scattered areas, the Communists did not have the luxury of "blind commandism" dictated solely from above. Guerrilla-style policy-making required flexibility, autarky, a united front, and the securing of mass support. The survival imperative facilitated attention to local initiatives and regional variations, whereas the urge for bureaucratic standardization was carefully restrained.[13]

The unusual experiences and legacies of the pre-1949 revolutionary period were to be cherished and remembered as the recipe for successful local administration in the People's Republic. Whenever hard times fell upon the population, these legacies were called upon for inspiration and encouragement. Yet overemphasis on local experiments and initiatives can be misleading since in reality the implementation dynamics were as much dictated by Beijing as by the localities. That is, stark differences in the political circumstances and policy environments need to be duly recognized when assessing the actual applicability of these revolutionary legacies and precedents to the post-revolution years.[14]

THE MAOIST ERA

A popular perspective on Maoist China (1949–76) suggests that the centrifugal tradition was largely suspended during this period in Chinese history. On the one hand, this assessment is not unreasonable because there were no discernible trends toward local assertiveness vis-à-vis Beijing at the time, nor any explicit regional defiance. On the other hand, this period was not only relatively brief — less than thirty years — from a macro-historical viewpoint, but also quite extraordinary due to the utopian group-think that the elite and the masses shared in the frantic processes of policy-making and implementation.[15]

Although the founding of the People's Republic led to the eradication of regional warlords and local bandits, deep-rooted regionalism remained. The

Communist leaders built extensive roads and railways to overcome the territorial fragmentation and cultural parochialism characteristic of traditional China. The temporary scheme of six "great administrative regions" (*daxing zhengqu*, 大行政区) was implemented to incorporate numerous sub-national localities into the new Communist state.[16] Once the task of territorial integration was completed through the "great administrative regions," Beijing sought tighter political integration by relying increasingly on centralized command and ideological control in its management of the provinces.[17]

Since 1957 in particular, after the traumatic anti-rightist purges against those intellectuals and cadres who had voiced concerns about Communist rule, local incentives and variations were dictated solely from above (i.e., Mao and the party center). Although there was some provincial variation and intergovernmental friction, particularly during the 1955–57 period when the provinces were even encouraged to exercise discretion, we know of few outright central-local conflicts during the Maoist era. Due to rigid — often black-and-white — ideological norms and harsh punishments against local foot-dragging and deviation, "compliance-in-advance" was the dominant pattern of local response to Beijing.[18]

It is worth elaborating on the decentralization experiences during the Great Leap Forward and the Cultural Revolution periods that are commonly associated with the extensive devolution of resource-allocation and policy-implementation authority. As one scholar aptly puts it, "[M]any analysts conclude that the decentralization measures of 1957–58 led to more provincial autonomy. . . . Instead, the decentralization in 1958 seemed more apparent than real."[19] Given the sheer lack of comparative advantage, local discretion, and adaptive implementation in Maoist China, provincial compliance was extremely rapid and highly standardized, and provincial deviation was rare. We may conclude that the Greap Leap Forward decentralization did not in any meaningful way expand the real scope of local discretion.[20]

Another period commonly associated with extensive decentralization is the Cultural Revolution (1966–76). However, even in the middle of organizational breakdown and administrative disruption, the self-policing Maoist norms operated effectively to ensure mechanical conformity and to detect even slight deviations at the local levels. The numerous factions and rivalries induced many to take advantage of the ever-changing ideological winds to advance their own careers by bringing down their foes, thereby preventing local officials from voicing concerns that might be viewed as even remotely in opposition to Mao and the party center.[21]

Despite the prevailing rhetoric of decentralization, willful neglect of "implementing according to local conditions" was rampant. Localities had no choice but to emulate national models such as Dazhai and Daqing without due regard to their local conditions. Comparative advantage was rarely considered as nationwide application of standardized policies — such as "taking grain as the key link" and "mechanization is the only way out for Chinese agriculture" — was stressed.[22] Beijing's unyielding emphasis on local autarky led to a nationwide isomorphic structure whereby provincial per capita agricultural and industrial outputs were increasingly highly correlated (from −0.16 in 1957 to 0.75 in 1980), thereby further reducing the basis for comparative advantage and inter-provincial trade.[23]

How was central control effectively maintained even during this unusual period of bureaucratic breakdown and administrative paralysis? The CCP's ability to impose its policy priorities on localities remained fairly intact because its ideological control was highly independent of the bureaucratic institutions and mostly self-policing in its mode of operation. Therefore, despite the breakdown of formal institutions, the party center was still able to whip up ideologically motivated "policy winds" to force controversial policies onto the agenda for provincial implementation without foot-dragging.[24]

In short, during the Maoist era, despite the successive formalistic commitments to both fiscal and administrative decentralization, the localities had little genuine discretion of their own. Although Beijing's commitment to the revolutionary legacy of implementing according to local conditions may not have been simply rhetorical, its urge to control the localities and local fears of persecution worked as key obstacles to genuine decentralization. Thus, Beijing was largely able to enforce its preferences with regard to most national policies. Without first weakening the center's ideological control mechanisms (i.e., unless norms of decentralization became widely accepted and shared), local discretion and regional variation would always be deemed ideologically problematic and politically unsafe.[25]

THE REFORM FACTOR

The post-Mao reform brought about a sea-change in the way the central party and government viewed and dealt with the localities. The foremost change focused on the weakening of Beijing's omnipresent and omnipotent ideological grip over the localities and the considerable reduction of frantic mass campaigns in the process of policy implementation. To borrow from

Amos Perlmutter, China's "totalitarian phase of authoritarianism" was over.[26] This crucial change is attributed to the post-Mao leadership's painful recognition that its reform platform was bound to fail without first transforming the prevailing norms of local policy implementation.[27] Hence, the most distinctive aspect of the post-Mao reforms is related to the leadership's persistent efforts to "emancipate the mind" (*sixiang jiefang*, 思想解放) in order to redress the pernicious effects of excessive ideological control over both human relations and economic management.[28]

The reformist leadership's efforts to transform the norms governing central-local relations soon led to a strong emphasis, reminiscent of the Yan'an tradition, on the principle of implementing according to local conditions.[29] Beijing's reemphasis on this principle meant that local discretion in implementing central policy was permitted to account for the variation in local conditions and the practice of imposing "blanket policies" (*yidaoqie*, 一刀切) for all localities was avoided by all means. This time, unlike during the Maoist era, the regime moved beyond mere rhetoric and single models for the entire nation (e.g., Dazhai and Daqing) were subsequently abolished for good.[30] Of course, it took some time for the *yindi zhiyi* principle to take real effect in the actual implementation of central policy.

In efforts to shake the ideological yoke off local implementers, the post-Mao leadership rehabilitated many of those who had been stigmatized and persecuted as "rightists" and other "bad elements" during the successive campaigns since 1957.[31] These included a large number of former local officials who had dared to speak out against Beijing's policies because they were regarded as unsuitable for their respective localities. These measures, along with the leadership's continued efforts to weed out "leftists" and the beneficiaries of the Cultural Revolution, contributed to mitigation of the suspicions and doubts held by many local cadres and reinforced trust in the intentions and vision of the new leadership.

Along with the diluting of Beijing's ideological indoctrination came the reformist leadership's concerted effort to weaken central planning and fiscal centralism. The planned allocation of resources to the localities, one of Beijing's most crucial instruments of control in the past, became increasingly irrelevant as the overall level of marketization increased to over 90 percent.[32] The power of the State Planning Commission, dubbed the "little State Council," in charge of imposing macro-plan items and micro-quotas, was steadily curtailed and in 2003 the commission was finally restructured as the State Development and Reform Commission. For the first time, the Eleventh Five-Year Socio-Economic Plan for 2006–2010 was designated a "directional guideline" (*guiha*, 规划) as opposed to an "operational plan" (*jihua*, 计划). The era of centralized state planning is gradually nearing its end.

A considerable amount of discretion was also granted to sub-national units to approve large-scale investment projects without prior endorsement from Beijing. Several ministries — such as the ministries of Machinery, Metallurgy, Electricity, and Electronics — were either abolished or reorganized as bureaus and were no longer allowed to approve local investment projects.[33] Central-local budgetary arrangements were also radically readjusted so that the provinces had sufficient funds at their disposal. Despite the "tax-assignment" reform of 1994, there is no doubt that the localities can now earn and spend more freely much more revenue than they could during the Maoist era.[34] One crucial difference, however, between the Yan'an period and the post-Mao era is that, despite extensive — and genuine — decentralization, the province has become the principal unit for local policy-making and the overall policy environment is not as favorable to the former guerrilla-style policy-making at the county level.[35]

The inefficacy of the Communist ideology and lax party discipline, as well as the widening economic opportunities and fiscal autonomy, increasingly emboldened the localities in reformist China. Keenly aware that Beijing is not likely to dampen the overall reform atmosphere because of a few non-compliant localities, the provinces are often tempted to venture into a hitherto unaccepted realm of discretion, foot-dragging, and even defiance. Accordingly, evidence of local assertiveness and implementation slippage is widely reported in the literature.[36]

The impact of the post-Mao reforms on central-local relations is highly complex in nature. Although the localities have indeed attained a considerably expanded scope of discretion, the balance of power between Beijing and the localities has not uniformly tilted toward the latter. Generally, Beijing still commands and the localities still listen, though this is done *selectively*. Two principal variations are noted with respect to the term "selectively." First, with respect to those issues about which the center cares, the localities generally tend to comply, although some localities with legitimate economic reasons may choose to drag their feet in the hope of securing a special exemption.[37] Second, regarding issues for which some localities have crucial interests at stake and Beijing does not require national compliance, local leaders may choose to circumvent central regulations to safeguard their interests. In such a contingency, Beijing generally will not pursue or punish them, even if it is aware of such local deviations.[38] In the reform era, as compared to the Maoist period, the revolutionary mass-line legacy has largely become a rhetorical formality and local initiatives and discretion have become more genuine.

INSTRUMENTS OF AUTHORITARIAN RESILIENCE: DISCOVERING HISTORICAL CONTINUITIES

The foregoing analysis has demonstrated that the CCP paid genuine attention to certain legacies of the revolutionary period so that the scope of local discretion was considerably expanded during the post-Mao era. Despite such notable changes, however, Beijing is still capable of commanding the localities fairly effectively. What enables the center to gather reliable information about local affairs and to constrain local deviations? What constitutes Beijing's *tentacle*s that are used to investigate the local state of affairs, to prevent excessive local deviations, and to punish serious violations? In discussing the three principal functions of Beijing's tentacles — investigation, prevention, and suppression — this section explores the historical linkages and continuities between traditional and revolutionary China on the one hand and reformist China on the other.

INVESTIGATIVE INSTRUMENTS

Local information is a valued commodity regardless of time and space. It is particularly so for a continent-sized nation like China, with its huge population. Therefore, to govern effectively the central government must be well-tuned to local affairs. For this purpose, a wide range of networks and channels has been created and sustained to facilitate central-local communications. Some of these networks originated in traditional China, such as operation of the formal document system and personal investigative visits by emperors and high-level officials. Others have their roots in the Yan'an and Maoist years, such as the dispatch of work teams, telephone calls, specialized meetings of lower-level officials convened at higher levels, statistical surveys, and so on.[39]

The formal document system — the central document series (*zhongfa*, 中发) in particular — still commands a critical status in central-local communication processes, as it carries official power and ultimate authority throughout the entire state jurisdiction and administrative hierarchy. At the same time, it is widely known that, due to its heavy reliance on "formalized language" (*tifa*, 提法), dissemination (*chuanda*, 传达) generally entails considerable variation and distortion at the local levels.[40]

In order to reduce the degree of local variation and distortion (i.e., a "local remake" of central policy), Beijing typically relies on several instruments. Editorials in the *People's Daily* and *Qiushi* are frequently used to highlight the spirit of central policy and the major contents to be implemented at the local levels. Beijing also utilizes local branches of the New China News Agency to serve the special information needs of the central party and government elite through the internal reference (*neibu cankao*, 内部参考) series.[41]

The center does not rely solely on the formal document system, however, since the elite are keenly aware of its inevitable limitations and potential loopholes. Just as the Qing dynasty's Kangxi Emperor left the Forbidden City on six occasions for grand inspection tours during his reign, Mao Zedong, Deng Xiaoping, Jiang Zemin, and Hu Jintao all carried out frequent personal inspection (*kaocha*, 考察) trips to gain a better understanding of local affairs and to provide on-site instructions for important — and often controversial — policy issues.[42] In fact, the frequency of personal inspection trips by top leaders (such as members of the Politburo Standing Committee) has considerably increased in recent years.[43] In addition, just as the emperors sent their trusted envoys (*qinchai*, 钦差) to check on the different corners of the nation on their behalf in traditional China, from the days of the Jiangxi Soviet and the Yan'an base areas, the Communist party center has frequently utilized ad-hoc work teams and investigative units to "squat on a point" (*dundian*, 蹲点) or tour a region to ascertain valuable local information (*diaocha*, 调查) to serve Beijing.[44]

Although the rapid advances in transportation and communication technologies in recent years have largely overshadowed the historical continuities between traditional, revolutionary, and contemporary China, certain linkages and legacies can be found in Beijing's constant search for specific local information for effective governance and regime survival.

PREVENTIVE MECHANISMS

Equally interesting are Beijing's diverse arrangements and mechanisms for preventing and containing conflicts with localities. Above all, structurally China maintains a highly stable provincial system (*shengzhi*, 省制).[45] Although as many as fifty-three provincial-level units were ruling the counties in 1953, the number was reduced to twenty-nine for much of the Maoist era. Even during the three decades of the reform era, only four changes were introduced to the provincial system, compared to several hundred changes in the sub-provincial system. These four changes include the establishment of Hainan as a province in 1988, the creation of Chongqing as the fourth centrally administered municipality in 1997, and the establishment of Hong Kong and Macau as special administrative regions in 1997 and 1999, respectively.[46]

Given China's huge land mass and population, the total number of provincial-level units — thirty-three as of 2010 — is by no means large. This can be compared with fifty in the United States, forty-seven in Japan, and eighty-three in Russia. One cannot help but wonder why there has been so little change in the Chinese provincial system. An informed guess may be that the rulers of contemporary China are still very much concerned about the centrifugal tendencies of the Chinese body politic that continuously haunted their imperial predecessors. Were it not for such persistent memories and preoccupations, the People's Republic would not have so fervently insisted on its current unitary system by defying even a nominally federal structure as that adopted in the former Soviet Union.[47]

Let us briefly reflect on the often-discussed topic of federalism. In his report to the Seventh National Party Congress in 1945, Mao stated, "[A]ll the nationalities within China's boundaries should, on the basis of voluntarism and democracy, organize the Chinese Federation of a Democratic Republic" (Zhonghua minzhu gongheguo lianbang, 中华民主共和国联邦). For obvious reasons, this passage was deleted from the post-1949 edition of the *Selected Works of Mao Zedong*. Furthermore, the 1954 Constitution stressed the primacy of the central government, thereby repudiating the need for a federalist structure. Unlike during the revolutionary era when a united front and a maximum winning coalition were a prerequisite for CCP survival, in the post-revolutionary phase there was simply no room for federalism or any other institutional arrangement that might weaken or challenge the authority of the center.[48]

In delineating regional and provincial boundaries, the principle of the "jagged teeth of a dog" (*quanya xiangru*, 犬牙相入) is often used. That is to say, instead of using natural environments like rivers, mountains, and lakes as the points of demarcation (*shanchuan xingbian*, 山川形便), emperors occasionally relied on an artificial imposition of man-made boundaries and borders between localities. The benefit of course was to prevent the rise of localism embedded in different dialects, cultures, and customs that had been cultivated over many years. The case of putting Shandong, long a stronghold of communism in North China, together with the provinces in East China that traditionally were more favorable to the Guomindang forces in the framework of the great administrative regions (1949–54) is a key example.[49]

Related to the Chinese rulers' inherited concern with the centrifugal tendencies is the establishment of administrative areas specifically designed to manage the ethnic minorities. Where the Han, Tang, Yuan, and Qing dynasties designated special areas for the ethnic minorities and the Republic of China (*minguo*, 民国) established two "regions" (*difang*, 地方) for the management of Mongolia and Xinjiang, a full-scale redesign took place under the People's Republic.[50] As of 2005, there were five provincial-level autonomous regions, thirty autonomous prefectures (*zizhizhou*, 自治州), 117 autonomous counties (*zizhixian*, 自治县), three autonomous Mongolian counties (*zizhiqi*, 自治旗), five urban ethnic minority districts (*chengshi minzuqu*, 城市民族区), and over 1,500 ethnic minority townships (*minzuxiang*, 民族乡). These areas jointly accounted for 65 percent of China's land mass and 75 percent of all the ethnic minority populations.[51]

Additionally, the CCP strictly prohibited the provinces and cities from organizing collective action against Beijing. In efforts to avoid the charge of "divisive factionalism" (*paixing*, 派性), localities had to engage in dyadic bargaining and negotiations with the central government, thereby mostly tipping the power balance in favor of Beijing. Although many inter-provincial associations and inter-city networks emerged during the reform era, often at the initiative of the central government, their functions are almost always economic.[52]

Of course, more important is the personnel system by which the center has been able to wield formidable influence over the localities. Since much has already been written on the *nomenklatura* system run by the Central Organization Department of the CCP, we focus here only on the historical linkages and institutional resilience.[53] Two features are particularly noteworthy. One focuses on the practice of assigning provincial leaders to their home provinces: the so-called "native" dimension. In stark contrast, traditional China had a strict system of "avoidance" (*huibi*, 回避), whereby provincial leaders were prohibited from serving in their native provinces for fear they might work for the interests of their families and relatives.[54]

The rule of avoidance was completely ignored during the People's Republic for two reasons. First, irrespective of the actual outcome, at least rhetorically the Communist regime almost always emphasized the principle of "implementing according to local conditions." Naturally, "natives" were generally deemed more familiar with local conditions and thus were better able to enhance local adaptability for policy implementation. Second, if there still were remnants of concerns about centrifugal localism (as was the case in Beijing's perceptions of South and Northeast China during the

1950s), Communist and party discipline, accompanied by intermittent rectification campaigns, were implemented to overcome them.[55] Thus, during the 1949–98 period 35 percent of all provincial party secretaries and deputy secretaries, governors, and deputy governors were appointed to rule their home provinces.[56]

If we place the relevant data along a time dimension, an interesting trend emerges. Although the native proportion in the top provincial positions continued to decline during the Maoist era (i.e., 50 percent in the 1950s, 40 percent in the 1960s, and 18 percent at the height of the Cultural Revolution), the figure rose again during the early years of the reform era to 41 percent in 1986.[57] In terms of only the provincial party secretaries, the native proportion was 34 percent in 1965 and 41 percent in 1988 and a similar increase occurred among the mayors of the large cities.[58] An important change has taken place since the 1990s, however, as the native proportion began to decline, again due to Beijing's growing concern with rampant localism. Consequently, the share of provincial party secretaries serving in their home provinces declined sharply from 32 percent in 1999 to 18 percent in 2002.[59] Although Beijing has not formally adopted the rule of avoidance per se, with respect to personnel appointments it appears to pay attention to the problems of localism.[60]

TOOLS OF SUPPRESSION

If all these preventive mechanisms should fail and anti-Beijing forces should cause grave instability or even threats to the survival of the regime, the final solution undoubtedly lies in the use of the physical force at the center's disposal. The public security and military organizations of the People's Liberation Army (PLA) constitute the last resort for securing local and social control in China, as was vividly demonstrated during the later years of the Cultural Revolution and the Tiananmen tragedy in 1989. Therefore, for Beijing, unlikely as it may be, the worst nightmare would be collusion between provincial governments and local PLA units against the center, which might pave the way for the beginning of another dynastic cycle in contemporary China.

Since the early 1990s, some concern has been voiced with regard to the presence of regionalism and localism within the PLA. The highly profitable "military-run businesses" (*junshang*, 军商) that spread to every province considerably strengthened the PLA's financial ability, whereas PLA professionalism underwent a corresponding decline. Subsequently, it was feared that Beijing's loss of control over local PLA forces would lead to their collusion with regional authorities to obtain more autonomy from Beijing. In the late 1990s, however, the center effectively intervened to eliminate such concerns by prohibiting all military-run businesses above the division level.[61]

Almost all available studies on PLA regionalism stop short of linking its regionalism with disobedience to Beijing. In fact, many argue that PLA forces would still be highly compliant with Beijing even if they were to be subject to a complex situation similar to that in June 1989.[62] In fact, the People's Republic maintains several mechanisms and arrangements, with historical precedents, designed specifically to prevent local-military collusion against the center.

First, the highest sub-national organization of the PLA consists of seven regional commands (*dajunqu*, 大军区), whereas their civilian counterparts are situated one level down in the provinces. One can speculate that the absence of a return of the great administrative regions at the beginning of the reform era may also have been related to the leadership's concern with local-military collusion at the supra-provincial level.[63] Such an intentional "mismatch" arrangement naturally reduces the chances for meaningful local collusion against Beijing. Furthermore, a teaming up of provincial governments with provincial-level military districts at best would pose an insignificant threat, since the latter possess little control over the PLA's main force units.[64] This arrangement is reminiscent of the vice-regal system during the Qing dynasty, when Manchu viceroys (*zongdu*, 总督) shared rule with or often superseded Han governors (*xunfu*, 巡抚) to control the provinces.[65] Furthermore, from the days of the Jiangxi Soviet local governments were not allowed to carry out military-related policies.[66]

Second, during Mao's rule, regional military commanders and political commissars often stayed in one locality for as long as ten years or more. Since the early 1990s, especially after the PLA's involvement in the Tiananmen suppression, in an effort to reduce the chances of local-military collusion, regional military commanders average only three years in one place before they are transferred to a different geographical location.[67] Interestingly, in traditional China there was also the rule of "short-term stay" (*luntiao*, 轮调) for high-level local military officials. For instance, the average tenure for viceroys during the Qing dynasty was three years.[68]

Third, Beijing has dispatched a large number of PLA and People's Armed Police forces to be stationed in ethnic minority regions where anti-Beijing separatist and independence movements have long been active — most notably in the Tibetan and Xinjiang autonomous regions. This practice is also reminiscent of the Manchu imperial court stationing Tartar garrisons at key strategic points to the northwest of Beijing.[69] Although concrete evidence as to whether PRC leaders consciously reflected on the historical precedents remains to be substantiated, given the similar dilemmas that the rulers of contemporary China face the institutional resilience does indeed have a historical resonance. Some traditional and revolutionary legacies were selectively and creatively adapted by the Communist party-state.

Fourth, paradoxically, the conscious efforts by the central party apparatus to rein in any possibility for local-military collusion further highlight the presence of centrifugal dangers lurking in the background and the leaders' perceptions as such. Given that the movement of PLA troops larger than a battalion, even for the purpose of conducting a regular drill, must be authorized in writing beforehand by the Central Military Commission, Beijing's preoccupation with local-military collusion is as real as its staunch control over local military forces.[70]

Challenges for Resilient Authoritarianism

The political resilience of the People's Republic rests very much on the Communist Party and its leaders' adaptive strategies for survival. The tasks of nation-building and social engineering undoubtedly were daunting, and they deserve much credit for the recent remarkable success of economic development, which mainly can be attributed to their astute adaptability.[71] It should be noted, however, that what worked in the past does not necessarily guarantee continual success in the future as the organizational principles of the Yan'an era prove difficult to implement in the People's Republic. In fact, new problems are constantly being generated that will continue to pose grave threats to the People's Republic's chances for survival.

China's central-local dynamics from a macro perspective reveal successive cycles replete with decentralization and recentralization. Overall, at the end of each cycle a set of structures, norms, and institutional arrangements have been generated that are more favorable to the promotion of local incentives, provincial discretion, and regional variation. Although signs of effective recentralization are often visible in certain sectors, if the tenure of the current transitional reform is further elongated, the overall breathing space for local governments is likely to become larger at t+2 rather than that at t+1, with the formal legislation of local prerogatives.[72]

Aside from strengthened local voices, multiple sources of instability are likely to distract Beijing's attention and resources. These include increasingly turbulent conditions in the ethnic minority regions (Xinjiang and Tibet in particular), growing institutional decay at the grassroots level caused in large part by the return of local clans, the nationwide spread of popular protests and "collective public security incidents" (*quntixing shijian*, 群体性事件), and the rise of unofficial religious sects and criminal organizations.[73] With the advances in telecommunication technologies — the Internet and mobile phones in particular — organizing large-scale protests has become much easier and less costly, thereby posing a greater threat to resilient authoritarianism.[74]

In the years to come, the deepening of marketization and ownership diversification may well closely interact with the decentralization reform in ways that we cannot foresee. That is to say, as the marketization and privatization reforms intensify, a wide range of national socio-economic programs — i.e., welfare provision, poverty alleviation, inter-regional equalization, and so on — may become increasingly bottom-heavy in terms of their resource and informational requirements.[75] This hitherto unforeseen connection may situate central-local dynamics much closer to the crucial concerns of state-society relations. This is not to suggest that an economic logic will completely replace the political logic of central-local dynamics. Rather, the economic logic will become increasingly mixed with the political logic to produce tensions and conflicts during the elongated process of transitional reforms, dictating the cultivation of new norms and rules to govern central-local relations.[76]

Despite these uncertainties, the future of the People's Republic as a resilient authoritarian system is still very much an open-ended question. China's intermittent adaptation of traditional and revolutionary legacies, the CCP's persistent learning from the fall of the Soviet Union, and Beijing's adeptness at placing blame on local governments for many policy failures, as well as China's conscious reflections on its own mismanagement during the 2003 SARS crisis, offer ample room for some optimism. In fact, some go so far as to argue that the People's Republic will be more durable than most of the short-lived dynasties in Chinese history.[77]

The two key questions in this regard are: (1) what will make the future of the People's Republic more durable? and (2) is the People's Republic more Chinese than Communist?[78] The first question is crucial since certain radical adaptations, such as institutionalized democracy and the rule of law, are likely to increase the survivability of the regime, even though the specific route for making such a transition possible is not easy to identify. The second question is also highly relevant because, in the long run, the features of a

Chinese dynasty may eventually overshadow the features of a Communist regime. If that should indeed occur, the contrast between institutional resilience and historical continuities will be useful to interpret the future path of China's central-local dynamics.

* The author would like to thank Sebastian Heilmann, Liz Perry, Steven Levitsky, and the participants at the Fourth Annual Workshop of the Asian Network for the Study of Local China (*ANSLoC*), held in Taipei, May 8–9, 2009, for their helpful comments.

Endnotes

1. See Robert I. Rotberg, ed., *When States Fail: Causes and Consequences* (Princeton, NJ: Princeton University Press, 2004); Robert H. Bates, *When Things Fell Apart: State Failure in Late-Century Africa* (Cambridge: Cambridge University Press, 2008).

2. Sixty years may not be a very long period of time for a state's lifespan in general terms, but it certainly is for regimes in many newly established developing nations.

3. See Frederic Wakeman, Jr., *The Fall of Imperial China* (New York: Free Press, 1975); James E. Sheridan, *China in Disintegration: The Republican Era in Chinese History, 1912–1949* (New York: The Free Press, 1975). Also see Jae Ho Chung, "Assessing the Odds Against the Mandate of Heaven: Do the Numbers (on Instability) Really Matter?" in Jae Ho Chung, ed., *Charting China's Future: Political, Social and International Dimensions* (Lanham, MD: Rowman and Littlefield, 2006), pp. 107–128.

4. For a study that disputes the role of decentralization in generating China's economic growth, see Hongbin Cai and Daniel Treisman, "Did Government Decentralization Cause China's Economic Miracle?" *World Politics*, 58, no. 4 (July 2006): 505–535. For studies with contrasting findings, see Gabriella Montinola, Yingyi Qian, and Barry R. Weingast, "Federalism, Chinese Style: The Political Basis for Economic Success in China," *World Politics*, 48, no. 1 (October 1995): 50–81; and Jae Ho Chung, "Reappraising Central-Local Relations in China: Decentralization, Dilemmas of Control and Diluted Effects of Reform," in Chien-min Chao and Bruce J. Dickson, eds., *Remaking the Chinese State: Strategies, Society, and Security* (London: Routledge, 2001), pp. 46–75.

5. See David Shambaugh, "Losing Control: The Erosion of State Authority in China," *Current History*, 92, no. 575 (September 1993): 253–259; Edward Friedman, "China's North-South Split and the Forces of Disintegration," *Current History*, 92, no. 575 (September 1993): 270–274; Maria Hsia Chang, "China's Future: Regionalism, Federation, or Disintegration," *Studies in Comparative Communism*, 25, no. 3 (September 1992): 211–227; Arthur Waldron, "Warlordism versus Federalism: The Revival of a Debate," *The China Quarterly*, no. 121 (March 1990): 116–128; Shaoguang Wang, "The Rise of the Regions: Fiscal Reform and the Decline of Central State Capacity in China," in Andrew G. Walder, ed., *The Waning of the Communist State: Economic Origins of Political Decline in China and Hungary* (Berkeley: University of California Press, 1995), pp. 87–113; Jack Goldstone, "The Coming Chinese Collapse," *Foreign Policy*, no. 99 (Summer 1995): 35–52; Gordon G. Chang, *The Coming Collapse of China* (New York: Knopf, 2001); Ni Jianzhong

(倪建中), ed., *Daguo zhuhou* (大国诸侯) (Feudal Princes in China) (Beijing: Zhongguo shehui chubanshe, 1996); Tong Zhongxin (童中心), *Shiheng de diguo* (失衡的帝国) (The Empire Off Balance) (Guiyang: Guizhou renmin chubanshe, 2001); Ma Jianzhong (马建中), *Zhengzhi wendinglun* (政治稳定论) (On Political Stability) (Beijing: Zhongguo shehui kexue chubanshe, 2003); Zhang Xianglin (张翔林), *Wendinglun* (稳定论) (The Theory of Stability) (Beijing: Zhongyang wenxian chubanshe, 2004); and Li Peilin (李培林) et al., eds., *Zhongguo shehui hexie wending baogao* (中国社会和谐稳定报告) (Report on Social Harmony and Stability in China) (Beijing: Shehui kexue wenxian chubanshe, 2008).

6. For the quote, see John Fitzgerald, "Reports of My Death Have Been Greatly Exaggerated," in David S. G. Goodman and Gerald Segal, eds., *China Deconstructs: Politics, Trade and Regionalism* (London: Routledge, 1994), pp. 21–58. For exemplary assessments that are supportive of Beijing's sustained capacity for local governance, see Yasheng Huang, *Inflation and Investment Controls in China: The Political Economy of Central-Local Relations during the Reform Era* (Cambridge: Cambridge University Press, 1996); Jae Ho Chung, *Central Control and Local Discretion: Leadership and Implementation during Post-Mao Decollectivization* (Oxford: Oxford University Press, 2000); and Barry J. Naughton and Dali L. Yang, eds., *Holding China Together: Diversity and National Integration in the Post-Deng Era* (Cambridge: Cambridge University Press, 2004).

7. The specific timing of resonance between different periods is difficult to pinpoint. On the ambiguities of a historical watershed, see Paul A. Cohen, *China Unbound: Evolving Perspectives on the Chinese Past* (London: RoutledgeCurzon, 2003), ch. 5.

8. Owen Lattimore, *The Making of Modern China* (New York: W. W. Norton, 1944), p. 186.

9. According to a study, 44 percent of the 2,132 years from the start of the Qin dynasty to the demise of the Qing belong to a divided and disintegrated China. See Zhang Xianglin, *Wendinglun*, p. 14.

10. Prior to 1949, no regime in China was ever able to rule the nation below the county (*xian*, 县) effectively. Due to the land reform and associated political struggles, the political reach of the People's Republic was extended to the townships (*xiangzhen*, 乡镇) and, very often, to the villages (*cun*, 村). See Jan Myrdal, *Report from a Chinese Village* (New York: Pantheon, 1965); Ezra Vogel, *Canton under Communism: Programs and Politics in a Provincial Capital, 1949–1968* (Cambridge, MA: Harvard University Press, 1969), ch. 3; and Yuan-tsung Chen, *The Dragon's Village* (New York: Penguin Books, 1980). Also see Joseph Fewsmith's chapter in this volume.

11. Ilpyong J. Kim, *The Politics of Chinese Communism: Kiangsi under the Soviets* (Berkeley: University of California Press, 1973), pp. 18–19, 114–116, 160–178.

12. Mark Selden, *The Yenan Way in Revolutionary China* (Cambridge, MA: Harvard University Press, 1971), chs. 1–4.

13. For the flexibility of the Yan'an system, see Elizabeth J. Perry, *Rebels and Revolutionaries in North China, 1845–1945* (Stanford, CA: Stanford University Press, 1980), pp. 225–239; and Ralph Thaxton, *China Turned Rightside Up: Revolutionary Legitimacy in the Peasant World* (New Haven, CT: Yale University Press, 1983), pp. 185–190. For a temporal comparison, see Chalmers Johnson, "Chinese Communist Leadership and Mass Response: The Yenan Period and the Socialist Education Campaign Period," in Ping-ti Ho and Tang Tsou, eds., *China in Crisis* (Chicago: University of Chicago Press, 1968), 1: 401–407.

14. For a discussion of this environmental contrast, see Sebastian Heilmann, "From Local Experiments to National Policy: The Origins of China's Distinctive Policy Process," *The China Journal*, no. 59 (January 2008): 9, 13–15.

15. See Chung, *Central Control and Local Discretion in China*, ch. 2.

16. At the dawn of the People's Republic, there were fifty-two provincial-level units, as opposed to thirty-three in 2010.

17. See Lowell Dittmer, "Political Development: Leadership, Politics, and Ideology," in Joyce E. Kallgren, ed., *The People's Republic of China after Thirty Years: An Overview* (Berkeley: Center for Chinese Studies, University of California, 1979), pp. 27–47; and Wu Li (武力), "Mao Zedong dui xin Zhongguo zhongyang yu difang jingji guanxi de tansuo" (毛泽东对新中国中央与地方经济关系的探索) (An Exploration of Mao Zedong on New China's Central-Local Economic Relations), *Dang de wenxian* (党的文献) (CCP Literature), no. 5 (2006): 49–50.

18. See Frederick C. Teiwes, *Politics and Purges in China: Rectification and the Decline of Party Norms, 1950–1965* (White Plains, NY: M.E. Sharpe, 1979), pp. 349–366; and Peter R. Moody, Jr., "Policy and Power: The Career of T'ao Chu, 1956–66," *The China Quarterly*, no. 54 (April–June 1973): 267–293. Also see Chung, *Central Control and Local Discretion in China*, ch. 2.

19. The quotation is from Alfred L. Chan, "The Campaign for Agricultural Development in the Great Leap Forward: A Study of Policy-Making and Implementation in Liaoning," *The China Quarterly*, no. 129 (March 1992): 54–55.

20. See William A. Joseph, "A Tragedy of Good Intentions: Post-Mao Views of the Great Leap Forward," *Modern China*, 12, no. 4 (October 1986): 419–457; Jean-Luc Domenach, *The Origins of the Great Leap Forward: The Case of One Chinese Province* (Boulder, CO: Westview, 1995), pp. 157–160; Chu Han (楚汉), *Zhongguo 1959–1961: Sannian ziran zaihai changbian jishi* (中国1959–1961: 三年自然灾害长编纪实) (China 1959–1961: Record of the Three Years of Natural Calamities) (Chengdu: Sichuan renmin chubanshe, 1996), pp. 105–142; Li Rui (李锐), "*Dayuejin" qinli ji* ("大跃进"亲历记) (Personal Recollections of the "Great Leap Forward") (Shanghai: Shanghai yuandong chubanshe, 1996), pp. 119–128; and Alfred L. Chan, *Mao's Crusade: Politics and Policy Implementation in China's Great Leap Forward* (Oxford: Oxford University Press, 2001).

21. For the Maoist norms that were self-policing, see Dorothy J. Solinger, "Politics in Yunnan Province in the Decade of Disorder: Elite Factional Strategies and Central-Local Relations, 1967–1980," *The China Quarterly*, no. 92 (December 1982): 628–662; Anita Chan, Richard Madsen, and Jonathan Unger, *Chen Village: The Recent History of a Peasant Community in Mao's China* (Berkeley: University of California Press, 1984); Anne F. Thurston, *Enemies of the People* (Cambridge, MA: Harvard University Press, 1987); and Keith Forster, *Rebellion and Factionalism in a Chinese Province: Zhejiang 1966–1976* (Armonk, NY: M.E. Sharpe, 1990).

22. Tang Tsou, Marc Blecher, and Mitch Meisner, "National Agricultural Policy: The Dazhai Model and Local Change in the Post-Mao Era," in Mark Selden and Victor Lippit, eds., *The Transition to Socialism in China* (Armonk, NY: M.E. Sharpe, 1982), pp. 269–272; Sun Qitai (孙启泰) and Xiong Zhiyong (熊志勇), *Dazhai hongqi de shengqi yu duoluo* (大寨红旗的升起与坠落) (The Rise and Fall of Dazhai's Red Banner) ([Zhengzhou]: Henan renmin chubanshe, 1990), pp. 258–268; Jae Ho Chung, "The Politics of Agricultural Mechanization in the Post-Mao Era, 1977–87," *The China Quarterly*, no. 134 (June 1993):

264–290; and Marc Blecher and Wang Shaoguang, "The Political Economy of Cropping in Maoist and Dengist China: Hebei Province and Shulu County, 1949–90," *The China Quarterly*, no. 137 (March 1994): 73–80.

23. Thomas P. Lyons, *Economic Integration and Planning in Communist China* (New York: Columbia University Press, 1987), p. 174.

24. Victor Falkenheim, "Continuing Central Predominance," *Problems of Communism*, 21, no. 4 (July–August 1972): 82–83; and David Zweig, "Strategies of Policy Implementation: 'Policy Winds' and Brigade Accounting in Rural China, 1968–1978," *World Politics*, 37, no. 2 (January 1985): 267–293.

25. Stuart R. Schram, "Decentralization in a Unitary State: Theory and Practice, 1940–1984," in S. R. Schram, ed., *The Scope of State Power in China* (Hong Kong: Chinese University Press and New York: St. Martin's Press, 1985), pp. 98–122; and David S. G. Goodman, "Political Perspectives," in David S. G. Goodman, ed., *China's Regional Development* (London: Routledge, 1989), pp. 22–26.

26. See Amos Perlmutter, *Modern Authoritarianism: A Comparative Institutional Analysis* (New Haven, CT: Yale University Press, 1981), p. 71.

27. See *Guanyu jianguo yilai dangde ruogan lishi wenti de jueyi* (关于建国以来党的若干历史问题的决议) (Resolution on Some Problems in the History of Our Party since the Founding of the State) (Beijing: Renmin chubanshe, 1985); and Bo Yibo (薄一波), *Ruogan zhongda juece yu shijian de huigu* (若干重大决策与实践的回顾) (Recollections of Some Crucial Decisions and Events) (Beijing: Zhonggong zhongyang dangxiao chubanshe, 1993), 2: 777–779.

28. See Dai Yuanchen (戴园晨), "Sixiang jiefang tuidongle gaige kaifang he jingji fazhan" (思想解放推动了改革开放和经济发展) ("Emancipation of the Mind Promoted Reform, Opening, and Economic Development), *Zhongguo shehui kexue* (中国社会科学) (Social Sciences in China), no. 1 (1999): 12–20; and Chung, "Reappraising Central-Local Relations in China," pp. 47–52.

29. Also see Sebastian Heilmann's chapter in this volume.

30. Sun Qitai and Xiong Zhiyong, *Dazhai hongqi de shengqi yu duoluo*, pp. 285–363.

31. See Hong Yung Lee, *From Revolutionary Cadres to Party Technocrats in China* (Berkeley: University of California Press, 1991), chs. 7–8.

32. "Guanyu Zhongguo shichanghua jincheng de yanjiu" (关于中国市场化进程的研究) (A Study of China's Marketization Process), *Diaocha yanjiu baogao* (调查研究报告) (Investigative Research Report), no. 1747 (July 26, 2002): 5.

33. Zeng Peiyan (曾培炎), ed., *Zhongguo touzi jianshe 50 nian* (中国投资建设50年) (50 Years of Investment in China) (Beijing: Zhongguo jihua chubanshe, 1999), pp. 233–237; Zhang Dexin (张德信), Bo Guili (薄贵利), and Li Junpeng (李军鹏), *Zhongguo zhengfu gaige de fangxiang* (中国政府改革的方向) (The Direction of China's Government Reforms) (Beijing: Renmin chubanshe, 2003), pp. 95–96; and *Guowuyuan guanyu touzi tizhi gaige de jueding* (国务院关于投资体制改革的决定) (State Council Decision Regarding Reform of the Investment System) (Beijing: Zhongguo shichang chubanshe, 2004), pp. 15–22.

34. Chung, "Reappraising Central-Local Relations in China," pp. 54–58.

35. See Chung, *Central Control and Local Discretion in China*, chs. 4–6.

36. See Suisheng Zhao, "From Coercion to Negotiation: The Changing Central-Local Economic Relationship in Mainland China," *Issues and Studies*, 28, no. 10 (October 1992):

1–22; and Shaun Breslin, *China in the 1980s: Centre-Province Relations in a Reforming Socialist State* (London: Macmillan, 1996), chs. 4, 6, and 7. Also see note 5 above.

37. Beijing's efforts to contain the Falun Gong, ethnic uprisings, and collective protests allowed little local discretion or variation, whereas its opposition to inflationary trends, and the implementation of the household responsibility system in the early 1980s and of the tax-assignment system in the early 1990s allowed a bit more local variation. For issue-based variation in local discretion, see Jae Ho Chung, "Studies of Central-Provincial Relations in the People's Republic of China: A Mid-Term Appraisal," *The China Quarterly*, no. 142 (June 1995): 497–508.

38. See Wang Linsheng (王林生), *Zhongguo difang zhengfu juece yanjiu* (中国地方政府决策研究) (A Study of Decision-Making in China's Local Government) (Guangzhou: Huanan ligong daxue chubanshe, 2005), pp. 163–164.

39. For details, see Michel Oksenberg, "Methods of Communication within the Chinese Bureaucracy," *The China Quarterly*, no. 57 (January–March 1974): 1–39; and Yasheng Huang, "The Statistical Agency in China's Bureaucratic System: A Comparison with the Former Soviet Union," *Communist and Post-Communist Studies*, 29, no. 1 (March 1996): 59–75.

40. See Kenneth Lieberthal, *Central Documents and Politburo Politics in China* (Ann Arbor: Center for Chinese Studies, University of Michigan, 1978), pp. 26, 32, 51, 63, 71; and Michael Schoenhals, *Doing Things with Words in Chinese Politics: Five Studies* (Berkeley: Institute for East Asian Studies, University of California, 1992), ch. 1.

41. Michael Schoenhals, "Elite Information in China," *Problems of Communism*, 34, no. 5 (September-October 1985): 65–71; Schoenhals, *Doing Things with Words in Chinese Politics*, pp. 37–44; and Guoguang Wu, "Command Communication: The Politics of Editorial Formulation in the *People's Daily*," *The China Quarterly*, no. 137 (March 1994): 194–211.

42. Given that Mao carried out more inspection tours during the catastrophic Great Leap Forward than at any other time, those trips were certainly used more to impose his ideals and preferences than to become better acquainted with local situations.

43. See http://www.xinhuanet.com/newscenter/ldrbdzj (accessed July 14, 2010).

44. Kim, *The Politics of Chinese Communism*, p. 50; and Selden, *The Yenan Way*, p. 226.

45. This system applied to traditional China too, as the number of provinces during rule by the Yuan, Ming, and Qing dynasties was 16, 15, and 18, respectively. See Zhou Zhenhe (周振鹤), *Zhongguo difang xingzheng zhidu shi* (中国地方行政制度史) (A History of China's Local Administrative Institutions) (Shanghai: Shanghai renmin chubanshe, 2005), ch. 3.

46. See Jae Ho Chung, "The Evolving Hierarchy of China's Local Administration: Traditions and Changes," in Jae Ho Chung and Tao-chiu Lam, eds., *China's Local Administration: Traditions and Changes in the Sub-National Hierarchy* (London: Routledge, 2010), pp. 4–6.

47. For China's perceptive resistance to a federalist structure, see Tao-chiu Lam, "The Federalist Possibility? Breaking the Chinese Exceptionalism," in Chung, ed., *Charting China's Future*, pp. 81–106.

48. See Schram, "Decentralization in a Unitary State," pp. 82–95, 98.

49. For the two principles of regional boundary demarcation, see Zhou Zhenhe, *Zhongguo difang xingzheng zhidu shi*, pp. 236–249. For the case of Shandong, see Dorothy J. Solinger, *Regional Governments and Political Integration in Southwest China, 1949–1954* (Berkeley: University of California Press, 1977), p. 29.

50. For the ethnic minority regions in traditional China, see Tian Suisheng (田穗生), Luo Hui (罗辉), and Zeng Wei (曾伟), *Zhongguo xingzheng quhua gailun* (中国行政区划概论) (Overview of China's Administrative Divisions) (Beijing: Beijing daxue chubanshe, 2005), pp. 91–92.

51. Dai Junliang (戴均良), *Chengxiang dazhuanxing shiqi de sikao* (城乡大转型时期的思考) (Thoughts on the Era of Great Transformation in the City and Countryside) (Beijing: Zhongguo shehui chubanshe, 2006), pp. 207–208; Jin Binghao (金炳浩) and Zhang Yong (张勇), "Chengshi minzuqu de falü diwei handai mingque" (城市民族区的法律地位涵待明确) (The Legal Status of the Urban Ethnic Minority Districts Needs to Be Clarified), *Neibu canyue* (内部参阅) (Internal Reference), no. 846 (January 26, 2007): 11–18; and Hongyi Lai, "Ethnic Autonomous Regions: A Formula for a Unitary Multiethnic State," in Chung and Lam, eds., *China's Local Administration*, pp. 62–85.

52. See Jae Ho Chung, "Vertical Support, Horizontal Linkages, and Regional Disparities in China: Typology, Incentive Structure, and Operational Logic," *Issues and Studies*, 37, no. 4 (July–August 2001): 121–148.

53. The *locus classicus* on this subject includes John P. Burns, *The Chinese Communist Party's Nomenklatura System* (Armonk, NY: M.E. Sharpe, 1989); and Melanie Manion, *Retirement of Revolutionaries in China: Public Policies, Social Norms, Private Interests* (Princeton, NJ: Princeton University Press, 1993). Also see Xu Songtao (徐颂陶) and Sun Jianli (孙健立), eds., *Zhongguo renshi zhidu gaige sanshinian* (中国人事制度改革三十年) (Thirty Years of Reform of China's Personnel System) (Beijing: Zhongguo renshi chubanshe, 2008).

54. See Wei Xiumei [Hsiu-mei] (伟秀美), *Qingdai zhi huibi zhidu* (清代之回避制度) (The System of Avoidance during the Qing Dynasty) (Taipei: Zhongyang yanjiuyuan jindai yanjiushi, 1992).

55. For Beijing's distrust of local cadres in South China during the 1950s, see Yang Kuisong, "CCP Cadre Policy in the Early Years of the PRC," paper presented at the conference on "Adaptive Authoritarianism," Harvard University, July 14–16, 2008.

56. Zhiyue Bo, *Chinese Provincial Leaders: Economic Performance and Political Mobility since 1949* (Armonk, NY: M.E. Sharpe, 2002), p. 44.

57. Ibid., p. 45.

58. Cheng Li and David Bachman, "Localism, Elitism, and Immobilism: Elite Formation and Social Change in Post-Mao China," *World Politics*, 42, no. 1 (October 1989): 71; and Xiaowei Zang, "Provincial Elite in Post-Mao China," *Asian Survey*, 31, no. 6 (June 1991): 516.

59. The decline of "natives" during the 1990s is noted in Bo, *Chinese Provincial Leaders*, p. 45. For the figures on the "native" provincial party secretaries in 1999 and 2002, see Dali L. Yang, *Remaking the Chinese Leviathan: Market Transition and the Politics of Governance in China* (Stanford, CA: Stanford University Press, 2004), p. 5.

60. According to the "Tentative Measures for Government Officials" (*Guojia gongwuyuan zanxing tiaoli*, 国家公务员暂行条例), August 14, 1993, Article 63 stipulates that leading officials at the county level or below are not to be assigned to their "native places" (*yuanji*, 原籍). But there are no such provisions for prefecture- or province-level officials.

61. See Tai-Ming Cheung, "Profits over Professionalism: The PLA's Economic Activities and the Impact on Military Unity," in Richard H. Yang et al., eds., *Chinese Regionalism:*

The Security Dimension (Boulder, CO: Westview, 1994), pp. 85–110. For measures to shut down businesses run by high-level PLA units, see James Mulvenon, *Soldiers of Fortune: The Rise and Fall of the Chinese Military-Business Complex, 1978–1998* (Armonk, NY: M.E. Sharpe, 2001), chs. 6–7.

62. See, for instance, David S. G. Goodman, "The PLA in Guangdong Province: Warlordism and Localism," in Yang et al., eds., *Chinese Regionalism*, pp. 220–221; and Gerald Segal, *China Changes Shape: Regionalism and Foreign Policy* (London: International Institute for Strategic Studies, 1994), pp. 24–25.

63. For the rumored return of the great administrative regions, see Dorothy J. Solinger, "Some Speculations on the Return of the Regions: Parallels with the Past," *The China Quarterly*, no. 75 (September 1978), pp. 623–638.

64. See Michael D. Swaine, "Chinese Regional Forces as Political Actors," in Yang et al., eds., *Chinese Regionalism*, pp. 63–67.

65. Wei-chin Mu, "Provincial-Central Government Relations and the Problem of National Unity in Modern China," Ph.D. dissertation, Princeton University, 1948, p. 59.

66. Kim, *The Politics of Chinese Communism*, p. 160.

67. David Shambaugh, "China's Military in Transition: Politics, Professionalism, Procurement and Power Projection," *The China Quarterly*, no. 146 (June 1996): 283; and David Shambaugh, *Modernizing China's Military: Progress, Problems, and Prospects* (Berkeley: University of California Press, 2002), pp. 22, 29.

68. Mu, "Provincial-Central Government Relations and the Problem of National Unity in Modern China," p. 56.

69. Ibid., p. 59.

70. Shambaugh, "China's Military in Transition," p. 283.

71. See Bruce J. Dickson, "The Future of the Chinese Communist Party: Strategies of Survival and Prospects for Change," in Chung, ed., *Charting China's Future*, ch. 2.

72. See Jude Howell, *China Opens Its Doors: The Politics of Economic Transition* (Boulder, CO: Lynne Rienner, 1993), pp. 5–6; and Chung, "Reappraising Central-Local Relations in Deng's China," p. 66.

73. See Elizabeth J. Perry and Mark Selden, eds., *Chinese Society: Change, Conflict and Resistance* (London: Routledge, 2000); Peter Hays Gries and Stanley Rosen, eds., *State and Society in 21st Century China: Crisis, Contention, and Legitimation* (London: RoutledgeCurzon, 2004); and Jae Ho Chung, Hongyi Lai, and Ming Xia, "Mounting Challenges to Governance in China: Surveying Collective Protestors, Religious Sects and Criminal Organizations," *The China Journal*, no. 56 (July 2006): 1–31.

74. See Eric Harwit, "Spreading Telecommunications to Developing Areas in China: Telephones, the Internet and the Digital Divide," *The China Quarterly*, no. 180 (December 2004): 1010–1030; and Jae Ho Chung, "Challenging the State: Falungong and Regulatory Dilemmas in China," in John D. Montgomery and Nathan Glazer, eds., *Sovereignty under Challenge: How Governments Respond* (New Brunswick, NJ: Transaction Publishers, 2002), pp. 83–106.

75. Ding Kaijie, "The Crucial Role of Local Governments in Setting up a Social Safety Net," *China Perspectives*, no. 48 (July–August 2003): 37–49.

76. Vivienne Shue, "Grasping Reform: Economic Logic, Political Logic, and the State-Society Spiral," *The China Quarterly*, no. 144 (December 1995): 1174–1185.

77. For Beijing learning from the collapse of the Soviet Union, see *Xingshuai zhi lu: Waiguo butong leixing zhengdang jianshe de jingyan yu jiaoxun* (兴衰之路: 外国不同类型政党建设的经验与教训) (The Road to Rise and Decline: Experiences and Lessons from Different Types of Political Parties Abroad) (Beijing: Zhonggong zhongyang dangxiao chubanshe, 2002); and Lu Nanquan (陆南泉), *Sulian xingwang shilun* (苏联兴亡史论) (Historical Overview of the Demise of the Soviet Union) (Beijing: Renmin chubanshe, 2nd ed., 2004). For Beijing's learning from the SARS crisis, see Wenfang Tang, *Public Opinion and Political Change in China* (Stanford, CA: Stanford University Press, 2005), pp. 197–198. For an optimistic projection of the People's Republic's survivability, see Hongyi Harry Lai, "The Life Span of Unified Regimes in China," *China Review*, 2, no. 2 (Fall 2002): 93–124. For Beijing's buck-passing to local governments, see Yongshun Cai, "Managed Participation in China," *Political Science Quarterly*, 119, no. 3 (Fall 2004): 425–451.

78. The second question has been sensitized by Simon de Beaufort, *Yellow Earth, Green Jade: Constants in Chinese Political Mores* (Cambridge, MA: Center for International Affairs, Harvard University, 1978); and Victoria Tin-bor Hui, "How China Was Ruled," *The American Interest*, 3, no. 4 (March-April 2008): 53–65.